An Annotated Checklist
of the Birds of Tennessee

John C. Robinson

An Annotated Checklist of the Birds of Tennessee

The University of Tennessee Press

KNOXVILLE

Publication of this book has been aided by grants from the Tennessee Wildlife Resources Agency, the Tennessee Ornithological Society, and the Warioto Chapter of the Audubon Society.

The paper in this book meets the minimum requirements of the American National Standard for Permanence of Paper for Printed Library Materials. ∞ The binding materials have been chosen for strength and durability.

Library of Congress Cataloging-in-Publication Data

Robinson, John C., 1959–
  An annotated checklist of the birds of Tennessee /
John C. Robinson. — 1st ed.
      p.   cm.
  Includes bibliographical references.
  ISBN 0-87049-642-5 (cloth: alk. paper)
  1. Birds—Tennessee.   I. Title.
QL684.T2R63   1990
598.29768—dc20   89-77251   CIP

Contents

Figures

Tables

Appendix: Species Maps

Acknowledgments

I am grateful to James J. Dinsmore, Hank and Linda Zaletel, Kim Norris, and Moe, all of whom encouraged me to study birds. I also wish to thank those persons who provided me direct or indirect access to data in the following collections: J.V. Remsen, Steven Cardiff, and Donna Dittman (Louisiana State University Museum of Zoology); David Snyder (Austin Peay State University); David Pitts (University of Tennessee at Martin); Portia MacMillan (Cumberland Science Museum); M. Ralph Browning (National Museum of Natural History); Gary Wallace (Milligan College); and Jim Tanner (University of Tennessee at Knoxville).

I owe special thanks to Michael Bierly, Rick Knight, Brainard Palmer-Ball, Jr., Burline Pullin, Steve Stedman, Jim Tanner, Martha Waldron, and Ed Warr, who reviewed and commented on earlier drafts of this manuscript. I also wish to extend thanks to the many observers in Tennessee and surrounding states who submitted to me details and published or unpublished accounts of the distribution and occurrence of various bird species. I am particularly grateful to all of the Tennessee birders, past and present, who contributed their findings to the scientific community; without their work, this book would not have been possible.

I am indebted to Walker's Printed Images and the staff of the Tennessee Department of Conservation, Division of Geology, who provided invaluable assistance in the preparation of the maps used in this book.

I thank the members of the Tennessee Ornithological Society who encouraged me throughout the course of this project. I would like to thank the Tennessee Wildlife Resources Agency, the Tennessee Ornithological Society, the Warioto Chapter of the Audubon Society, and Warioto Chapter members Art and Patty Bieber, Nita and Annie Heilman, Louise S. Podell, and Ellen J. Walker for their generous support.

But, most of all, I thank my mother, who spurred my curiosity at an early age by telling me, "there were no hummingbirds."

Introduction

How to Use This Book

This book has been prepared to meet, at a minimum, the following basic objectives:

1. To provide, in one volume, a list of all bird species which have been reported in the state, including all hypothetical and provisional records;
2. To provide information on where, when, in what numbers, and in what type of habitat a bird can be found;
3. To list notably early and late arrival and departure dates for transient species;
4. To list the maximum one-day totals which have been recorded for each species;
5. To encourage the study of birds in Tennessee so that we may continue to fill in the gaps in our knowledge of the ecology and life history of each species that occurs in the state; and
6. To serve as a reference for anyone conducting research on the birds of Tennessee.

This book may be used by field observers prior to, during, or after birding activity. Prior to birding activity, it can be used as a planning aid to determine when and where an observer must be to see a given species. Alternatively, it can be used during or after birding activity to determine whether an observation which has just been made represents a notably early or late date, an unusually high number, or an unusual geographic location/habitat for a species.

For ease in interpreting the data, I have divided the state into three geographic regions: west Tennessee, middle Tennessee, and east Tennessee (see Figure 1). West Tennessee includes all counties west of the Tennessee River, including western Hardin County. Middle Tennessee includes all counties east of the Tennessee River, including eastern Hardin County; its eastern border is roughly defined by the Cumberland Plateau and includes most areas west of the following counties: Scott, Morgan, Cumberland, Van Buren, Grundy and Marion. East Tennessee encompasses all counties east of middle Tennessee, including the eastern mountains.

All species are listed in American Ornithologists' Union (1983, 1985) checklist order. An index to common names is provided at the end of the book. Once you have found the name of the species in which you are interested, turn to the appropriate page for the species account. In the species account, the bird's status and abundance in the state are described first (see the Definition of Terms section for the meanings of the status and abundance designations used throughout the text). For migrant species, abundance is further described by listing arrival and departure dates for each applicable season of the year. The season is defined first, followed by the *expected* dates of occurrence for the species. *A bird seen outside the expected dates of occurrence should be considered a noteworthy sighting.* Following the expected dates of occurrence, three arrival and/or three departure dates are listed (usually one date for each of the three regions of the state). In some instances, representative arrival or departure dates were not available for or applicable to a certain region of the state. Frequently, the dates listed here fall outside the expected period of occurrence for a given species; this is because these dates usually, but not always, represent the extreme arrival or departure dates for the applicable region.

For each species which breeds or is suspected to breed in the state, general information regarding its breeding status is given in the "Summer" or "Remarks" sections of the species account. In the appendix following the species accounts, maps of selected species show the counties in which these species have bred.

A "Remarks" section is included in each species account, which may provide various types of information. One such item is the high count(s) of individuals found in one day. Many of the high counts listed were made on Christmas Bird Counts or Spring Bird Counts. However, an attempt was made to use counts which were made only during a one-day period. As a result, data from Spring Bird Counts collected over a two- or three-day period are not included in this book.

The final section of each species account is the "Substantiation," which describes to what level the species has been documented in the state. Substantiation details generally describe when and where the species was collected or photographed. Abbreviations are used to identify the institution currently holding the photograph or specimen, and the name of the photographer. When appropriate, documentations on file with the state Bird Records Committee are also indicated. When substantiating evidence was not applicable (Hypothetical species) nor readily available (Regular or Irregular species lacking an accessible extant specimen, photograph, or sound recording), this section of the species account was omitted.

Persons conducting research on the birds of Tennessee should find the species accounts helpful in determining the abundance and the seasonal and geographic distribution of species which occur in the state. Those conducting field surveys or making routine observations of birds in Tennessee should find this book extremely helpful in determining when noteworthy, rare, or unusual sightings have been made. Such sightings should be published in the state's ornithological journal, *The Migrant*, and thus should be submitted to the appropriate regional compiler of *The Migrant* in a timely manner. Guidelines establishing the style and format in which bird records should be documented and submitted to *The Migrant* were described by Stedman and Robinson (1987).

The species accounts in this book represent the synthesis of unpublished records and published records in *The Migrant* (1930–1988) and other professional journals and books. The information is current through May 1988, but a few noteworthy observations from the June–September 1988 period are also included. I estimate that I created over twenty-five thousand individual notes on bird sightings made in the state of Tennessee. In the course of handling such a prodigious volume of data, a certain number of mistakes are to be expected. I recognize in advance that I may have missed some records, interpreted other records incorrectly, or recorded an incorrect date or reference for some sightings. This manuscript has been circulated and reviewed by several prominent Tennessee field workers. I welcome the submission of comments about errors in the text and remarks about any previously published or unpublished records which do not appear to have been used. Certain records, the validity of which I regarded as questionable, were omitted from the text.

History of the Tennessee Ornithological Society

On 7 October 1915 the Tennessee Ornithological Society (hereafter TOS) was founded at Nashville, Tennessee. The TOS originated on that day at a meeting in Faucon's Restaurant called by Dixon Merritt, then editor of the Nashville *Tennessean and American*. The meeting was attended by five other men: Albert F. Ganier, chief draughtsman engineer of N.C. and St. Louis Railway; Dr. George R. Mayfield, professor of German at Vanderbilt University; Dr. George M. Curtis of the Vanderbilt School of Medicine; Court of Appeals Judge H.Y. Hughes; and A. C. Webb, writing and drawing supervisor of Nashville City Schools. Each of these men expressed a deep interest in the study of birds; as a result of their meeting, the idea of a state ornithological organization, the TOS, became a reality.

The purposes of the TOS were well defined when the Society was created and hinged on the following four objectives: (1) to promote the science of ornithology in Tennessee; (2) to publish the results of its investigations; (3) to stand for the passage and enforcement of wise and judicious laws for bird protection; and (4) to promote bird study and protection by any other means that may from time to time be deemed advisable.

The TOS was officially recognized as a corporation by the state of Tennessee on 14 December 1938. A set of bylaws and a constitution were developed for the Society, and TOS chapters were established across the state, including Nashville in 1915, Knoxville in 1923, and Memphis in 1930. There are currently fourteen TOS chapters throughout Tennessee. The Society meets twice (spring and fall) annually and manages its business and property via an elected board of directors.

During the more than seventy years of its existence, the TOS has been instrumental in many ornithological accomplishments. In 1932 and 1933, the Society was instrumental in publicizing the campaign to select a state bird; a list of fifteen bird species was developed and presented to school children. The Northern Mockingbird received 15,533 votes and thus became the state bird of Tennessee. The TOS has also been directly involved in Chimney Swift banding projects, Eastern Bluebird nest box projects, coordinated statewide or regional surveys of selected species (e.g., House Wren, Chuck-will's-widow, and Whip-poor-will), Bald Eagle, Osprey and Peregrine Falcon hacking projects, the North American Nest Record Card Program (sponsored by the Laboratory of Ornithology at Cornell University), and annual statewide autumn hawk counts. Society members have been directly involved in the operation of Christmas Bird Counts since 1915, Breeding Bird Survey Routes since 1966, a five-year (1986–1990) Breeding Bird Atlas Project, and a cooperative statewide Common Barn-Owl nesting census in 1987 and 1988. The TOS has supported the Tennessee Wildlife Resources Agency's establishment of a network of Wildlife

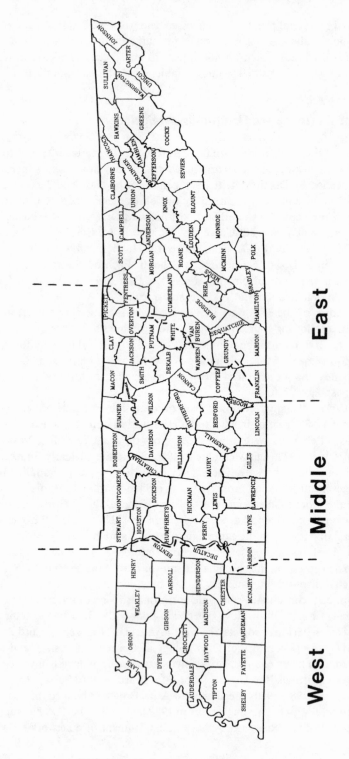

Figure 1. The three geographic regions of the state.

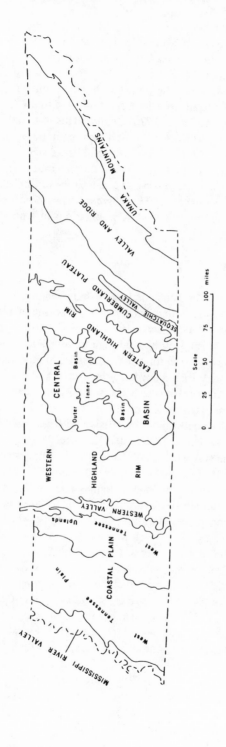

Figure 2. The eight natural topographic divisions of the state (adapted from Miller [1979]).

Observation Areas throughout the state. The Society has always had an active voice in environmental/conservation issues affecting the general environment or specific bird populations, and it coordinates many of its efforts with state and federal agencies as well as with non-profit conservation groups such as the Tennessee Chapter of The Nature Conservancy and the Tennessee Environmental Council.

Perhaps the most significant contribution of the TOS to the scientific community is the official journal of the Society, *The Migrant*. This journal has been published four times annually since 1930, and without it the present book would not have been possible. The existence of this large volume of published sight records, articles, and ornithological material is a tribute to the founding members of the TOS who had the foresight to create a journal to serve as a repository for the work of the Society. With the information published in *The Migrant*, it has been possible to monitor the numbers and distribution of many bird populations in Tennessee.

History of the State List

The state list of Tennessee birds has undergone many changes during the past two centuries. Alexander Wilson visited Tennessee in the spring of 1810 from late April to early May. Nicholson (1986) summarized the various bird species Wilson encountered on his trip, which took him through middle Tennessee via Sumner and Robertson counties, Nashville, southwest Williamson County, and southward along the Natchez Trace to the Alabama border. John James Audubon made several trips through Tennessee, primarily on the Mississippi River, between 1810 and 1830. Deaderick (1940) summarized the list of about twenty-seven species which were recorded on Audubon's flatboat trip on the Mississippi River when he passed through Tennessee between 22 November 1820 and 2 December 1820.

The only substantial statewide list of Tennessee birds prepared prior to 1900 was developed by Rhoads (1895) in the late nineteenth century. Samuel N. Rhoads spent part of the spring and summer of 1895 in Tennessee surveying bird life from Reelfoot Lake to Roan Mountain. He collected 60 birds to take back to the Academy of Natural Sciences and prepared an annotated checklist which gave accounts of 214 species and subspecies, 10 of which were assigned a "doubtful" or hypothetical status (Table 1). Ganier (1917) prepared a "Preliminary List of the Birds of Tennessee" in 1917 that listed 270 species and subspecies of birds. This work was revised sixteen years later (Ganier 1933) and was entitled, "A Distributional List of the Birds of Tennessee." This version listed 272 species, including about 16 species assumed to occur in Tennessee based on their occurrence in surrounding states, but for which there were no valid state records. Also included in this list were three accidental, three introduced, one extirpated, and two extinct species (Table 1).

The state list was prepared in field checklist format in the early 1960s, after which nearly a decade passed before Alsop (1972) prepared a revised version and established criteria for acceptability of a species to the Tennessee state bird list. Alsop's list totaled 342 species and included 255 regularly occurring species, 26 accidental species, 41 casual species, 4 introduced species, and 16 species in three other cate-

Table 1. Number of species recorded on previous Tennessee state bird lists.

Author	Regular	Provisional/ Hypothetical	Introduced	Extirpated	Extinct
Rhoads (1895)	203	10	1		
Ganier (1933)	250*	0/16	3	1	2
Alsop (1972)	322*	11	4	3	2
Bierly (1980)	331	1	5	2	2
Nicholson (1983)	324	14/0	6	2	2

*Total includes species classified as Casual or Accidental by the author.

Table 2. Number of species representing each status category defined in the text.

Status	Number of Species
Regular	250
Irregular	29
Extremely Rare	27
Accidental	39
Extirpated	4
Extinct	2
Escape	2
Provisional	16
Hypothetical	4
TOTAL:	373

gories (Table 1). Bierly (1980) prepared a list which totaled 341 species, one less than the list prepared by Alsop eight years earlier. Bierly's list included 5 introduced, 2 extirpated and 2 extinct species (Table 1). The first official list of Tennessee birds (Nicholson 1983) was prepared in 1983 by the Tennessee Ornithological Society's Bird Records Committee. As seen in Table 1, this list describes 348 species, of which 334 are confirmed and 14 are of provisional occurrence.

The present volume presents an annotated list of 373 species (Regular, Accidental, Extinct, Hypothetical, or otherwise) for which a reference was applicable to Tennessee (Table 2). This total includes 10 Introduced species. Four additional species are known only from fossil evidence and are discussed at the end of the main list. Some of the species discussed hereinafter have been omitted from previous lists but are included here so that the reader has access to accounts of all bird species that have been reported in Tennessee.

Physical Features and Topographic Divisions in Tennessee

The study of bird life in Tennessee is especially challenging because of the diverse topography found across the state. From east to west, Tennessee covers a distance of approximately 760 kilometers. By contrast, from north to south the state spans a maximum linear distance of only 192 kilometers. Bierly (1980) described the highest and lowest elevations in the state, respectively, as Clingman's Dome in the Great Smoky Mountains National Park (2,023 meters above sea level) and Memphis, along the Mississippi River (55 meters above sea level). Both Ganier (1933) and Bierly (1980) recognized that these extremes in elevations are responsible for the occurrence of some species as breeders in one region of the state which in the other regions of the state are not found at all or occur only as transients.

As already discussed, the three geographic regions of the state are west, middle and east Tennessee. Eight recognized natural topographic divisions also occur in Tennessee (Figure 2). These divisions have a profound impact on the distribution of bird species in the state. In the western region of the state, the **Mississippi River Valley** division, characterized by oxbow lakes, backwater swamps, and natural levees, occurs along the Mississippi River bottoms between Memphis and Reelfoot Lake. The elevations of this division range from about 55 to 90 meters above sea level (hereafter m MSL). The remainder of west Tennessee occurs within the **Coastal Plain** and **Western Valley** divisions, the elevations of which range from about 105 to over 210 m MSL. The **Coastal Plain** includes the West Tennessee Uplands and the West Tennessee Plain. The **Western Valley** was formed by the Tennessee River and in some places is up to 32 kilometers wide.

In middle Tennessee, the **Central Basin** division is surrounded by the **Highland Rim** division. The Eastern Rim is generally characterized by nearly level terrain, while the Western Rim has a more rolling topography. The elevation of lands within the **Highland Rim** ranges from about 210 to 305 m MSL. The **Central Basin** is lower in elevation, averaging about 182 m MSL in the Inner Basin and 230 m MSL in the Outer Basin.

The **Cumberland Plateau**, whose western escarpment divides middle Tennessee from east Tennessee, has a general elevation of about 515 to 580 m MSL, with some mountainous areas reaching as high as 1,065 m MSL. The Sequatchie Valley and the Cumberland Mountains occur within this division. The **Eastern Valley and Ridge** follows the valleys of the Tennessee, French Broad, Holston and Clinch rivers northeastward from Chattanooga to upper east Tennessee. The elevations of the valleys within this division average between 210 m and 305 m MSL; some of the ridges are as high as 940 m MSL. Along the extreme eastern border of the state lies the **Unaka (Eastern) Mountains** division, a portion of the Appalachian Mountain chain. This division is characterized by rugged terrain and heavily forested slopes. Elevations range from 305 m in the valleys to over 2,000 m MSL.

Each of the three geographic regions of the state has a unique set of habitats that is a direct result of the influence of the eight topographic divisions described above. Average annual rainfall across the state varies from 51.5 centimeters (cm) at Memphis to 48.5 cm at Nashville and 47.3 cm at Knoxville. Temperature extremes, the relative evenness or unevenness of the land, and the susceptibility of the land to flooding also vary across the state and are therefore important environmental factors that influence the abundance and distribution of bird species.

The effects of the diversity of Tennessee's habitat and topography on bird populations cannot be overemphasized. When posed with the problem of finding a particular species, a seasoned ornithologist with an acute awareness of habitat and of the physical features of the land can usually go directly to the site where the bird occurs, much to the surprise of novice birders who may accompany him or her. Tennessee's many rivers and mountains have a pronounced influence on where and when birds are found. Many species migrate along rivers and mountain ridges, and oftentimes a birder can find a rare or unusual species simply by being in these habitats at the right time of year or during the appropriate weather conditions. The Mississippi River area in west Tennessee is well known for its ability annually to attract a large number of common and rare species alike; "water" birds and "land" birds are perhaps equally affected by this major physical feature of west Tennessee. In the east, the Appalachian Mountain region can almost be viewed as a miniature state within a state. In the higher elevations of these mountains a Canadian zone of plant life occurs, including hemlock and spruce-fir forests. Many birds found breeding in these mountains are not found at lower elevations until one reaches latitudes far to the north of Tennessee.

Definition of Terms

A standard set of terms has been used to describe each species in this book. These terms are grouped under five basic categories: Status, Abundance, Seasonal Occurrence, Remarks, and Substantiation. Table 3 defines the various terms used to describe a species' status. The status of Regular, Irregular, Extremely Rare, and Accidental species was defined based on the number of times a given species had been *reported* in Tennessee in the past twenty years (since 1968, in this case). I acknowledge that there are probably a number of unpublished records that would upgrade the status of a species (e.g., from Extremely Rare to Irregular), but I chose to structure this book around evidence that was directly available to me. In all instances, the history of a species' occurrence in the state prior to 1968 was not ignored. I found the twenty-year index easy to use and I believe that future researchers of Tennessee birds will be able to use it to determine when a need exists to change the status of a given species.

For Regular and Irregular species, the abundance, or frequency of occurrence, is specifically defined (see Table 4). Some species found in Tennessee have a limited or local distribution. In these instances, the word "locally" is used to modify the appropriate abundance term (e.g., the Common Raven is locally uncommon in east Tennessee). The abundance codes assigned to each species described in this book are applicable when the species is looked for in the proper habitat.

The seasonal occurrence is described in conjunction with the abundance for Regular and Irregular species. The five terms used to describe the seasonal occurrence of a species are defined (see Table 5).

Table 3. Status definitions.

Term	Definition
Regular	Species found yearly or nearly every year in the state.
Irregular	Species recorded in the state at least 16 times in the last 20 years (i.e., seen only once or twice a year on average).
Extremely Rare	Species recorded in the state at least 6 times, with 3-15 records in the last 20 years (i.e., seen once every few years, or less).
Accidental (Vagrant)	Species recorded five or fewer times in the state; or two or fewer records in the last 20 years.
Extirpated	Species formerly occurred in the state but can no longer be found; may occur again, but only as a vagrant.
Extinct	Species formerly occurred in the state but can no longer be found anywhere.
Escape	Species suspected to have escaped from confinement.
Provisional	Species recorded in the state, and has been accepted by the state Bird Records Committee on the basis of one or two documented sight records.
Hypothetical	Species reported in the state but has not been documented beyond a reasonable doubt.

Table 4. Abundance (frequency of occurrence) definitions.

Term	Definition
Common	Species easily detected and often occurs in considerable numbers or large flocks.
Fairly Common	Species usually easily detected but is not often found in considerable numbers or large flocks.
Uncommon	Species not easily detected and most often occurs in small numbers.
Rare	Species hard to detect and may go unreported for an entire season or year.
Very Rare	Species not expected during the specified season for which at least one sight record exists.

Table 5. Seasonal occurrence definitions*.

Term	Definition
Permanent Resident	Species present all year, although local abundance and distribution may vary widely from season to season as a result of ingress and egress of migrants and seasonal residents.
Summer Resident	Species present during the summer months, usually with a noticeable spring and fall migration period.
Winter Resident	Species present during the winter months, usually with a noticeable fall and spring migration period.
Migrant	Species regularly passing through the state *en route* to or from wintering or breeding areas.
Visitor	Species encountered during the specified season, although breeding, overwintering or regular occurrence as a migrant has not been established.

*The four seasons of the year are loosely defined as: spring = March-May; summer = June and July; fall = August-November; winter = December-February. As it is not always easy to describe each species within the limits of these definitions, there occasionally will be instances when July or December records are discussed under the "fall" season, when February or June records are discussed under the "spring" season, etc.

The "Remarks" and "Substantiation" sections of the species accounts are described separately under Format of Text. Although the authors of other books summarizing the regional occurrence of birds have used or defined the terms in Tables 3, 4, and 5 in diverse ways, the definitions as presented here represent a general and basic approach to categorizing the status, abundance, and occurrence of Tennessee birds. Additional terms could have been used but were avoided to make the text readily interpretable by all audiences.

Format of Text

The text of the species accounts in this book has been prepared using a standard format. The first line gives the species' common name and, in italics, its scientific name. Brackets [ ] placed at the beginning and end of this line designate species of hypothetical occurrence. An asterisk (*) placed at the beginning of this line denotes that the species has been introduced directly or indirectly into Tennessee by humans.

The status of the species is described on the second line of the species account. The third line of text is then used to describe the abundance of a species within the state. Although abundance ratings are often applicable to the entire state or the entire year, the abundance of some species is described separately for the western, middle, and eastern regions of the state and/or for specified seasons of the year.

A paragraph entitled "Remarks" usually follows the status and abundance definition lines for each permanent resident and for species falling into any of the following categories: Extremely Rare, Accidental, Extirpated, Extinct, Escape, Provisional, or Hypothetical. For all other species, the abundance definition line is immediately followed by a season-by-season account of the species' occurrence in the state. These season-by-season accounts include representative and notable arrival or departure dates for each migrant species. Although an attempt has been made to include, for each season, one arrival and one departure date from each of the three regions of the state, there were times when such dates were unavailable for or not applicable to a certain region. The "Remarks" section of the species account is used to describe a number of items, including the habitat(s) in which the bird is found; behavioral traits characteristic of the species; field identification problems; changes in population levels or distribution; date when the species was added to the state list; past or ongoing management or research programs or activities; and the maximum number (high counts) of individuals found in one day.

Following the "Remarks" paragraph is a brief section entitled "Substantiation." This section is used to describe the degree to which the species has been documented in the state of Tennessee. The highest level of documentation is represented by a verifiable, extant specimen or fossil collected in Tennessee and adequately labeled (i.e., includes species name, date, site name and name of collector). The second highest level of documentation is represented by a photograph that has been adequately labeled. The third highest level of documentation ideally would consist of a sound recording of the bird's voice. Lacking these three levels of documentation, a species can be substantiated in written form as an acceptably documented sight record. Acceptably documented sight records must include the name of the species, date seen, the site name, the name of the observer, and convincing details of the observation.

Species Maps

Maps for thirty-three selected species have been prepared and are included in an appendix following the species accounts. These maps show either all counties from which positive breeding evidence is known for a given species or all counties in which a given species has been observed or collected. The map number for each species so represented is given on the status line of the species account.

The Tennessee Bird Records Committee

The Tennessee Ornithological Society's (TOS) Bird Records Committee was formed in the fall of 1981 to establish and verify an official list of Tennessee birds. The Committee currently consists of three voting members (one each for west, middle, and east Tennessee) and three alternates. Records reviewed by the Committee currently involve only first, second, or third state records for a given species. A species is placed on the confirmed or official list of Tennessee birds if documented by one or more of the following:

1. Extant verified specimen;
2. Extant verified photograph;
3. Extant verified sound recording; or
4. Three independent verifiable observations of the species or a verifiable observation by three independent observers of the same individual bird at different times.

Observations accompanied by any of the above types of documentation are accepted to the state list pending a unanimous decision from the three voting members of the Committee. A species is given provisional status when only one or two acceptably documented sight records exist.

The Bird Records Committee published the first official state list in 1983 (Nicholson 1983). An addendum to the official state list was published five years later (Nicholson and Stedman 1988).

The Study of Birds in Tennessee

One may ask the question, "How long must we study the birds of Tennessee before we can see the 'big picture,' the grand design of the ornithological arena in the state?" This question is difficult to answer, but only because of its limitless implications. Since bird populations are always in a state of flux, it is certain we will never reach a total understanding of Tennessee's avifauna. This is not to say, however, that the study of birds within Tennessee, or anywhere in the world, is a fruitless effort. Indeed, the study of birds must continue, and at an ever-increasing rate. Without the work that has gone before and the work that still needs to be done, effective management of threatened and endangered species will not be possible, and the ability to detect population declines before they reach detrimentally low threshold levels will be lost.

The study of birds in Tennessee can be accomplished by many different methods, the most important of which is the regular submission of bird sightings to the appropriate regional compiler of *The Migrant*. *The Migrant* is published four times a year and its contents include a report entitled, "The Season," wherein are published the field records of Tennessee observers. "The Season" includes a report for each of the following regions of the state: Western Coastal Plain, Highland Rim and Basin, Eastern Ridge and Valley, and Eastern Mountain.

In 1986, Tennessee joined a growing number of states which have completed or are conducting Breeding Bird Atlas projects. The Tennessee Atlas project is scheduled for completion in 1990. Its purpose is to inventory and map the distribution and abundance of breeding birds in Tennessee. Atlas field work is conducted during the breeding season in an Atlas Block which measures about 5.6 kilometers by 4.6 kilometers. Its major goal is to survey at least 701 target Atlas Blocks over the five-year period. All species found in a block will be assigned a breeding code indicating (from lowest to highest certainty of breeding) whether it is a possible, probable or positive breeding species. The code ultimately assigned to a species is directly dependent on the type of breeding evidence that is collected. An adequate survey of a block includes sixteen to twenty hours spent searching for nests or other breeding evidence plus one and a half hours spent running a fifteen-stop mini-route conducted in the same manner as a Breeding Bird Survey (see below). The Atlas Project is a cooperative effort, and the TOS will coordinate the publication of the results once all of the field work is completed.

Other bird study opportunities in the state include the statewide annual Autumn Hawk Counts coordinated by the TOS. Results from these autumn hawk counts have been published in *The Migrant* since about 1950 and include observations of the more commonly found raptor species, most notably the Broad-winged Hawk. Although most hawk count stations have traditionally been established in east Tennessee, the phenomenon of fall raptor migration can be monitored anywhere in the state.

Bird banding is another activity that has the potential to generate much important data. Tennesseans, including members of the TOS, have been banding birds since at least the late 1920s. Chimney Swifts were banded in large numbers during the fall throughout the 1930s and 1940s, the results of which were in part responsible for the location of that species' wintering grounds in northeastern Peru. A number of ornithologists and TOS members across the state currently have banding permits and are actively involved in banding projects. Mist nets are commonly used to trap smaller birds during migration; bal-chatri traps are used to capture shrikes and other birds of prey; and bait traps and rocket or cannon nets are used to capture larger birds such as geese, ducks, and Wild Turkeys. A number of state and federal conservation agencies also have master banding permits and attempt to achieve annual banding quotas for waterfowl and migratory upland game species. Since 1984, the Kentucky-Tennessee Eagle Management Team (consisting of personnel from the U.S. Fish and Wildlife Service, U.S. Army Corps of Engineers, Tennessee Valley Authority, Kentucky Department of Fish and Game, Tennessee Wildlife Resources Agency, and the Tennessee Department of Conservation) has placed leg bands on no less than twenty-five young Bald Eagles in nests located in middle and west Tennessee. The eagles are banded before they are capable of flight, usually at about seven weeks of age. If you are interested in bird banding, you should contact a local bander and inquire about how you may assist in his/her banding project. Mortality rates, survival rates, population recruitment rates, and distribution of migratory pathways are examples of the types of important data provided by bird banding activities.

Many coordinated field surveys are conducted throughout Tennessee to gather important information on all of Tennessee's migrant, wintering, summering, and permanent resident birds. These surveys provide considerable enjoyment to everyone — novice or seasoned ornithologist — who participates in them. The TOS's Spring Bird Counts have been conducted annually since 1932 and have accumulated data which allow for inter- and intra-specific comparisons of bird abundance. A number of long-term trends have thus been established, especially for migratory species such as the warblers and vireos. Spring bird counts are conducted at a variety of sites across the state. Each count was initially limited to a twenty-four-hour period during April or May. However, many counts have now expanded to include observations over a two-day period. Currently about thirteen counts are conducted annually in Tennessee. The sites at which the counts are made range from Memphis to Elizabethton.

Christmas Bird Counts are another type of annual survey conducted in Tennessee. Unlike Spring Bird Counts, the Christmas Bird Counts are designed to survey populations of winter residents. The Christmas Counts are conducted primarily in the United States and Canada over a three-week period during the latter half of December and the beginning of January. The counts have been conducted annually since 1900, when they were established as an alternative to the custom of some sportsmen in the late 1800s of shooting as many birds of any species as they could in one day during the Christmas season. These counts are published annually in *American Birds*, a journal of the National Audubon Society, the organization which oversees the collection and tabulation of all Christmas Bird Count data. The first Christmas Count in Tennessee was conducted by Magnolia Woodward in 1902 at Knoxville; six species were recorded (Trabue 1965). Judge H. Y. Hughes conducted a count in 1909 at Tazewell, Tennessee (Claiborne County), and Albert F. Ganier conducted the first Nashville Christmas Count in 1914. By 1938 there were at least seventeen Christmas Bird Counts being conducted within the state (Trabue 1965). Currently, about twenty-three to twenty-five Christmas Bird Counts are run annually in Tennessee. A total of 213 different bird species has been recorded over the years on the various Tennessee Christmas Counts (Simbeck 1987). As with the Spring Bird Counts, the establishment of long-term trends in population levels of many winter residents is a direct result of the data accumulated on the Christmas Bird Counts. The interested reader should consult the analyses of changes in bird abundance in Tennessee prepared by Tanner (1985, 1986) from data collected by these two types of annual surveys.

Breeding Bird Surveys, coordinated cooperatively by the U.S. Fish and Wildlife Service and the Canadian Wildlife Service, are conducted annually in Tennessee during the early summer period. These surveys are conducted throughout the United States and Canada by skilled amateur and professional ornithologists. Breeding Bird Survey routes are 39.2 kilometers long, consisting of fifty stops placed at 0.8 kilometer intervals. All birds seen or heard within a 0.4 kilometer radius of each stop during a three-minute interval are recorded during the survey. A tabulated summary of each route is sent to the U.S. Fish and Wildlife Service's Office of Migratory Bird Management in Laurel, Maryland, where the data are verified and entered into a computer database. Since these surveys are conducted along roadside habitats, species that typically occur in the interior of large forests or wetlands are not as easily detected as species occurring in other habitats. Approximately forty-two Breeding Bird Survey routes have been operated in Tennessee each year since 1966. Long-term trend analysis of breeding bird populations is probably the most important result of data collected for a broad geographic area. Robbins *et al.* (1986) discussed population trends of 230 bird species in North America for the 1965–79 period. Species for which the 1966–87 Tennessee data indicate significant annual population increases or decreases exceeding 5 percent are listed in Table 6, and the locations of the forty-two routes run in Tennessee are shown in Figure 3.

Table 6. Breeding species which are increasing or decreasing significantly (% annual change greater than 5%) in Tennessee.*

Species	Status Increasing	Status Decreasing	Percent Annual Change	Significance Level
Great Blue Heron	X		5.8	p < 0.10
White-breasted Nuthatch	X		7.4	p < 0.01
Song Sparrow	X		5.1	p < 0.01
Bewick's Wren		X	-6.6	p < 0.01
Loggerhead Shrike		X	-7.0	p < 0.01
American Redstart		X	-7.1	p < 0.01
Grasshopper Sparrow		X	-10.3	p < 0.01

* Data adapted from information prepared by the U.S. Fish and Wildlife Service, Office of Migratory Bird Management.

A recently established survey focused on birds of prey is the Winter Roadside Raptor Survey, organized by Stephen J. Stedman during the winter of 1985–86. These raptor surveys were conducted between 1 December and the end of February each winter along predominantly rural roadsides for a minimum linear distance of one hundred kilometers. Species which were surveyed included the Loggerhead Shrike and all raptors except owls. Observers were requested to determine the age for most species of hawks and the sex of Northern Harriers and American Kestrels. By March 1988 the Winter Roadside Raptor Surveys had been conducted for three consecutive winters, thus providing a reservoir of much-needed data on the winter abundance of raptors in Tennessee. Stedman (1988) discussed the results of the 1986–87 Winter Roadside Raptor Survey. The results of these surveys, generally expressed in the number of birds per hundred kilometers, will eventually allow for inter- and intra-specific comparisons of abundance between the three regions of the state, over the three months of the winter, and between different years.

Abbreviations

To conserve space, the following abbreviations are used throughout the text.

Place Names

Chat.	Chattanooga, Tennessee
GSMNP	Great Smoky Mountains National Park
HRA	Hiwassee River Area
Memp.	Memphis, Tennessee
Nash.	Nashville, Tennessee
LBL	Land-Between-the-Lakes National Recreation Area

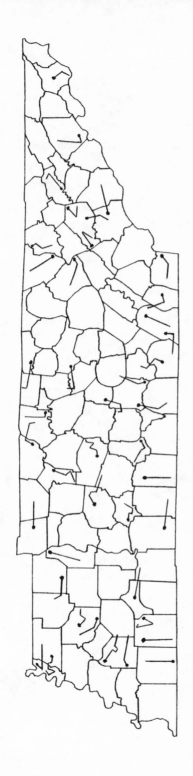

Figure 3. Locations of Tennessee's forty-two Breeding Bird Survey routes.

Museums

APSU	Austin Peay State University Museum of Zoology
CSM	Cumberland Science Museum, Nashville
LSUMZ	Louisiana State University Museum of Zoology
UTMB	University of Tennessee at Martin
UTK	University of Tennessee at Knoxville
USNM	United States National Museum of Natural History

Publications

BNA	Birds of the Nashville Area, 4th edition, (Parmer *et al.* 1985)
MIG	*The Migrant*, the state ornithological journal

Symbols

*	Denotes an Introduced species when placed at the beginning of the species account
[ ]	Brackets denote Hypothetical species when placed at the beginning and end of a species name (first line of species account)

Miscellaneous

ad.	Adult
imm.	Immature
Co.	County
L.	Lake
NWR	National Wildlife Refuge
WMA	Wildlife Management Area
S.P.	State Park
Res.	Reservoir
CBC	Christmas Bird Count
SBC	Spring Bird Count
TOS	Tennessee Ornithological Society
TBRC	Tennessee Bird Records Committee

Observers

DPB	Diane P. Bean
MLB	Michael L. Bierly
DWB	Donald W. Blunk
CHB	Carolyn H. Bullock
BBC	Ben B. Coffey, Jr.
LCC	Lula C. Coffey
JPC	J. Paul Crawford

DAD	Dollyann Daily
CGD	C. Gerald Drewry, Jr.
KHD	Kenneth H. Dubke
LHD	Lillian H. Dubke
AFG	Albert F. Ganier
JDH	J. David Hassler
RCH	Robbie C. Hassler
DRJ	Daniel R. Jacobson
WNJ	William N. Jernigan
RLK	Richard L. Knight
CPN	Charles P. Nicholson
VBR	Virginia B. Reynolds
JCR	John C. Robinson
DJS	Damien J. Simbeck
CAS	Christopher A. Sloan
BHS	Barbara H. Stedman
SJS	Stephen J. Stedman
MGW	Martha G. Waldron
GOW	Gary O. Wallace
JRW	Jeff R. Wilson
TWRA	Tennessee Wildlife Resources Agency

Tennessee Site Names Used in the Text

The following site names are used repeatedly throughout the text of this book. The county(ies) in which each site is found is given. Please refer to Figure 1 for the location of each county. The reader should note that several of the locations listed (e.g., Cherokee Lake, GSMNP, etc.) occur in more than one county; many of the species records attributed to such locations lacked sufficient information to determine the exact county of observation.

Location	*County(ies)*
Alcoa Marsh	Blount
Amnicola Marsh	Hamilton
Ashland City Marsh	Cheatham
Austin Springs	Washington
Bear Creek Wildlife Management Area	Stewart
Boone Lake	Sullivan and Washington
Bristol	Sullivan
Britton Ford Unit, Tennessee NWR	Henry
Brownsville	Haywood
Buena Vista Marsh	Davidson

Location	County(ies)
Bush Lake	Davidson
Byrdstown	Pickett
Camden	Benton
Chattanooga	Hamilton
Cheatham Lake	Cheatham
Cherokee Lake	Grainger, Hamblen and Hawkins
Chickamauga Lake	Hamilton
Clarksville	Montgomery
Columbia	Maury
Cove Lake	Campbell
Cross Creeks National Wildlife Refuge	Stewart
Douglas Lake	Jefferson and Cocke
Dover	Stewart
Duck River Unit, Tennessee NWR	Humphreys
Dyersburg	Dyer
Eagle Bend Fish Hatchery	Anderson
Elizabethton	Carter
Erwin	Unicoi
Fort Loudoun Lake	Knox
Fort Pillow State Park	Lauderdale
Gallatin Steam Plant	Sumner
Gatlinburg	Sevier
Goose Pond	Grundy
Great Smoky Mountains National Park	Blount and Sevier
Greeneville	Greene
Hatchie National Wildlife Refuge	Haywood and Lauderdale
Hiwassee River Area	Meigs, Bradley, McMinn and Rhea
Island 13	Lake
Johnson City	Washington
Kentucky Lake	Henry and Stewart
Kingsport	Hawkins and Sullivan
Kingston Steam Plant	Roane
Knoxville	Knox
Lake Phillip Nelson	Carter
Land-Between-the-Lakes	Stewart
Lebanon	Wilson
Lilydale	Clay
Martin	Weakley
Memphis	Shelby
Monsanto Ponds	Maury
Mud Lake	Shelby
Murfreesboro	Rutherford
Nashville	Davidson
Natchez Trace State Park	Carroll and Henderson

Location	County(ies)
Nickajack Lake	Marion and Hamilton
Norris	Anderson
Norris Lake dam	Anderson and Campbell
Norris Lake	Union
Oak Ridge	Anderson and Roane
Old Hickory Lake	Davidson, Sumner and Wilson
Pace Point	Henry
Paris Landing State Park	Henry
Patrick Henry Lake	Sullivan
Penal Farm	Shelby
Percy Priest Lake	Davidson, Rutherford and Wilson
Pickwick Landing State Park	Hardin
Radnor Lake	Davidson
Reelfoot Lake	Lake and Obion
Reelfoot National Wildlife Refuge	Lake and Obion
Roan Mountain	Carter
Roans Creek	Johnson
Savannah	Hardin
Savannah Bay	Hamilton
Sequatchie Valley	Marion and Sequatchie
Shelby Forest	Shelby
Smyrna	Rutherford
South Holston Lake	Sullivan
Tennessee National Wildlife Refuge	Humphreys and Henry
Tennessee River Gorge	Marion and Hamilton
Two Jays	Davidson
Warner Parks	Davidson
Watauga Lake	Carter and Johnson
Watauga River	Carter
Watts Bar Lake	Rhea and Meigs
Wilbur Lake	Carter
Woodbury	Cannon
Woods Reservoir	Franklin

Species Accounts

ORDER GAVIIFORMES

FAMILY GAVIIDAE: Loons

Red-throated Loon, *Gavia stellata*
Status: Irregular.
Abundance: Rare migrant, very rare winter visitor.
Spring: Early Apr to early May; considerably fewer birds are found in the spring than in the fall.
    Arrivals: 29 Mar 1971, Chickamauga L., MIG 42:46
                    5-10 Apr 1987, Chickamauga L., MIG 58:101
                    6 Apr 1950, Watauga L., (Herndon 1950)
    Departures: 4-5 May 1974, Pickwick Landing S.P., MIG 45:45
                    7 May 1950, Watauga L., (Herndon 1950)
                    7-8 May 1976, Columbia SBC, MIG 47:90
Fall: Late Oct to mid Dec.
    Arrivals: 21 Oct 1971, Woods Res., MIG 42:92
                    22 Oct 1979, Cherokee L., Grainger Co., MIG 51:17
                    23 Oct 1971, Knoxville, MIG 42:93
    Departures: 26 Dec 1958, Kingsport CBC, MIG 29:70
                    29 Dec 1984, Bristol CBC, MIG 56:6
                    30 Dec-2 Jan 1960/61, Boone L., MIG 31:78
Winter: One bird was at Roans Creek, Johnson Co., on 15-22 Feb 1975 (MIG 46:47).
Remarks: Usually found on large bodies of water. Of the more than thirty records for the state, there are only seven middle Tennessee and two west Tennessee records. Scan large lakes or rivers for a small loon with a light gray crown and hindneck and a slightly upturned bill. Bill and head are usually tilted at a slight upward angle. First state record was of five to six birds at Watauga L. on 6 Nov 1949 (Herndon 1950). High count: eight on 22 Apr 1950 at Watauga L. (Herndon 1950).
Substantiation: Adequately documented sight records.

Pacific Loon, *Gavia pacifica*
Status: Accidental (Provisional).
Remarks: One winter-plumaged bird lacking a white flank patch was found at Percy Priest L., Davidson Co., on 6 Mar 1988 and lingered until 19 Mar 1988, for a first state record (CGD). The details of this sighting are under review by the TBRC.

Common Loon, *Gavia immer*

Status: Regular.

Abundance: Fairly common migrant, uncommon to rare winter resident, rare summer visitor.

Fall: The arrival of fall migrants begins in early Oct and reaches a peak during the late Oct to mid Nov period. Concentrations of large numbers of loons are not uncommon at this time (e.g., 350 at Woods Res. on 12 Nov 1979, MIG 51:38; and 400 at Roans Creek, Johnson Co., on 12 Nov 1986, MIG 58:30). Many birds remain on the larger reservoirs and lakes into the winter.

Winter: Winter records exist from all across the state and usually involve birds on large bodies of water. A notable concentration involved forty-three birds on the Hickory-Priest CBC on 4 Jan 1986 (MIG 57:9). More birds are found in Dec and Jan than in Feb.

Spring: The arrival of spring migrants usually occurs by late Mar. The peak of the migration occurs in Apr when many sightings of small numbers of birds are usually made. A small number of migrants may linger well into June.

Summer: Summer loons have been detected as early as 1935 when one bird was present at Radnor L. on 16 June 1935 (Woodring 1935); however, the great majority of summer records have occurred since 1970. Summering birds are usually in non-breeding plumage and have been detected all across the state (e.g., 28 June 1979, Douglas L., MIG 50:88; 13-31 July 1975, Percy Priest L., MIG 46:88; and 2-22 Aug 1986, Kentucky L., MIG 58:19).

Remarks: Although most often encountered on large bodies of water, the species can also be found on smaller lakes and reservoirs. Large numbers of birds are most often found in the fall, usually after the passage of a cold front. Occasionally seen migrating high overhead. High count: 465 on 3 Nov 1973, Old Hickory L. (MIG 45:21).

Substantiation: Specimen: 1 imm. male, Watauga River, 14 Nov 1904 (USNM, 195681).

ORDER PODICIPEDIFORMES

FAMILY PODICIPEDIDAE: **Grebes**

Pied-billed Grebe, *Podilymbus podiceps*

Status: Regular. (Map A-1)

Abundance: Fairly common migrant and winter resident, rare summer resident.

Fall: Fall migrants usually arrive by early August. The appearance of Pied-billeds in July may represent very early migrants or dispersals from local breeding populations (see Summer below). Notable concentrations of birds can sometimes be found in Nov.

Pied-billed Grebe, continued

Winter: Can be found statewide throughout the winter wherever open water remains. Peak populations are usually recorded at this time (e.g., 145 on 21 Feb 1970 at Woods Res., MIG 41:42; and 265 on 25 Jan 1982 at Chickamauga L., MIG 53:47).

Spring: Most migrants and winter residents depart for northern breeding areas by late Apr. Some birds may linger throughout May and into June (e.g., 24 June 1969, HRA, MIG 40:69; and 28 June 1986, Bear Creek WMA, MIG 57:105).

Summer: There are many June and July sightings with breeding records from east, west and middle Tennessee. The species has been found breeding in the following counties: Davidson, Dyer, Franklin, Hamilton, Knox, Maury, Meigs, Rutherford, Shelby, and Warren. Breeding records range from 1934 in Franklin Co. to as recently as 1988 in Meigs Co. Breeding evidence (nests, eggs, or young) is usually detected from Apr through June.

Remarks: The species can be encountered on almost any size body of water and also in a variety of habitats ranging from dense emergent vegetation to open water. Usually escapes danger by diving and swimming away rather than flying. A surprisingly large number of breeding records exist for the state; natural and artificial wetlands and marshes with an abundance of emergent vegetation and cover should be checked regularly for possible nesting. High counts: 350 on 3 Jan 1987, Nickajack L. CBC (MIG 58:2) and 311 on 18 Dec 1972, Woods Res. (MIG 44:22).

Substantiation: Specimen: 1, Reelfoot L., 26 Nov 1915 (LSUMZ, 75661).

Horned Grebe, *Podiceps auritus*

Status: Regular.

Abundance: Fairly common migrant and winter resident, very rare summer visitor.

Fall: Fall migrants usually arrive by mid Oct. Occasionally large numbers of birds may be found. There are four Aug records ranging from 7 Aug 1921 at Radnor L. (BNA:14) to 31 Aug 1977 at Kingsport (MIG 49:20).

Arrivals: 20 Sept 1969, Radnor L., MIG 40:89
            27 Sept 1975, Nickajack L., MIG 47:20
            13 Oct 1985, Pace Point, MIG 57:22

Winter: Found wintering statewide wherever there are large bodies of open water. Notable concentrations are often found at this time (e.g., 225 on 11 Jan 1971, Woods Res., MIG 42:18).

Spring: Spring migrants and winter residents usually depart the state by late Apr. There are a handful of May records.

Departures: 30 Apr 1961, Chat. SBC, MIG 32:29
              4 May 1985, Gallatin Steam Plant, MIG 56:75
              23 May 1974, Tennessee NWR, MIG 45:100

Summer: There are two summer records for the state. One bird remained at L. Phillip Nelson near Elizabethton from 30 May through 19 June 1954

Horned Grebe, continued

(Behrend 1954). One to two birds remained at Bush L. from 8 May through 1 June 1967 (MIG 38:47).

Remarks: Found most often on large bodies of water, but may also be encountered on small lakes and ponds. During the peak of the migration and throughout the winter, sizeable rafts of Horned Grebes are occasionally found in suitable habitat. Molting birds in the spring are sometimes mistaken for Eared Grebes. High count: 405 on 23 Nov 1971, Booker T. Washington S.P. (MIG 43:26).

Substantiation: Specimen: 1, near Chattanooga, Hamilton Co., winter 1972-73 (UTMB, 200).

Red-necked Grebe, *Podiceps grisegena*
Status: Extremely Rare.
Spring: There are three spring records as follows: 26 Mar-2 Apr 1979, Chickamauga L. (MIG 50:69); 30 Apr-1 May 1977, Lebanon SBC (MIG 48:90); and 1 May 1920, Radnor L. (Dubke and Dubke 1975).
Fall: There are three fall records as follows: 7 Sept 1975, Nash. (MIG 47:18); 31 Oct-2 Nov 1976, Old Hickory L. (MIG 48:18); and 24 Nov 1984, Nickajack L. (Parks 1985).
Winter: All but one of the seven winter records have occurred in the eastern third of the state. These sightings include:

2 Dec 1956, Laurel L., Blount Co., MIG 28:10

17 Dec 1983, Chat. CBC, MIG 55:8

28 Dec, 15 Jan 1985/86, Roans Creek, MIG 57:62

2 Feb 1948, Tennessee NWR, (Cypert 1955)

18 Feb 1975, Booker T. Washington S.P., MIG 46:45

27 Feb-20 Mar 1978, Roans Creek, MIG 49:47, 71

Remarks: Of the fourteen known records, only once has this species been observed in west Tennessee. In 1895 a bird was reported by Rhoads (1895) from Reelfoot L. Eight of the records are from east Tennessee, a proportion consistent with the species' diagonal migration pattern across the eastern United States. All sightings are of one or two birds except for 12-27 Feb 1988 when up to six birds were present at Chickamauga L. (RLK, LHD).
Substantiation: Photographs: 1, Old Hickory L., 31 Oct 1976 (JPC–TBRC).

Eared Grebe, *Podiceps nigricollis*
Status: Extremely Rare. (Map A-2)
Spring: There are only two spring records: 12 Mar 1988, Percy Priest L., Davidson Co. (RLK) and 3 Apr 1977, Patrick Henry L. (MIG 48:77).
Fall: Observations of this species in the fall range from late Aug to late Nov, with at least four records from Radnor L. in Davidson Co. All six records follow:

26 Aug–2 Oct 1983, Kingston Steam Plant, MIG 55:23

4–9 Sept 1987, Radnor L., MIG 59:34

Eared Grebe, continued
  21 Sept 1981, Kingston Steam Plant, MIG 53:18
  4-9 Oct 1975, Radnor L., MIG 47:18
  12-19 Oct 1987, Radnor L., MIG 59:34
  1-21 Nov 1980, Radnor L., MIG 52:47
Winter: Two winter records exist: 14 Jan 1923 at Nash. (Ganier 1935) and 9-10 Jan 1981 in Knox Co. (MIG 52:48).
Remarks: Following the first state record in 1923, fifty-two years elapsed before the species was recorded again in 1975. All records are of single birds except for the 21 Sept 1981 sighting of a flock of three birds at the Kingston Steam Plant. Although it may occur on large bodies of water, this grebe has a tendency to use smaller lakes and ponds.
Substantiation: Photographs: 1, Radnor L., Davidson Co., 5 Oct 1975 (JPC−TBRC).

Western/Clark's Grebe, *Aechmophorus* (Genus)
Status: Accidental.
Remarks: Usually found on large bodies of water. There are five records of this genus in the state beginning with the observation of one bird at Woods Res. from 18 Nov 1973 to 10 Feb 1974 (MIG 45:21). Other records include: 20 Dec 1975, Reelfoot L. CBC (MIG 47:35); two birds on 20 Dec 1980, Chat. CBC (MIG 52:13); 19 Jan 1981, Chickamauga L. (MIG 52:48) and 1-2 Jan 1983, Hickory-Priest CBC (MIG 54:13). All of the records occurred when two "color phases" of the Western Grebe were recognized. The species was split into light phase Clark's (*A. clarkii*) and dark phase Western (*A. occidentalis*) Grebes in 1985. Documentation on the above sightings lacks enough detail to determine which species has occurred in Tennessee.

ORDER PROCELLARIIFORMES

FAMILY HYDROBATIDAE: **Storm-Petrels**

Band-rumped Storm-Petrel, *Oceanodroma castro*
Status: Accidental.
Remarks: Known from one record: on 24-26 Sept 1975 three birds were found dead or dying at GSMNP (MIG 47:23). The occurrence of this oceanic species was directly related to the passage of Hurricane Eloise. An unidentified storm-petrel with a forked tail and white rump was also noted at Collegedale following the hurricane on 24 Sept 1975 (MIG 47:20).
Substantiation: Specimen: 1, GSMNP, Sevier Co., 26 Sept 1975 (USNM, 526349).

ORDER PELECANIFORMES

FAMILY SULIDAE: Gannets

Northern Gannet, *Sula bassanus*
Status: Accidental (Provisional).
Remarks: Known from one record: on 29 Nov 1987 a well described imm. was observed along Interstate 65 in Robertson Co. The bird was observed flying from Kentucky into Tennessee (Braun 1988).
Substantiation: Adequately documented sight record (TBRC).

FAMILY PELECANIDAE: Pelicans

American White Pelican, *Pelecanus erythrorhynchos*
Status: Irregular.
Abundance: Very rare spring migrant, summer visitor and winter visitor; rare fall migrant.
Spring: There are only about five records from across the state as follows:
    23 Apr 1975, Cheatham L., MIG 46:66
    24-25 May 1975, Lauderdale Co., (Coffey 1976)
    6-8, 22 May 1983, Reelfoot L. SBC, MIG 54:51, (CGD)
    8 May 1935, Knoxville, (Johnson 1935)
    9-10 May 1971, Kentucky L., MIG 42:67
Summer: Three June records include 6 June 1945 at Tennessee NWR (Cypert 1955), 7 June 1945 near Pickwick L. dam (Weakley 1945), and 22-30 June 1985 at Fort Loudoun L., Knox Co. (MIG 56:113). There are also three July records: 9 July 1948, Tennessee NWR (Cypert 1955); 11 July 1934, Mud L. (MIG 5:62); and 31 July 1944, Mud L. (MIG 15:55).
Fall: Early Oct to late Nov. There is a handful of Aug and Sept records, most of them occurring prior to 1950.
    Arrivals: 18 Sept 1932, Mud L., (Coffey 1932)
                21 Sept 1937, GSMNP, (Stupka 1963)
                10 Oct 1948, Tennessee NWR, (Cypert 1955)

American White Pelican, continued

Departures: 27 Oct 1985, Tennessee NWR, MIG 57:25
24 Nov 1979, Reelfoot L., MIG 51:38
30 Nov 1985, Nickajack L., MIG 57:31

Winter: There are at least six Dec records with the latest being 29 Dec 1984 (MIG 56:6). There are no Jan or Feb records.

Remarks: Frequently uses shallow water areas and can be found resting on exposed shorelines. In the 1930s and 1940s the species was regularly reported from the Mud L. area of Shelby Co. where the high count for the state was obtained on 24 Aug 1941 when four hundred birds were seen (MIG 12:58). The species is reported twice as often in west Tennessee as it is in middle or east Tennessee.

Substantiation: Photographs: 22, Mississippi River, Lauderdale Co., 25 May 1975 (GOW—Milligan College).

Brown Pelican, *Pelecanus occidentalis*

Status: Accidental.

Remarks: Only three state records: 17 May 1936 at the Tennessee/Mississippi state line in Shelby Co. (M'Camey 1936); 6 June 1937 at Norris L. (Foster 1937); and 12 Apr 1983, Memp. (MIG 54:59). All sightings are of single birds. The 1983 bird was captured and released on 3 May 1983 at Gulfport, Mississippi.

Substantiation: Photograph: 1, Norris L., 6 June 1937 (I. G. Tupfer, MIG 8:82).

FAMILY PHALACROCORACIDAE: Cormorants

Double-crested Cormorant, *Phalacrocorax auritus*

Status: Regular. (Map A-3)

Abundance: East: uncommon migrant and winter resident, very rare summer visitor.

Middle and West: fairly common migrant, uncommon winter resident, rare summer visitor; formerly bred.

Fall: Migrants usually arrive by mid Aug. The appearance of birds in July may represent very early migrants or non-breeding summering birds. The peak of the migration occurs in Oct. Small numbers of cormorants often linger into the winter months.

Winter: Formerly wintered in large numbers at Reelfoot L. and the Duck River Unit of the Tennessee NWR (e.g., three thousand on 3 Jan 1954, Tennessee NWR, MIG 24:81). In recent years winter flocks have generally numbered fewer than one hundred birds. Fewer birds are found after midwinter.

Double-crested Cormorant, continued

Spring: Migrants usually arrive by late Mar. The peak of the migration occurs in Apr and May. Most migrants and winter residents depart for northern breeding areas by late May, but some birds linger well into the summer.

Summer: Has not nested in the state since 1955, when ten nests were in use in Benton Co. on Kentucky L. (Alsop 1980). Formerly nested at Reelfoot L. in the 1920s and 1930s with approximately 250 nests still in use as late as 1939 (Whittemore 1939). In 1949, a rookery that is no longer used by cormorants was established at the Duck River Unit of the Tennessee NWR, Humphreys Co.; this site had about one hundred nests on 3 Apr 1949 (Cypert 1949). A small number of recent non-breeding summer records exist for middle and west Tennessee. Very rarely seen in the east in the summer (e.g., 6 June 1986, HRA, MIG 57:113; and 5 July 1987, Chickamauga L. [JCR]).

Remarks: Usually found in or near large bodies of water where it perches in dead trees or snags to dry its wings. Nests in colonies. Occasionally observed soaring or migrating overhead in "V" formation. High count: 4,500 on 20 Dec 1952, Reelfoot L. CBC (MIG 23:69).

Substantiation: Specimen: 1 male, Reelfoot L., 27 Apr 1919 (LSUMZ, 80269).

FAMILY ANHINGIDAE: **Darters**

Anhinga, *Anhinga anhinga*

Status: Irregular. (Map A-4)

Abundance: West: rare migrant and summer resident.

Spring: Arrives by late Apr.

Arrivals: mid Mar 1980, Big Hill Pond S.P., (Waldron 1980)

17 Apr 1938, Reelfoot L., (Pitelka 1939)

24 Apr 1954, Tennessee NWR, MIG 25:28

Summer: Formerly nested at Reelfoot L. in the 1930s. The species had been virtually absent from this site for almost forty years when a nest was discovered near the lake in Lake Co. in 1977 (Pitts 1982). Incubating birds have been observed at this site in most years since 1981. One nest record exists for McNairy Co. in 1980 at Big Hill Pond S.P. (Waldron 1980), and the species was reported as nesting in Humphreys Co. at the Tennessee NWR in 1953 (Cypert 1955). Rhoads (1895) stated that Benjamin C. Miles found nesting evidence in the Mississippi River bottoms of Haywood and Lauderdale Counties. All recent summer records are from west Tennessee.

Fall: The departure of summering birds is poorly documented but probably occurs by late Aug. There are virtually no Sept records. The latest record is of thirteen birds on 29 Oct 1950 at President's Island, Shelby Co. (MIG 22:12).

Anhinga, continued
Remarks: Found along lakes, rivers and cypress swamps. Formerly more common, especially in west Tennessee where a high count of fifty on 29 May 1933 was made on the Reelfoot L. SBC (MIG 4:15). There are no published middle Tennessee records since 1959, and there is only one east Tennessee record: 11 Oct 1987, Amnicola Marsh, Hamilton Co. (LHD).
Substantiation: Egg set: Reelfoot L., Obion Co., 26 Apr 1919 (AFG–LSUMZ).

FAMILY FREGATIDAE: **Frigatebirds**

Magnificent Frigatebird, *Fregata magnificens*
Status: Accidental.
Remarks: Known from two records, both of which can probably be attributed to the passage of Hurricane Gilbert through the Gulf of Mexico in mid Sept 1988. A female was photographed in Hamblen Co. on Cherokee L. on 24 Sept 1988 (Joyce Haigh). Three days later, on 27 Sept 1988, another individual was found at Columbia (WNJ).
Substantiation: Photograph: 1 female, Cherokee L., Hamblen Co., 24 Sept 1988 (Joyce Haigh–TBRC).

ORDER CICONIIFORMES

FAMILY ARDEIDAE: **Bitterns and Herons**

American Bittern, *Botaurus lentiginosus*
Status: Regular. (Map A-5)
Abundance: Uncommon migrant, rare summer resident, very rare winter resident.
Spring: Usually not encountered in the spring until mid Mar when early migrants can be found by walking shallow marshes or drainage ditches lined with dense vegetation. The peak of the migration occurs in Apr and May. Most migrants depart by late May. Determination of actual departure dates is not possible due to the presence of breeding and non-breeding summering birds.

American Bittern, continued

Summer: June and July records exist for Buena Vista Marsh, Radnor L., Goose
  Pond in Grundy Co., Sumner Co., and Amnicola Marsh. Nesting evidence is
  not easily found. Four breeding records for the state. At Goose Pond,
  Grundy Co., the following nests were found: three nests with young on 26
  May 1935 (Ganier 1935a); a nest with four eggs on 14 May 1939 (Todd 1944)
  and a nest with eggs and young on 22 May 1976 (MIG 47:99). Also on 26
  May 1935, two additional nests were found in Coffee Co. (Ganier 1935a).
  Considered by Pitelka (1939) to be a summer resident at Reelfoot L.

Fall: Late Sept to mid Nov.

  Arrivals: 10 Sept 1948, Nash., (Spofford 1949)
                  16 Sept 1970, Amnicola Marsh, MIG 41:87
                  24 Sept 1985, Cross Creeks NWR, MIG 57:25
  Departures: 31 Oct 1971, Reelfoot L., MIG 42:90-91
                  19 Nov 1972, Cross Creeks NWR, MIG 44:22
                  29 Nov 1938, GSMNP, (Stupka 1963)

Winter: A very limited number of Dec and Jan records exist and range from 9
  Dec 1978 at Nash. (BNA:15) to 2 Jan 1961 on the Lebanon CBC (MIG
  31:74). One overwintering record, at Chat.: 17 Dec 1983-11 Mar 1984 (MIG
  55:49, 72-73). Three mid Feb records from Hamilton Co. as early as 14 Feb
  1976 (MIG 47:47) may represent very early spring migrants.

Remarks: Found in marshes and meadows with dense vegetative cover. Usually
  allows close approach before flushing because it relies on its cryptic coloration to conceal it in surrounding vegetation. High count: seven on 17 Apr
  1972, Goose Pond, Grundy Co. (MIG 43:50).

Substantiation: Specimen: 1 female, Nash., Davidson Co., 14 Sept 1922
  (LSUMZ, 75672).

Least Bittern, *Ixobrychus exilis*

Status: Regular. (Map A-6)

Abundance: Uncommon migrant and summer resident.

Spring: Arrives by early May.

  Arrivals: 4 Apr 1968, Knoxville, MIG 39:44
                  17 Apr 1972, Goose Pond, Grundy Co., MIG 43:50
                  29 Apr 1967, Reelfoot L. SBC, MIG 38:46

Summer: Has bred across the state in the following counties: Blount,
  Cheatham, Davidson, Dyer, Gibson, Grundy, Hamilton, Humphreys, Maury,
  Obion, Putnam, and Shelby. May sometimes occur in small colonies (e.g.,
  sixteen nests near Samburg at Reelfoot L. on 28 June 1971, MIG 42:67).

Fall: Departs by late Sept.

  Departures: 8 Oct 1932, Radnor L., BNA:15
                  10 Oct 1937, Knox Co., (Howell and Monroe 1957)
                  29 Sept-23 Oct 1979, Austin Springs, MIG 51:17

Remarks: Found in dense vegetation (e.g., creeping primrose-willow, cattails,
  sedges, *Phragmites*, etc.) bordering water. A much overlooked species,

Least Bittern, continued

breeding habitat still exists in many areas across the state. Mengel (1965) regarded the local population at Reelfoot L. as the largest in the southern U.S. High count: eighteen on 28 June 1971 near Samburg (MIG 42:67). There are no winter records.

Substantiation: Specimen: 1 female, Reelfoot L., 21 May 1923 (LSUMZ, 75671).

Great Blue Heron, *Ardea herodias*
Status: Regular. (Map A-7)
Abundance: Fairly common to common permanent resident.
Remarks: Found along rivers, ponds and lakes. Breeds in colonies. Influxes of spring and fall migrants are readily detected in Mar and Oct-Nov, respectively. Occurs as a non-breeder or post-breeding wanderer at many wetland locations statewide from late spring through early fall. Breeding evidence exists for Benton, Carroll, Hardin, Henry, Lake, Marion, Weakley, and Obion Counties. Nesting occurred regularly at Reelfoot L. through 1963 after a heronry was discovered there in 1921 (Ganier 1951; Pitts 1982). A new colony was discovered near this site in 1976. Ganier (1951) noted that no breeding evidence existed in 1950 for areas east of the Tennessee River. However, in 1949, Cypert (1949) documented the establishment of a Great Blue Heron colony consisting of about 500 nests at the Tennessee NWR in Humphreys Co. This colony is still active. A colony in Coffee Co. is described by Pitts (1973) and is also still active. A colony in Meigs Co. described by Pitts (1977) may have been established in 1965; it had 520 active nests in 1987 (MIG 58:144). Nesting has also been documented in Hamilton Co. since 1982, in McMinn Co. since 1986, in Rhea Co. since 1979, and in Roane Co. since 1983 (Pullin 1986). High count: five hundred on 24 Apr 1954, Tennessee NWR (MIG 25:28).
Substantiation: Specimen: 1 male, Reelfoot L., 28 May 1933 (LSUMZ, 75663).

Great Egret, *Casmerodius albus*
Status: Regular. (Map A-8)
Abundance: East and Middle: uncommon migrant and summer visitor, rare winter visitor.
West: fairly common migrant and summer resident, rare winter visitor.
Spring: Arrives by late Mar.
Arrivals: 10 Mar 1973, Gallatin, BNA:15
              13 Mar 1957, Shelby Co., MIG 28:7-8
              27 Mar 1973, Battle Creek, Marion Co., MIG 44:52
Summer: Occurs regularly in June and July in middle and east Tennessee, most likely as a result of post-breeding dispersal. Once nested in Humphreys Co. where approximately 150 nests were discovered on the Tennessee NWR on 3 Apr 1949 (Ganier 1951). No recent nest records exist for middle Tennessee. Commonly nested at Reelfoot L. between 1932 and the early 1950s (Ganier 1951). After this colony was disbanded in 1963, nesting was not documented

Great Egret, continued

again in Lake Co. until 1981 (Pitts 1982). Nests of this species were discovered near Dyersburg in 1964 (Coffey 1964) but this heronry was disbanded after 1969 (Leggett 1970). There are no east Tennessee nest records.

Fall: The largest numbers of birds are usually recorded in Aug and Sept, especially in west Tennessee. Fewer birds are found in Oct. Most birds have left the state by late Nov but small numbers may linger well into Jan or Feb.

Winter: There are over twenty Dec records and a handful of Jan and Feb records, the majority of which probably represent stragglers of the fall migration; some birds have successfully wintered (e.g., 21 Dec-25 Feb 1985-86, Cross Creeks NWR, MIG 57:56).

Remarks: Found along lakes, ponds or rivers. Usually breeds in colonies. High count: 1,219 on 6 Aug 1988, Ensley Bar, Shelby Co. (Robinson 1988a).

Substantiation: Egg set: Reelfoot L., Lake Co., 13 May 1934 (AFG−LSUMZ).

Snowy Egret, *Egretta thula*
Status: Regular. (Map A-9)
Abundance: East and Middle: rare migrant and summer visitor.
West: uncommon migrant and summer resident, very rare winter visitor.
Spring: Arrives by late Apr.

Arrivals:　　29 Mar 1988, Putnam Co., MIG 59:96
　　　　　　12 Apr 1987, Lake/Dyer Co., MIG 58:92
　　　　　　16 Apr 1986, Boone L., MIG 57:84

Summer: Occurs in east and middle Tennessee as a post-breeding wanderer. Most if not all recent sightings in west Tennessee represent post-breeding dispersals. Breeding was first documented for the state in 1950 when about 70-100 nests were found in a heronry located in a swamp 1.6 km east of Ridgely in Lake Co. (Ganier 1951). This colony disbanded sometime during the 1950s (Ganier 1960). It is not clear whether a colony near Redmond Bar on the Mississippi River containing about 150 nests of this species in 1952 was located in Tennessee (Shelby Co.) or Arkansas (Coffey 1952).

Fall: Departs by late Sept.

Departures:　20 Sept 1985, Cross Creeks NWR, MIG 57:25
　　　　　　26 Sept 1982, Shelby Co., MIG 54:19
　　　　　　6 Oct 1986, Austin Springs, MIG 58:27

Winter: One winter record: 24 Dec 1955, Reelfoot L. CBC (MIG 26:59).

Remarks: Found along lakes, rivers and ponds. Formerly less frequently observed in east Tennessee but now occurs there in most years. High count: 156 on 11 Aug 1988, Ensley Bar, Shelby Co. (Robinson 1988a).

Little Blue Heron, *Egretta caerulea*
Status: Regular. (Map A-10)
Abundance: East and Middle: uncommon migrant and summer resident, very rare winter visitor.

Little Blue Heron, continued
West: fairly common migrant and summer resident, very rare winter visitor.
Spring: Arrives by early Apr.
  Arrivals: 25 Mar 1968, Old Hickory L., MIG 39:43
  26 Mar 1973, Savannah Bay, MIG 44:52
  29 Mar 1969, Reelfoot L., MIG 40:44
Summer: Present during June and July across the state with post-breeding
  dispersals becoming most evident in July. There are no east Tennessee
  breeding records. Ganier discovered a small breeding colony of this species
  at Reelfoot L. in 1919 and a larger heronry in Lake Co. east of Ridgely in
  1950 (Ganier 1951). Although the Ridgely colony ceased to exist after the
  1950s, Ganier (1960) felt is was probable that some of these birds moved to
  a large heronry near Dyersburg, Dyer Co., which was discovered in 1960 and
  contained about five hundred Little Blue Heron nests. This colony remained
  in existence until 1969 (Leggett 1970). It is not clear whether a colony near
  Redmond Bar on the Mississippi River containing about six hundred nests
  of this species in 1952 was located in Tennessee (Shelby Co.) or Arkansas
  (Coffey 1952). Seventy-five young successfully hatched at the Tennessee NWR
  in Humphreys Co. from 1962 through 1970 (Pitts 1973). A small active
  nesting colony was discovered in Benton Co. in 1982 (Pullin et al. 1982). A
  single nest in Houston Co. in 1984 hatched three young that later died when
  the nest was abandoned (MIG 55:90).
Fall: Departs by mid Oct. Four Nov records exist, the latest of which is 23 Nov
  1977, Nash. (MIG 49:42).
  Departures: 21 Oct 1974, HRA, MIG 46:21
  21 Oct 1977, Dyersburg, (Criswell 1979)
  23 Oct 1979, Nash., MIG 51:16
Winter: There are at least three Dec records as follows: 26 Dec 1936, Memp.
  CBC (MIG 8:7); 28 Dec 1970, Lebanon CBC (MIG 42:8); and 19 Dec 1971,
  Knoxville CBC (MIG 43:11).
Remarks: Found along lakes, rivers and ponds. Although uncommon in middle
  Tennessee, it has been encountered in flocks of as many as 70-100 birds at
  the Tennessee NWR in Humphreys Co. and the Cross Creeks NWR. High
  count: three thousand on 30 June 1962, Dyersburg (MIG 33:47).
Substantiation: Specimen: 1 male, Wooten Farm, Montgomery Co., 27 July
  1968 (APSU, 2312).

Tricolored Heron, *Egretta tricolor*
Status: Extremely Rare.
Remarks: Found along lakes, rivers and ponds. There are at least fourteen
  records from locations spanning the entire width of the state. First recorded
  on 18 July 1948 at Mud L. (Coffey 1948), then not recorded for a period of
  fourteen years. Earliest arrival is 1-2 Apr 1988, Great Lakes Pond, Carter
  Co. (MIG 59:103). Latest departure is 31 Aug-16 Sept 1978, HRA (MIG
  50:22). Other records:

Tricolored Heron, continued
9 Apr 1972, Old Hickory L., MIG 43:50
1 May 1978, Holston River, Hawkins Co., MIG 49:69
8 May 1967, Amnicola Marsh, MIG 38:50
15 May 1971, Memphis, MIG 42:67
4 July-7 Sept 1985, Shelby Co., MIG 56:107/57:22
23-24 July 1973, HRA, MIG 44:86
26 July-4 Aug 1987, Cross Creeks NWR (JCR)
10-24 Aug 1970, HRA, MIG 41:87
27 Aug 1974, Tennessee NWR, MIG 46:18
8 Sept 1962, Ashland City Marsh, (Parmer 1962)
All of the above records are of single birds. During the 31 July-14 Aug 1988 period, as many as twenty-six birds were found using a heron roost on Ensley Bar in the Mississippi River, Shelby Co. (Robinson 1988a).
Substantiation: Photograph: 1 imm., Cross Creeks NWR, Stewart Co., 26 July 1987 (JCR—TBRC).

Cattle Egret, *Bubulcus ibis*
Status: Regular. (Map A-11)
Abundance: East and Middle: uncommon migrant, rare summer visitor.
West: fairly common migrant and summer resident.
Spring: Arrives by early Apr. Summers in west Tennessee but a majority of the birds depart east and middle Tennessee by late May.
Arrivals: 7 Mar 1976, Memp., MIG 47:45
              8 Mar 1974, Cove L., MIG 45:23
              2 Apr 1979, Old Hickory L., MIG 50:68
Summer: Summers regularly in west Tennessee and is a rare post-breeding wanderer in most of middle and east Tennessee. Eight nests were discovered in 1964 at the Dyersburg heronry, Dyer Co. (Coffey 1964), a nesting site that was last used in 1969 (Leggett 1970). Four nests were discovered in a colony on Cherokee L., Grainger Co., in 1975 (Pitts 1977). Photographs were taken of a nest with two young which was observed from 3 July to 19 Aug 1987 at the Gallatin Steam Plant in Sumner Co. (MIG 58:139).
Fall: More frequently found in Sept and Oct. Late fall stragglers depart by late Nov. However, there are three Dec records the latest of which includes one bird on the 22 Dec 1973 Reelfoot L. CBC (MIG 45:11).
Departures: 25 Nov 1965, Chickamauga L., MIG 36:95
               28 Nov 1972, Cannon Co., MIG 44:22
               22 Dec 1984, Reelfoot L. CBC, MIG 56:6.
Remarks: Found in pastures and near lakes and ponds. A self-introduced species that first appeared in North America in 1941 or 1942 (Terres 1980); the first state record was on 5-6 May 1961 in Anderson Co. (Olson 1961).
High count: 1,884 on 6 Aug 1988, Ensley Bar, Shelby Co. (Robinson 1988a).
Substantiation: Specimen: 1 ad. male, Dyer Co., 22 May 1988 (UTMB, 411).

Green-backed Heron, *Butorides striatus*
Status: Regular.
Abundance: Fairly common migrant and summer resident, rare winter resident.
Spring: Arrives by late Mar.
    Arrivals: 11 Mar 1979, Radnor L., BNA:15
                     12 Mar 1983, Red Bank, Hamilton Co., MIG 54:64
                     21 Mar 1987, Shelby Co., MIG 58:92
Summer: Breeds widely throughout the state. This species is typically a solitary nester. However, of note are two colonies described for Shelby Co. during 1933-1935 (Coffey 1981) and Sullivan Co. in 1966 (Coffey 1966).
Fall: Departs by early Nov, but may linger well into midwinter.
    Departures: 8 Nov 1966, near Elizabethton, MIG 37:85
                     12 Nov 1971, Cross Creeks NWR, MIG 43:24
                     28 Nov 1963, Knoxville, MIG 34:74
Winter: There are more than forty winter records, about 80% of which occurred in Dec. Late winter records include: 14 Feb 1968, Fort Loudoun dam (MIG 39:44); 4 Jan and 21 Feb 1983, Chickamauga L. (MIG 54:45); and 15 Jan 1971, Knoxville (MIG 42:20).
Remarks: Found along streams, ponds and small lakes. The surprising number of winter records represents a tendency for fall migrants to linger where suitable habitat and open water remain available. High count: fifty-five on 4 Aug 1985, HRA (MIG 57:31).
Substantiation: Specimen: 1 female, Montgomery Co., 5 May 1968 (APSU, 2311).

Black-crowned Night-Heron, *Nycticorax nycticorax*
Status: Regular. (Map A-12)
Abundance: East and Middle: fairly common migrant and summer resident, rare winter resident.
West: uncommon migrant and summer resident, very rare winter visitor.
Spring: Arrives by mid Mar (some birds overwinter near traditional breeding areas).
    Arrivals: 6 Mar 1980, Old Hickory L., MIG 51:39
                     6 Mar 1988, Memp. (CHB, JRW)
                     11 Mar 1962, near Kingsport, MIG 33:17
Summer: Post-breeding wanderers become evident in early July. Formerly bred in west Tennessee at the Lake Co. heronry at Reelfoot L. where Ganier (1951) found it nesting in 1933 and Gersbacher (1939) counted 45 nests in 1938. Several colonies, some quite large, have been documented in middle and east Tennessee in Blount, Davidson, Knox, Loudon, Monroe, Roane, Sevier, and Sumner Counties. The Bordeaux heronry in Davidson Co. has been in existence since 1908 (Pitts 1973). A colony in Grainger Co. established in 1974 (Pitts 1977) became inactive in 1986 (Pullin 1986). Pullin (1986) counted 493 nests in a Sevier Co. colony near Sevierville in 1985,

Black-crowned Night-Heron, continued
reported that 174-324 nests were used in the Bordeaux heronry in 1986, and reported active colonies from Loudon and Sumner Counties in 1986.

Fall: Found regularly in migration through mid to late Sept, after which numbers conspicuously drop off. Most birds have departed by mid Nov; however, there are many Dec and early Jan records, indicating that some birds remain into or through the winter.

Winter: Overwinters in small numbers in middle and east Tennessee. At least one record for west Tennessee. Becomes extremely scarce by late winter. Considered a permanent resident in the Nash. area (BNA:15). Representative dates include:

26 Dec 1986, Shelby Co., MIG 58:53
2 Jan 1982, Kingsport CBC, MIG 53:6
10 Nov-Mar 1955-1956, near Bush L., MIG 27:17
23 Feb 1962, Elizabethton, MIG 33:18

Remarks: Found in wooded swamps and around lakes and ponds. Non-breeders and migrants are often encountered at dusk or dawn. Also active at night. There is a likelihood that additional colonies may become established. High count: seven hundred (from an aerial photograph during the summer of 1984 at the Bordeaux heronry, BNA:15).

Substantiation: Specimen: 1 female, near Nash., Davidson Co., 17 Nov 1921 (LSUMZ, 75669).

Yellow-crowned Night-Heron, *Nycticorax violaceus*
Status: Regular. (Map A-13)
Abundance: Uncommon migrant and summer resident, very rare winter visitor.
Spring: Arrives by late Mar.
Arrivals:　　7 Mar 1988, Memp., MIG 59:94
　　　　　　21 Mar 1977, Shelby Bottoms, Davidson Co., MIG 48:76
　　　　　　23 Mar 1980, Gap Creek, Carter Co., MIG 51:63

Summer: Found breeding in all three regions of the state. However, may nest singly or in small colonies and thus be overlooked as a breeder. A review of the literature resulted in satisfactory breeding documentation in the following counties: Blount, Carter, Davidson, Greene, Hamilton, Hardeman, Hardin, Henry, Madison, Maury, Meigs, Obion, Rutherford, Sevier, and Shelby. Sixty-seven nests were counted at a Memp. colony in 1977 (MIG 48:75).

Fall: Departs by late Oct.
Departures:　26 Oct 1973, HRA, MIG 44:101
　　　　　　19 Nov 1972, Cross Creeks NWR, MIG 44:22
　　　　　　21 Nov 1970, Cross Creeks NWR, MIG 42:19

Winter: Five Dec records, the earliest of which is 16 Dec 1979, Memp. CBC (MIG 51:31), and the latest of which is 30 Dec 1978, Highland Rim CBC (MIG 50:10). Two Feb records: 27 Feb 1976, Gallatin (MIG 47:45) and 24 Feb 1980, Nash. (MIG 51:39). All winter records should be documented.

Yellow-crowned Night-Heron, continued

Remarks: Found in swamps and along wooded ponds and streams. Active at night; often encountered at dawn or dusk going to or from foraging areas. High count: twenty-nine on 15 June 1985, Hatchie NWR (MIG 56:107).

Substantiation: Specimen: 1 male, Shiloh National Military Park, Hardin Co., 30 May 1926 (LSUMZ, 75670).

FAMILY THRESKIORNITHIDAE: **Ibises and Spoonbills**

White Ibis, *Eudocimus albus*
Status: Irregular.
Abundance: Rare fall migrant.
Fall: Early July to late Sept.
    Arrivals: 27 June 1973, Sequatchie Valley, MIG 44:86
                   2 July 1981, near Dyersburg, MIG 52:95
                   8 July 1970, Giles Co., (Williams 1971)
    Departures: 3 Sept 1978, Hickman Co., MIG 50:20
                   1-6 Oct 1978, Cove L., MIG 50:22
                   13 Oct 1977, Dyersburg, (Criswell 1979)

Remarks: Found along shallow marshes, pools and swamps. Usually feeds and roosts with other herons. All records indicate post-breeding wanderers; there are no spring records. High count: 103 on 7 Aug 1980, Dyersburg (MIG 51:91).

Glossy Ibis, *Plegadis falcinellus*
Status: Extremely Rare.
Remarks: Found in marshes and along lakes and ponds. All records are listed below.
Spring: 21 Apr 1984, Penal Farm, MIG 55:67
       25-30 Apr 1971, near Reelfoot L., MIG 42:67
       3 May 1985, Sumner Co., MIG 56:75
       8 May 1971, Kingsport SBC, MIG 42:37
       8-10 May 1967, Amnicola Marsh, (Dubke 1968)
       10-11 May 1988, Stewart Co. (DWB, JCR)
       11 May 1983, Shelby Co., MIG 54:59
       24-25 May 1975, Lauderdale Co., (Coffey 1976)
       25 May 1971, Philadelphia, MIG 42:71
Summer: One record: 30 June 1976, Haywood Co. (MIG 47:99).
Fall: 28 Aug 1978, Eagle Bend Fish Hatchery, MIG 50:22
     31 Aug 1975, HRA, MIG 47:20
     6 Nov 1973, Woods Res., MIG 45:21

Glossy Ibis, continued
The first *Plegadis* record for the state was an unidentified bird at Mud L. on 24 Aug 1941 (MIG 12:58). Documentation on some of the above-listed records was often less than desirable. Fall birds should be identified with care as most birds are indistinguishable from the White-faced Ibis at this time of the year. Two birds were reported at Cross Creeks NWR on 4-7 May 1969 without details (Robinson and Blunk 1989). High count: fourteen on 8 May 1971 at Kingsport.
Substantiation: Adequately documented sight records (TBRC).

[White-faced Ibis, *Plegadis chihi*]
Status: Hypothetical.
Remarks: Mount (1945) described a bird of this species at Mud L. on 23 Sept 1945 at the Tennessee/Mississippi border. Not enough detail was provided to allow separation from the Glossy Ibis. Both of these species are virtually indistinguishable at this time of year. The first *Plegadis* record for the state was an unidentified bird at Mud L. on 24 Aug 1941 (MIG 12:58).

Roseate Spoonbill, *Ajaia ajaja*
Status: Accidental (Provisional).
Remarks: Known from one record. A juvenile bird was present at the Duck River Unit of the Tennessee NWR in Humphreys Co. from 29 June 1972 through 13 July 1972 (Rauber 1972).
Substantiation: Adequately documented sight record.

FAMILY CICONIIDAE: **Storks**

Wood Stork, *Mycteria americana*
Status: Extremely Rare (Federally Endangered).
Spring: Represented by about four records:
      16 Apr 1937, Knox Co., (Howell and Monroe 1958)
      17 Apr 1945, Reelfoot L., (Spofford 1945)
      17 May 1944, Lauderdale Co., (Monroe 1944)
      25 May 1975, Stewart Co., (Dinsmore 1975)
Summer: Represented by three records:
      13 June 1932, Claiborne Co., (Ogden 1933)
      14 June 1984, Reelfoot L., MIG 55:87
      June 1966, Chat., MIG 37:82
Fall: Mid July to mid Oct.

Wood Stork, continued

Arrivals: 14 July 1934, Reelfoot L., (Coffey 1934)

                17 July 1985, Shelby Co., MIG 56:107

                25 July 1925, Radnor L., BNA:16

Departures: 7 Oct 1983, Knoxville, MIG 55:24

                16 Oct 1938, Mud L., MIG 9:95

                20 Nov 1963, Shelby Forest, MIG 34:71

Remarks: Found along rivers, swamps and shallow pools and lakes. Most records indicate this species occurs in Tennessee as a post-breeding wanderer. Formerly more frequently seen; only about twelve records since 1960, which correlates with a then all-time low stork population in 1957 (Terres 1980). About two-thirds of the state records have come from west Tennessee, with many sightings from Mud L. in Shelby Co. There are about six east and six middle Tennessee records. High count: five hundred on 27 Sept 1953, Lauderdale Co. (MIG 25:15).

Substantiation: Photographs: 2, Cross Creeks NWR, Stewart Co., Aug 1983 (Fabian F. Romero — TBRC).

ORDER ANSERIFORMES

FAMILY ANATIDAE: **Swans, Geese and Ducks**

Fulvous Whistling-Duck, *Dendrocygna bicolor*

Status: Extremely Rare.

Remarks: Found in marshes and adjacent agricultural areas. First state record and high count was of thirty-one birds on 29 Jan 1965 at Norris dam; the species may have been seen a few years prior to this on Cove L. in Campbell Co. (Olson 1965). Several other records exist for 1965: 23 Mar 1965, Amnicola Marsh (Crownover 1965); 4 Apr-20 June 1965, Cross Creeks NWR (Ryan 1968); and 9 Sept 1965, Indian Creek, Humphreys Co. (Petit 1967). Other records: 11 Apr 1972, Sequatchie Valley (MIG 43:52); 13-21 May 1976, near Gallatin, Sumner Co. (MIG 47:76) and 27 Nov 1970, Tennessee NWR (MIG 42:19).

Substantiation: Photograph: 1, Green's L., Sumner Co., 15 May 1976 (JPC — TBRC).

Black-bellied Whistling-Duck, *Dendrocygna autumnalis*

Status: Accidental.

Remarks: First state record was of two adults on Broad Slough near Reelfoot L. from 1 Aug-8 Oct 1978; these birds apparently bred and raised eight young which were seen on 7-8 Oct 1978 (Pitts 1982a). One bird was present

Black-bellied Whistling-Duck, continued
at the Penal Farm in Shelby Co. from 24 Nov-18 Dec 1985 (MIG 57:22, 51).
Four birds were discovered in Ensley Bottoms, Shelby Co., on 17 June 1988
(JRW).
Substantiation: Photographs: 1-2, Reelfoot L., 31 Aug 1978 (JPC—TBRC).

Tundra Swan, *Cygnus columbianus*
Status: Regular.
Abundance: Rare migrant and winter resident.
Fall: Arrives by early Nov.
　　Arrivals:　　25 Oct 1959, Hiwassee Bridge, (West 1959)
　　　　　　　　7 Nov 1971, Cross Creeks NWR, MIG 43:24
　　　　　　　　22 Nov 1978, Obion Co., MIG 50:41
Winter: Has been found in all three regions of the state during Dec, Jan and
　　Feb. Notable concentrations include fifteen on 3-24 Jan 1976 at Hatchie
　　NWR (MIG 47:45) and twelve on 14 Jan 1979 near Memp. (MIG 50:41).
Spring: Departs by mid Mar.
　　Departures:　15 Mar 1986, Gooch WMA, MIG 57:74
　　　　　　　　15 Mar 1973, Jonesborough, MIG 44:25
　　　　　　　　18 Mar 1967, Cross Creeks NWR, (Ryan 1968)
Remarks: Found on lakes and ponds. Occasionally travels in family groups. A
　　minor invasion was detected in the winter of 1973-1974 and a major invasion
　　was evident in the winter of 1978-1979, when a high count of twenty-seven
　　on 27 Nov 1978 at Woods Res. (MIG 50:42) was made. The average flock
　　size in Tennessee is three birds.
Substantiation: Specimen: 1, Reelfoot L., 1895 (LSUMZ, 9152).

Trumpeter Swan, *Cygnus buccinator*
Status: Extirpated.
Remarks: Known from two sightings made by John James Audubon during his
　　flatboat trip on the Mississippi River in 1820. One swan was sighted in west
　　Tennessee on the Mississippi River on 26 Nov 1820 and another was seen on
　　30 Nov near the Third Chickasaw Bluff by the Shelby/Tipton Co. line
　　(Alsop 1972; Deaderick 1940).

*Mute Swan, *Cygnus olor*
Status: Extremely Rare.
Spring: Known from at least three records:
　　　　　2 Mar 1985, South Holston L., MIG 56:81
　　　　　9-20 Mar 1985, Chickamauga L., MIG 56:79
　　　　　9-12 May 1985, Ashland City, BNA:16
Winter: Late Dec to late Feb.
　　Arrivals:　　20 Dec 1980, Chat. CBC, MIG 52:13
　　　　　　　　26 Dec 1983, Hickory-Priest CBC, BNA:16
　　　　　　　　28 Dec 1985, Bristol CBC, MIG 57:9

*Mute Swan, continued
Departures: 7 Feb 1988, Stewart Co. (JCR)
21 Feb 1970, Boone L., MIG 41:45
22 Feb 1984, Boone L., MIG 55:49

Remarks: Introduced into the United States around the middle of the nineteenth century, this swan is an extremely rare visitor in Tennessee. Apparently migrates into and out of Tennessee on its own; however, some birds may be of local origin (escapes). There undoubtedly have been many observations of this species that are unpublished due to doubts about the birds' status. Midwinter birds probably accompany southward bound geese and other waterfowl during the latter stages of the fall migration. First state record was of one bird on 16 Jan 1970 on the South Holston River Embayment, Sullivan Co. (Coffey 1970). High count: six on 3 Feb 1985, South Holston L. (MIG 56:58).
Substantiation: Specimen: 1, Reelfoot L., Dec 1985 (UTMB, 407).

Greater White-fronted Goose, *Anser albifrons*
Status: Irregular.
Abundance: Rare migrant and winter resident.
Fall: Arrives by early Nov.
Arrivals: 5 Oct 1971, Shelby Co., (Waldron 1987)
26 Oct 1984, Cross Creeks NWR, MIG 56:19
3 Nov 1974, HRA, MIG 46:45

Winter: Sightings are more or less evenly distributed among Dec, Jan and Feb. Records are concentrated more in middle and west Tennessee.
Spring: Departs by late Mar.
Departures: 14 Mar 1985, Dyer Co., MIG 56:74
30 Mar 1985, Lawrence Co., MIG 56:75
1 Apr 1961, Cove L., (Olson 1961a)

Remarks: Found along lakes, shorelines and in wheat and corn fields. Most often encountered with other geese at state and federal refuges. First state record was of three birds at Memp. on 11 Mar 1945 (Hoyt 1945). More than fifty state records; average flock size in Tennessee is three birds. High count: fifteen on 24 Dec 1978, Concord, Knox Co. (MIG 50:44). Domesticated geese are sometimes misidentified as this species. Atypical (late spring and early fall) records include: 26 Apr 1980, Elizabethton SBC (MIG 51:55); 2-3 May 1986, Columbia SBC (MIG 57:66); and 21 Aug and 24-25 Sept 1973, HRA (MIG 44:102).

Snow Goose, *Chen caerulescens*
Status: Regular.
Abundance: East: uncommon migrant and winter resident.
Middle and West: fairly common migrant and winter resident, very rare summer visitor.
Fall: Arrives by late Sept.

Snow Goose, continued

Arrivals: 21 Sept 1976, Percy Warner Park, MIG 48:18

22 Sept 1965, near Greeneville, MIG 36:97

12 Oct 1967, Reelfoot L., MIG 38:94

Winter: Occurs in small numbers during Dec, Jan and Feb throughout the state. Larger numbers are usually found in middle and west Tennessee (e.g., four hundred on 31 Dec 1982, Tennessee NWR, MIG 54:13).

Spring: Exact dates of departure are difficult to determine due to the presence of lingering birds. Most migrants and winter residents leave for northern breeding areas by late Mar; however, there are at least seventeen records for Apr and May ranging from 12 Apr 1978, Cove L. (MIG 49:69) to 15 May 1960, Shelby Co. (MIG 31:30). See comments under Summer.

Summer: Apparently some non-breeding individuals do not complete the northward migration in the spring. Two ad. and six imm. were at the Tennessee NWR from 6-18 July 1951 (Cypert 1955). Also recorded at Ashland City on 1 June 1975. One bird was present at Memp. from 15 May through 21 Aug 1960 (MIG 31:44).

Remarks: Found in open habitats around grain fields, lakes and rivers. Easily flushed by low-flying aircraft or eagles. Most frequently encountered at the federal and state waterfowl refuges. Blue phase birds usually arrive first in the fall. High count: two thousand on 19 Oct 1970, Tennessee NWR (MIG 41:84).

Substantiation: Specimen: 1, Stewart Co., 6 Nov 1967 (APSU, 1616).

Ross' Goose, *Chen rossii*

Status: Accidental.

Remarks: Known from three records: 20 Nov 1986 (1 ad.), Cross Creeks NWR (Robinson 1988b); 23 Dec-24 Jan 1987/88 (1 ad.), Cross Creeks NWR (JCR); and 25-26 Feb 1988 (3 ad.), Britton Ford area of the Tennessee NWR, Henry Co. (JCR). Frequents the same habitat as Snow Geese and almost always occurs with that species. Traditional wintering grounds include the San Joaquin and Sacramento Valleys of California; however, in recent years it has been regularly found throughout much of the Mississippi Flyway. Has become an annual migrant in Illinois (Peterjohn 1987) and was discovered in Kentucky in 1986 (Palmer-Ball and Robinson 1987). May soon prove to be a rare migrant in Tennessee. Field marks and methods used to identify this species are summarized by Robinson (1982).

Substantiation: Photographs: 1 ad., Cross Creeks NWR, Stewart Co., 23 Dec 1987 (JCR – TBRC).

Brant, *Branta bernicla*

Status: Extremely Rare.

Remarks: Normally winters along the Atlantic and Pacific coasts. First state record: one bird on 22-26 Oct 1939 at Elkmont, Sevier Co. (Stupka 1963). High count: nineteen birds on 29 Dec 1952 and 9 Jan 1953 at the Duck

Brant, continued

River Unit of the Tennessee NWR, Humphreys Co. (Cypert 1955). Other records include: 20 Oct 1959, Chat. (West 1959a); 29 Oct-21 Nov 1974, HRA (MIG 46:21); 31 Oct 1965, Hiwassee Island (DeVore and Dubke 1966) and one shot at this site in Nov 1965 (DeVore 1969); 2 Mar-28 May 1974, Memp. (Coffey 1974); and two birds from 17 Dec 1981 to 28 Feb 1982 with one bird remaining throughout the year and lingering until 4 Jan 1983, Cross Creeks NWR (Robinson and Blunk 1989).

Substantiation: Photograph: 1, Arlington, Shelby Co., 6 May 1974 (JPC—TBRC).

Barnacle Goose, *Branta leucopsis*

Status: Accidental.

Remarks: An Old World species which nests in Greenland (Terres 1980), it was first recorded in Tennessee on 10 Feb-17 Mar 1968 at Cove L. (MIG 39:44). Placed on the state list of confirmed species by the TOS Bird Records Committee in 1983 (Nicholson 1983). Other records include: 1 Mar-24 Apr 1970, Tennessee NWR (MIG 41:42); 24-27 Jan 1976, Cross Creeks NWR (MIG 47:45); and 11 Jan 1983, Tennessee NWR (Nicholson 1983a). One or two birds were present in each sighting.

Substantiation: Photographs: 1, Tennessee NWR, Humphreys Co., 23 Mar 1970 (J.N. Riggins—TBRC).

Canada Goose, *Branta canadensis*

Status: Regular.

Abundance: Fairly common to common migrant and winter resident, uncommon summer resident.

Fall: Early migrants from northern breeding areas usually arrive by mid Sept. By late Nov, areas in middle and west Tennessee have acquired notable concentrations (e.g., 22,000 on 24 Nov 1970 at Tennessee NWR, MIG 42:19).

Arrivals: 4 Sept 1967, Hiwassee Island, MIG 38:97
              9 Sept 1973, Cove L., MIG 44:102
              26 Sept 1985, Cross Creeks NWR (JCR)

Winter: Usually found in comparatively small numbers in east Tennessee but can be found in large concentrations in middle and west Tennessee (e.g., 36,000 on 28 Jan 1986 at Cross Creeks NWR, MIG 57:56).

Spring: Migrants and winter residents usually depart by mid Mar but actual dates when wintering birds leave are not well documented due to the presence of a breeding population. Recently hatched young may be seen swimming with adults as early as late Apr.

Summer: Distribution of breeding birds is not well documented in the literature. However, several notable breeding locations include the Percy Priest/Old Hickory L. area, Stewart Co., upper east Tennessee, Melton Hill, Cordell Hull and Chickamauga Lakes, Woods and Tims Ford Reservoirs, and the Watts Bar L. area. There are also many small, local populations

Canada Goose, continued

distributed across the state. There are fewer resident birds in west Tennessee during the summer. Breeding still occurs at Reelfoot L. where Ganier (1933a) noted the occurrence of a number of reliable nest records. Bierly (1980) reported that the success of the Old Hickory L. population (which began in the 1950s as a small captive breeding flock on a private Sumner Co. farm) was responsible for the stocking of Canada Geese throughout Tennessee. Many reports of successful breeding, especially in upper east Tennessee, have occurred since the stocking program began in the mid-1970s. Currently, the size of the statewide resident population is estimated to range from ten to fifteen thousand birds (Ed Warr, pers. comm.).

Remarks: Found in grain fields and along lakes, ponds and rivers; resident birds may also occur on residential lawns, golf courses and other similar areas. Wintering birds primarily include representatives of the Mississippi Valley Population of Canada Geese which are found in west Tennessee and as far east as the Cross Creeks and Tennessee NWRs; and the Tennessee Valley Population of Canada Geese, the birds of which are distributed throughout east and middle Tennessee. Breeding birds are generally of the Giant race of Canada Geese (*B. canadensis maxima*) (Bierly 1980). A summer flock at Cross Creeks NWR, which was surveyed in 1987 (236 ad. and 39 goslings), was also started with the acquisition of 17 Giant Canada Geese between 1967 and 1970. Population concentration areas include many of the state and federal waterfowl refuges. High count: 112,500 on 20 Dec 1975, Reelfoot L. CBC (MIG 47:35).

Substantiation: Specimen: 1, near Big Sandy, Henry Co., 28 Nov 1971 (UTMB, 120).

Wood Duck, *Aix sponsa*

Status: Regular.

Abundance: Fairly common migrant and summer resident, uncommon winter resident.

Spring: Arrival and departure dates are obscured by the presence of wintering birds and a breeding population. Spring migrants usually arrive by mid Feb. Small flocks of as many as 25-40 birds can be found throughout Mar and into early Apr. Resident birds begin seeking out nesting sites by mid Mar.

Summer: Nesting records are well distributed across all three regions of the state. Broods of young ducks are usually found by early May, but broods from late nesters can be seen in late July and into early Aug. An estimated 358-1,647 young were produced each year in a nest box program at Hatchie NWR, Lauderdale and Haywood Counties, from 1967 through 1972 (Waldron 1982).

Fall: By Aug, resident birds and fledged young form evening roosts that are used daily throughout Aug and Sept. Migrants from breeding areas north of Tennessee usually arrive by mid Sept. By late Oct most birds have departed for southern wintering areas.

Wood Duck, continued

Winter: Becomes less common in winter, especially in east Tennessee. Found consistently in small numbers in middle and west Tennessee. Since 1980, it has been recorded on an average of 11 CBCs each year.

Remarks: Found on lakes, ponds and wooded streams and swamps. Nests in tree cavities or where active nest box programs are adequately maintained. Formerly occurred in unusually large concentrations at Reelfoot L., including a high count of 4,850 on 10 Oct 1967 (MIG 38:94). A notable concentration in the east was of 396 on 9 Sept 1969, HRA (MIG 40:92).

Substantiation: Specimen: 1, near Clarksville, Montgomery Co., 2 June 1940 (LSUMZ, 75673).

Green-winged Teal, *Anas crecca*

Status: Regular.

Abundance: Fairly common migrant and winter resident, very rare summer visitor.

Fall: Arrives by mid Aug.

Arrivals: 23 July 1983, Shelby Co., MIG 54:86

1 Aug 1965, Amnicola Marsh, MIG 36:68

9 Aug 1986, Monsanto Ponds, Maury Co., MIG 58:23

Winter: May be found in sizeable flocks in Dec and Jan at state and federal waterfowl refuges (e.g., six hundred on 1 Jan 1957, Tennessee NWR, MIG 27:71; and two thousand on 1 Jan 1983, Hiwassee CBC, MIG 54:13). Becomes slightly less detectable by midwinter across the state.

Spring: Departs by late Apr after an influx of migrating flocks in Mar.

Departures: 28 Apr 1968, Knoxville SBC, MIG 39:31

2 May 1987, Memp. SBC, MIG 58:81

14 May 1955, Nash. SBC, MIG 26:27

Summer: Known from two records: a pair on 3 June 1986 at the Tatumville Marsh in Dyer Co. (MIG 57:103), and an ad. male on 2 June-31 July 1988 at Cross Creeks NWR (JCR).

Remarks: Found on mudflats and in shallow pools, lakes and bays. High count: 4,400 on 26 Oct 1967, Reelfoot L. (MIG 38:94).

Substantiation: Specimen: 1 female, Barkley L., Stewart Co., 9 Sept 1970 (APSU, 2509).

American Black Duck, *Anas rubripes*

Status: Regular.

Abundance: East: fairly common migrant and winter resident, very rare summer resident.

Middle and West: common migrant and winter resident, very rare summer resident.

Fall: Arrives by late Aug.

American Black Duck, continued
Arrivals:　　6 Aug 1972, Savannah Bay, MIG 43:101
　　　　　　　9 Aug 1987, Cross Creeks NWR (JCR)
　　　　　　　20 Aug 1986, Cross Creeks NWR, MIG 58:23
Winter: A widespread winter resident throughout middle and west Tennessee
　　where large concentrations are regularly found (e.g., 5,000 on 28 Dec 1964,
　　Dyersburg CBC, MIG 35:111; and 11,000 on 20 Jan 1984, Cross Creeks
　　NWR, MIG 55:45). Fewer birds are found in the eastern third of the state,
　　where the species is also widespread.
Spring: Departs by mid May.
　　Departures:　　18 May 1978, Watauga River, MIG 49:95
　　　　　　　　　19 May 1960, Bush L., (Parmer 1962a)
　　　　　　　　　25 May 1986, Gallatin Steam Plant, MIG 57:76
Summer: Breeding occurred in the 1960s at the Cross Creeks NWR in Stewart
　　Co. (Robinson and Blunk 1989). The first east Tennessee nest was discovered
　　at Alcoa Marsh, Blount Co., in 1972 when a hen and a nest with ten eggs
　　were found (MIG 43:52). Has nested occasionally in Blount Co. since then
　　and also at Fort Loudoun L. in 1974 (MIG 45:77). There are over ten non-
　　breeding summer records ranging from 2 June 1955 at Radnor L. (BNA:17)
　　to 30 July 1987, Robertson Co. (MIG 58:140). Non-breeding birds also have
　　been found recently at the Tennessee and Cross Creeks NWRs and at Mon-
　　santo ponds in Maury Co.
Remarks: Found on lakes and ponds and in forested wetlands. Hybridizes with
　　the Mallard; birds showing plumage characteristics of both species are occa-
　　sionally found. Large numbers are frequently encountered at the federal and
　　state waterfowl refuges. High count: 29,000 on 28 Dec 1966, Reelfoot L.
　　CBC (MIG 37:64).
Substantiation: Specimen: 1, Kentucky L., Henry Co., winter 1969-1970
　　(UTMB, 99).

Mallard, *Anas platyrhynchos*
Status: Regular.
Abundance: Common migrant and winter resident, uncommon summer
　　resident.
Remarks: Found on lakes, ponds, rivers and in forested wetlands. Winter
　　residents are usually present from Oct through Feb, at which time the
　　species is especially numerous across the state. Arrival and departure dates
　　are not well described in the literature. Larger numbers are generally
　　reported from middle and west Tennessee, with 16,138 on 31 Dec 1983,
　　Hiwassee CBC (MIG 55:49) representing an unusually large count in the
　　east. Nest records exist for all three regions of the state. Hybrids of this
　　species and the American Black Duck are occasionally found. Domestic
　　"Mallards" kept on farms and about resort areas may sometimes be

Mallard, continued

mistaken for birds of breeding populations. High count: 265,000 on 23 Dec 1979, Reelfoot L. CBC (MIG 51:31).

Substantiation: Specimen: 1, Benton Co., 20 Dec 1976 (UTMB, 327).

Northern Pintail, *Anas acuta*
Status: Regular.
Abundance: Fairly common migrant, uncommon winter resident, very rare summer visitor.
Fall: Arrives by late Aug.
Arrivals: 15 Aug 1965, Chat., MIG 36:68
             21 Aug 1987, Island 13 (JCR)
             28 Aug 1975, Gallatin, MIG 47:18
Winter: Becomes noticeably less numerous in the winter with a detectable northward migration by mid Feb. Overwinters in small numbers at state and federal waterfowl refuges.
Spring: Most migrants depart by late Mar, but some birds may linger well into May.
Departures: 15 Apr 1956, Radnor L., BNA:17
             23 May 1981, McNairy Co., (Nicholson 1984)
             26 May 1986, HRA, MIG 57:84
Summer: Known from two records: two birds on 19 July 1984, Tennessee NWR (MIG 55:91) and one ad. on 29 June 1988, Cross Creeks NWR (JCR).
Remarks: Found on lakes, ponds and in flooded grain fields. Recent decline in continental population has probably caused an overall drop in the numbers of birds observed across the state. High counts: seventeen thousand on 27 Dec 1960, Reelfoot L. CBC (MIG 31:74); and nine thousand on 31 Dec 1982, Tennessee NWR (MIG 54:13).
Substantiation: Specimen: 1 male, Dover, Stewart Co., 31 Dec 1986 (Cross Creeks NWR.)

Garganey, *Anas querquedula*
Status: Accidental.
Remarks: This Old World teal is known only from one record: one male at the Darwin sewage ponds, Shelby Co., on 1-5 Apr 1978 (MIG 49:65). Placed on the confirmed list of Tennessee birds in 1983 (Nicholson 1983). The origin of the bird is still unknown but presumed to be wild.
Substantiation: Photographs: 1, Shelby Co., 3 Apr 1978 (JPC−TBRC).

Blue-winged Teal, *Anas discors*
Status: Regular. (Map A-14)
Abundance: Common migrant, rare summer and winter resident.
Fall: Most early migrants arrive by early Aug. Departure dates are obscured by the presence of wintering birds. Blue-wings are very infrequently encountered after Oct and most birds have left the state by late Dec.

Blue-winged Teal, continued

Arrivals: 20 July 1941, Mud L., MIG 12:58

28 July 1982, Nash., MIG 57:81

2 Aug 1982, Kingston Steam Plant, MIG 54:24

Winter: There is a large number of winter records, including a few sightings of surprisingly large flocks (i.e., 100-200 birds). It is likely that some birds are misidentified. Most winter sightings involve considerably fewer birds. Becomes less detectable by midwinter. Two birds in Carter Co. on 10 Feb 1954 (MIG 25:19) may have overwintered.

Spring: Spring migrants arrive by late Feb. Can occasionally be found well into late May, but actual dates of departure are obscured by the presence of summering birds.

Arrivals: 20 Feb 1982, Ashland City, MIG 53:45

25 Feb 1963, near Greeneville, MIG 34:11

25 Feb 1986, Cross Creeks NWR, MIG 57:76

Summer: There are over thirty summer sightings including several breeding records. Nesting has been documented as early as 1936, when a nest with eight eggs in Maury Co. was discovered (Todd 1944); and as recent as 1986, when one ad. and four young were found in Shelby Co. (MIG 57:103). Nesting has also been documented for Anderson, Coffee, Davidson, Grundy, and Rutherford Counties. Possible nesting occurred in 1980 in Sumner Co. (MIG 57:81).

Remarks: Found in marshes, shallow lakes and ponds. High counts: 5,350 on 21 Sept 1967, Reelfoot L. (MIG 38:94) and 1,500 on 17 Sept 1956, Memp. (MIG 27:67).

Substantiation: Specimen: 1 male, Wooten Farm, Montgomery Co., 27 July 1968 (APSU, 2371).

Cinnamon Teal, *Anas cyanoptera*

Status: Accidental.

Remarks: Known from three records: 10-21 Apr 1972, Tennessee NWR, Humphreys Co. (Rauber 1972a); 26 Mar 1974, Cross Creeks NWR (Snyder 1974); and 15 Jan 1987, two birds shot on the Tennessee (Shelby Co.)/Arkansas (Crittendon Co.) line (MIG 58:53). The 1974 bird apparently stayed at Cross Creeks NWR for about a month (Bierly 1980).

Substantiation: Photograph: 1 male, Cross Creeks NWR, Stewart Co., 7 Apr 1974 (JPC−TBRC).

Northern Shoveler, *Anas clypeata*

Status: Regular.

Abundance: Fairly common migrant, uncommon winter resident, very rare summer visitor.

Fall: Arrives by late Aug.

Northern Shoveler, continued

Arrivals: 8 Aug 1981, Nash., MIG 53:15

8 Aug 1985, HRA, MIG 57:32

23 Aug 1987, Island 13 (JCR)

Winter: Becomes less numerous during the winter. Overwinters at most of the state and federal waterfowl refuges where open water is available.

Spring: An influx of migrants is usually noted by mid Feb. Most birds depart by early May.

Departures: 29 Apr 1962, Memp. SBC, MIG 33:28

17 May 1967, Nash., MIG 38:48

22 May 1967, Amnicola Marsh, MIG 38:50

Summer: Known from two records: one male on 5 July 1967, Austin Springs (MIG 38:68), and one to two birds on 1 June and 24 July 1986, Dyer Co. (MIG 57:103).

Remarks: Found in marshes, shallow ponds and lakes. High counts: 3,200 on 23 Dec 1972, Reelfoot L. CBC (MIG 44:10), and 3,100 on 23 Nov 1967, Reelfoot L. (MIG 38:94).

Substantiation: Specimen: 1, near Reelfoot L., Obion Co., 13 Nov 1971 (UTMB, 116).

Gadwall, *Anas strepera*

Status: Regular.

Abundance: Fairly common migrant and winter resident, very rare summer visitor.

Fall: Arrives by mid Sept.

Arrivals: 14 Aug 1977, Nickajack L., MIG 49:20

29 Aug 1988, Cross Creeks NWR (JCR)

8 Sept 1968, Reelfoot L., MIG 39:89

Winter: Frequently encountered along rivers and on state and federal waterfowl refuges throughout the winter. Usually found in larger numbers in middle and west Tennessee, but 1,213 were at Chickamauga L. and HRA on 12 Dec 1986 (MIG 58:59) in east Tennessee.

Spring: Most migrants depart by mid Apr, but small numbers may linger into May.

Departures: 9 May 1954, Reelfoot L. SBC, MIG 25:28

26 May 1980, Kingston Steam Plant, MIG 51:93

28 May-1 June 1963, near Nash., MIG 34:50

Summer: Two records of single birds: 1 July 1976, Patrick Henry L. (MIG 47:101) and 13, 17 July 1977, Sumner Co. (MIG 48:103).

Remarks: Found on ponds, lakes, rivers and forested wetlands. High counts: 9,600 on 2 Jan 1960, Reelfoot L. CBC (MIG 30:64) and 750 on 15 Nov 1971, Woods Res. (MIG 43:24).

Substantiation: Specimen: 1 female, Camden WMA, Benton Co., 1 Dec 1965 (APSU, 1620).

Eurasian Wigeon, *Anas penelope*
Status: Extremely Rare.
Remarks: Nine state records. First recorded on 21 Feb 1944 when three birds
were found at Chickasaw S.P., Chester Co. (Witt 1944). Sometime during the
hunting seasons of 1950 through 1954, one bird was shot at Reelfoot L.
(Pitts 1981). Not recorded again until the 1980s. Five of these records are
from Cross Creeks NWR as follows: 8-20 Mar 1983 (MIG 54:61); 30 Dec-16
Jan 1983/84 (MIG 55:45); 19 Oct-25 Nov 1984 (MIG 56:19); 22-25 Jan 1986
(MIG 57:56); and 21 Nov-30 Dec 1987 (JCR, DWB). Possibly, the same bird
has returned to this wintering site for five consecutive years. Other records
include: 20-30 Nov 1982, Savannah Bay (MIG 54:24) and 23 Dec 1984, Tennessee NWR, Humphreys Co. (MIG 56:51). All records are of male birds except the 1944 sighting, which was of two males and one female.
Substantiation: Adequately documented sight records.

American Wigeon, *Anas americana*
Status: Regular.
Abundance: Fairly common migrant and winter resident, very rare summer
visitor.
Fall: Arrives by late Sept.
    Arrivals: 24 Aug 1987, Henry Co. (JCR)
                4 Sept 1988, Cross Creeks NWR (DWB)
                5 Sept 1980, Kingston Steam Plant, MIG 52:24
Winter: Becomes somewhat less detectable by Jan, especially in the east.
However, some larger flocks have been found in recent years (e.g., 1,889 on 7
Jan 1985, Chickamauga L., MIG 56:55). Concentration areas include all of
the waterfowl refuges.
Spring: An influx of migrants usually is noted by mid Feb. Departs by early
May.
    Departures: 21 May 1975, Austin Springs, MIG 46:89
                24 May 1972, Radnor L., MIG 43:76
                30 May 1987, Cross Creeks NWR, MIG 58:96
Summer: June records include 8 June 1963, Watauga L. (MIG 34:53), 6-30 June
1977, Sumner Co. (MIG 48:103), and one ad. male on 29 June 1988 at Cross
Creeks NWR (JCR). July records include 21 July 1974, Campbell Co. (MIG
45:102) and 24 July 1968, Boone L. (MIG 39:65).
Remarks: Found on ponds, lakes, rivers and in grain fields or on mudflats.
High count: 15,300 on 27 Dec 1960, Reelfoot L. CBC (MIG 31:74).
Substantiation: Specimen: 1 ad. male, Woods Res., Franklin Co., Jan 1959
(USNM, 430872).

Canvasback, *Aythya valisineria*
Status: Regular.
Abundance: Uncommon migrant and winter resident.
Fall: Arrives by late Oct.

Canvasback, continued
Arrivals: 29 Sept 1935, Knox Co., (Howell and Monroe 1957)
26 Oct 1964, Bush L., MIG 35:101
29 Oct 1968, Reelfoot L., MIG 39:89
Winter: Uncommon in most areas across the state, but may be locally common where suitable habitat and food are available. A well-known annual concentration area is the Pace Point/Britton Ford area of the Tennessee NWR, Henry Co., where 1,232 birds were found on 16 Jan 1987 (MIG 58:53) and where 2,002 were present the following winter on 15 Jan 1988 (JCR).
Spring: Departs by late Mar, but may occasionally be seen into May.
Departures: 28 Apr 1985, Memp. SBC, MIG 56:68
13 May 1961, Kingsport SBC, MIG 32:30
19 May 1976, Gallatin, BNA:17
Summer: One male present from 23-25 July 1976 in Sumner Co. (MIG 47:99-100) was apparently sick or injured (BNA:17).
Remarks: Found on deeper lakes, ponds and rivers. High count: three thousand on 27 Dec 1960, Reelfoot L. CBC (MIG 31:74).

Redhead, *Aythya americana*
Status: Regular.
Abundance: Uncommon migrant and winter resident, very rare summer visitor.
Fall: Arrives by early Nov.
Arrivals: 12 Oct 1985, Cross Creeks NWR, MIG 57:25
13 Oct 1977, Savannah Bay, MIG 49:20
25 Oct 1968, Reelfoot L., MIG 39:89
Winter: Occurs uncommonly statewide in the winter, but an influx of migrants is usually detectable by Feb. Notable winter counts: five hundred on 28 Dec 1967, Lebanon CBC (MIG 38:87) and six hundred on 20 Dec 1975, Reelfoot L. CBC (MIG 47:35).
Spring: Departs by late Apr.
Departures: 4 May 1986, Chat. SBC, MIG 57:66
5 May 1963, Reelfoot L. SBC, MIG 34:30
24 May 1980, Cedar Hill L., BNA:17
Summer: One bird on 31 Aug 1985 in Lake Co. (MIG 57:22) summered in the area. One bird was present on 3 July 1983 in Greene Co. (MIG 54:90). A bird found on 1 Aug 1965 at Chat. (MIG 36:68) may have summered there.
Remarks: Found on deeper lakes and ponds. High count: 1,500 on 12 Nov 1979, Woods Res. (MIG 51:39).

Ring-necked Duck, *Aythya collaris*
Status: Regular.
Abundance: Fairly common migrant and winter resident, rare summer visitor.

Ring-necked Duck, continued

Fall: Arrives by early Oct. There are several Sept records. Three Aug records range from 25 Aug 1973 (MIG 44:99) to 28 Aug 1968 (MIG 39:92) and could possibly represent summering birds.

Arrivals: 10 Sept 1978, Kingston Steam Plant, MIG 50:22

20 Sept 1987, Henry Co. (JCR)

1 Oct 1984, Cross Creeks NWR, MIG 56:19

Winter: Found in rafts in middle and west Tennessee that occasionally exceed several thousand birds. Smaller numbers generally are recorded in the east.

Spring: Most migrants and winter residents depart for northern breeding areas by late Apr. However, some birds may linger well into May, and occasionally Ring-necks are encountered during the summer.

Summer: There are more than ten summer (June/July) records of non-breeding birds, mostly from east and middle Tennessee. Only record from the west was on 27 June 1977, Shelby Co. (MIG 48:102).

Remarks: Found on lakes, ponds, flooded grain fields and forested wetlands. Often occurs with Lesser Scaup in large rafts. Frequently occurs in the shallower portions of lakes, usually more often than other diving ducks. High counts: 25,000 on 30 Dec 1958, Reelfoot L. CBC (MIG 30:16) and 3,000 on 5 Mar 1978, Cheatham L. (MIG 49:42).

Substantiation: Specimen: 1 male, Nash., Davidson Co., 27 Nov 1922 (LSUMZ, 75674).

Greater Scaup, *Aythya marila*

Status: Regular.

Abundance: East: uncommon migrant and winter resident, very rare summer visitor.

Middle and West: rare migrant and winter resident.

Fall: Arrives by late Nov.

Arrivals: 17 Oct 1987, HRA (Albert M. Jenkins)

30 Oct 1983, Old Hickory L., MIG 55:19

4 Nov 1967, Hamilton Co., MIG 38:97

Winter: Locally common in east Tennessee, especially on Chickamauga L. at Booker T. Washington S.P. Not easily detected elsewhere in the state. Should be identified only when definitive field marks are well seen. There are only about twelve winter records for the middle and west regions of the state.

Spring: Departs by mid Apr.

Departures: 13 Apr 1962, Bush L., MIG 33:48

1 May 1978, Kingsport SBC, MIG 49:56

3 May 1970, Chat. SBC, MIG 41:36

Summer: Two records: one bird at Fort Loudoun L. from 16 May-8 July 1976 (MIG 47:101) and one bird on 7 June 1983 at the Kingston Steam Plant (MIG 54:90).

Remarks: Found on rivers and lakes. There are at least fourteen middle Tennessee records and at least seven west Tennessee records. About half of

Greater Scaup, continued

middle Tennessee's records occurred between 1959 and 1963 in the Nash. area, including nineteen at Bush L. on 1-4 Dec 1959 (Parmer 1960) and six birds on 28 Dec 1963, Nash. CBC (MIG 34:82). High counts: 500 on 26 Jan 1971 (MIG 42:20) and 450 on 4 Mar 1974 (MIG 45:23), both Chickamauga L.

Lesser Scaup, *Aythya affinis*

Status: Regular.

Abundance: Fairly common migrant and winter resident, rare summer visitor.

Fall: Arrives by late Oct.

Arrivals: 6 Oct 1938, North L., Shelby Co., MIG 9:95

                 6 Oct 1984, Radnor L., MIG 56:19

                 9 Oct 1976, Wilbur L., MIG 48:23

Winter: Although more conspicuous in the spring and fall, large concentrations can also be found in midwinter: 490 on 26 Jan 1986, Henry Co. (JCR) and 1,000 on 1 Jan 1955, Reelfoot L. CBC (MIG 25:77).

Spring: Most migrants and winter residents depart for northern breeding areas by early May. However, some birds may linger well into late May (e.g., 31 May 1955, Grundy Co., [Yeatman 1955]).

Summer: More than twenty summer (June/July) records of non-breeding birds exist from all across the state. Most sightings are of single birds or small flocks of fewer than ten birds. Aug sightings include at least four records, all of which were summering birds.

Remarks: Found on ponds, lakes and rivers. Often found in large rafts with other diving ducks, especially during migration. High counts: 6,800 on 23 Dec 1972, Reelfoot L. CBC (MIG 44:10) and 2,000 on 16 Nov 1970, Woods Res. (MIG 42:19).

King Eider, *Somateria spectabilis*

Status: Accidental.

Remarks: Known from one record: a female, taken sometime between the 1964 and 1967 waterfowl hunting seasons in the Opossum Branch area of Woods Res. (Bierly 1976).

Substantiation: Specimen: 1 female, Woods Res., Coffee Co., shot sometime between 1964 and 1967 (CSM, AV-267).

Harlequin Duck, *Histrionicus histrionicus*

Status: Accidental.

Remarks: Two birds of this species were shot on Norris L. on 8 Jan 1984 (MIG 55:49), constituting the first state record. Another bird, a male, was shot on 5 Jan 1985 at Cheatham L. (MIG 56:51).

Substantiation: Specimen: 1 female, Norris L., Campbell Co., 8 Jan 1984 (USNM, uncatalogued).

Oldsquaw, *Clangula hyemalis*
Status: Irregular.
Abundance: Rare migrant and winter resident.
Fall: Arrives by mid Nov.
  Arrivals: 26 Oct 1985, Pace Point, MIG 57:22
                30 Oct 1980, Boone L., MIG 52:24
                31 Oct 1975, Radnor L., MIG 47:18
Winter: There are many records for each of the three winter months. A portion
  of the Dec sightings probably represents late-arriving fall migrants, and a
  portion of the Feb sightings probably represents early spring migrants.
Spring: Departs by late Mar. One May record: 3 May 1930, Radnor L. (Monk
  1932).
  Departures: 5 Apr 1964, Boone L., MIG 35:42
                12 Apr 1946, Reelfoot L., (Steenis 1946)
                12 Apr 1972, Radnor L., MIG 43:50
Remarks: Found on deeper lakes and rivers. Seen more often in middle and
  east Tennessee than in the west. High count: thirty-one on 3 Feb 1929, Rad-
  nor L. (Monk 1932).
Substantiation: Specimen: 1 male, Jackson, Madison Co., 25 Nov 1937
  (LSUMZ, 75675).

Black Scoter, *Melanitta nigra*
Status: Extremely Rare. (Map A-15)
Remarks: Found on lakes and large bodies of water. About seventeen records
  for the state. Usually observed during Oct and Nov. First found when one
  was shot sometime between 13 and 18 Nov 1945 at Reelfoot L. (Pickering
  1945), then not recorded again until 1967, when the only summer record was
  obtained: 14 May-14 June 1967, Cardwell's L., near Knoxville (Alsop and
  Wallace 1970). High count was twenty on 19 Apr 1985, Stewart Co. (Robinson and Blunk 1989). Only Dec sighting was 17 Dec 1983, Chat. CBC (MIG
  55:8). Most sightings are of single birds. All other records follow:
    21-26 Oct 1987, Paris Landing S.P., MIG 59:32
    29 Oct-10 Nov 1977, Radnor L., MIG 49:42
    30 Oct 1977, HRA, MIG 49:20
    6 Nov 1977, Nickajack L., MIG 49:45
    6 Nov 1983, Sumner Co., MIG 55:19
    6-10 Nov 1985, Radnor L., MIG 57:25
    9 Nov 1979, Chickamauga L., MIG 51:41
    11 Nov 1986, Boone L., MIG 58:27
    11-12 Nov 1986, Franklin Res., MIG 58:23
    13 Nov 1981, Kingston Steam Plant, MIG 53:18
    15 Nov 1987, Lawrence Co., MIG 59:34
    18 Nov 1981, Radnor L., MIG 53:15
    29 Apr 1988, Dickson Co. (CGD)
Substantiation: Adequately documented sight records.

Surf Scoter, *Melanitta perspicillata*
Status: Irregular.
Abundance: Rare migrant.
Fall: Mid Oct to late Dec.
    Arrivals: 1 Oct 1984, Austin Springs, MIG 56:24
                   8 Oct 1980, Radnor L., BNA:18
                   22 Oct 1987, Paris Landing S.P., MIG 59:32
    Departures: 22 Dec 1984, Chickamauga L., MIG 56:55
                   29 Dec 1979, Nash. CBC, MIG 51:31
                   5 Jan 1980, Radnor L., MIG 51:39
Spring: Mid Feb to late Apr.
    Arrivals: 6 Feb 1974, Radnor L., MIG 45:21
                   16 Feb 1986, Watauga River, MIG 57:62
                   18 Feb 1988, Pickwick L., Hardin Co. (DJS)
    Departures: 29 Apr 1988, Dickson Co. (CGD)
                   11 May 1975, Savannah Bay, MIG 46:67
                   15 May 1960, Alcoa L., Blount Co., (Campbell 1967)
Remarks: Found on deeper lakes and rivers. Noted by Monk at Radnor L.
    from 1929 to 1931 (MIG 27:78) and then not recorded again until the 1950s.
    Sightings in Feb are presumed to be of northbound migrants. Spring migra-
    tion is not as pronounced as the fall migration; there are about fifteen
    spring records. Of the four west Tennessee records, three are from Paris
    Landing S.P.: 28 Oct-11 Nov 1984 (MIG 56:16); 8-9 Nov 1986 (MIG 58:19);
    and 22-29 Oct 1987 (MIG 59:32). High counts: seven on 16 Nov 1970,
    Woods Res. (MIG 42:19) and again on 29 Oct 1987, Paris Landing S.P.
    (JCR).
Substantiation: Adequately documented sight records.

White-winged Scoter, *Melanitta fusca*
Status: Irregular.
Abundance: Rare migrant and winter resident.
Fall: Arrives by early Nov.
    Arrivals: 21 Oct 1949, Tennessee NWR, (Cypert 1955)
                   25 Oct 1986, Old Hickory L., Sumner Co., MIG 58:23
                   2 Nov 1982, Savannah Bay, MIG 54:24
Winter: There are a number of records for each of the three winter months in-
    cluding a few birds which stayed for an appreciable length of time (e.g., 29
    Jan to 26 Feb 1979, Chickamauga L., MIG 50:44; and 20-28 Jan 1968, Con-
    cord, MIG 39:21).
Spring: Departs by late Mar.
    Departures: 26 Mar 1979, Chickamauga L., MIG 50:70
                   27 Apr 1968, Fort Loudoun L., MIG 39:45
                   29 Apr 1988, Dickson Co. (CGD)
Remarks: Found on deeper lakes and rivers. Most of the records are from east
    Tennessee. First available record was of six birds at Radnor L. on 10 Nov

White-winged Scoter, continued

1917 (Monk 1932). Not recorded again in the state until 1932. Currently is the most frequently seen scoter in Tennessee. Rarely seen in the west where there are only about five records. High counts: twenty-eight on 30 Dec 1981, Chickamauga L. (MIG 53:47) and fifteen on 24 Feb 1968, Boone L. (MIG 39:45).

Substantiation: Specimen: 1, Kentucky L., Benton Co., Dec 1977 (UTMB, 300).

Common Goldeneye, *Bucephala clangula*

Status: Regular.

Abundance: Uncommon to fairly common migrant and winter resident, very rare summer visitor.

Fall: Arrives by early Nov.

Arrivals: 16 Oct 1953, Kingsport, (Switzer 1957)
3 Nov 1984, Woods Res., MIG 56:19
8 Nov 1986, Paris Landing S.P., MIG 58:19

Winter: Found uncommonly throughout the state during Dec, Jan and Feb. However, may be locally common in certain areas (e.g., 543 on 11 Jan 1986 at Tennessee NWR, MIG 57:51; and 261 on 9 Feb 1987 at Cherokee L., MIG 58:59).

Spring: Departs by early Apr. There are several May records.

Departures: 29 Apr 1972, Nash. SBC, MIG 43:45
7 May 1978, Knoxville SBC, MIG 49:56
11 May 1975, Reelfoot L. SBC, MIG 46:56

Summer: One bird present on 12 June 1963 at Wilbur L. (Dubke 1963a) apparently lingered until 14 Sept 1963 and throughout the 1964 summer; it is not clear if this is the same bird that arrived on the lake on 30 Sept 1962 (MIG 34:13). Records of a single bird at Wilbur L. on 12 May 1965 and 18 July 1965 are possibly of the same individual that was seen and noted as apparently injured on 5 Aug-11 Oct 1966 (MIG 37:85).

Remarks: Found on ponds, deeper lakes and rivers. High counts: 3,000 on 28 Dec 1964, Dyersburg CBC (MIG 35:111) and 1,204 on 24 Jan 1988, Paris Landing S.P. (JCR).

Substantiation: Specimen: 1 female, Kentucky L., Stewart Co., 2 Jan 1967 (APSU, 1636).

[Barrow's Goldeneye, *Bucephala islandica*]

Status: Hypothetical.

Remarks: One male was described on the Cumberland River in Montgomery Co. on 21 Jan 1940 (Clebsch 1940), but was considered hypothetical by Alsop (1972). Another bird, a female, was photographed at Radnor L. sometime between 18 Nov and 30 Dec 1978 (MIG 50:42) and was identified by its predominantly yellow bill. However, absolute verification from the photographs was never obtained. The status of this species is considered

Barrow's Goldeneye, continued

Provisional by the State Bird Records Committee (Nicholson 1983), but is treated as Hypothetical here.

Bufflehead, *Bucephala albeola*
Status: Regular.
Abundance: Fairly common to uncommon migrant and winter resident, very rare summer visitor.
Fall: Arrives by late Oct.
  Arrivals: 9 Oct 1983, Wilbur L., MIG 55:27
              20 Oct 1981, Radnor L., MIG 53:15
              21 Oct 1987, Paris Landing S.P. (JCR)
Winter: Winters throughout the state. Seldom found in flocks exceeding a hundred birds. Notable counts include: 165 on 21 Dec 1985, Reelfoot L. CBC (MIG 57:9), and 106 on 27 Mar 1968, HRA (MIG 39:45).
Spring: Departs by late Apr.
  Departures: 3 May 1964, Reelfoot L. SBC, MIG 35:45
              9 May 1988, Radnor L. (CAS)
              24 May 1975, Wilbur L., MIG 46:91
Summer: Occasionally summers in east Tennessee, most frequently at Wilbur L., where there are at least five different summer records between 1966 and 1982. These records include two birds seen from May-July 1970 (MIG 41:72) and two birds that were present throughout the summer of 1969 (MIG 40:93). On 20 June 1972, one bird was seen on Nickajack L. (MIG 43:78).
Remarks: Found on ponds, rivers and lakes. High counts: 1,000 on 14 Jan 1940, Norris L. (MIG 11:27) and 310 on 23 Dec 1972, Reelfoot L. CBC (MIG 44:10).
Substantiation: Specimen: 1, near Chat., Hamilton Co., winter 1972-73 (UTMB, 309).

Hooded Merganser, *Lophodytes cucullatus*
Status: Regular.
Abundance: Fairly common migrant, uncommon winter resident, locally rare summer resident.
Fall: One bird shot on 5 Sept 1936 in Rutherford Co. (DeVore 1975) was likely an early fall migrant. However, most migrants do not arrive until late Oct.
Winter: Found uncommonly in each of the three regions throughout the winter. Concentrations of a hundred or more birds appear annually at some locales, including Hiwassee River Area, Cross Creeks NWR, Tennessee NWR and Reelfoot NWR.
Spring: Most migrants depart by early May. Birds found in late May (e.g., 30 May 1960 at Bush L. [Parmer 1962a]) probably remain to summer as breeding or non-breeding individuals.
Summer: Non-breeding summer records for east and middle Tennessee include 4 June 1963, Roans Creek (Dubke 1963a), 2 June 1985, Nickajack L. (MIG

Hooded Merganser, continued

56:113), 10 July 1978, Coffee Co. (MIG 49:91-92), 4-5 June 1988, Cross Creeks NWR (JCR), and 3 June 1976, Old Hickory L. (MIG 47:100). The only nest record for the east was in 1982 at Chat., Hamilton Co. (MIG 53:67-68). Apparently nested in Shelby Co. in 1934 (MIG 5:26). One imm. was seen at the Tatumville Marsh, Dyer Co., in 1986 (MIG 57:103), and nest records exist for Reelfoot L. (Lake and/or Obion Co.) for 1941 and 1983 (Sights 1943; and MIG 54:49). An ad. female and four young were found at Monsanto Ponds, Maury Co., in June and July 1987 (MIG 58:140). Waldron (1982) summarized nesting as a result of a Wood Duck box program in Lauderdale and Haywood Counties at Hatchie NWR during the 1967 to 1972 period. During this period there were 231 successful nests and an estimated 3,021 young produced. Recent records from the Hatchie NWR (12 nests in 1986 and 28 nests in 1987) indicate that the population has declined since the early 1970s but is still nesting annually (Marvin Nichols, pers. comm.).

Remarks: Found on ponds, lakes and wooded swamps. Nests in natural or artificial cavities. High counts: 3,000 on 2 Jan 1955, Tennessee NWR (MIG 25:77) and 2,002 on 26 Dec 1955, Reelfoot L. CBC (MIG 26:61).

Substantiation: Specimen: 1, Kentucky L., Henry Co., winter 1970-71 (UTMB, 100).

Common Merganser, *Mergus merganser*

Status: Regular.

Abundance: Uncommon to rare migrant and winter resident; formerly bred.

Fall: Arrives by mid Nov.

Arrivals:　　16 Oct 1953, near Kingsport, (Switzer 1957)

　　　　　　26 Oct 1974, Old Hickory L., MIG 46:19

　　　　　　9 Nov 1967, Reelfoot L., MIG 38:94

Winter: Infrequently encountered in each of the three regions of the state. Usually only small numbers are seen; concentrations of birds do not usually appear until after mid Dec (e.g., 100 on 2 Jan 1955, Tennessee NWR, MIG 25:77; and 125 on 24 Feb 1979, Norris L., MIG 50:44).

Spring: Departs by early Apr, but may linger well into May.

Departures:　　7 May 1967, Paris Landing S.P., MIG 38:31

　　　　　　　23 May 1973, Austin Springs, MIG 44:86

　　　　　　　24 May 1971, Lilydale, Clay Co., MIG 42:69

Remarks: Found on deeper lakes and rivers. Identification in early fall when males are still in eclipse plumage should take into account this species' resemblance to Red-breasted Merganser. There are no recent summer records for the state. However, Kiff (1989) provided good details for five sets of eggs collected in Smith County in 1897, 1898, and 1899. One bird described as apparently injured was found on Watauga L. on 24 Aug 1980 (MIG 52:27). High count: two hundred on 29 Feb 1964, Old Hickory L. (MIG 35:14).

Substantiation: Specimen: 1, John Sevier L., Hawkins Co., 6 Dec 1970 (UTK).

Red-breasted Merganser, *Mergus serrator*
Status: Regular.
Abundance: Uncommon migrant, rare winter resident, very rare summer visitor.
Fall: Arrives by mid Nov. There are two Aug records: 3 Aug 1985, Anderson
  Co. (MIG 57:32) and 19 Aug 1971, Roans Creek (MIG 42:95). Departure
  dates are not clear due to the presence of small numbers of birds in the
  winter.
Arrivals: 29 Sept 1974, Percy Priest L., MIG 46:19
              4 Oct 1969, South Holston L., MIG 40:92
              29 Oct 1985, Woods Res., MIG 57:26
Winter: Becomes noticeably less detectable after Dec and usually only found in
  small numbers until late Feb to early Mar, when spring migrants move north
  into Tennessee. Has been reported annually on CBCs since 1971.
Spring: Departs by early May.
Departures: 11 May 1977, Gallatin, MIG 48:76
              30 May 1982, Watauga L., MIG 53:70
              31 May 1967, Reelfoot L., MIG 38:46
Summer: There are at least four summer records for the state as follows: 20
  May-27 June 1984, Old Hickory L. (MIG 55:91); 18 and 24 June 1975,
  Clinch River (MIG 46:89); 3-28 June 1973, Nickajack L. (MIG 44:86); and
  one ad. male on 22 June-9 July 1988, Paris Landing S.P. (DJS, JCR).
Remarks: Found on lakes and rivers. May be mistaken for Common Merganser
  in early fall. High count: six hundred on 21, 27 Nov 1972, Woods Res. (MIG
  44:22).
Substantiation: Specimen: 1, Kentucky L., Benton Co., 27 Mar 1976 (UTMB,
  354).

Ruddy Duck, *Oxyura jamaicensis*
Status: Regular.
Abundance: Fairly common migrant, uncommon winter resident, very rare
  summer visitor.
Fall: Arrives by mid Oct.
Arrivals: 5 Sept 1964, near Greeneville, MIG 35:103-104
              16 Sept 1979, Maury Co., MIG 51:16
              14 Oct 1968, Reelfoot L., MIG 39:89
Winter: Winters in small numbers throughout most of the state. Large numbers
  have been reported at Reelfoot L. since about 1960 (e.g., 3,500 on 23 Dec
  1972, MIG 44:10) and at Robco L., Shelby Co., since about 1980 (e.g., 2,600
  on 15 Dec 1982, MIG 54:40).
Spring: Departs by early May.
Departures: 11 May 1958, Reelfoot L. SBC, MIG 29:30
              22 May 1981, Kingston Steam Plant, MIG 52:97
              27 May 1976, Maury Co., MIG 47:100
Summer: Most summer records are from Shelby Co., including 25 June 1978
  (MIG 49:90), 18 June and 3 July 1981 (MIG 52:95), 7-12 June 1983 (MIG

Ruddy Duck, continued
54:86), and 20 July 1982 (MIG 53:87). Also seen in Lake Co. on 12 July 1987 (MIG 58:137) and at Nickajack L. on 4 June 1980 (MIG 51:93).

Remarks: Found on ponds, lakes and rivers. Formerly infrequently observed in the east, but 76 on 4 Apr 1977, HRA and Savannah Bay (MIG 48:77) and 125 on 6 Dec 1986, Chickamauga L. (MIG 58:59) indicate an increase in recent years. High counts: 4,700 on 20 Dec 1986, Reelfoot L. CBC (MIG 58:2) and 3,800 on 20 Dec 1980, Reelfoot L. CBC (MIG 52:13).

Substantiation: Specimen: 1, Reelfoot L., Lake Co., Nov 1977 (UTMB, 302).

Masked Duck, *Oxyura dominica*
Status: Accidental.
Remarks: Known from one record: a one-year-old male was at Reelfoot L., Obion Co., on 11-15 Apr 1974 (Fintel 1974).
Substantiation: Photograph: 1, Reelfoot L., Obion Co., 15 Apr 1974 (JPC – TBRC).

ORDER FALCONIFORMES

FAMILY CATHARTIDAE: Vultures

Black Vulture, *Coragyps atratus*
Status: Regular.
Abundance: Uncommon permanent resident.
Remarks: Found in wooded areas, near cliffs and bluffs, and near open fields. Also frequents roadsides, where it can be seen feeding on the remains of road-killed vertebrates. Often found roosting in trees or on power lines with Turkey Vultures. Some roost sites may contain a hundred or more birds. Slightly more detectable in middle and west Tennessee than in the east. However, three hundred were seen in Marion Co. on 24 Nov 1985 (MIG 57:32). Withdrawal from certain breeding areas occurs annually during the winter. Nests of this species are difficult to locate and often overlooked. A review of *The Migrant* from 1930 to 1987 resulted in satisfactory breeding documentation from as far east as the GSMNP (Williams 1977) and near Washington Co. (Lyle and Tyler 1934), to as far west as Reelfoot L. (Spofford 1942). There are also breeding records for Carroll, Davidson, Hamilton, Marion, Meigs, Rutherford, Smith, Stewart, Sumner, and Wilson Counties. It is not clear whether a nest with eggs in 1982 (MIG 53:68) was

Black Vulture, continued

in Anderson or Roane Co. High counts: 450 on 12 Dec 1951, 24 km north-east of Nash. (Ganier 1952) and 450 on 1 Nov 1986, Gallatin Steam Plant (MIG 58:23).

Substantiation: Specimen: 1, St. Bethlehem, Montgomery Co., 15 May 1968 (APSU, 2302).

Turkey Vulture, *Cathartes aura*
Status: Regular.
Abundance: Fairly common permanent resident.
Remarks: Found in wooded areas, near cliffs and bluffs, and near open fields. Occasionally found roosting in large numbers. Some individuals, feeding on the remains of road-killed animals, are themselves struck by passing vehicles. In the summer, some birds visit small impoundments or oxbows, where they feed on the fish that die and are exposed by rapidly receding water levels. Loose flocks of migrant birds are regularly seen during the early spring and late fall. Encountered regularly at all elevations in the Roan Mt. area of northeast Tennessee (Eller and Wallace 1984). The distribution of birds across the state becomes more localized in the winter, when a withdrawal from most breeding areas occurs; however, the species is readily found in all three regions of the state throughout the winter. Nests of the species are difficult to locate, often overlooked and poorly reported in the literature. A review of *The Migrant* revealed satisfactory breeding documentation only for the following counties: Hamilton, Lawrence, McMinn, and Rutherford. Nest records are also described for an area in or near Washington Co. (Lyle and Tyler 1934) and for the GSMNP, Sevier Co. (Stupka 1963). Undoubtedly breeds in west Tennessee, where Ganier (1933) described it as a common permanent resident. High count: 1,845 on 21 Oct 1982, Blount Co. (MIG 54:36).
Substantiation: Specimen: 1, Model, Stewart Co., 6 June 1965 (APSU, 1258).

FAMILY ACCIPITRIDAE:
Kites, Eagles, Hawks and Allies

Osprey, *Pandion haliaetus*
Status: Regular (State Endangered). (Map A-16)
Abundance: Uncommon migrant, locally uncommon summer resident, rare winter visitor.
Spring: Spring migrants usually arrive by late Mar; however, there is a handful of early Mar records. Nesting birds appear to arrive earlier than migrant birds. Most birds are found throughout Apr and early May. A few Ospreys

Osprey, continued

linger until late May (e.g., 24 May 1941, Reelfoot L., [Spofford 1941]), and some non-breeding individuals are occasionally found during the summer.

Summer: There are over twenty non-breeding summer records for June and July between 1940 and 1986, indicating a tendency for the species to linger within the state during this period. Has bred or attempted to breed on Watts Bar L., Meigs Co., annually since about 1961. In recent years, breeding activity at this site has increased substantially, and as many as seventeen simultaneously active nests from the Watts Bar L. area have been reported (MIG 58:145). Successful nests in Hawkins Co. and Anderson Co. were documented in 1988. Unsuccessful nesting attempts were described for Knox Co. in 1937 (Walker 1937), Greene Co. in 1940 (White 1956) and Cummings L., Tennessee River Gorge, in 1984 (MIG 55:73). Breeding was attempted in Davidson Co. in 1986 on Percy Priest and Old Hickory Lakes (MIG 57:106). One young bird was found on Old Hickory L., Sumner Co., in 1987 (MIG 58:140). A site with at least two successful nest attempts has also been documented at the Tennessee NWR, Humphreys Co., between 1984 and 1987. At Reelfoot L. two birds were observed at a nest in Obion Co. on 16 May 1963 (Ellis 1963); a nest in Lake Co. was found in 1964 (Alsop 1979); one nest had three young in 1970 (MIG 41:68); and three active nests were reported and two imm. were later sighted in 1981 (MIG 52:95). Pitts (1985) indicated that Ospreys have apparently nested regularly at Reelfoot L. since the 1930s, although nest success has been poorly documented.

Fall: Migrant Ospreys usually arrive by early Sept, but some birds can be observed in late Aug. The peak of the migration occurs in Sept. Fewer birds are found in Oct. Sightings after mid Nov are rare.

Winter: Only three of the more than twenty-five Dec and Jan records for this species occurred prior to 1968. There are only about six Jan sightings. Winter records exist for all three regions of the state. The latest record appears to be 28 Jan 1980, Chickamauga L. (MIG 51:42).

Remarks: Usually found near lakes and rivers. Hacking programs have existed since at least 1983 in Sumner and Clay Counties, at Percy Priest L. and Woods Res., and at several sites in west Tennessee. These programs have already resulted in birds attempting to breed in Davidson Co. and will possibly result in further nesting attempts across the state. High counts: fifteen on 26 Apr 1987, Knoxville SBC (MIG 58:81) and fifteen on 25 Apr 1987, Elizabethton SBC (MIG 58:81).

Substantiation: Specimen: 1 male, Dunbar Cave, Montgomery Co., 22 Apr 1940 (LSUMZ, 75704).

American Swallow-tailed Kite, *Elanoides forficatus*
Status: Extremely Rare.
Remarks: First recorded in the state on 5 May 1810 in Maury Co. by Alexander Wilson as he crossed the Duck River (Yeatman 1965). There are about eleven records for the state. Yeatman (1965) noted that O. M. Pindar found eight or ten birds on 9 Aug 1886 near Woodland Mills, Tennessee, approximately 3.2

American Swallow-tailed Kite, continued

km south of the Kentucky state line. A "small flock" was observed around 1900 a "few miles north of Nashville" by A. C. Webb (BNA:19). One of two birds observed along the South Harpeth River southwest of Nash. on 15 Aug 1929 was shot, and another bird along the South Harpeth River was shot on 25 Sept 1933 (Ganier 1933b). An imm. female was found in Franklin Co. on 12 Aug 1965 (Yeatman 1965). Other records, all of single birds, follow:

    11 Aug 1968, Donelson, near Nash., (Ganier 1968)
    10 Apr 1977, Shelby Co., MIG 48:75
    7 Sept 1981, Sequatchie Valley, MIG 53:19
    19 Sept 1983, Memp., MIG 55:17
    19-28 Aug 1986, Polk Co., MIG 58:31

Substantiation: Specimen: 1 female, Winchester, Franklin Co., 13 Aug 1965 (LSUMZ, 75676).

Mississippi Kite, *Ictinia mississippiensis*
Status: Regular (State Endangered).
Abundance: East and Middle: rare migrant.
West: uncommon to fairly common summer resident.
Spring: Arrives by late Apr.
    Arrivals: 30 Mar 1985, Memp., MIG 56:74
                 9 Apr 1955, Radnor L., BNA:19
                 17 Apr 1980, Savannah Bay, MIG 51:61
Summer: Actual nests of this species have been described only for Shelby Co., where recently fledged young were seen as early as the 1930s (Coffey 1940). Breeding probably also occurs in Dyer, Lauderdale, Lake and Obion Counties.
Fall: Most birds depart by early Sept.
    Departures: 26 Sept 1981, Signal Pt., Hamilton Co., (Stringer 1982)
                  28 Sept 1976, Audubon Park, Shelby Co., MIG 48:17
                  13 Oct 1983, Cross Creeks NWR, MIG 55:19
Remarks: Found along rivers and wooded swamps. Most numerous along the Mississippi River. Coffey (1979) summarized the occurrence of this species in west Tennessee in the following counties: Shelby, Madison, Henderson, Lauderdale, Dyer, Obion, Lake, Tipton, Haywood, and Hardeman. He also described the first authenticated record for the state, which was seen by Ganier in north central Henderson Co. on 11 Aug 1926. Kalla and Alsop (1983) described the habitat preference of this species in the west Tennessee floodplains. There are eight middle Tennessee and six east Tennessee records, four of which have been described above in the migration dates. The other records follow:

    2 May 1987, Reflection Riding, Chat., MIG 58:102
    3 May 1983, Chat., Hamilton Co., MIG 54:64
    9 May 1987, Lawrence Co., MIG 58:81

Mississippi Kite, continued

 13 May 1951, Overton Co., (Ganier 1951a)

 12 June 1941, Nash., (Burdick 1941)

 14 June 1987, Robertson Co., MIG 58:140

 24 June 1988, Stewart Co. (DWB)

 27 Aug 1979, near Decatur, Meigs Co., MIG 51:17

 27 Aug 1980, Nash., BNA:19

 22 Sept 1978, Hamilton Co., (Stringer 1982)

At least eighty-five Mississippi Kites have been released since 1983 as a result of a hacking program in Shelby Co. High count: 197 on 22 Aug 1987, Island 13 (MIG 59:32).

Substantiation: Specimen: 1 male, Memphis, Shelby Co., 7 July 1944 (LSUMZ, 9535).

Bald Eagle, *Haliaeetus leucocephalus*

Status: Regular (Federally Endangered). (Map A-17)

Abundance: East and West: rare summer resident, uncommon migrant and winter resident.

Middle: locally uncommon summer resident, uncommon migrant and winter resident.

Remarks: Found along lakes and rivers. Migrants may arrive as early as mid Aug and usually depart by mid May. Most migrants and winter residents are seen from Sept through Apr. Noticeably less detectable in the east. Winter concentration areas include Kentucky L. in Humphreys, Benton, Stewart and Henry Counties, Dale Hollow L. and Reelfoot L. Considered by Ganier (1933) to be a very rare summer resident in the west, a very rare resident in the eastern mountains and a very rare transient in middle Tennessee. Nesting activity within the state was undoubtedly affected by the presence of DDT in the environment. Nested at Reelfoot L. as early as 1916 (Alsop 1979) and fairly regularly thereafter from about 1932 (MIG 3:16) until about 1963 (Alsop 1979). Also nested in Stewart Co. in 1948 and 1949 (Ganier 1951b). Specific details for nests in Clay, Pickett, Meigs, Hardin, and Shelby Counties are lacking. There were no nests in the state from 1963 through the early 1980s. However, a total of ten active nests have been identified in middle and west Tennessee since 1983. From 1983 through 1988, three active nests in Stewart Co. fledged twenty young, and a nest in Benton Co. fledged three young between 1985 and 1988. In Jackson Co., five young have fledged from a nest which was active during the 1986, 1987 and 1988 nesting seasons. Three nests were active at Reelfoot L. in Obion and Lake Co. in 1988, fledging seven young. An unsuccessful nest attempt occurred at Reelfoot L. in 1987. Nesting was attempted in Coffee and Humphreys Co. in 1986 (MIG 57:107). Hacking programs at Reelfoot L. and LBL from 1980 through 1987 have resulted in the release of 76 eagles (Hatcher 1987). At least one nest in Stewart Co. has been built by a hacked eagle. Eagles are rare summer visitors to the east Tennessee lakes (Norris L., Chickamauga L., Nickajack

Bald Eagle, continued

L., and South Holston L.) where a number of June/July observations has been made since the mid 1960s. High count: 297 (175 ad. and 122 imm.) on 5 Feb 1987, Reelfoot L. (MIG 58:53).

Substantiation: Specimen: 1 ad., Reelfoot L., late 1930s (TWRA office, Nashville).

Northern Harrier, *Circus cyaneus*
Status: Regular (State Threatened).
Abundance: Fairly common to uncommon migrant, uncommon winter resident, very rare summer visitor.
Fall: Arrives by late Aug.

Arrivals: 3 Aug 1969, Ashland City Marsh, MIG 40:89
13 Aug 1985, Elizabethton, MIG 57:35
19 Aug 1941, Memp., MIG 12:59

Winter: Found uncommonly across most of the state. More detectable in middle and west Tennessee than in the east. Usually found in small numbers, but twenty-one birds were found on 2 Jan 1956, Tennessee NWR (MIG 26:61).

Spring: Departs by early May.

Departures: 12 May 1985, Knox Co., MIG 56:79
21 May 1986, Putnam Co., MIG 57:78
29 May 1975, Hatchie NWR, MIG 46:87

Summer: Known from seven records:
15 June 1984, near Elizabethton, MIG 55:95
19 June 1982, Trenton, Gibson Co., MIG 53:87
21 June 1987, Carter Co., MIG 58:147
4 July 1970, Byrdstown, Pickett Co., MIG 41:69
6 July 1952, Williamson Co., BNA:19
7 July 1987, Lake Co., MIG 58:137
16 July 1950, Knox Co., MIG 21:52

Remarks: Found in open, agricultural areas, usually over large, brushy fields. Active throughout the day as well as in dim light (dawn and dusk). High count: twenty-four on 9 Mar 1986, Humphreys Co. (MIG 57:78).

Substantiation: Specimen: 1 male, near Nash., Davidson Co., 11 Nov 1921 (LSUMZ, 75703).

Sharp-shinned Hawk, *Accipiter striatus*
Status: Regular (State Threatened).
Abundance: East and Middle: fairly common migrant, uncommon winter resident, rare summer resident.
West: fairly common migrant, uncommon winter resident, rare summer visitor.
Remarks: Found statewide in wooded areas and along woodland edge. Usually nests in conifers. Nests are probably overlooked even though suitable coniferous habitat is scattered throughout the middle and eastern regions of the

state. Becomes much less detectable during the summer in middle and east
Tennessee. However, in recent years its presence in the east has been well
documented at several locations including Marion, Blount, Knox, Jefferson,
Washington, and Carter Counties. It is encountered regularly at all elevations within the Roan Mt. area of northeast Tennessee (Eller and Wallace
1984). Nests are documented for a number of counties throughout middle
and east Tennessee. Ganier (1933) considered it a permanent resident only in
the middle and east. Alsop (1980) and Bierly (1980) considered it to be a
permanent resident in the west; however, no nest records are described in the
literature, and the presence of the species during the summer in that part of
the state is poorly documented. Calhoun (1941) found one bird in a
Hardeman Co. pine forest between 22 June and 27 July 1939. Fall migration
occurs primarily in Sept and Oct, but may be detected as early as Aug.
Migrating hawks along the eastern mountain chains are notable and may
sometimes include counts of twenty or more Sharp-shinned Hawks in one
day. Spring migration has been little documented; winter residents depart for
northern breeding areas by late Apr or early May. High count: sixty-seven
on 15 Oct 1977, Kyle's Ford Fire Tower, Hawkins Co. (MIG 49:50).
Substantiation: Specimen: 1 female, near Nash., Davidson Co., 3 Mar 1924
(LSUMZ, 75683).

Cooper's Hawk, *Accipiter cooperii*
Status: Regular (State Threatened).
Abundance: Uncommon permanent resident.
Remarks: Found in wooded areas and along woodland edge. Nests in con-
iferous and deciduous forests. Consistently seen during the summer
throughout the state, but nests are overlooked and seldom reported. There
are nest records for Cheatham, Maury, Rutherford, Sullivan, and Williamson
Counties. Also nested in McMinn Co. between 1897 and 1909 (Ijams and
Hofferbert 1934), in Bradley Co. in 1986 (MIG 57:113) and near Washington
Co. ca. 1930 (Lyle and Tyler 1934). It is listed as a breeding species in the
Roan Mt. area of northeast Tennessee, where it is encountered regularly at
all elevations (Eller and Wallace 1984). The species is less numerous in the
west during the breeding season. There are only two west Tennessee nest
records: three young in Henderson Co. in 1986 (MIG 57:103) and a nest with
young in Shelby Co. in 1945 (Coffey 1945). There is an influx of migrants into the state in Sept and Oct, especially notable in the east where eleven birds
were seen on 25 Sept 1977 at the Kyle's Ford Fire Tower, Hawkins Co. (MIG
49:50). Spring migration has been less well documented. High count: thirteen
on 26 Apr 1981, Knoxville SBC (MIG 52:64).
Substantiation: Specimen: 1 male, Murfreesboro, Rutherford Co., 13 Jan 1934
(LSUMZ, 75689).

Northern Goshawk, *Accipiter gentilis*

Status: Irregular.

Abundance: Rare migrant, very rare winter resident and summer visitor.

Remarks: Found in wooded areas and along woodland edge between mid Dec and late Mar. Treated here primarily as a migrant as most birds rarely linger and are often not relocated. First recorded in the state on 19 Oct 1918, when one bird was shot in Cheatham Co. (Ganier 1937). There are at least forty-five state records. More frequently observed in the east, especially the north-eastern end of the state. Most early fall and late spring dates are also from the east. May arrive in the east as early as Aug (e.g., 13 Aug 1981, Roan Mt., MIG 53:22; and 21-25 Aug 1982, Elizabethton, MIG 54:27). There are at least three Aug records and two Sept records (all from the east), four Oct records and four Nov records. Most of the migrants arrive in Dec, and there are considerably fewer sightings after Dec. Late spring dates include 19 Mar 1941, Warner Parks, Nash. (Laskey 1941), 28 Apr 1973, Elizabethton SBC (MIG 44:45) and 8 May 1988, Butler, Johnson Co. (Glen D. Eller, Harry H. Farthing). There are at least seventeen records for middle Tennessee. There are only five West Tennessee records:

> 30 Oct 1982, Memp., MIG 54:19
> 17 Nov 1984, Lake Co. (Randy Stringer)
> 18 Dec 1987, Memp. (VBR, MGW)
> 8 Jan 1984, Henry Co., MIG 55:43
> 2 Apr 1974, Hatchie NWR, MIG 54:19

One summer record exists, also from east Tennessee: 18 June 1971, Indian Gap, GSMNP (MIG 42:72). All observations within the state have been of single birds. One bird overwintered at Roans Creek from 4 Oct 1975 through 24 Apr 1976 (MIG 47:79). All sightings (particularly of birds found in late spring, summer or early fall) should be carefully documented; Cooper's Hawks and Red-shouldered Hawks are occasionally misidentified as imm. Goshawks.

Substantiation: Specimen: 1 male, Sycamore, Cheatham Co., 19 Oct 1918 (LSUMZ, 75681).

Red-shouldered Hawk, *Buteo lineatus*

Status: Regular.

Abundance: Uncommon permanent resident.

Remarks: Found in lowland deciduous forests, deciduous forested wetlands and cypress swamps. Less detectable in the east, especially the northeastern end of the state. Considered by Alsop (1980) to be very rare in upper east Tennessee, especially in the summer months. Ganier (1933) also found it to be a very rare resident in the east. It is usually more frequently encountered in the middle and west, especially in the Mississippi River floodplain from Reelfoot L. to Memp. A highly vocal raptor, its calls are often imitated by Blue Jays. Nesting has been documented throughout the state. A notable number of nests has been found along the Tennessee River floodplain above

Red-shouldered Hawk, continued

Chat. in Rhea, Meigs, Hamilton, and McMinn Counties. Fall migration is detectable but never includes large concentrations of birds (Fowler 1985). High counts: seventeen on 26 Dec 1936, Memp. CBC (MIG 8:7); and sixteen on 20 Dec 1986, Reelfoot L. CBC (MIG 58:2).

Substantiation: Specimen: 1 female, Nash., Davidson Co., 19 Nov 1940 (LSUMZ, 75693).

Broad-winged Hawk, *Buteo platypterus*

Status: Regular.

Abundance: Fairly common to common migrant, uncommon summer resident, very rare winter visitor.

Spring: Usually arrives by late Mar. There are two early Mar records: 1 Mar 1967, Waconda Bay, Hamilton Co. (MIG 38:50) and 3 Mar 1969, Savannah (MIG 40:44). Smaller concentrations of birds are observed in the spring than in the fall.

Arrivals: 12 Mar 1961, Nash., MIG 32:5
              12 Mar 1973, HRA, MIG 44:25
              23 Mar 1975, Shelby Co., MIG 46:65

Summer: On a statewide basis, breeding birds are usually found where large tracts of forest provide food, cover and habitat to meet minimum home range requirements. Fewer nests are reported from the west.

Fall: Departs by early Oct. Migration may be noted as early as mid Aug.

Departures: 2 Nov 1937, Giles Co., (Wetmore 1939)
              10 Nov 1986, Shelby Co., MIG 58:19
              24 Nov 1987, Union Co., MIG 59:40

Winter: There are four winter records, only two of which have acceptable details: one bird at Cox's L., Johnson Co., from 1 Dec 1935 through mid Jan 1936 (Tyler and Lyle 1936) and one bird on 22 Dec 1984, Nash. CBC (MIG 56:51). All winter sightings should be thoroughly documented.

Remarks: Found in wooded areas. In Sept, during the fall migration, it is often found in large migratory flocks or "kettles," especially in east Tennessee. Behrend (1952) discussed the migration in the east in the fall, noting that Clinch Mountain (running from Bristol to Knoxville) and Bays Mountain northwest of Greeneville offered good viewing opportunities for this species in the fall. Clinch Mountain in Hawkins Co., the Chilhowee Mountain at Look Rock in Blount Co., and Signal Mountain in Hamilton Co. usually yield the most broad-wings, but the species has been seen in respectable numbers on most of the mountain chains east of the Highland Rim (e.g., 4,246 on 25 Sept 1970, near Fall Creek Falls S.P., MIG 42:3). Fall migration in the middle and west is detectable but not usually spectacular. High counts: 5,632 on 19 Sept 1981, Chilhowee Mountain (MIG 53:22) and 4,985 on 25 Sept 1960, Elder Mountain (MIG 32:27).

Substantiation: Specimen: 1 female, Sycamore, Cheatham Co., 8 Oct 1919 (LSUMZ, 75698).

Swainson's Hawk, *Buteo swainsoni*
Status: Accidental (Provisional).
Remarks: Known from one record: one bird on 27 Sept 1980, Chilhowee Mountain (Stedman and Stedman 1981). Observed in good light migrating with a group of Broad-winged Hawks.
Substantiation: Adequately documented sight record.

Red-tailed Hawk, *Buteo jamaicensis*
Status: Regular.
Abundance: Fairly common permanent resident.
Remarks: Found in wooded areas and along clearings and roadsides. Usually nests on the edge of wooded areas. Nests throughout Tennessee from the eastern mountains to the Mississippi River valley. Seen in greater numbers during the winter with the arrival of winter residents from northern breeding areas. Red-tails are generally more abundant in the western two-thirds of the state during the winter. The Harlan's race, *B. j. harlani*, is not often seen east of the Mississippi River but has been recorded in Tennessee at least fifteen times, with reports ranging in distribution from Chattanooga (West 1966) and Franklin Co. (Yeatman 1979) to the Mississippi River valley from Memphis to Reelfoot L.; most of the records are from Shelby Co. where it was first noted in 1940 (MIG 12:15) and seen as recently as 1986 (MIG 58:53); also recorded in Humphreys Co. (MIG 42:43). Dark phase birds of western breeding populations have been more regularly reported recently, with as many as six birds being found in middle Tennessee during the 1986-87 winter (MIG 58:56). Dark phase birds and Rough-legged Hawks are occasionally misidentified as "Harlan's" Hawks. High counts: 74 on 20 Dec 1981, Memp. CBC (MIG 53:6); 54 on 22 Dec 1984, Reelfoot L. CBC (MIG 56:7); and 45 on 14 Nov 1979, Chickamauga L. dam (MIG 51:82).
Substantiation: Specimen: 1 female, Nash., Davidson Co., 23 Nov 1916 (LSUMZ, 75691).

Rough-legged Hawk, *Buteo lagopus*
Status: Regular.
Abundance: Rare migrant and winter resident.
Fall: Arrives by mid Nov. There are at least two Sept sightings and only a handful of Oct records.
Arrivals:　　24 Sept 1957, Joelton, Davidson Co., BNA:20
　　　　　　26 Sept 1975, Rockwood, Roane Co., MIG 47:26
　　　　　　6 Oct 1985, Shelby Co., MIG 57:22
Winter: More frequently observed in the middle region than in the east or west; least observed in the east. Most individuals seen in Tennessee are light phase birds; however, dark phase birds are occasionally found.
Spring: Departs by late Mar.

Rough-legged Hawk, continued
Departures: 27 Mar 1968, Dyersburg, MIG 39:42
                4 Apr 1987, Williamson Co., MIG 58:96
                29 Apr 1956, Greeneville SBC, MIG 27:32
Remarks: Found in wide, open areas. Often perches at the tops of trees and tall shrubs. First recorded in the state on 22 Dec 1934 at Nash. (Ganier 1935b). An irruptive species; more frequently reported in an invasion year as was the case during the 1977-78 season when at least thirty-eight individuals were reported from thirteen counties in middle Tennessee (MIG 49:42). Many records are a result of CBC efforts. Most consistently reported at Memp., Reelfoot L. and Fort Campbell Military Reservation, Montgomery Co. High count: five on 15 Jan 1983, Fort Campbell, Montgomery Co. (MIG 54:44).
Substantiation: Photographs: 1, Piney Flats, Sullivan Co., 17 Feb 1979 (GOW—Milligan College).

Golden Eagle, *Aquila chrysaetos*
Status: Regular (State Endangered).
Abundance: Uncommon migrant and winter resident, very rare summer visitor; formerly bred.
Fall: Arrives by mid Nov. There are several Aug, Sept and Oct records.
Arrivals: 6 Sept 1964, Greene Co., MIG 35:104
             2 Oct 1969, Rutherford Co., (DeVore 1975)
             15 Nov 1970, Tennessee NWR, MIG 41:83
Winter: May be found in any of the three regions throughout the winter months wherever habitat is available. Most consistent reporting areas are Woodbury (Cannon Co.), and along the northern reaches of the Tennessee and Cumberland Rivers (Stewart, Henry and Humphreys Counties).
Spring: Departs by early Mar.
Departures: 6 Mar 1982, Reelfoot L., MIG 53:66
                 17 Apr 1955, Bristol SBC, MIG 26:28
                 29 Apr 1971, Rutherford Co., (DeVore 1975)
Summer: A number of sightings exist for the May to Aug period, primarily from the east. Along the Cumberland Plateau, there are summer records from Fentress Co. between 1927 and 1930, and Overton Co. in 1951 (Ganier 1951a). Also seen on 21 Aug 1970 in Rutherford Co. (DeVore 1975). In the east, summer records include at least nine published accounts from as early as 1924 in Sevier Co. (Stupka 1963) to as recent as 1986 in the GSMNP (MIG 58:31). All May-Aug records should be thoroughly documented. See comments on breeding under Remarks.
Remarks: Found near wooded areas interspersed with patches of open habitat. When soaring, tends to flap less often than the Bald Eagle. Apparently was once a permanent resident in a few select areas of the the Cumberland Plateau and in the eastern mountains. Rhoads (1895) noted a report by Lemoyne that a set of eggs and nesting birds was collected on Bald Mountain, Blount Co., around the late 1800s. Two birds were taken from a nest on Walden's Ridge in the Cumber-

Golden Eagle, continued

land Mountains (Bent 1937). Ganier reported finding a nest in Van Buren Co. in Oct 1935 (MIG 7:47), and another nest from the same area is described in 1940 (Ganier and Clebsch 1940). There are no recent nest records. High count: seven on 3 Jan 1954, Tennessee NWR (MIG 24:77).

Substantiation: Specimen: 1, near Lynchburg, Moore Co., 12 Apr 1935 (LSUMZ, 75702).

FAMILY FALCONIDAE: Falcons

American Kestrel, *Falco sparverius*
Status: Regular.
Abundance: Fairly common to uncommon permanent resident.
Remarks: Found in open areas and along roadsides. Often seen hovering in mid air in search of prey. Frequently perches on telephone wires, a habit that is rarely observed in other falcons. Abundance varies throughout the year; occurs in greater numbers in the winter. Nests in cavities across the state but is not especially numerous during the summer in any of the three regions.
High count: 85 on 27 Dec 1986, Murfreesboro CBC (MIG 58:3).
Substantiation: Specimen: 1 female, Nash., Davidson Co., 17 Oct 1922 (LSUMZ, 75711).

Merlin, *Falco columbarius*
Status: Regular.
Abundance: Uncommon migrant, rare winter resident.
Fall: Arrives by mid Sept.
  Arrivals: 21 Aug 1985, Eagle Bend Fish Hatchery, MIG 57:32
        28 Aug 1974, Nash., MIG 46:20
        15 Sept 1951, Mud L., MIG 22:46
Winter: More than thirty winter records; there are at least ten records for each of the three winter months. The species is equally reported in each of the three regions of the state. Most birds are not relocated, but a few linger for a month or longer (e.g., 9 Dec to 9 Jan 1977-78, Lascassas, Rutherford Co., MIG 49:42).
Spring: Departs by late Apr.
  Departures: 6 May 1961, near Tiptonville, Lake Co., MIG 32:41
        6 May 1984, Nash. area, BNA:20
        13 May 1957, Knoxville, MIG 28:43
Remarks: Found in open areas and along rivers. Formerly less numerous, now reported more frequently. There are no summer records. Most sightings are of single birds.
Substantiation: Specimen: 1, near Nash., Davidson Co., ca. 1900 (LSUMZ, 75709).

Peregrine Falcon, *Falco peregrinus*

Status: Regular (Federally Endangered). (Map A-18)

Abundance: Uncommon migrant, rare winter resident, very rare summer visitor; formerly bred.

Fall: Arrives by mid Sept. The best time to see this raptor in Tennessee is late Sept-early Oct.

Arrivals: 4 Aug 1972, Percy Priest L., MIG 43:99

     11 Aug 1985, Shelby Co., MIG 57:22

     6 Sept 1986, Kingston Steam Plant, MIG 58:27

Winter: Formerly recorded more frequently in the winter. More likely to be found in Dec than in Jan or Feb. Most birds are not relocated, but some occasionally linger (e.g., 10 Nov-8 Dec 1985, Nickajack L., MIG 57:60; and 24 Feb-2 Mar 1968, Knoxville, MIG 39:45).

Spring: Departs by mid May.

Departures: 9 May 1987, Williamson Co., MIG 58:96

      15 May 1986, Cross Creeks NWR, MIG 57:78

      26 May 1984, Reelfoot L., MIG 55:67

Summer: See notes on breeding under Remarks. There are several recent non-breeding summer records as noted below:

 1 June 1980, Ashwood, Maury Co., (Yeatman 1980)

 7 June 1977, Austin Springs, MIG 48:105

 12 July 1987, Island 13, MIG 58:137

 20 July 1986, Shelby Co., MIG 57:103

 22 July 1972, Tennessee NWR, MIG 43:75

The July records probably represent very early fall migrants or wandering birds from hacking or reintroduction programs.

Remarks: Found in open areas and along lakes, rivers and bluffs. Formerly bred in the state, then became less numerous due to the widespread use of DDT. Now reported regularly as a migrant. Past breeding records are restricted to the Cumberland Plateau region, the eastern mountain region and the northern Mississippi River valley. Formerly nested in Fentress, Grundy, Knox, Lake, Marion, Sevier, and Van Buren Counties. Also nested in Sullivan and Washington Co. in the early 1930s (Alsop 1979), and near Lauderdale Co. (Spofford 1947). Up to 15 pairs of birds may have nested in the state at one time (MIG 9:29). The last known nest in Tennessee was at Reelfoot L. in 1947, and the last known nesting in the GSMNP was in 1943 (Alsop 1979). In 1984 and 1986 at least seven birds were hacked at the GSMNP in an attempt to reestablish a nesting population there. Most sight records are of one or two birds.

Substantiation: Specimen: 1 female, Chat., Hamilton Co., 30 Sept 1966 (LSUMZ, 75706).

Gyrfalcon, *Falco rusticolus*
Status: Accidental (Provisional).
Remarks: Known from one record: one well-described white phase bird observed chasing European Starlings in Jefferson Co. on 13 Jan 1978 (Koella 1985).
Substantiation: Adequately documented sight record (TBRC).

Prairie Falcon, *Falco mexicanus*
Status: Accidental.
Remarks: Usually found in wide, open areas. Known from five records. First state record was on 5 Oct 1958, Memp. (Coffey 1981a). Other records include:
    12 Oct 1980, Memp., (Coffey 1981a)
    15, 19 Oct 1984, Island 13, MIG 56:17
    6 Sept 1986, Mound City, TN/ARK state line, MIG 58:19
    11 Sept 1987, Island 10, Lake Co. (CGD)
All records are of single birds. Based on records from midwestern states, the likely period of occurrence is during the Oct to Nov period.
Substantiation: Adequately documented sight records.

ORDER GALLIFORMES

FAMILY PHASIANIDAE: **Partridges, Grouse, Turkeys and Quail**

*Chukar, *Alectoris chukar*
Status: Extirpated.
Remarks: Solyom (1940) described the introduction of this bird into Tennessee during 1939. In 1937 the Tennessee Game and Fish Division obtained eggs of the Chukar in preparation for a release effort to establish a huntable game population. During 1939, 2,400 birds were released throughout the state. Released in the east at: Roan Mt., Kingsport, Rockford, Maryville, Edgemore, Orebank, Crossville, and Pikeville; in the middle at: Standing Stone, Sparta, Hartsville, Murfreesboro, Lawrenceburg, Centerville, and Hohenwald; and in the west at: Lexington, Huntingdon, Henderson, Selmer, Whiteville, Gallaway, Millington, Covington, Dyersburg, and Union City. The birds at Gallaway (Fayette Co.) nested and produced 30-60 young. However, several dead birds were found on several of the release sites and the species never became established in the wild anywhere in Tennessee. One

*Chukar, continued

recent report (most likely of an escaped bird) is of one bird at Percy Warner Park on 2 June 1986 (MIG 57:107). The species has probably been extirpated from Tennessee.

*Japanese Quail, *Coturnix japonica*

Status: Extirpated.

Remarks: About 29,000 of these game birds were released in various parts of the state ca. 1956 by the Tennessee State Game and Fish Commission. However, the birds tended to wander and migrate and in 1959 the stocking program was abandoned (Tenn. State Game and Fish Comm. 1959). There are no recent records.

*Ring-necked Pheasant, *Phasianus colchicus*

Status: Extremely Rare.

Remarks: The species was stocked as a game bird at several locations across the state, but never became well established. Now rarely encountered anywhere within the state. In Oct 1949, 24 birds were released near Kingsport at the Holston Defense area (MIG 22:69). Another 422 birds were released on Hiwassee Island on 5 Nov 1959. A large number was also released at the Old Hickory WMA, near Lebanon (MIG 29:68). The species has nested in Campbell, Greene, and Johnson Counties, and at the HRA. Reported once in the west on 29 Dec 1965, Reelfoot L. CBC (MIG 36:88). Apparently local propagators continue to occasionally release birds.

Substantiation: Specimen: 1 ad. female, Rutledge, Grainger Co., 28 June 1963 (USNM, 488572).

Ruffed Grouse, *Bonasa umbellus*

Status: Regular.

Abundance: East: uncommon permanent resident.

Middle: locally uncommon permanent resident.

Remarks: Found in wooded areas. Former distribution probably extended as far west as the Tennessee River in Humphreys, Houston and Stewart Counties, based on a statewide survey conducted by Schultz (1953). Schultz (1953) found grouse to be essentially nonexistent in Hardin, Wayne and Perry Counties and concluded that grouse may have originally been found in the Central Basin region of the state but in fewer numbers than reported elsewhere on the Highland Rim. He described the primary range of grouse to include the Cumberland Plateau, the upper Tennessee River valley and the Unaka Range (extreme east Tennessee). White and Dimmick (1979) found the current range of the Ruffed Grouse to be more restricted than that reported by Schultz. The current range was found generally not to extend much beyond the Cumberland Plateau in the following counties: Putnam, Cumberland, White, Warren, Grundy, and Franklin. Grouse were absent from Loudon, Meigs and Bradley Counties; and restricted to mountains and

Ruffed Grouse, continued

ridges surrounding the Tennessee River valley in Rhea, McMinn, and Hamilton Counties (White and Dimmick 1979). In middle Tennessee, recent reports of one to three birds have been made in Cannon Co. (MIG 43:45), Putnam Co. (MIG 49:56 and MIG 56:51), Pickett Co. (MIG 57:81), White Co. (MIG 57:81), Coffee Co. (MIG 58:23), Williamson Co. (MIG 54:61) and Wilson Co. (BNA:20). White and Dimmick (1979) also found a few birds to occur west of the Plateau in Clay, Jackson, and Overton Counties. Between 1980 and 1983, more than eighty birds were released in Humphreys Co. and in Benton Co. in the Nathan Bedford S.P. High count: twenty-five on 19 Dec 1937, GSMNP CBC (MIG 9:7).

Substantiation: Specimen: 1 female, Rocky River, Van Buren Co., 30 Dec 1939 (LSUMZ, 75717).

Greater Prairie-Chicken, *Tympanuchus cupido*

Status: Extirpated.

Remarks: Considered by Ganier (1933) to have been seen by Alexander Wilson in May 1810 near the Kentucky/Tennessee state line. However, Nicholson (1986) noted that Wilson never specifically mentioned personally observing the species in Tennessee. Wilson described the range of the prairie-chicken to include the Barrens of Kentucky, an area which extended into Tennessee (Nicholson 1986). Parmalee and Klippel (1982) found fossil evidence of the species' occurrence in cave deposits in Maury Co.

Substantiation: Fossil evidence (Parmalee and Klippel 1982).

Wild Turkey, *Meleagris gallopavo*

Status: Regular.

Abundance: Uncommon permanent resident.

Remarks: Found in open woods and adjacent clearings. "Gobbling" males are most frequently heard in Apr and May. Schultz (1955) summarized the range of the Wild Turkey in Tennessee in the early 1950s to include the Unaka Range, the Cumberland Plateau, portions of the western Highland Rim and portions of the Mississippi River valley. He listed observations between 1940 and 1951 from about forty-five counties. Apparently over-harvested because turkeys were reported from only seventeen counties in 1952 (Jack Murrey, pers. comm.) and only twenty-three counties had native populations by 1962, when the statewide population was estimated at 3,700 birds (Lewis 1962). Restoration efforts by the Tennessee Game and Fish Commission and the TWRA since 1951 are still ongoing and have succeeded in reestablishing the Wild Turkey throughout the majority of its former range. The source for most of the released birds are native birds which were trapped and relocated to other sites; however, close to 100 birds from Florida, Missouri, Arkansas and Kentucky were released in the state between 1973 and 1988 (Jack Murrey, pers. comm.). In 1988, turkeys were present in all counties except Crockett, Meigs, Loudon, Knox, and Jefferson (Jack Murrey, pers. comm.).

Wild Turkey, continued

Current size of population is apparently healthy with recent statewide harvest totals averaging between 1,500 and 2,000 birds per year (TWRA 1987). Breeding records are currently well distributed across the entire state (TWRA 1987). High counts: 78 on 16 Nov 1973, Cades Cove, GSMNP (MIG 45:25-26) and 53 on 22 Dec 1984, Reelfoot L. CBC (MIG 56:7).

Substantiation: Specimen: 1, Anderson Tully WMA, Lauderdale Co., winter 1979 (UTMB, 408).

Northern Bobwhite, *Colinus virginianus*
Status: Regular.
Abundance: Fairly common permanent resident.
Remarks: Found in agricultural areas, brushland and areas with scattered woodlands. Nests throughout the state. At Roan Mt., it is regularly encountered at elevations as high as 1,800 m (Eller and Wallace 1984). More detectable in spring (Apr-May) when coveys begin to break up and males begin calling, and throughout summer. Generally slightly less numerous in the east with the exception of the Knoxville area where larger concentrations are frequently encountered. High counts: 209 on 28 Apr 1968, Knoxville SBC (MIG 39:31) and 183 on 21 Dec 1958, Memp. CBC (MIG 29:70).
Substantiation: Specimen: 1 male, near Germantown, Shelby Co., 23 Dec 1941 (LSUMZ, 6118).

ORDER GRUIFORMES

FAMILY RALLIDAE: **Rails, Gallinules and Coots**

Yellow Rail, *Coturnicops noveboracensis*
Status: Extremely Rare. (Map A-19)
Remarks: Found in dry or wet grassy fields. There are at least fourteen state records, seven of these being tower/window kills (noted by a "*" below). Most likely to be found in migration in late Sept or early Oct. First state record was on 15 Oct 1953, Nash. suburbs (Ganier 1954). Other records include:

27 Sept 1986, Davidson Co., MIG 58:23
*28 Sept 1960, Nash., (Bierly 1980)
*29 Sept 1957, Nash., (Laskey 1957)
29 Sept 1957, Knox Co., (Howell and Monroe 1958)
*30 Sept 1960, Nash., (Bierly 1980)
7 Oct 1967, Cannon Co., MIG 38:95

Yellow Rail, continued
   *13 Oct 1980, Chat., MIG 52:24
   *18 Oct 1960, Nash., (Bierly 1980)
   *31 Oct 1970, Nash., MIG 41:84
   *30 Apr 1979, Martin, Weakley Co., MIG 51:20
   4 May 1985, Columbia SBC, MIG 56:68
One winter record: 8 Dec 1983, Pickett Co., observed at close range (Hassler 1984). One bird was regularly observed over a two week period at the Cross Creeks NWR, 4-17 Oct 1987 (MIG 59:35). All records are of single birds. Parmalee and Klippel (1982) provided fossil evidence of the species' occurrence in Maury Co. dating back to the Pleistocene epoch.
Substantiation: Specimen: 1 female, Nash., Davidson Co., 15 Oct 1953 (LSUMZ, 75734).

Black Rail, *Laterallus jamaicensis*
Status: Accidental.
Remarks: Found in wet, grassy meadows or fields. All records are from the east, including a breeding record of two ad. and five young at Roaring Fork in western Greene Co. in 1964 (Nevius 1964). First recorded in the state in 1915 when a bird was found in Cocke Co. near Del Rio between 10 June and 20 June (Walker 1935). Other records include:
   spring 1948, Bluff Mt., Greene Co., (Nevius 1964)
   27 Apr 1980, Knoxville SBC, MIG 51:55
   5 May 1980, Jefferson Co., MIG 51:62
   1 May 1983, Knoxville SBC, MIG 54:51
   Also known from fossil evidence in a Maury Co. cave dating back to the Pleistocene epoch (Parmalee and Klippel 1982).
Substantiation: Adequately documented sight records.

Clapper Rail, *Rallus longirostris*
Status: Accidental.
Remarks: Known from one record: 8 Apr 1986, one captured, photographed and released (on 17 Apr 1986), Elizabethton (MIG 57:87). Photographs were confirmed by the Tennessee Bird Records Committee.
Substantiation: Photographs: 1, Elizabethton, Carter Co., 9 Apr 1986 (GOW— Milligan College).

King Rail, *Rallus elegans*
Status: Regular. (Map A-20)
Abundance: Rare migrant and summer resident, very rare winter visitor.
Spring: Arrives by early Apr.
   Arrivals: 1 Mar 1961, Bristol, MIG 32:10
            29 Mar 1956, Buena Vista Marsh, BNA:21
            27 Apr 1987, Hooper Marsh, Dyer Co., MIG 58:92

King Rail, continued

Summer: Has been found breeding in the middle and east in the following counties: Blount, Coffee, Davidson, Grundy, Hamilton, Humphreys, Knox, Maury, Robertson, Rutherford, Stewart, and Warren. The most consistently reported nesting sites are Alcoa Marsh (Blount Co.), Amnicola Marsh (Hamilton Co.), and Goose Pond (Grundy Co.). There is no recent breeding evidence from the west, but suitable habitat is still available (see Remarks).

Fall: Departs by early Oct.

Departures: 30 Oct 1975, Alcoa Marsh, MIG 47:21

3 Nov 1942, Nash., MIG 13:71

17 Nov 1976, Alcoa Marsh, MIG 48:49

Winter: There are at least four winter records: 24 Dec 1940, Knox Co. (MIG 12:18); 2 Jan 1943, near Nash. (MIG 13:71); 4 Dec 1952, Nash. (BNA:21); and one bird that remained at Alcoa Marsh from Nov 1974 through Mar 1975 (MIG 46:46).

Remarks: Found in marshy areas with dense vegetation. Breeding records in west Tennessee exist for Chester Co. (MIG 12:35) and Shelby Co. (Smith 1952). Ganier (1933a) reported a nest at Reelfoot L. on 25 May 1921. Calhoun (1941) found one to two birds in June and July in Hardeman Co.

Substantiation: Specimen: 1 female, Buena Vista Marsh, Davidson Co., 21 May 1938 (LSUMZ, 75721).

Virginia Rail, *Rallus limicola*

Status: Regular. (Map A-21)

Abundance: Uncommon migrant, rare summer and winter resident.

Spring: Late Apr to mid May.

Arrivals: 13 Mar 1987, Sullivan Co., MIG 58:102

18 Mar 1978, Buena Vista Marsh, MIG 49:67

10 Apr 1980, Memp., MIG 51:60

Departures: 14 May 1955, Reelfoot L. SBC, MIG 26:28

16 May 1976, Ashland City Marsh, MIG 47:76

18 May 1981, Chat., MIG 52:97

Summer: One bird was found on 16 July 1950, Knox Co. (MIG 21:52). Most other summer records are of breeding birds. First nest was discovered in Hamilton Co. in 1963 (West 1963). Other eastern nest records are from Alcoa Marsh (Blount Co.) and the Holston River (Hawkins Co.) in 1974, from Sullivan Co. in 1987 (MIG 58:102) and near Kingsport in 1976 (MIG 47:77). Nested in middle Tennessee in 1984 and 1985 at Monsanto Ponds, Maury Co. (Lochridge and Lochridge 1984; and MIG 56:110).

Fall: Mid Sept to late Oct.

Arrivals: 14 Aug 1976, Buena Vista Marsh, MIG 48:19

24 Aug 1964, near Greeneville, MIG 35:64

3 Sept 1974, Savannah Bay, MIG 46:22

Virginia Rail, continued

Departures: 26 Oct 1966, Nash., (Laskey 1966)
                    2 Nov 1983, Shelby Co., MIG 55:17
                    16 Nov 1986, Monroe Co., MIG 58:31

Winter: There are more than twenty records, most of them from Dec, suggesting many birds may be late migrants. Seen at Alcoa Marsh on 3 Feb 1974 (MIG 45:24). Winter sightings exist for Reelfoot L., Bays Mt., and Roane, Blount, Knox, Maury, and Stewart Counties. Close to half of the winter records are from Monsanto Ponds, Maury Co., where it was found in nine of the past twelve winters beginning in Dec 1976, with as many as eight birds being counted at once (MIG 55:9).

Remarks: Found in marshes and along the edges of lakes and ponds. High count: eight on 23 Dec 1974, Alcoa Marsh (MIG 46:46).

Substantiation: Specimen: 1 female, Nash., Davidson Co., 18 Apr 1951 (LSUMZ, 75723).

Sora, *Porzana carolina*

Status: Regular.

Abundance: Fairly common migrant, rare winter resident, very rare summer visitor.

Spring: Early Apr to mid May.

Arrivals: 6 Mar 1951, near Bristol, MIG 22:19
                13 Mar 1987, Hardin Co., MIG 58:92
                23 Mar 1985, Maury Co., MIG 56:76

Departures: 22 May 1956, Elizabethton, MIG 27:52
                    27 May 1985, Lawrence Co., MIG 56:76
                    30 May 1986, Shelby Co., MIG 57:74

Summer: Known from three records: 21 June 1956, Greene Co. (MIG 27:52); 22 July 1972, Tennessee NWR (MIG 43:75); and 23 July 1972, Buena Vista Marsh (MIG 43:76). The July records are probably early migrants.

Fall: Late Aug to early Nov.

Arrivals: 2 Aug 1961, Goose Pond, Grundy Co., MIG 32:43
                20 Aug 1964, Knoxville, MIG 35:63
                21 Aug 1978, Shelby Co., MIG 50:19

Departures: 8 Nov 1976, Daus, Sequatchie Co., MIG 48:49
                    11 Nov 1971, Buena Vista Marsh, MIG 43:25
                    16 Nov 1986, Percy Priest L., MIG 58:23

Winter: There are more than twenty winter records, most of them from Dec, suggesting that many of the sightings are of lingering fall migrants. February records include: 3 Feb 1974, Alcoa Marsh (MIG 45:24) and 27 Feb 1971, Amnicola Marsh (MIG 42:46). Has been found in Jan and Dec at Bristol, Nash., Alcoa and Amnicola Marshes, Cumberland City Steam Plant in Stewart Co., Reelfoot L., and Cheatham L. As with the preceding species, about half of all the winter records are from the Monsanto Ponds, Maury Co., between 1976 and 1987.

Sora, continued
Remarks: Found in marshes, and along the edges of lakes and ponds. Can often be stimulated to call by throwing rocks into a marsh or other suitable habitat. High count: thirty-seven on 6 May 1988, Stewart Co. (JCR, DWB).
Substantiation: Specimen: 1 male, Nash., Davidson Co., 10 Apr 1943 (LSUMZ, 75731).

Purple Gallinule, *Porphyrula martinica*
Status: Irregular. (Map A-22)
Abundance: Rare migrant, very rare summer resident.
Remarks: Found in marshes and ponds with dense growths of emergent vegetation (e.g., American lotus or creeping primrose-willow). May be found somewhere in the state one to three times each year; some years not seen at all. Most sightings are made in the spring and early summer from late Apr through mid June. Seldom seen after July.

Arrivals:	16 Mar 1936, Coffee Co., MIG 7:47
	7 Apr 1983, Memp., MIG 54:59
	18 Apr 1964, near Kingsport, MIG 35:40
Departures:	10 Sept 1981, HRA, MIG 53:19
	5 Oct 1975, Nash., MIG 47:18
	12 Oct 1958, Knox Co., MIG 30:9
	10 Nov 1923, Radnor L., BNA:21

Records are scattered across all three regions of the state with representative sites including Knox Co., Gatlinburg, Oak Ridge, Nash., Austin Springs, Stewart Co., Memp., and Ashland City. However, there are many records for Reelfoot L., where a nesting colony was found in 1923 (Ganier 1933a) and periodically thereafter. Found nesting there in 1984 (Pitts 1985). Other nest records include two active nests at Goose Pond, one in 1935 (Ganier 1935a) and one in 1964 (Dubke 1974); and an empty, apparently used, nest in Warren Co. in 1952 (Ganier 1952a). Most sightings are of single birds.
Substantiation: Specimen: 1 female, Nash., Davidson Co., 27 Apr 1920 (LSUMZ, 75736).

Common Moorhen, *Gallinula chloropus*
Status: Irregular. (Map A-23)
Abundance: Rare migrant and summer resident, very rare winter visitor.
Spring: Late Apr to mid May.

Arrivals:	19 Mar 1956, Memp., MIG 27:17
	7 Apr 1988, Nash. (Mark H. Mayfield)
	14 Apr 1973, Erwin Fish Hatchery, MIG 44:52

Summer: Summer records are scattered across all three regions of the state with representative sites including Humphreys Co., Greene Co., Blount Co., the HRA, and Norris L. However, it is primarily seen at Reelfoot L., where it nested in 1941 (Spofford 1941) and again in 1984 (Pitts 1985). Ganier (1933a) found several nests there in 1921. A nest with eggs was also found at Powell

Common Moorhen, continued

Airport in Knox Co. (Williams 1975). An ad. with young was found in Meigs Co. in 1988 (Mark Armstrong). In recent years it has been found at Monsanto Ponds (MIG 56:110 and 57:107), although nesting has not been documented at this location. The discovery of additional nesting sites is likely.

Fall: Late Sept to early Oct. There are several Aug records.

Departures: 21 Oct 1937, Reelfoot L., (Wetmore 1939)

               27 Oct 1984, Maury Co., MIG 56:20

               2 Nov 1982, HRA, MIG 54:24

Winter: Known from one record: 26 Dec 1949, Reelfoot L. CBC (MIG 20:61).

Remarks: Found in marshes and on ponds with dense growths of emergent vegetation (e.g., American lotus or creeping primrose-willow). Slightly more numerous than the preceding species. High count: twenty-five on 30 May 1932, Reelfoot L. (Ganier 1933a).

Substantiation: Specimen: 1 male, Nash., Davidson Co., 19 Oct 1953 (LSUMZ, 75738).

American Coot, *Fulica americana*

Status: Regular.

Abundance: Fairly common to common migrant and winter resident, rare summer resident.

Remarks: Found on marshes, lakes and ponds primarily from early Sept to early May. There are records for every month of the year, but the largest concentrations are reported during the Oct to Apr period. Summer records are scattered across all three regions of the state with representative sites including Knoxville, Ashland City, Sullivan Co., Savannah, Cove L., Carter Co., Franklin Co., Kingston Steam Plant, and the GSMNP. Nested in 1971 in Hamilton Co. on Nickajack L. (MIG 42:46) and in Benton Co. at Camden (MIG 42:68). A young bird accompanied by an ad. was seen on Old Hickory L. near Nash. in the summer of 1984 (MIG 55:91). Nested at Reelfoot L. in 1984 (Pitts 1985); Rhoads (1895) described it as a breeding species at Reelfoot L. and Ganier (1933a) found several nests there in 1923. May occur in very large concentrations during the winter. Historical areas of abundance are Reelfoot L., Woods Res., Nickajack L., and Kentucky L. at Paris Landing S.P. High counts: 36,000 on 29 Dec 1965, Reelfoot L. CBC (MIG 36:88) and 16,400 on 28 Oct 1975, Woods Res. (MIG 47:18).

Substantiation: Specimen: 1, Reelfoot L., 26 Nov 1915 (LSUMZ, 75739).

Caribbean Coot, *Fulica caribaea*

Status: Accidental.

Remarks: Known from one record: one bird was present at the Chickamauga L. Boat Harbor, Hamilton Co., from 8 Nov 1981 through 18 Dec 1982 (McLean 1982). It was photographed and judged to have a broken or crippled left wing. Placed on the confirmed list of Tennessee birds in 1983 (Nicholson 1982a). The validity of the Caribbean Coot as a distinct species

Caribbean Coot, continued

is questionable, and the relationship of this species with the American Coot is still not completely understood.

Substantiation: Photograph: 1, Chickamauga L., Hamilton Co., Nov. 1981 (H. K. McLean—TBRC).

FAMILY ARAMIDAE: **Limpkins**

Limpkin, *Aramus guarauna*

Status: Accidental.

Remarks: Known from one record: one bird was at Radnor L. on 10-11 June 1961; the plumage and behavior of this bird were well described (Morlan 1961).

Substantiation: Adequately documented sight record.

FAMILY GRUIDAE: **Cranes**

Sandhill Crane, *Grus canadensis*

Status: Regular.

Abundance: East: fairly common migrant, rare winter resident, very rare summer visitor.

Middle: uncommon migrant, very rare winter resident and summer visitor.

West: rare migrant, very rare winter visitor.

Fall: Mid Oct to late Dec.

Arrivals: 21 Sept 1987, Memp., MIG 59:32

                 28 Sept 1978, Norris L., MIG 50:22

                 16 Oct 1986, Byrdstown, MIG 58:23

Departures: 3 Jan 1981, Murfreesboro CBC, MIG 52:13

                 9 Jan 1985, HRA, MIG 56:56

                 13 Jan 1986, Cross Creeks NWR, MIG 57:57

Winter: There is a short interval of time between early Jan and mid Feb when cranes are generally not reported in the state. However, there appears to be a recent tendency for the species to overwinter. Such records include: 13 Nov 1959 to 28 Feb 1960, Knox Co. (Owen 1960); 9 Jan-15 Mar 1976, Sullivan Co. (DeVore 1980); 16 Jan-22 Feb 1981, Obion Co. (MIG 52:72); 4-16 Jan 1985, Woods Res. (MIG 56:52); winter, 1987-1988, HRA (MIG 59:69); and 5 Jan-28 Feb 1986, Maury Co. (MIG 57:57).

Sandhill Crane, continued
Spring: Mid Feb to late Mar.
  Arrivals: 1 Feb 1953, Shelby Co., (Barbig 1953)
                  10 Feb 1984, HRA, MIG 55:49
                  17 Feb 1988, Overton Co. (RCH, JDH)
  Departures: 2 May 1982, Murfreesboro SBC, MIG 53:54
                  16 May 1986, HRA, MIG 57:84
                  18 May 1986, Fort Pillow S.P., MIG 57:74
Summer: Summer records include the first state record, taken near Chat. on
  1 June 1935 (Butts 1936). Another bird was taken in Aug 1936 in Bedford
  Co. (DeVore 1972), and one was found near Chat. on 1 Aug 1965 (DeVore
  1966). A bird was present from July through 24 Sept 1985, Loudon Co.
  (MIG 57:32), and an apparently sick bird was present from 31 May through
  6 June 1982 at Nash. (MIG 57:81-82).
Remarks: Found along rivers, on mudflats and in grain fields; most observations are of birds in flight. A historical record includes Audubon's observation of large flocks of cranes in the vicinity of the Shelby/Tipton Co. line in
  Nov of 1820 (Deaderick 1940). Migrates through the state along a definite
  corridor that is centered approximately on Pickett and Clay Counties and
  which runs south-southeastwards toward Bradley and Monroe Counties;
  western and eastern edges of this corridor are Davidson Co. and Sevier and
  Knox Counties (DeVore 1980). Formerly less abundant; DeVore (1980) noted
  a sudden increase in the number of sightings beginning in 1968. There are
  many records for Byrdstown (Pickett Co.), Barnes Hollow (Putnam Co.) and
  the HRA near Chat. High counts: 700 on 5 Mar 1988, HRA (KHD); 650 on
  3 Nov 1986, Pickett Co. (MIG 58:23); and 590 on 5 Mar 1987, Putnam Co.
  (MIG 58:96).
Substantiation: Specimen: 1 imm., near Joelton, Davidson Co., 15 June 1982
  (CSM, F82-11).

ORDER CHARADRIIFORMES

FAMILY CHARADRIIDAE: **Plovers**

Black-bellied Plover, *Pluvialis squatarola*
Status: Regular.
Abundance: Uncommon migrant, very rare summer visitor.
Spring: Early May to late May.

Black-bellied Plover, continued

Arrrivals: 15 Mar 1986, Lawrence Co., MIG 57:78

2 Apr 1972, Jefferson Co., MIG 43:53

27 Apr 1986, Memp. SBC, MIG 57:66

Departures: 29 May 1978, Dyersburg, MIG 49:91

29 May 1983, Gallatin Steam Plant, MIG 54:61

31 May 1980, Anderson Co., MIG 51:94

Summer: Birds found in early June are probably late spring migrants while birds found after mid July are likely to be early fall migrants. Three June records include: 4-5 June 1968, Columbia (MIG 39:64); 12 June 1977, Sumner Co. (MIG 48:103); and 24 June 1977, near Hopefield, Shelby Co. (MIG 48:102).

Fall: Mid Aug to mid Nov.

Arrivals: 18 July 1987, Kingston Steam Plant, MIG 58:145

29 July 1979, Gallatin Steam Plant, MIG 50:87

11 Aug 1986, Pace Point, MIG 58:19

Departures: 15 Nov 1970, Kingston Steam Plant, MIG 42:21

24 Nov 1984, Tennessee NWR, MIG 56:20

30 Nov 1987, Henry Co., MIG 59:32

Remarks: Found on sandbars, mudflats and edges of lakes and ponds. First state record was on 6 Oct 1932, near Knoxville (Ijams 1932). Apparently not recorded in the 1940s; there are at least five published records for the 1950s. Has been observed regularly since 1960. Compared to the Lesser Golden-Plover, the Black-bellied is usually not found in groups of more than ten or fifteen birds. High count: nineteen on 17 May 1980, Kingston Steam Plant (MIG 51:94).

Lesser Golden-Plover, *Pluvialis dominica*

Status: Regular.

Abundance: East: uncommon migrant.

Middle and West: fairly common migrant; very rare summer visitor in west.

Spring: Early Mar to late Apr.

Arrivals: 28 Feb 1971, Tennessee NWR, MIG 42:43

4 Mar 1955, Penal Farm, MIG 26:46

14 Mar 1967, Savannah Bay, MIG 38:50

Departures: 11 May 1975, Reelfoot L. SBC, MIG 46:56

14 May 1979, Kingston Steam Plant, MIG 50:70

31 May 1988, Sumner Co. (JPC)

Summer: Known from three records of single birds: 14 June 1987, Lake Co. (MIG 58:137); 17 June 1984, Lake Co. (Brainard Palmer-Ball, Jr.); and 18-20 June 1988, Shelby Co. (JRW, JCR).

Fall: Late Aug to mid Nov. There is a handful of July records.

Arrivals: 5 July 1975, Lake Co., MIG 46:87

22 July 1986, Cross Creeks NWR, MIG 58:23

11 Aug 1973, Sequatchie Co., MIG 44:102

Lesser Golden-Plover, continued
Departures: 20 Nov 1954, Bush L., BNA:22
                28 Nov 1978, Shelby Co., MIG 50:41
                2 Dec 1979, Savannah Bay, MIG 51:42
Remarks: Found on sandbars, mudflats and in grain fields; often found in
plowed fields in the spring. First state record was 9 Oct 1938, Mud L.
(Coffey 1939); was not recorded in the east until 1953 (Stupka 1954) and not
recorded in middle Tennessee until 1954 (Ganier 1954a). The largest concen-
trations of birds occur in the spring in the Mississippi River floodplain.
High counts: 1,200 on 27 Mar 1988, Lake Co. (MLB, CGD) and 540 on 26
Mar 1955, Penal Farm (MIG 26:46).

Snowy Plover, *Charadrius alexandrinus*
Status: Accidental.
Remarks: Known from two records: 19-25 May 1977, Gallatin Steam Plant
    (Crawford and Crawford 1977); and 9-18 Sept 1985, Island 13 (MIG 57:22).
Substantiation: Photographs: 1, Gallatin Steam Plant, Sumner Co., 20 May
    1977 (JPC–TBRC).

Wilson's Plover, *Charadrius wilsonia*
Status: Accidental (Provisional).
Remarks: One acceptably documented record: 17 Apr 1988, Ensley sewage
    lagoons, Shelby Co. (MGW, et al.). There are also two hypothetical records
    of single birds at Chat.: 22 Sept 1957 (West 1957) and 26 June 1961 (MIG
    32:44). No plumage description is given for either of these two sightings.
Substantiation: Adequately documented sight record (TBRC).

Semipalmated Plover, *Charadrius semipalmatus*
Status: Regular.
Abundance: East: uncommon migrant, very rare winter visitor.
Middle and West: fairly common migrant; very rare summer visitor in middle.
Spring: Late Apr to late May.
    Arrivals: 6 Mar 1978, Shelby Co., MIG 49:65
                   15 Apr 1985, Williamson Co., MIG 56:76
                   23 Apr 1978, HRA, MIG 49:69
    Departures: 29 May 1974, Buena Vista Marsh, MIG 45:101
                   31 May 1986, Savannah Bay, MIG 57:84
                   31 May-1 June 1977, Dyer Co., MIG 48:102
Summer: One bird remained near Hillsboro, Coffee Co., from 21 May through
    9 July 1977 (MIG 48:103). Other records include:
    3 June 1972, Tennessee NWR, MIG 43:75
    4 June 1984, Austin Springs, MIG 55:94
    11 June 1975, Gallatin Steam Plant, MIG 46:88

Semipalmated Plover, continued

11 June 1979, Gallatin Steam Plant, MIG 50:87

22 June 1985, Tennessee NWR, MIG 57:27

Early June records are probably late spring migrants.

Fall: Late July to mid Oct.

Arrivals: 16 July 1972, Gallatin Steam Plant, MIG 43:76

17 July 1985, Island 13, MIG 56:107

20 July 1980, Cocke Co., MIG 51:94

Departures: 22 Oct 1980, Kingston Steam Plant, MIG 52:24

1 Nov 1982, Gallatin Steam Plant, MIG 54:22

22 Nov 1987, Henry Co., MIG 59:32

Winter: Known from two records: two birds on 21 Dec 1969, Knoxville CBC (MIG 41:8); and six birds from 23 Dec 1971 through 1 Jan 1972, Cherokee L. (MIG 43:27).

Remarks: Found on mudflats, sandbars and lake edges. High count: 114 on 15 May 1979, Gallatin Steam Plant (MIG 50:87).

Substantiation: Specimen: 1 female, Mud L., Shelby Co., 25 Aug 1940 (LSUMZ, 8991).

Piping Plover, *Charadrius melodus*

Status: Irregular (Federally Threatened).

Abundance: Rare migrant.

Spring: Early Apr to early May (all records listed).

9 Apr 1955, Nash., (Weise 1958)

28 Apr-6 May 1984, Columbia SBC, MIG 55:69

3 May 1973, Columbia SBC, MIG 44:45

5 May 1935, Shelby Co., (Coffey 1935)

7 May 1984, Lake Co. (SJS, BHS)

Fall: Late July to early Oct.

Arrivals: 22 July 1972, Tennessee NWR, MIG 43:75

24 July 1979, Kingston Steam Plant, MIG 50:89

28 July 1985, Gallatin Steam Plant, MIG 57:27

Departures: 23 Sept 1984, Island 13, MIG 56:17

3 Oct 1977, Hiwassee Island, MIG 49:21

15 Oct 1983, Gallatin Steam Plant, MIG 55:20

Remarks: Found on sandbars, mudflats and lake edges. Most sightings occur in the fall. Slightly less detectable in the east but has occurred as far east as Cocke Co. (Koella 1975). First state record was on 5 May 1935, Shelby Co. (Coffey 1935); only four records prior to 1970, but currently more than fifty records for the state. Most observations are of one or two birds.

Substantiation: Adequately documented sight records.

Killdeer, *Charadrius vociferus*

Status: Regular.

Abundance: Common permanent resident.

Killdeer, continued

Remarks: Often found near water, but also in grain fields, pastures and urban areas. Seen at 1,830 m elevation flying over Roan Mt. on 28 Dec 1985 (MIG 57:63). In mixed species shorebird flocks, the Killdeer is usually the first to take alarm and flush, often causing the other birds to do the same. Nests across the state from Mar through Aug; some nests may even be found in Feb (e.g., four nests on 27-28 Feb 1932, Davidson Co., [Crook 1932]). Especially common during migration in Mar-Apr and Sept-Nov. Also occurs in large flocks in the winter, most notably at Memp. and the HRA. High counts: 681 on 1 Jan 1985, Hiwassee CBC (MIG 56:7) and 486 on 21 Dec 1986, Memp. CBC (MIG 58:3).

Substantiation: Specimen: 1 male, Nash., Davidson Co., 26 Apr 1916 (LSUMZ, 75744).

FAMILY RECURVIROSTRIDAE: **Stilts and Avocets**

Black-necked Stilt, *Himantopus mexicanus*

Status: Irregular.

Abundance: East and Middle: very rare fall visitor.

West: locally uncommon summer resident.

Remarks: First recorded in the state on 21 Mar 1981 in Shelby Co. near Millington, when two birds were found (MIG 52:71). Has been found annually in Shelby Co. through 1988, but no subsequent arrival dates are earlier than 25 Mar. After 1981, birds were found annually at the Ensley sewage lagoons, where nesting took place in 1982 and 1984 through 1988. At least four young were seen in 1982 on 1 Aug (Coffey 1985); and three young were found in 1984 on 22 Aug (Coffey 1985). As many as nine ad. birds have been seen at this location at one time (MIG 57:103). Departure dates for this local colony average late Aug to mid Sept, with 19 Sept 1982 (Coffey 1985) being the latest. Other state records include one bird at the Eagle Bend Fish Hatchery, Anderson Co., on 1 Aug 1985 (Fowler 1986); and one bird which appeared after the passage of Hurricane Juan on 2-4 Nov 1985 at the Cumberland City Steam Plant, Stewart Co. (MIG 57:27).

Substantiation: Photograph: 1, Eagle Bend Fish Hatchery, Anderson Co., 1 Aug 1985 (CPN, MIG 57:19).

American Avocet, *Recurvirostra americana*

Status: Regular.

Abundance: Rare spring migrant, uncommon fall migrant, very rare summer visitor.

Spring: Mid Apr to early May.

American Avocet, continued
Arrivals: 16 Apr 1982, Chickamauga L., MIG 53:68
                     18 Apr 1977, Old Hickory L., MIG 48:76
                     21 Apr 1979, Gallatin Steam Plant, MIG 50:69
Departures: 9 May 1984, Dyer Co., MIG 55:67
                     10 May 1971, Pace Point, MIG 42:68
                     21 May 1983, Gallatin Steam Plant, MIG 54:62
Summer: Two records: two birds in Washington Co. on 19 June 1977 (MIG 48:105) and one bird on 28 June 1987 in Polk Co. (MIG 58:147). The latter sighting most likely represents an early fall migrant.
Fall: Mid Aug to early Nov.
Arrivals: 9 July 1987, Cross Creeks NWR, MIG 59:35
                     20 July 1981, Kingston Steam Plant, MIG 52:98
                     1 Sept 1985, Island 13, MIG 57:22
Departures: 24 Oct 1971, Fayette Co., MIG 42:91
                     7 Nov 1974, Tennessee NWR, MIG 46:44
                     22 Nov 1975, Johnson City, MIG 47:48
Remarks: Found on mudflats, sandbars, and at the edges of ponds and lakes. More frequently found in the fall than the spring, and more often observed in the middle and east than in the west. First state record was 7 Nov 1948, Clinch River, Knox Co. (Howell and Meyerriecks 1948). There are currently more than sixty-five state records but only six records prior to 1970. High counts: thirty-six on 16 Apr 1982, Chickamauga L. (MIG 53:68) and twenty-seven on 9 May 1984, Dyer Co. (MIG 55:67).
Substantiation: Photograph: 1 ad., Cross Creeks NWR, Stewart Co., 9 July 1987 (JCR – TBRC).

FAMILY SCOLOPACIDAE: **Sandpipers,**
Phalaropes and Allies

Greater Yellowlegs, *Tringa melanoleuca*
Status: Regular.
Abundance: Uncommon migrant, very rare summer and winter visitor.
Spring: Early Mar to mid May.
Arrivals: 21 Feb 1983, HRA, MIG 54:46
                     23 Feb 1955, Buena Vista Marsh, BNA:22
                     28 Feb 1977, Dyersburg, MIG 48:45
Departures: 15 May 1932, Memp., MIG 3:14
                     19 May 1981, Kingston Steam Plant, MIG 52:98
                     27 May 1988, Cross Creeks NWR (JCR)

Greater Yellowlegs, continued

Summer: Known from two records: 4 June 1963, Roans Creek (Dubke 1963a) and 22 June 1985, Lawrence Co. (MIG 57:27). These observations probably represent late spring and early fall migrants, respectively.

Fall: Mid July to mid Nov.

    Arrivals: 3 July 1987, Kingston Steam Plant, MIG 58:145

                     4 July 1972, Old Hickory L., MIG 43:76

                     12 July 1987, Lake Co. (JCR)

    Departures: 7 Nov 1959, Penal Farm, MIG 31:10

                     30 Nov 1975, Buena Vista Marsh, MIG 47:46

                     25 Nov-1 Dec 1977, HRA, MIG 49:46

Winter: There are fewer than ten winter records, ranging in dates from 7 Dec 1982, HRA (MIG 54:46) and 17 Dec 1972, Hickory-Priest CBC (MIG 44:11) to 22 Dec 1984, Reelfoot L. CBC (MIG 56:7) and 3 Jan 1980, HRA (MIG 51:42).

Remarks: Found on mudflats and at the edges of lakes and ponds. High counts: three hundred on 20 Apr 1986, Lake Co. (Brainard Palmer-Ball, Jr.) and two hundred on 25 Apr 1955, Nash. (Weise 1958).

Substantiation: Specimen: 1, Memp., Shelby Co., 13 Sept 1942 (LSUMZ, 75754).

Lesser Yellowlegs, *Tringa flavipes*

Status: Regular.

Abundance: Fairly common migrant, very rare summer and winter visitor.

Spring: Mid Mar to mid May.

    Arrivals: 14 Feb 1987, Lake Co., MIG 58:53

                     8 Mar 1975, Cheatham L., BNA:22

                     9 Mar 1981, HRA, MIG 52:49

    Departures: 22 May 1988, Shelby Co. (CHB, VBR, MGW)

                     30 May 1988, Cross Creeks NWR (JCR)

                     31 May 1979, Savannah Bay, MIG 50:89

Summer: At least ten June records for the state, probably representing late spring migrants, early fall migrants, or non-breeding summering birds. Records range in dates from 2 June 1982, Kingston Steam Plant (MIG 53:89) to 26 June 1987, Cross Creeks NWR (JCR) and 24-30 June 1977, near Hopefield, Shelby Co. (MIG 48:102).

Fall: Early July to mid Nov.

    Arrivals: 1 July 1973, Sequatchie Valley, MIG 44:86

                     2 July 1972, Tennessee NWR, MIG 43:75

                     4 July 1986, Lake Co., MIG 57:103

    Departures: 14 Nov 1973, Savannah Bay, MIG 45:24

                     15 Nov 1986, Shelby Co., MIG 58:20

                     29 Nov 1972, Buena Vista Marsh, MIG 44:23

Lesser Yellowlegs, continued

Winter: Probably less than ten records, ranging in dates from 9 Dec 1984, Shelby Co. (MIG 56:48) and 21 Dec 1969, Knoxville CBC (MIG 41:8) to 23 Dec 1923, Nash. (Walker 1932) and 3 Jan 1987, Hickory-Priest CBC (MIG 58:3).

Remarks: Found on mudflats and at the edges of lakes and ponds. High counts: 600 on 6 Apr 1941, Mud L. (MIG 12:36) and 470 on 6 May 1985, Tennessee NWR (MIG 56:76).

Substantiation: Specimen: 1 male, Nash., Davidson Co., 7 May 1916, (LSUMZ, 75755).

Solitary Sandpiper, *Tringa solitaria*

Status: Regular.

Abundance: Uncommon migrant, very rare winter visitor.

Spring: Late Mar to mid May.

Arrivals:	1 Mar 1973, Woodbury, Cannon Co., MIG 44:23
	18 Mar 1934, Mud L., MIG 5:26
	20 Mar 1974, Carter Co., MIG 45:79
Departures:	18 May 1986, Shelby Co., MIG 57:74
	26 May 1968, Knoxville, MIG 39:66
	7 June 1978, Cannon Co., MIG 49:92

Fall: Early July to late Sept.

Arrivals:	28 June 1972, Ashland City Marsh, MIG 43:76
	1 July 1972, Reelfoot L., MIG 43:75
	3 July 1987, Carter Co., MIG 58:147
Departures:	3 Nov 1964, Bristol, MIG 35:104
	22 Nov 1986, Shelby Co., MIG 58:20
	27 Nov 1975, Buena Vista Marsh, MIG 47:46

Winter: Known from two records: 15 Dec 1956, Bush L. (BNA:23) and 3 Nov 1973 through 8 Jan 1974, Buena Vista Marsh (MIG 45:21).

Remarks: Found on mudflats, along creeks and along edges of lakes and ponds. Usually found singly or in small numbers, but may become locally common for brief periods during migration. High counts: 114 on 3 May 1986, Shelby Co. (MIG 57:74) and 82 on 26 Apr 1980, Elizabethton SBC (MIG 51:55).

Substantiation: Specimen: 1 female, Nash., Davidson Co., 28 Apr 1963 (LSUMZ, 75758).

Willet, *Catoptrophorus semipalmatus*

Status: Regular.

Abundance: Rare migrant, very rare summer visitor.

Spring: Late Apr to mid May.

Arrivals:	2 Apr 1972, Jefferson Co., MIG 43:53
	17 Apr 1983, Shelby Co., MIG 54:60
	18 Apr 1978, Old Hickory L., MIG 49:67

Willet, continued

Departures: 10 May 1987, Island 13, MIG 58:92

                13 May 1969, Clay Co., MIG 40:68

                17 May 1980, Kingston Steam Plant, MIG 51:94

Summer: Two June records exist, both of which may actually represent early fall migrants: 22 June 1985, Tennessee NWR (MIG 57:27) and 30 June 1986, Lawrence Co. (MIG 58:23).

Fall: Early Aug to mid Sept. There are about ten July records.

Arrivals: 3 July 1965, Amnicola Marsh, MIG 36:68

                9 July 1987, Cross Creeks NWR, MIG 59:36

                15 July 1983, Lake Co., MIG 54:86

Departures: 15 Sept 1984, Tennessee NWR, MIG 56:20

                19 Sept 1984, Island 13, MIG 56:17

                8 Nov 1986, Roans Creek, MIG 58:31

Remarks: Found on sandbars, mudflats and along edges of ponds and lakes. Formerly less numerous; becoming more regularly seen. First state record was of one bird shot in Cocke Co. in the summer of 1934 (Walker 1935). Usually found singly or in small numbers in the fall; occasionally recorded in larger numbers in the spring. High counts: 175 on 3 May 1979, Center Hill L. (MIG 50:69) and 77 on 6 May 1984, Ashland City Marsh (BNA:23).

Substantiation: Specimen: 1 male, Mud L. (state line), Shelby Co., 12 Aug 1939 (LSUMZ, 3394).

Spotted Sandpiper, *Actitis macularia*

Status: Regular. (Map A-24)

Abundance: Fairly common migrant, rare summer resident, very rare winter resident.

Spring: Mid Apr to late May.

Arrivals: 15 Mar 1976, Carter Co., MIG 47:50

                1 Apr 1988, Henry Co. (DWB)

                3 Apr 1971, Rickman, Overton Co., MIG 42:44

Summer: There are many summer records for the state, primarily for the middle and east, but it has also been found in the west. Representative sites include: Roans Creek, Austin Springs, Knox Co., Kingston Steam Plant, Stewart Co., Coffey Co., Humphreys Co., Maury Co., Gallatin Steam Plant, Benton Co., Hatchie NWR, Shelby Co., and Lake Co. A nest with four eggs was found near Johnson City on 10 June 1934 (Lyle and Tyler 1934), and another Washington Co. nest record was of two ad. and two young at Austin Springs on 29 June 1971 (MIG 42:71). One ad. and two young were found near Ashland City (Cheatham Co.) on 26 June 1954 (Weise 1955). Has nested successfully in Nash. at Buena Vista Marsh in 1977 (MIG 48:103), and at Metro Center from 1979 through 1984. At least one bird was fledged from a nest in Shelby Co. in 1988 (*fide* MGW).

Spotted Sandpiper, continued

Fall: An influx of fall migrants usually occurs by mid July. By late July and throughout Aug and Sept, many individuals are regularly found in suitable wetland habitat. Fewer sightings are made in Oct, but a few birds linger well into Nov.

Winter: There are about twenty winter sightings, with multiple records from Memp., Savannah, Chat., and the HRA. The records range in dates from 1 Dec 1985, Penal Farm (MIG 57:51) and 20 Dec 1980, Lebanon CBC (MIG 52:13) to 11 Jan 1987, HRA (MIG 58:59) and 18 Feb 1967, Hardin Co. (Patterson 1967). One bird was present at Chat. from 18 Dec 1982 through 28 Feb 1983 (MIG 54:45-46).

Remarks: Found on mudflats, along creeks and along edges of ponds and lakes; often frequents shorelines with exposed stones and pebbles. High count: 109 on 8 May 1976, Kingsport SBC (MIG 47:90).

Substantiation: Specimen: 1 male, Nash., Davidson Co., 7 May 1916, (LSUMZ, 75763).

Upland Sandpiper, *Bartramia longicauda*

Status: Regular.

Abundance: Uncommon migrant.

Spring: Late Mar to early May.

Arrivals:	10 Mar 1937, Murfreesboro, (Todd 1937)
	12 Mar 1950, Memp., MIG 21:13
	2 Apr 1972, Jefferson Co., MIG 43:53
Departures:	4 May 1976, Penal Farm, MIG 47:75
	8 May 1971, Kingsport SBC, MIG 42:37
	18 May 1960, Rutherford Co., (DeVore 1975)

Fall: Mid July to mid Sept. A handful of late June sightings exists, all of which probably represent early fall migrants.

Arrivals:	18 June 1972, Nash., MIG 43:76
	21 June 1953, Penal Farm, MIG 24:55
	2 Aug 1972, Tri-Cities Airport, MIG 43:101
Departures:	16 Oct 1950, Elizabethton, MIG 22:18
	22 Oct 1964, Buena Vista (Nash.), MIG 35:102
	13 Nov 1943, Memp., MIG 15:76

Remarks: Found in grassy pastures and fields; frequents airports. Less frequently reported in the east than the middle and west. Reported in Jan 1958 without adequate details (MIG 28:65). High count: one hundred on 28 June 1946, Rutherford Co. (Layne 1946).

Whimbrel, *Numenius phaeopus*

Status: Extremely Rare. (Map A-25)

Remarks: Found on mudflats and in marshes and flooded fields. First recorded in the state on 8 July 1934, Mud L. (Ganier and Coffey 1934); then not recorded again until 1971. An unusual record was of two birds at 1,520 m

Whimbrel, continued
   MSL on Big Bald Mt., Unicoi Co., on 30-31 Aug 1980 (Mayfield 1981). High
   count: eighteen on 27 May 1979, Kingston Steam Plant (Stedman 1980). All
   other records follow:
      24 May 1980, Kingston Steam Plant, (Stedman 1980)
      4 June 1977, Austin Springs, MIG 48:105
      24 July 1971, Ashland City Marsh, (Riggins and Riggins 1972)
      24 July 1971, Buena Vista Marsh, (Riggins and Riggins 1972)
      10-13 Aug 1985, Kingston Steam Plant, MIG 57:33
      11 Aug 1985, Shelby Co., MIG 57:22
      20 Sept 1971, Buena Vista Marsh, (Bierly 1972)
      26 Sept 1975, Gallatin Steam Plant, MIG 47:18
   Most sightings are of one or two birds.
Substantiation: Adequately documented sight records.

Long-billed Curlew, *Numenius americanus*
Status: Accidental (Provisional).
Remarks: One bird was seen at Island 13, Lake Co., on 1 Sept 1985 (MIG
   57:22). The call and the plumage of this bird were well described (Blunk
   1986).
Substantiation: Adequately documented sight record (TBRC).

Hudsonian Godwit, *Limosa haemastica*
Status: Extremely Rare.
Remarks: Found on exposed mudflats and wet grassy areas near water. First
   state record was of one bird which was found in Kentucky just north of
   Reelfoot L. on 8 May 1971; the bird was observed flying while it was still in
   Tennessee (Manning and Manning 1971). High counts: two birds on 13 May
   1978, Gallatin Steam Plant (MIG 49:67) and two birds on 8 May 1983,
   Reelfoot L. SBC (Brown 1985). There are only eight state records. Addi-
   tional records (all of single birds) follow:
      17 Apr 1982, Penal Farm, MIG 53:66
      13-14 May 1979, Kingston Steam Plant, MIG 50:70
      16 Aug 1982, Kingston Steam Plant, (Fowler 1983)
      5-7 Sept 1981, Bradley Co., (Haney 1981a)
      12 Nov 1983, HRA, MIG 55:24
Substantiation: Adequately documented sight records.

Marbled Godwit, *Limosa fedoa*
Status: Extremely Rare.
Remarks: Found on mudflats and lake edges; most sightings have occurred
   along major river systems. About fifteen state records, over half of which
   occurred in Aug. First recorded on 2-6 Sept 1970, Savannah Bay (MIG
   41:88). High counts: two birds on 26 Apr 1980, Nash. (MIG 57:82) and two

Marbled Godwit, continued
birds on 18 Apr 1988, Anderson Co. (Mike Smith, CPN). All other records were of single birds:

30 Apr-1 May 1982, Columbia SBC, MIG 53:54
16-17 July 1981, Kingston Steam Plant, MIG 52:98
2-4 Aug 1985, Cross Creeks NWR, MIG 57:27
3 Aug 1985, Island 13, MIG 57:22
10 Aug 1971, Buena Vista Marsh, (Bierly et al. 1973)
15-17 Aug 1987, Paris Landing S.P., MIG 59:32
17-24 Aug 1976, Sumner Co., MIG 48:19
24 Aug 1984, Kingston Steam Plant, MIG 56:25
26 Aug 1972, Pace Point, MIG 43:98
28 Aug 1977, Pace Point, MIG 51:38
10 Sept 1975, Norris L., MIG 47:21
6 Oct 1976, Douglas L., MIG 48:21

Substantiation: Photographs: 1, Green's L., Sumner Co., 17 Aug 1976 (JPC–TBRC).

Ruddy Turnstone, *Arenaria interpres*
Status: Regular.
Abundance: Rare migrant.
Spring: Early May to late May.

Arrivals:	18 Apr 1987, Old Hickory L., MIG 58:97
	24 Apr 1987, Washington Co., MIG 58:103
	7 May 1983, Lake Co., MIG 54:60
Departures:	22 May 1983, Lake Co., MIG 54:60
	24 May 1980, Kingston Steam Plant, MIG 51:94
	28 May 1979, Gallatin Steam Plant, MIG 50:87

Fall: Early Aug to mid Sept.

Arrivals:	28 July 1974, Pace Point, MIG 45:101
	29 July 1979, Gallatin Steam Plant, MIG 50:87
	1 Aug 1981, Cocke Co., MIG 53:19
Departures:	27 Sept 1975, Old Hickory L., MIG 49:68
	30 Sept 1980, Kingston Steam Plant, MIG 52:24
	13 Oct 1985, Shelby Co., MIG 57:22

Remarks: Found on sandbars and exposed mudflats. Formerly less numerous. First record was of one bird at Chickamauga L. dam on 24 Sept 1957 (West 1957); then recorded only three additional times prior to 1970. Currently there are more than eighty state records. Sightings are equally distributed across all three regions of the state. High count: twenty-one on 21 Sept 1985, Island 13 (MIG 57:22).

Substantiation: Specimen: 1, Tennessee NWR, Henry Co., 9 Sept 1973 (APSU, 2458).

Red Knot, *Calidris canutus*
Status: Irregular.
Abundance: Rare migrant.
Fall: Late Aug to mid Sept.
    Arrivals: 6 Aug 1955, Memp., MIG 26:47
                     16 Aug 1986, Douglas L., MIG 58:28
                     21 Aug 1981, Douglas L., MIG 53:19
    Departures: 15 Sept 1984, Island 13, MIG 56:17
                     5 Oct 1985, Kingston Steam Plant, MIG 57:33
                     10 Oct 1979, Gallatin Steam Plant, BNA:23
Remarks: Found on sandbars and exposed mudflats; appears to follow major river systems. About nineteen state records. First recorded on 11 Sept 1954, Memp. (Coffey 1955). Only recorded once in the spring: 28 May 1979, Gallatin Steam Plant (MIG 50:87). Most reports are from the east and west; only three middle Tennessee records. There are multiple records for Memp., Gallatin Steam Plant, Kingston Steam Plant, and Pace Point. High count: seven on 28 May 1979, Gallatin Steam Plant (MIG 50:87).
Substantiation: Specimen: 1 female, Nash., Davidson Co., 20 Sept 1960 (LSUMZ, 75770).

Sanderling, *Calidris alba*
Status: Regular.
Abundance: Rare spring migrant, uncommon fall migrant, very rare winter visitor.
Spring: Late Apr to mid May.
    Arrivals: 24 Apr 1971, Woodbury, Cannon Co., MIG 42:44
                     29 Apr 1961, Bristol, MIG 32:30
                     5 May 1983, Lake Co., MIG 54:60
    Departures: 28 May 1979, Gallatin Steam Plant, MIG 50:87
                     28 May 1979, Kingston Steam Plant, MIG 50:89
                     28 May 1987, Island 13, MIG 58:92
Fall: Early Aug to early Oct.
    Arrivals: 9 July 1985, Sumner Co., MIG 57:27
                     9 July 1988, Island 13 (JCR)
                     18 July 1981, Kingston Steam Plant, MIG 52:98
    Departures: 25 Oct 1986, HRA, MIG 58:28
                     6 Nov 1961, Bush L., MIG 33:13
                     11 Nov 1984, Island 13, MIG 56:17
Winter: Known from two records: 9 Dec 1984, Shelby Co. (MIG 56:48) and 1 Jan 1987, Hiwassee CBC (MIG 58:3).
Remarks: Found on sandbars, exposed mudflats and along edges of lakes and ponds. Appears to be most abundant along the Mississippi River during the fall migration. First state record was of one to two birds at Watauga L., Johnson Co., on 3-18 Sept 1955 (Herndon 1955). High count: forty-two on 22 Sept 1984, Island 13 (MIG 56:17).

Semipalmated Sandpiper, *Calidris pusilla*

Status: Regular.

Abundance: Fairly common migrant.

Spring: Late Apr to early June.

Arrivals: 5 Mar 1986, Savannah Bay, MIG 57:84

6 Apr 1972, Buena Vista Marsh, MIG 43:50

15 Apr 1934, Mud L., MIG 5:26

Departures: 10 June 1972, Amnicola Marsh, MIG 43:79

12 June 1954, Mud L., MIG 25:52

22 June 1985, Tennessee NWR, MIG 57:27

Summer: One to two birds stayed at Buena Vista from about 11 June 1972 through 31 July 1972 (MIG 43:76 and BNA:24).

Fall: Mid July to early Oct.

Arrivals: 5 July 1988, Cross Creeks NWR (JCR)

6 July 1981, Kingston Steam Plant, MIG 52:98

9 July 1988, Island 13 (JCR)

Departures: 7 Nov 1959, Memp., MIG 31:10

9 Nov 1970, Gallatin Steam Plant, MIG 42:19

28 Nov 1968, Cherokee L., MIG 40:22

Remarks: Found on exposed mudflats and along edges of lakes and ponds. There are at least five winter records. However, all birds found after Oct should be closely examined to separate this species from the similar Western Sandpiper. Most birds of both species have acquired their basic plumage by the end of Oct and are resultantly very difficult to separate from one another. A good discussion of the plumage differences between these two species is presented by Veit and Jonsson (1987). High count: two thousand on 22 May 1983, Lake Co. (MIG 54:60).

Substantiation: Specimen: 1 female, Buena Vista Marsh, Davidson Co., 23 May 1934 (LSUMZ, 75772).

Western Sandpiper, *Calidris mauri*

Status: Regular.

Abundance: Rare spring migrant, uncommon fall migrant, very rare winter visitor.

Spring: Early May to late May.

Arrivals: 3 Apr 1972, Buena Vista Marsh, MIG 43:50-51

17 Apr 1988, Shelby Co. (CHB, VBR, MGW)

28 Apr 1979, St. John's Pond, Carter Co., MIG 50:70

Departures: 22 May 1983, Lake Co., MIG 54:60

28 May 1979, Kingston Steam Plant, MIG 50:89

4 June 1972, Gallatin Steam Plant, MIG 43:76

Fall: Mid July to mid Oct.

Arrivals: 29 June 1986, Shelby Co., MIG 57:103

4 July 1985, Gallatin Steam Plant, MIG 57:27

11 July 1948, Carter Co., (Herndon 1950)

Western Sandpiper, continued

Departures: 15 Nov 1986, Shelby Co., MIG 58:20

23 Nov 1968, Cherokee L., MIG 40:22

25 Nov 1973, Buena Vista Marsh, MIG 45:21

Winter: Known only from two records: 12 Jan 1981, Dyer Co. (MIG 52:45) and 1, 30 Jan 1983, Shelby Co. (MIG 54:40). All birds in the winter should be identified with care (see Remarks under Semipalmated Sandpiper).

Remarks: Found on exposed mudflats and along edges of lakes and ponds; difficult to detect outside of traditional high-use shorebird areas. First state record was of four birds at North L., Shelby Co., on 7 Aug 1935 (M'Camey 1935). High counts: one hundred on 5 Sept 1937, Mud L. (MIG 8:58) and fifty on 6 Sept 1984, Island 13 (MIG 56:17).

Substantiation: Specimen: 1 female, Memp., Shelby Co., 11 Aug 1935 (LSUMZ, 75777).

Least Sandpiper, *Calidris minutilla*

Status: Regular.

Abundance: Common migrant, rare winter resident.

Spring: Most migrants are observed from mid Apr to late May.

Arrivals: 2 Mar 1957, Nash., MIG 28:8

11 Mar 1950, Penal Farm, MIG 21:13

13 Mar 1987, Savannah Bay, MIG 58:103

Departures: 2 June 1979, Kingston Steam Plant, MIG 50:89

4 June 1986, Memp. (C. Kinian Cosner)

18 June 1968, Columbia, MIG 39:64

Fall: Most migrants are found from early July to mid Oct; determination of departure dates is not possible due to presence of lingering birds.

Arrivals: 26 June 1977, Amnicola Marsh, MIG 48:105

26 June 1971, Tennessee NWR, MIG 42:68

29 June 1988, Cross Creeks NWR (JCR)

Winter: A wintering population has become established at Savannah Bay and, in recent years, in Memp. As many as 61 birds were at the Savannah Bay area on 27 Jan 1976 (MIG 47:48); and 346 birds were discovered at the Ensley sewage lagoons in Memp. on 1 Jan 1983 (MIG 54:40). Most winter records are from these two areas, but sightings have also occurred at Nash., Cumberland City Steam Plant (Stewart Co.) and Britton Ford (Henry Co.). Observed more frequently in Dec and Jan than in Feb; there are many CBC records.

Remarks: Found on exposed mudflats and along edges of lakes and ponds. One of the first shorebirds to arrive in the fall. High count: 2,600 on 25 Oct 1986, Ensley sewage lagoons, Shelby Co. (MIG 58:20).

Substantiation: Specimen: 1 male, Nash., Davidson Co., 14 May 1960 (LSUMZ, 75780).

White-rumped Sandpiper, *Calidris fuscicollis*
Status: Regular.
Abundance: Uncommon spring migrant, rare fall migrant.
Spring: Early May to early June.
    Arrivals: 27 Apr 1984, Sumner Co., MIG 55:69
                    27 Apr 1986, Memp., MIG 57:66
                    28 Apr 1979, Austin Springs, MIG 50:70
    Departures: 9 June 1985, Shelby Co., MIG 56:107
                    19 June 1969, Austin Springs, MIG 40:70
                    23 June 1972, Gallatin Steam Plant, MIG 43:76
Fall: Mid Aug to mid Sept.
    Arrivals: 3 July 1975, Gallatin Steam Plant, MIG 46:88
                    17 July 1980, Kingston Steam Plant, MIG 51:94
                    20 July 1986, Shelby Co., MIG 57:103
    Departures: 1 Oct 1951, Radnor L., MIG 23:10
                    25 Oct 1970, HRA, MIG 41:88
                    1 Nov 1986, Shelby Co., MIG 58:20
Remarks: Found on exposed mudflats and along edges of ponds and lakes. Most observations are of spring migrants; fall sightings are rare. High counts: 132 on 7 June 1982, Kingston Steam Plant (MIG 53:89) and 60 on 23 May 1985, Sumner Co. (MIG 56:76).

Baird's Sandpiper, *Calidris bairdii*
Status: Regular.
Abundance: Rare spring migrant, uncommon fall migrant.
Spring: Late Apr to mid May.
    Arrivals: 6 Apr 1985, Tennessee NWR, MIG 56:76
                    8 Apr 1971, Carter Co., MIG 42:48
                    21 Apr 1988, Shelby Co. (JRW)
    Departures: 6 June 1971, Tennessee NWR, MIG 42:68
                    8 June 1971, Amnicola Marsh, MIG 42:71
                    11 June 1980, Sumner Co., BNA:24
Fall: Late Aug to late Sept.
    Arrivals: 13 July 1981, Kingston Steam Plant, MIG 52:98
                    15 July 1985, Lawrence Co., MIG 57:27
                    29 July 1985, Island 13, MIG 57:23
    Departures: 3 Nov 1985, Gallatin Steam Plant, MIG 57:27
                    15 Nov 1986, Shelby Co., MIG 58:20
                    29 Nov 1972, Austin Springs, MIG 44:26
Remarks: Found on sandbars, exposed mudflats and along edges of lakes and ponds; often seen in the drier, grassier areas of mudflats. More frequently found in the fall than in the spring. Formerly less numerous; first state record was of one to two birds on 27 Aug-9 Sept 1936 at Caryville (Cove) L., Campbell Co. (Foster 1936); then recorded only three additional times prior to 1970. High count: twelve on 12 Oct 1985, Island 13 (MIG 57:23).

Pectoral Sandpiper, *Calidris melanotos*
Status: Regular.
Abundance: Common migrant, very rare winter visitor.
Spring: Early Mar to mid May.
    Arrivals: 2 Feb 1957, Union City airfield, MIG 28:7
                    11 Feb 1968, Knoxville, MIG 39:45
                    19 Feb 1975, Tennessee NWR, MIG 46:44
    Departures: 17 May 1976, HRA, MIG 47:101
                    31 May 1987, Maury Co., MIG 59:99
                    2 June 1988, Shelby Co. (MGW)
Fall: Mid July to late Oct.
    Arrivals: 20 June 1986, Kingston Steam Plant, MIG 57:113
                    22 June 1985, Tennessee NWR, MIG 57:27
                    4 July 1985, Shelby Co., MIG 56:107
    Departures: 21 Nov 1986, Britton Ford, Henry Co., MIG 58:20
                    26 Nov 1986, Stewart Co., MIG 58:24
                    30 Nov 1971, HRA, MIG 43:27
Winter: There are very few winter records. Sightings include one bird on the
    Memp. CBC on 16 Dec 1979 (MIG 51:32); 1 Jan 1976, HRA (MIG 47:48)
    and 28 Jan 1987, Stewart Co. (MIG 58:56).
Remarks: Found on exposed mudflats, in plowed agricultural fields and along
    edges of lakes and ponds. Frequently occurs in large numbers. High counts:
    1,100 on 5 Apr 1987, Shelby Co. (MIG 58:92) and 490 on 16 Aug 1986,
    Douglas L., Jefferson Co. (MIG 58:28).
Substantiation: Specimen: 1 male, Nash., Davidson Co., 5 Apr 1916 (LSUMZ,
    75786).

Purple Sandpiper, *Calidris maritima*
Status: Accidental.
Remarks: Four records, all of single birds: 25 Nov 1962, Hiwassee Island
    (Alsop 1972); 8 June 1967, Bays Mt. Lake, Sullivan Co. (Alsop 1972); 6 June
    1975, Gallatin Steam Plant (Crawford and Crawford 1975); and 29-30 Nov
    1976, Shelby Co. on the TN/ARK state line (Holt 1979).
Substantiation: Adequately documented sight records.

Dunlin, *Calidris alpina*
Status: Regular.
Abundance: Uncommon migrant, rare winter resident.
Spring: Early May to late May.
    Arrivals: 7 Apr 1973, Reelfoot L., MIG 44:50
                    11 Apr 1987, Sumner Co., MIG 58:97
                    16 Apr 1972, HRA, MIG 43:53
    Departures: 22 May 1967, Pickwick L., MIG 38:47
                    1 June 1986, Kingston Steam Plant, MIG 57:113
                    12 June 1971, Gallatin Steam Plant, MIG 42:69

Dunlin, continued
Fall: Early Oct to late Nov. There are several Aug and Sept records.
Arrivals: 1 Aug 1976, Sumner Co., MIG 55:22
                  10 Aug 1978, Kingston Steam Plant, MIG 50:22
                  23 Aug 1936, Mud L., (Coffey 1939)
Departures: 18 Dec 1976, Ashland City CBC, MIG 48:32
                  19 Dec 1982, Memp. CBC, MIG 54:13
                  19 Dec 1967, Hiwassee CBC, MIG 38:88
Winter: Has wintered regularly in most years at the HRA since about 1968.
Birds are usually present at this site from late Dec throughout Mar. Very infrequently encountered in other areas of the state during the winter. Additional sightings include: 14 Jan 1956, Nash. (MIG 27:17); 4 Feb 1961, Old Hickory L. (MIG 32:5); 12 Feb 1966, Boone L. (MIG 37:10); and 30 Jan 1983, Shelby Co. (MIG 54:40).
Remarks: Found on exposed mudflats and along edges of lakes and ponds.
First state records were of single birds on 4 Oct 1936, Lake Andrew Jackson, Knoxville (Henry 1937) and on 23 Aug 1936, Mud L. (Coffey 1939). Much less numerous in the spring when it is not easily detected. Considerably large flocks have been consistently reported only from Douglas L. (Jefferson Co.) and the HRA. High counts: 390 on 27 Nov 1982, Douglas L. (MIG 54:25); 260 on 30 Nov 1980, Douglas L. (MIG 52:49); and 200 on 16 Nov 1973, HRA (MIG 45:24).
Substantiation: Specimen: 1, Savannah Bay, Hamilton Co., 14 Jan 1975 (Milligan College, 65).

Stilt Sandpiper, *Calidris himantopus*
Status: Regular.
Abundance: Rare spring migrant, uncommon fall migrant.
Spring: Early May to late May.
Arrivals: 10 Mar 1985, Shelby Co., MIG 56:74
                  3 Apr 1977, Savannah Bay, MIG 48:77-78
                  14 Apr 1987, Cross Creeks NWR, MIG 58:97
Departures: 20 May 1971, Old Hickory L., MIG 42:69
                  24 May 1971, Reelfoot L., MIG 42:68
                  2 June 1982, Kingston Steam Plant, MIG 53:89
Fall: Late July to early Oct.
Arrivals: 1 July 1980, Gallatin Steam Plant, BNA:24
                  3 July 1987, Kingston Steam Plant, MIG 58:145
                  4 July 1987, Shelby Co., MIG 58:137
Departures: 9 Oct 1972, HRA, MIG 43:102
                  2 Nov 1981, Gallatin Steam Plant, MIG 58:25
                  15 Nov 1986, Shelby Co., MIG 58:20
Remarks: Found on exposed mudflats and along edges of lakes and ponds. Apparently the first state record was on 9 Sept 1934, North L., Shelby Co. (M'Camey 1935). Very infrequently observed in the spring; most sightings

Stilt Sandpiper, continued

occur in the fall. Less detectable in the east than in the middle and west. High counts: forty-eight on 15 Sept 1988, Heloise, Dyer Co. (William G. Criswell) and thirty-three on 25 Aug 1984, Tennessee NWR (MIG 56:20).
Substantiation: Specimen: 1, Mud L., Shelby Co., 3 Sept 1939 (LSUMZ, 75794).

Buff-breasted Sandpiper, *Tryngites subruficollis*
Status: Regular.
Abundance: Rare fall migrant.
Spring: Known only from one record: 26 Apr 1981, Memp. SBC (MIG 52:64).
Fall: Late Aug to mid Sept.
    Arrivals: 1 Aug 1976, Britton Ford, Henry Co., MIG 48:17
                   2 Aug 1986, Cross Creeks NWR, MIG 58:24
                   23 Aug 1975, HRA, MIG 47:21
    Departures: 10 Oct 1973, Gallatin Steam Plant, MIG 44:100
                   17 Oct 1987, Shelby Co., MIG 59:32
                   22 Oct 1980, Kingston Steam Plant, MIG 52:25
Remarks: Found on dry sandbars and exposed mudflats, primarily where short vegetation has begun to grow. First state record was of two birds on 19 Sept 1943, Lauderdale Co. (Monroe 1944); then not recorded again until 1952. Spring sightings are few because the species' spring migration corridor is through the central United States west of the Mississippi River. High count: twenty-four on 8 Sept 1984, Tennessee NWR (MIG 56:20).

Ruff, *Philomachus pugnax*
Status: Accidental (Provisional).
Remarks: Three records, all of single birds: 6-9 Apr 1972, Sequatchie Valley, well described (Shafer 1972); and 7 Sept 1987 and 24 Apr 1988, Ensley sewage lagoons, Shelby Co. (JRW, DAD).
Substantiation: Adequately documented sight records.

Short-billed Dowitcher, *Limnodromus griseus*
Status: Regular.
Abundance: Uncommon migrant.
Spring: Late Apr to mid May.
    Arrivals: 13 Apr 1986, Shelby Co., MIG 57:74
                   18 Apr 1978, HRA, MIG 49:69
                   25 Apr 1973, Lebanon SBC, MIG 44:45
    Departures: 16 May 1986, Cross Creeks NWR, MIG 57:79
                   18 May 1986, Shelby Co., MIG 57:74
                   21 May 1983, Kingston Steam Plant, MIG 54:65
Fall: Mid July to late Sept.
    Arrivals: 4 July 1986, Lake Co., MIG 57:103
                   5 July 1987, Cross Creeks NWR (JCR)
                   21 July 1984, Kingston Steam Plant, MIG 55:94

Short-billed Dowitcher, continued
Departures: 20 Sept 1983, Anderson Co., MIG 55:25
25 Oct 1980, Shelby Co., MIG 52:22
27 Oct 1985, Gallatin Steam Plant, MIG 57:27
Remarks: Found on exposed mudflats and along edges of lakes and ponds. Seen more frequently in the fall than in the spring. High count: sixty-two on 12 May 1984, Chat. (MIG 55:73). Most observations in the state have occurred since the late 1950s, after the American Ornithologists' Union separated the "Eastern" and "Long-billed" races into two distinct dowitcher species. These species are extremely difficult to tell apart and, unless call notes are learned and used, a certain percentage of dowitchers should go unidentified. *L. g. hendersoni* is the race of Short-billed to be expected throughout most of Tennessee. Wilds and Newlon (1983) presented a definitive synopsis of field marks which can aid in identification of dowitchers. The expected dowitcher in Oct is Long-billed.
Substantiation: Specimen: 1 female, Mud L., Shelby Co., 24 Aug 1941 (LSUMZ, 75753).

Long-billed Dowitcher, *Limnodromus scolopaceus*
Status: Irregular.
Abundance: Rare migrant.
Spring: Late Apr to mid May.
Arrivals: 19 Apr 1975, Sequatchie Valley, MIG 46:68
28 Apr 1984, Chat. SBC, MIG 55:59
Departures: 13 May 1979, Nash., MIG 50:57
14 May 1967, Knox Co., (Alsop and Wallace 1970)
Fall: Late July to mid Oct.
Arrivals: 10 July 1977, Sumner Co., MIG 48:103
28 July 1986, Lake Co., MIG 58:20
31 July 1972, HRA, MIG 43:79
Departures: 8 Oct 1987, Cross Creeks NWR, MIG 59:36
17 Oct 1971, Paris Landing S.P., MIG 42:91
25 Oct 1976, Savannah Bay, MIG 48:21
Remarks: Found on exposed mudflats and along edges of lakes and ponds. Seen more often in the fall than in the spring. Most observations have occurred since the mid 1960s. It is rarely reported due in part to the difficulty in separating the two species of dowitchers apart in the field (see Remarks under Short-billed Dowitcher above). The dowitcher expected in Oct is this species.

Common Snipe, *Gallinago gallinago*

Status: Regular.

Abundance: Fairly common migrant and winter resident, very rare summer visitor.

Fall: Arrives by mid Aug. There are several July records.

Arrivals: 10 July 1975, Amnicola Marsh, MIG 46:90
10 July 1977, Sumner Co., MIG 48:103
13 Aug 1980, Memp., MIG 52:22

Winter: Recorded regularly throughout the winter across the state wherever suitable habitat occurs. Frequently found on exposed mudflats of the Tennessee and Cumberland River reservoirs during the low winter pool stage.

Spring: Departs by early May.

Departures: 22 May 1967, Amnicola Marsh, MIG 38:50
23 May 1961, Buena Vista Marsh, BNA:25
26 May 1979, Dyer Co., MIG 50:86

Summer: There are about five June records, all of single birds:

13 June 1964, Elizabethton, MIG 35:106
8 June 1971, Alcoa Marsh, Blount Co., MIG 43:78
4 June 1978, HRA, MIG 49:94
12-27 June 1979, Nash., MIG 50:87
14 June 1980, Nash., MIG 57:82

Remarks: Found on exposed mudflats, in shallow marshes, and along creeks and edges of lakes and ponds. Usually allows close approach before flushing because it relies on its cryptic coloration for concealment. Occasionally large numbers concentrate in a local area (e.g., 84 on 8 Mar 1987, Lawrence Co., MIG 58:97). Consistently recorded in large flocks in the HRA since about 1967. High count: 340 on 1 Jan 1986, Hiwassee CBC (MIG 57:10).

Substantiation: Specimen: 1 female, Nash., Davidson Co., 6 Apr 1967 (LSUMZ, 75751).

American Woodcock, *Scolopax minor*

Status: Regular. (Map A-26)

Abundance: Uncommon migrant and summer resident, rare winter resident.

Remarks: Found in lowland wooded areas, along streams and in brushy fields; uses wooded areas for daytime roosts and forages and displays in and over open fields at night. Often allows close approach before flushing because it relies on its cryptic coloration to conceal it in surrounding vegetation.

Migration in the spring is easily detectable, beginning about early to mid Feb, when singing males can be heard on warmer nights shortly after dusk. Encountered less frequently during the summer. However, breeding records are scattered across the state from Johnson and Cocke Counties in the east to Weakley and Shelby Counties in the west. Nesting in Tennessee occurs between early Mar and Apr and broods have been observed in Mar, Apr and May (Pitts 1978). Courtship flights have been reported for each month from Oct through May, with peak activity occurring in Feb (Pitts 1978). Fall

American Woodcock, continued

migration is unremarkable. Presence in winter is difficult to detect; many birds are probably overlooked. Most notable winter records are sixteen birds on 17 Dec 1967, Hardin Co. (MIG 39:19) and twenty-three birds on 30 Dec 1984, Duck River Res. CBC, near Columbia (MIG 56:7). Has been found in the east at high elevations, including 1,570 m in the GSMNP on 12 June 1935 (Fleetwood 1937) and at 1,675 m on Roan Mt. on 19 June 1983 (MIG 54:91). High count: see Duck River Res. CBC record above.

Substantiation: Specimen: 1, Memp., Shelby Co., 6 Mar 1982 (UTMB, 409).

Wilson's Phalarope, *Phalaropus tricolor*
Status: Regular.
Abundance: Rare migrant.
Spring: Early May to mid May.

Arrivals:	16 Apr 1983, Shelby Co., MIG 54:60
	27 Apr 1985, Tennessee NWR, MIG 56:76
	3 May 1963, Chat., MIG 34:31
Departures:	13 May 1978, Roans Creek, MIG 49:71
	28 May 1988, Shelby Co. (JRW)
	30 May 1985, Sumner Co., MIG 56:76

Fall: Mid Aug to mid Sept.

Arrivals:	11 July 1975, Gallatin Steam Plant, MIG 46:88
	25 July 1987, Shelby Co., MIG 58:137
	30 July 1977, HRA, MIG 48:105
Departures:	26 Sept 1970, Ashland City Marsh, MIG 41:85
	9 Oct 1938, Mud L., (Coffey 1939)
	9 Nov 1980, Douglas L., MIG 52:49

Remarks: Found in shallow pools of water and along edges of lakes and ponds. More frequently observed in the fall than in the spring. A very active shorebird; often resembles a wind-up toy thrown in the water. Most sightings are of one to three birds. An invasion occurred in the spring of 1978 with large numbers reported all across the state. High counts: 65 on 6 May 1978, Shelby Co. (MIG 49:66); 21 on 8 May 1978, Shelby Co. (MIG 49:66); 23 on 6-7 May 1978, Nash. SBC (MIG 49:56); and 13 on 4 May 1978, HRA and Chat. (MIG 49:69).

Substantiation: Specimen: 1 male, Mud L. (state line), Shelby Co., 30 Aug 1939 (LSUMZ, 3373).

Red-necked Phalarope, *Phalaropus lobatus*
Status: Irregular.
Abundance: Rare migrant.

Red-necked Phalarope, continued

Spring: Mid May to late May. Five records:

    16-17 May 1975, Austin Springs, MIG 46:90
    17, 21 May 1980, Kingston Steam Plant, MIG 51:94
    18 May 1976, Sumner Co., (Crawford and Crawford 1976)
    18 May 1969, Austin Springs, (Coffey 1970a)
    22-26 May 1979, Kingston Steam Plant, MIG 50:89

Fall: Late Aug to late Sept.

    Arrivals: 20 Aug 1969, Cades Cove, GSMNP, (Alsop 1970)
                    23 Aug 1987, Island 13, MIG 59:32
                    27 Aug 1976, Cross Creeks NWR, MIG 48:19
    Departures: 4 Oct 1984, Island 13, MIG 56:17
                    21 Oct 1959, Bush L., (Ogden 1959)
                    1 Nov 1981, Cocke Co., MIG 53:20

Remarks: Found on shallow pools of water and along edges of lakes and ponds. First recorded in the state on 21 Oct 1959, Bush L. (Ogden 1959). Around thirty total records for the state, about two-thirds of which are from the east. Most sightings occur in the fall and involve only one or two birds. High count: eight on 17 May 1980, Kingston Steam Plant (MIG 51:94).

Substantiation: Photograph: 1, Knoxville, Knox Co., 21 Sept 1982 (CPN, MIG 55:84).

Red Phalarope, *Phalaropus fulicaria*

Status: Extremely Rare.

Remarks: Found on ponds or lakes, often in deeper water than other phalaropes. About thirteen state records, the first two of which involved birds found dead on 17 Dec 1944, GSMNP CBC (MIG 15:70) and on 29 Nov 1959, near Maryville, Blount Co. (Monroe 1959). Usually occurs later in the fall than the other two phalaropes. There is only one west Tennessee record: 25 Oct 1987, Paris Landing S.P. (MIG 59:32). All sightings are of one to two birds:

    20-21 Sept 1970, Cove L., Campbell Co., MIG 41:88
    24-29 Sept 1964, Bush L., BNA:25
    26 Sept 1970, Percy Priest L., MIG 41:85
    6 Oct 1984, Radnor L., MIG 56:21
    26 Oct 1986, Old Hickory L., MIG 58:24
    1 Nov 1985, Fall Creek Falls S.P., MIG 57:33
    8 Nov 1972, Buena Vista Marsh, MIG 44:23
    4 Dec 1965, Woods Res., (McCrary and Wood 1966)
    12-13 Dec 1967, Savannah Bay, (Dubke 1968a)

Also recorded on 28 Apr 1963, Greeneville SBC (MIG 34:31) with details (Clemens 1963) that are unconvincing and inconsistent with the plumage of this species.

Substantiation: Adequately documented sight records.

FAMILY LARIDAE: Gulls, Terns and Skimmers

Pomarine Jaeger, *Stercorarius pomarinus*
Status: Accidental.
Remarks: At least one record. A bird found at Paris Landing S.P., Henry Co., on 28 June 1987 (MIG 58:137) is presumably the same individual present at this site from 15 Aug to 4 Sept 1987 (MIG 59:32). The latter sighting was of a subadult bird found foraging over the large expanse of water on Kentucky L. east and south of the park; this bird was accompanied by a Parasitic Jaeger during the last six days of the observation period.
Substantiation: Photograph: 1 subad., Paris Landing S.P., Henry Co., 15 Aug 1987 (JPC—TBRC).

Parasitic Jaeger, *Stercorarius parasiticus*
Status: Accidental.
Remarks: Found on large bodies of water. Three records: 16 Sept to 27 Oct 1978, Woods Res. (MIG 50:21); 6-22 Oct 1985, Pace Point (Stedman and Robinson 1986); and 29 Aug-5 Sept 1987, Paris Landing S.P., Henry Co. (JCR, DWB). The latter sighting was of interest in that the bird accompanied a Pomarine Jaeger during the six-day period from 29 Aug through 4 Sept 1987. The 1978 bird was initially identified only to genus, but upon submission of additional evidence, complete identification was possible (Stedman and Robinson 1987a).
Substantiation: Photographs: 1, Kentucky L., near Pace Point, Henry Co., Oct 1985 (Wallace Todd—TBRC).

Long-tailed Jaeger, *Stercorarius longicaudas*
Status: Accidental.
Remarks: Known from one record: an ad. bird in breeding plumage on 2-4 Sept 1984, Island 13, Lake Co. (Stedman 1985).
Substantiation: Photographs: 1 ad., Island 13, Lake Co., 2-3 Sept 1984 (SJS, JPC—TBRC).

Laughing Gull, *Larus atricilla*
Status: Irregular.
Abundance: Rare migrant.
Remarks: Found on or near large lakes and rivers. Has been observed in Tennessee in every month of the year except Jan. Most records involve one to three birds. Sightings are concentrated around early to mid May and from mid Aug through mid Sept. At least fifty records for Tennessee, over half of these from the eastern region of the state. First recorded in 1915 when one bird was taken on the French Broad River near Del Rio, Cocke Co., on an unknown date (Walker 1935). The number of records has increased dramatically in the 1980s. Several extreme dates are listed below:
  6 Feb 1983, Chickamauga L., MIG 54:46
  18 Feb 1973, Nickajack L., MIG 44:26
  3 June 1972, Tennessee NWR, MIG 43:75
  9 June 1979, Gallatin Steam Plant, MIG 50:87
  4 July 1972, Old Hickory L., MIG 43:76
  10 Nov 1983, Percy Priest L., MIG 55:21
  18 Nov 1985, Pace Point, MIG 57:23
  9 Dec 1971, Chickamauga L., MIG 43:27
High count: fifteen on 15 Dec 1971, Chickamauga L. (MIG 43:27).
Substantiation: Adequately documented sight records.

Franklin's Gull, *Larus pipixcan*
Status: Irregular.
Abundance: Rare migrant, very rare summer visitor.
Spring: Early Apr to early May.
  Arrivals: 5 Mar 1988, Shelby Co. (JRW)
                 13 Mar 1988, Dover, Stewart Co. (JCR)
                 5 Apr 1987, Chickamauga L., MIG 58:103
  Departures: 29 Apr 1988, Kingston Steam Plant (RLK)
                 7 May 1950, Shelby Co., MIG 21:26
                 30 May 1983, Gallatin Steam Plant, MIG 54:62
Summer: One record: 2 July 1972, Tennessee NWR (MIG 43:75).
Fall: Early Oct to mid Nov.
  Arrivals: 15 Sept 1963, Mud Island, MIG 34:50
                 3 Oct 1987, Tennessee NWR, MIG 59:36
                 5 Oct 1985, Britton Ford, Henry Co. (MIG 57:23)
  Departures: 3 Dec 1947, Memp., (Coffey 1947)
                 12 Dec 1985, Ft. Loudoun L., Blount Co., MIG 57:60
                 20 Dec 1960, Bush L., (Parmer 1962a)

Franklin's Gull, continued

Remarks: Found along lakes and rivers. More than thirty state records. First recorded in Tennessee at Memp. on 19 Nov 1947 (Coffey 1947). Observed more often in the west and middle than in the east. Has been found in the east only five times, at Nickajack L., Chickamauga L., Fort Loudoun L., Kingston Steam Plant, and the HRA. High count: eighteen on 17 Nov 1973, Woods Res. (MIG 45:21).

Substantiation: Adequately documented sight records.

Common Black-headed Gull, *Larus ridibundus*

Status: Accidental.

Remarks: Known from two records: an ad. bird in winter plumage was at Hamilton Creek, Percy Priest L., in Davidson Co., on 13-22 Mar 1987 (MIG 58:97); and a well-described molting ad. was found at the Kingston Steam Plant, Roane Co., on 1 May 1988 (MIG 59:101).

Substantiation: Photographs: 1 ad., Hamilton Creek, Percy Priest L., Davidson Co., 17 Mar 1987 (JPC–TBRC).

Bonaparte's Gull, *Larus philadelphia*

Status: Regular.

Abundance: Fairly common migrant, uncommon winter resident.

Fall: Arrives by late Oct. There are two Aug records: 20 Aug 1978 (MIG 50:19), and 30 Aug 1986 (MIG 58:20), both at Pace Point.

Arrivals: 23 Sept 1983, Austin Springs, MIG 55:25
              5 Oct 1985, Pace Point (JCR)
              17 Oct 1975, Old Hickory L., MIG 47:19

Winter: Becomes less detectable in the winter but may be locally common, especially along the Tennessee and Cumberland Rivers (e.g., 350 on 19 Feb 1965, Old Hickory L., MIG 36:8; and 233 on 14 Dec 1976, Chickamauga L., MIG 48:50). Observed only in small numbers in upper east Tennessee.

Spring: An influx of migrants occurs from mid to late Mar through early Apr. Most birds depart by early May.

Departures: 14 May 1978, Gallatin Steam Plant, BNA:26
              16 May 1937, Norris L., (Foster 1937a)
              30 May 1983, Shelby Co., MIG 54:60

Remarks: Found on lakes and rivers. There are no summer records. High count: one thousand on 20 Mar 1988, Shelby Co. (CHB, DPB, MGW).

Substantiation: Specimen: 1 male, Old Hickory L., Davidson Co., 27 Dec 1975 (APSU, 3374).

Ring-billed Gull, *Larus delawarensis*

Status: Regular.

Abundance: Common migrant and winter resident, rare summer resident.

Fall: Arrives by late Sept.

Arrivals: 10 Aug 1986, Island 13, MIG 58:20

                  22 Aug 1983, Chickamauga L., MIG 55:25

                  7 Sept 1988, Tennessee NWR (JCR)

Winter: Widely distributed throughout the state. Most detectable along the major river systems and associated lakes and reservoirs. Smallest concentrations are usually found in the northeastern region of the state.

Spring: Departs by early May.

Departures: 15 May 1939, Memp., (Coffey 1939a)

                  23 May 1985, Old Hickory L., MIG 56:76

                  28 May 1978, Watauga L., MIG 49:95

Summer: Small numbers of non-breeding birds are occasionally found during June and July. There are at least twenty-five summer records, primarily from Old Hickory L., Watauga L. and Cherokee L. Has also been observed at the following locations:

      18 June 1960, Pickwick L. dam, MIG 31:44

      26 June-18 July 1971, Tennessee NWR, MIG 42:68

      3 June 1972, Knoxville, MIG 43:79

      2 July 1982, Kingston Steam Plant, MIG 53:89

      1-4 July 1985, Shelby Co., MIG 56:107

      12 July 1987, Island 13, MIG 58:137

Remarks: Found on lakes and rivers; occasionally rests on islands or bare ground near water. High count: 3,800 on 31 Dec 1983, Hickory Priest CBC (MIG 55:9).

Substantiation: Specimen: 1, Kentucky L., Benton Co., winter 1977-78 (UTMB, 301).

Herring Gull, *Larus argentatus*

Status: Regular.

Abundance: Uncommon migrant and winter resident, very rare summer visitor.

Fall: Arrives by early Oct.

Arrivals: 23 Aug 1986, Stewart Co., MIG 58:24

                  6 Sept 1980, Pace Point, MIG 52:22

                  15 Sept 1986, Austin Springs, MIG 58:28

Winter: Occurs statewide in small to moderate numbers, with the fewest birds being found in upper east Tennessee. Seems to be more readily found in midwinter when the surface water on lakes begins to ice over.

Spring: Departs by early May.

Departures: 8 May 1971, Kingsport SBC, MIG 42:37

                  11 May 1958, Reelfoot L. SBC, MIG 29:31

                  31 May 1975, Old Hickory L., MIG 46:88

Herring Gull, continued

Summer: At least six records, all of single birds:

    30 July 1958, Old Hickory L., BNA:26

    4 July 1961, Old Hickory L., MIG 32:43

    4 June 1972, Gallatin Steam Plant, MIG 43:76

    6 June 1977, Dyer Co., MIG 48:102

    4 June 1986, Lawrence Co., MIG 57:108

    7 June 1986, Watauga L., MIG 57:115

Early June records likely represent late spring migrants.

Remarks: Found on large lakes and rivers; occasionally rests on islands or bare ground near water. More detectable in the middle and west than in the east. High count: 258 on 29 Dec 1984, Highland Rim CBC, near Tullahoma (MIG 56:7).

Iceland Gull, *Larus glaucoides*

Status: Accidental (Provisional).

Remarks: First verifiable state record was of one imm. bird on 27 Feb 1979, Old Hickory L. dam (MIG 50:42). Another imm. gull on 26 Jan-26 Mar 1979, Chickamauga L. (MIG 50:45), was photographed and initially identified as an Iceland Gull, but thought by some to be a Glaucous Gull.

Substantiation: Adequately documented sight record (TBRC).

Glaucous Gull, *Larus hyperboreus*

Status: Accidental.

Remarks: Found on large bodies of water. Four records:

    18 Jan-2 Feb 1969, Old Hickory L., (Parmer and Monk 1969)

    7-24 Mar 1971, Ft. Loudoun L., (Nicholson and Morton 1972)

    12 Jan 1984, Paris Landing S.P., MIG 55:43

    19 Jan 1985, Chickamauga L. dam (CGD, DRJ)

All sightings were of single birds in immature plumage. Another imm. gull on 26 Jan-26 Mar 1979, Chickamauga L. (MIG 50:45), was photographed and initially identified as an Iceland Gull, but thought by some to be a Glaucous Gull.

Substantiation: Photographs: 1 imm., Old Hickory L., Davidson Co., 26 Jan 1969 (Henry E. Parmer—TBRC).

Great Black-backed Gull, *Larus marinus*

Status: Extremely Rare.

Remarks: Found on large bodies of water. At least six records, all of imm. birds:

    19 Jan 1985, Chickamauga L. dam (CGD, DRJ)

    27 Jan 1985, Old Hickory L., MIG 56:52

    6-7 Feb 1977, Old Hickory L., MIG 48:47

    20 Feb 1984, Stewart/Henry Co., MIG 55:46

Great Black-backed Gull, continued
   2-8 Mar 1986, Paris Landing S.P., MIG 57:74
   19, 24 Mar 1984, Percy Priest L., MIG 55:70
The bird at Percy Priest L. in 1984 was injured. Because of the recent expansion of this species' breeding range, it is likely that more observations will be made. Future sightings should be thoroughly documented.
Substantiation: Adequately documented sight records (TBRC).

Black-legged Kittiwake, *Rissa tridactyla*
Status: Accidental.
Remarks: Found on large lakes. Most sightings appear to be of imm. birds. Known from five records:
   7-13 Dec 1971, Chickamauga L. dam, MIG 43:27
   21-22 Aug 1971, Percy Priest L., (Blunk 1984)
   10 Oct 1981, Cookeville, Putnam Co., MIG 53:16
   10-12 Dec 1983, Bard's L., Stewart Co., (Blunk 1984)
   15-17 Dec 1985, Fort Loudoun L., MIG 57:60-61
The bird at Cookeville was most unusual in that it landed on the playing field during a night football game at Tennessee Technological University and was photographed. High count: four on 13 Dec 1971, Chickamauga and Nickajack Lakes (MIG 43:27).
Substantiation: Adequately documented sight records.

[Ross' Gull, *Rhodostethia rosea*]
Status: Hypothetical.
Remarks: Recorded at Reelfoot L. on 19-28 Dec 1985. Imhof (1986) considered this a valid record, but the Tennessee Bird Records Committee found the documentation not to be totally convincing.

Sabine's Gull, *Xema sabini*
Status: Accidental (Provisional).
Remarks: One well-described ad. bird was present at Chickamauga L., Hamilton Co., on 20 Sept 1988 (Benton Basham). A review of this record by the Tennessee Bird Records Committee is pending.

Caspian Tern, *Sterna caspia*
Status: Regular.
Abundance: Uncommon migrant, very rare winter visitor.
Spring: Mid Apr to mid May.
   Arrivals: 26 Mar 1988, Percy Priest L., MIG 59:97
             11 Apr 1976, Savannah Bay, MIG 47:78
             13 Apr 1988, Paris Landing S.P. (DWB)
   Departures: 20 May 1957, Shelby Co., MIG 28:26
             14 June 1977, Austin Springs, MIG 48:105
             16 June 1963, Old Hickory L., (Dubke 1963a)

Caspian Tern, continued

Fall: Late July to early Oct.

Arrivals: 29 June 1979, Kingston Steam Plant, MIG 50:89

9 July 1979, Percy Priest L., MIG 50:87

18 July 1971, Tennessee NWR, MIG 42:68

Departures: 18 Oct 1972, Old Hickory L., MIG 43:100

22 Oct 1976, Shelby Co., MIG 48:17

10 Nov 1984, HRA, MIG 56:25

Winter: One record: 3 Dec 1972, Nickajack L. (MIG 44:26).

Remarks: Found along lakes and rivers. Seen more frequently in the fall, when large flocks are occasionally found (e.g., 100 on 17 Sept 1956, Memp., MIG 27:67). The presence of migrating birds high overhead is sometimes revealed by the loud, raucous call typical of this species. High count: 130 on 5 Sept 1964, Boone L. (MIG 35:106).

Common Tern, *Sterna hirundo*

Status: Regular.

Abundance: Uncommon migrant, rare summer visitor.

Spring: Late Apr to mid May.

Arrivals: 1 Apr 1972, Cherokee L., MIG 43:53

21 Apr 1972, Old Hickory L., MIG 43:51

23 Apr 1985, Paris Landing S.P., MIG 56:74

Departures: 27 May 1967, South Holston L., MIG 38:54

3 June 1972, Tennessee NWR, MIG 43:75

3 June 1968, Columbia, MIG 39:64

Summer: The following records are difficult to classify as either late spring migrants or early fall migrants and are possibly summering non-breeders: 12 June 1988, Cherokee L. (RLK); 13 June 1976, Alcoa Marsh (MIG 47:101); 23, 26 June 1961, Buena Vista Marsh and Bush L. (MIG 32:43); and 27 June 1987, Reelfoot L. (MIG 58:137).

Fall: Early Aug to late Sept.

Arrivals: 2 July 1972, Tennessee NWR, MIG 43:75

4 July 1972, Old Hickory L., MIG 43:76

7 July 1984, Savannah Bay, MIG 55:94

Departures: 28 Oct 1984, Paris Landing S.P., MIG 56:17

29 Oct 1980, Austin Springs, MIG 52:25

3 Nov 1984, Rutherford Co., MIG 56:21

Remarks: Found along lakes and rivers. Often difficult to separate from the similar Forster's Tern, especially in the fall. The Common Tern is rarely seen after Sept. Recent high count: 56 on 6 Sept 1987, Nickajack L. (MIG 59:40). Counts of 150 to 200 birds have been recorded but may have included a certain percentage of Forster's Terns.

Forster's Tern, *Sterna forsteri*

Status: Regular.

Abundance: Fairly common migrant, very rare summer and winter visitor.

Spring: Late Apr to mid May.

Arrivals: 26 Mar 1988, Percy Priest L., MIG 59:97-98

                1 Apr 1988, Paris Landing S.P., (DWB)

                9 Apr 1984, Watauga L., MIG 55:75

Departures: 13 May 1978, Boone L., MIG 49:69

                3 June 1972, Tennessee NWR, MIG 43:75

                7 June 1986, Lawrence Co., MIG 57:79

Summer: The following records are difficult to classify as either late spring migrants or early fall migrants and are possibly summering non-breeders: 15 June 1963, Old Hickory L. (MIG 34:51) and 24 June 1960, Bush L. (MIG 31:46).

Fall: Late July to early Oct.

Arrivals: 2 July 1972, Tennessee NWR, MIG 43:75

                3 July 1975, Old Hickory L., BNA:26

                7 July 1984, Savannah Bay, MIG 55:94

Departures: 27 Oct 1984, Douglas L., MIG 56:25

                15 Nov 1985, Tennessee NWR, MIG 57:28

                19 Nov 1985, Britton Ford, Henry Co., MIG 57:23

Winter: All winter records have occurred since 1983. Five records:

    31 Jan 1983, Chickamauga L., MIG 54:46

    2-16 Dec 1984, Shelby Co., MIG 56:48

    1 Jan 1985, Hiwassee CBC, MIG 56:7

    7 Dec 1986, Chickamauga L., MIG 58:60

    16 Jan 1987, Pace Point, MIG 58:53

Remarks: Found along lakes and rivers. Seen more frequently than Common Tern. More detectable in the fall, and may linger well into Nov. High count: forty-four on 27 Sept 1975, Nash. (MIG 47:19).

Substantiation: Specimen: 1 female, Bush L., Davidson Co., 9 Oct 1969 (LSUMZ, 75797).

Least Tern, *Sterna antillarum*

Status: Regular (interior race Federally Endangered). (Map A-27)

Abundance: East and Middle: rare migrant and summer visitor.

West: uncommon to locally common migrant and summer resident.

Spring: Arrives by mid May. One Mar record: 30 Mar 1969, near Nash. (MIG 40:46).

Arrivals: 2 May 1986, Columbia SBC, MIG 57:67

                2 May 1987, Memp. SBC, MIG 58:82

                9 May 1986, Island 13 (JCR)

Summer: Nesting colonies exist along the islands in the Mississippi River basin between Memp. and Reelfoot L. An active colony near Memp., Shelby Co., was documented in 1930 and 1931 (MIG 2:24), and nesting has occurred

Least Tern, continued

near this location as recently as 1985 (MIG 57:23). Breeding in Tipton Co. was documented in 1987 (*fide* MGW). Nesting has also been documented in Dyer Co., Lake Co. and Lauderdale Co. Over 160 young in colonies in Lake and Lauderdale Counties were banded in 1984 (MIG 55:88). No known nesting records are described east of these Mississippi River counties.

Fall: Departs by early Sept. There is one Oct record: 17 Oct 1983, Austin Springs (MIG 55:25).

Departures: 12 Sept 1958, Bush L., (Parmer 1959)
15 Sept 1945, Mud L., MIG 16:45
29 Sept 1974, Knoxville, MIG 46:22

Remarks: Found along rivers and oxbows and other adjacent bodies of water; nests on exposed sandbars. The number of observations substantially decreases east of a line running from Obion Co. to Fayette Co. Sightings in the east are primarily restricted to the fall (July to Sept); one exception is 5 June 1979, Savannah Bay (MIG 50:89). Most middle Tennessee sightings occur prior to Aug, with at least twelve records for May and June, suggesting a spring migration primarily in the Mississippi and western Tennessee River valleys and a tendency for some terns to migrate east of the Central Basin in the fall. There are more than twenty records each for east and middle Tennessee, primarily from the Nash. area, Cross Creeks NWR and the Chat. to HRA area. High count: 224 on 3 July 1984, Lauderdale Co. (MIG 55:88).

Substantiation: Specimen: 1 male, Ripley, Lauderdale Co., 19 June 1942 (LSUMZ, 75799).

Sooty Tern, *Sterna fuscata*
Status: Accidental (Provisional).
Remarks: Two records: an imm. male was picked up in a yard in Knoxville in an exhausted condition (and later died) on 20 June 1934 (Ijams 1934). Another specimen was discovered in the GSMNP on 30 July 1926 at an elevation of 610 m (Stupka 1963). The location of either specimen is not known. Both records occurred immediately following the passage of hurricanes (Bierly 1980).

Black Tern, *Chlidonias niger*
Status: Regular.
Abundance: Uncommon migrant, rare summer visitor.
Spring: Late Apr to mid May.
Arrivals: 11 Apr 1976, Savannah Bay, MIG 47:78
13 Apr 1978, Shelby Co., MIG 49:66
14 Apr 1928, Radnor L., BNA:27
Departures: 2 June 1959, Nash., MIG 30:37
3 June 1972, Tennessee NWR, MIG 43:75
7 June 1969, Watauga L., MIG 40:70

Black Tern, continued

Summer: The following records are difficult to classify as either late spring migrants or early fall migrants and are possibly non-breeding summering birds:

 12 June 1939, Memp., (Coffey 1939a)
 15 June 1975, Tennessee NWR, MIG 46:87
 20 June 1982, Douglas L., MIG 53:89
 21 June 1950, Benton Co., (Walker 1952)
 25 June 1960, Bush L., MIG 31:46

Fall: Mid July to late Sept.

Arrivals: 30 June 1987, Cross Creeks NWR, MIG 59:36
 1 July 1962, Lake Co., MIG 33:47
 13 July 1986, Chickamauga L., MIG 57:113

Departures: 29 Sept 1975, Old Hickory L., BNA:27
 1 Oct 1964, Bluff City, Sullivan Co., MIG 35:104
 14 Oct 1976, Shelby Co., MIG 48:17

Remarks: Found along lakes and rivers. High count: 230 on 30 Aug 1955, Nash. (MIG 26:48).

Substantiation: Specimen: 1 male, Reelfoot L., Obion Co., 21 May 1923 (LSUMZ, 75802).

Black Skimmer, *Rynchops niger*

Status: Accidental (Provisional).

Remarks: One record: one bird was found dead in 1890 in Obion Co. after a severe storm and was picked up by Mr. J. A. Craig (Rhoads 1895). The specimen was eventually placed in Albert Ganier's collection (Alsop 1972) but its current whereabouts are unknown.

ORDER COLUMBIFORMES

FAMILY COLUMBIDAE: Pigeons and Doves

*Rock Dove, *Columba livia*

Status: Regular.

Abundance: Common permanent resident.

Remarks: Found in urban areas, about farmlots, under large bridges and on cliff walls. A domesticated Old World species introduced into the United States over three centuries ago. A widespread permanent resident throughout

*Rock Dove, continued
Tennessee. High counts: 1,200 on 18 Dec 1982, Chat. CBC (MIG 54:13) and 500 on 31 Dec 1978, Kingsport CBC (MIG 50:11).
Substantiation: Specimen: 1, Clarksville, Montgomery Co., March 1965 (APSU, 1232).

Band-tailed Pigeon, *Columba fasciata*
Status: Accidental (Provisional).
Remarks: A well-described bird was found on 9 Apr 1974 at Nash. along the edge of Old Hickory L. (Fintel 1974a). Due to doubt about the origin of this bird, it was placed by the Tennessee Bird Records Committee on the list of provisional species (Nicholson 1983).
Substantiation: Adequately documented sight record.

*Ringed Turtle-Dove, *Streptopelia risoria*
Status: Escape.
Remarks: Introduced into the United States, its origin is apparently unknown; however it is now considered to be a domesticated form of the African Collared-Dove (*Streptopelia roseogrisea*) (Smith 1987). The following sightings have been made in Tennessee:
Apr 1965-17 Jan 1966, near Greeneville, (Darnell 1966)
June-Aug 1970, Knoxville, (Wallace 1971)
8 June 1980, Nash., MIG 57:82
29 May 1981, Bristol, MIG 52:99
30 Apr-31 May 1983, Columbia, MIG 54:62
There are good details for all sightings. Commonly kept in captivity; all sightings are probably of escaped birds. Undoubtedly, many observations of this species are unpublished due to doubts about the birds' origin. The 1980 sighting at Nash. included two birds with a nest and three eggs.

Mourning Dove, *Zenaida macroura*
Status: Regular.
Abundance: Common permanent resident.
Remarks: Found in open areas, along hedgerows and in grain fields. A widespread resident species throughout the state. Nests are commonly found from Mar through Sept. Occasionally found in flocks of 100 or more birds. High counts: 5,000 on 1 Jan 1958, Lebanon CBC (MIG 28:65) and 790 on 19 Dec 1976, Chat. CBC (MIG 48:32).
Substantiation: Specimen: 1 male, Nash., Davidson Co., 19 May 1945 (LSUMZ, 75803).

Passenger Pigeon, *Ectopistes migratorius*
Status: Extinct.
Remarks: Formerly a common migrant and winter resident found in or near forests; no nest records are known for Tennessee (Ganier 1933). Unlimited

Passenger Pigeon, continued

hunting, loss of forest lands, and harassment of nesting colonies (an activity that disrupted the reproductive process) apparently caused its extinction (Terres 1980; Blockstein and Tordoff 1985). Manlove (1933) described a flight of these wild pigeons that took place in the fall of 1870 ten km north of Nash. as follows:

> When a flock of pigeons approached a grove the column would wheel and the first birds would alight on the ground under the trees in perfect alignment and begin to feed. The birds following would hover a moment on the wing and then drop in front of the first rank. When the first had advanced to where the second rank had been feeding, it would again take wing and drop in front, as before. This constant movement gave to the flock the appearance of a great cylinder of fluttering birds, hundreds of yards long, rolling through the woods with machine-like precision, and at about the speed a man would walk.

Rhoads (1895) quoted a resident (Benjamin C. Miles) of Brownsville, TN, who wrote that the pigeons were last seen in that town in 1881 and that one out of a flock of eight was killed in 1893 near Brownsville. Mr. Miles also stated that "he feared their extinction" as early as 1866.

Substantiation: Historically recorded sight records.

Common Ground-Dove, *Columbina passerina*

Status: Extremely Rare.

Remarks: Found in open areas and along roadsides. At least ten state records. First recorded by Rhoads (1895) near Harriman, Roane Co., on 4 June 1895 (MIG 46:44). All other records have occurred in the fall and winter, with the exception of one spring record of two birds in Hardin Co. on 13 Mar 1987 (MIG 58:93). It is not clear why there were no records between 1895 and 1968. All other records follow:

    4 Oct 1986, Williamson Co., MIG 58:24

    17-22 Oct 1987, Shelby Co., MIG 59:32

    20 Oct, 7 Nov 1968, Savannah, MIG 39:89

    late Oct/early Nov 1984, Weakley Co., (Pitts 1987)

    3 Nov 1985, Cross Creeks NWR, MIG 57:28

    3-7 Dec 1974, Tennessee NWR, MIG 46:44, 71

    27 Dec 1979, Lawrence Co., (Bierly 1980)

    13 Jan 1986, Shelby Co., MIG 57:51

Substantiation: Specimen: 1, near Martin, Weakley Co., Oct-Nov 1984 (UTMB, 406).

ORDER PSITTACIFORMES

FAMILY PSITTACIDAE: **Parakeets**

*Monk Parakeet, *Myiopsitta monachus*
Status: Accidental.
Remarks: An introduced species considered by the Tennessee Bird Records
  Committee to be successfully established in the state (Nicholson 1983). A
  known agricultural pest. First state record was of one bird present from late
  Oct 1972 through 3 Feb 1973 at Memp. (Dinkelspiel 1973). Three other
  published records include:
  16-17 Oct 1977, Knox Co., MIG 49:21
  27 Oct 1979, Memp., MIG 51:15
  16 Dec 1979-18 May 1980, Nash., BNA:27
  The May 1980 sighting at Nash. included a nest, but no further evidence of
  breeding was reported.

Carolina Parakeet, *Conuropsis carolinensis*
Status: Extinct.
Remarks: Former inhabitant of wooded areas. Range was apparently restricted to
  river bottoms in west and middle Tennessee. Shot in large numbers by hunters
  and farmers. Recorded by several travelers along the Mississippi River between
  1673 and 1820, but no indication is given for which side of the river the birds
  were observed (McKinley 1979). Alexander Wilson observed "large flocks" of
  this species on 20 Apr 1810 along Mansker's Creek near the Sumner/Davidson
  Co. line; and later, on 25 Apr 1810, he shot three additional parakeets near
  Nash. (McKinley 1979; Rhoads 1895). Mr. Benjamin Miles, of Brownsville,
  recorded the following notable observations (Rhoads 1895): one hundred in
  1874 (unknown date) at Ashport, Lauderdale Co.; and one in 1876 (unknown
  date) at Brownsville. McKinley (1979) described other important references to
  this species, including an observation of a flock on the Cumberland River in or
  near Putnam Co. on 25 Nov 1799.
Substantiation: Historically recorded sight records.

Black-hooded Parakeet, *Nandayus nenday*
Status: Escape.
Remarks: A bird of this species seen on 7-8 Aug 1976 in Sumner Co. was adequately described (Crawford 1977). Although it lacked a leg band and ex-
  hibited a wild behavior, it is treated as a likely escaped bird here.

ORDER CUCULIFORMES

FAMILY CUCULIDAE: Cuckoos and Anis

Black-billed Cuckoo, *Coccyzus erythropthalmus*
Status: Regular.
Abundance: East and Middle: uncommon migrant, rare summer resident.
West: uncommon migrant, very rare summer resident.
Spring: Late Apr to early June.
    Arrivals: 8 Apr 1965, Elizabethton, MIG 36:65
                    14 Apr 1985, Murfreesboro, MIG 56:76
                    23 Apr 1975, Lauderdale Co., MIG 46:65
Summer: Spring migrants may be observed as late as early June. Occasionally
found in middle and east from mid June throughout July. One notable
record is from the west: 15 June 1984, near Camden, Benton Co. (MIG
55:88). Has nested in the following counties:
    Sequatchie, 1972, nest with eggs, MIG 43:53
    near Washington, 1920-1930s, nests, (Lyle and Tyler 1934)
    Campbell, 1971, nest with young, MIG 42:71
    Van Buren or Bledsoe, 1940, eggs, (Ganier and Clebsch 1940)
    Davidson, 1917, 1931, 1935, nests, BNA:27
    Davidson, 1950, nest with young, BNA:27
    Madison, 1950, nest with young, (Roever 1951)
The Madison Co. record in west Tennessee is most unusual and is apparently
the only nest record for that region of the state.
Fall: Mid Aug to early Oct.
    Arrivals: 2 Aug 1964, Knoxville, MIG 35:63
                    6 Aug 1974, Nash., MIG 46:20
                    14 Aug 1978, Penal Farm, MIG 50:19
    Departures: 22 Oct 1973, Old Hickory L., MIG 44:100
                    27 Oct 1957, Shelby Co., MIG 29:7
                    3 Nov 1974, near Erwin, MIG 46:24
Remarks: Found in shrubby open areas and in woodlands. High counts: nine
on 7 May 1950, Elizabethton SBC (MIG 21:26) and nine on 4 May 1958,
Kingsport SBC (MIG 29:31).
Substantiation: Specimen: 1 female, Nash., Davidson Co., 7 Oct 1951 (LSUMZ,
75815).

Yellow-billed Cuckoo, *Coccyzus americanus*
Status: Regular.
Abundance: Fairly common migrant and summer resident, very rare winter
visitor.
Spring: Arrives by late Apr.
    Arrivals: 29 Mar 1967, Reelfoot L., MIG 38:47
                    3 Apr 1985, Nash., MIG 56:77
                    10 Apr 1965, Elizabethton, MIG 36:65
Summer: Nests throughout the state. Found incubating eggs in Nash. as late as
early Sept (MIG 50:21).
Fall: Departs by mid Oct.
    Departures: 5 Nov 1980, Austin Springs, MIG 52:49
                    6 Nov 1977, Dyersburg, MIG 49:41
                    25 Nov 1973, Old Hickory L., MIG 45:21
'Winter: Three records. A weak bird was found on 23 Dec 1941 at Memp. (MIG
13:20). An injured bird was also found at Memp. on 9 Dec 1953 (MIG
25:15). A possible early spring overflight is one bird that was found at Nash.
on 25 Feb 1961 (MIG 32:5).
Remarks: Found along hedgerows, in woodlands and along woodland edge.
Abundance is often related to the availability of hairy or tent caterpillars.
High counts: 36 on 30 Apr 1961, Knoxville SBC (MIG 32:31); and 201 on
12-13 May 1979 (exact date not specified), Nash. SBC, MIG 50:58.
Substantiation: Specimen: 1 male, Nash., Davidson Co., 6 Sept 1942 (LSUMZ,
75811).

Groove-billed Ani, *Crotophaga sulcirostris*
Status: Accidental.
Remarks: Two records. A male of this species was shot by a hunter 16 km
north of Dyersburg on 29 Nov 1968 (Leggett 1969a). Another bird was
found at the Tigrett WMA, Dyer Co., on 17 Oct 1985 (Criswell 1986).
Substantiation: Specimen: 1 male, Dyersburg, Dyer Co., 29 Nov 1968 (LSUMZ,
75817).

ORDER STRIGIFORMES

FAMILY TYTONIDAE: **Barn-Owls**

Common Barn-Owl, *Tyto alba*
Status: Regular.
Abundance: Rare permanent resident.

Common Barn-Owl, continued

Remarks: Found locally throughout Tennessee in open areas, along woodland edge and in towns and cities; roosts in barns, tree cavities and grain silos. Fewer sightings occur in the western region of the state. There are many nest records from the eastern and middle regions, ranging from Carter and Blount Counties in the east to Davidson, Maury and Williamson Counties in middle Tennessee. Nests in the west are known from Weakley Co., Shelby Co. and Reelfoot L. (Alsop 1980). Strictly nocturnal. Certain nest sites have been used for many consecutive years. A few birds have been hacked by state wildlife officials and volunteers in recent years.

Substantiation: Specimen: 1 male, Dickson, Dickson Co., 2 Dec 1939 (LSUMZ, 75818).

FAMILY STRIGIDAE: **Typical Owls**

Eastern Screech-Owl, *Otus asio*

Status: Regular.

Abundance: Fairly common permanent resident.

Remarks: Found in wooded areas; also in cities and towns where suitable cavities are available. Utilizes Wood Duck boxes as well as boxes built specifically for screech-owls for roost sites in the winter, and may occasionally breed in these structures. Of 69 owls collected in or near the GSMNP over a fifteen-year period beginning in 1936, the ratio of red phase birds to gray phase birds was 4:1 (Stupka 1953). In a study that examined 127 road-killed owls and 225 owls banded at nests, Fowler (1985a) also found a higher frequency of red phase birds in Tennessee. Large numbers have been reported on the CBCs and SBCs since the early 1970s when 'owling' with owl tapes became popular. High count: 31 on 20 Dec 1981, Knoxville CBC (MIG 53:7).

Substantiation: Specimen: 1 female, near Nash., Davidson Co., 13 Sept 1935 (LSUMZ, 75823).

Great Horned Owl, *Bubo virginianus*

Status: Regular.

Abundance: Fairly common permanent resident.

Remarks: Found in wooded areas. Nests throughout the state. Most detectable in Dec and Jan when vocalizations are given by nesting birds during the establishment of breeding territories. Eggs are laid by Feb and nests with young are frequently found in Mar. Although easily identified by its five- to six-note hoot, some birds (presumably immatures) give a single, high-pitched scream. Was usually recorded in small numbers prior to the 1970s; however,

Great Horned Owl, continued

a notable count of twelve birds was found on 22 Dec 1956, Nash. CBC (MIG 27:72). Larger numbers have been recorded since the mid-1970s, due in part to the use of tape recorders to stimulate birds to call. High count: eighteen on 27 Dec 1986, Bristol CBC (MIG 58:3).

Substantiation: Specimen: 1 male, Reelfoot L., 25 Nov 1915 (LSUMZ, 75832).

Snowy Owl, *Nyctea scandiaca*

Status: Accidental.

Remarks: Found in open areas. There are nine state records. First recorded at Paris, Henry Co., on 3 Feb 1918, when one bird was shot (MIG 2:7). An "invasion" occurred during the winter of 1930-31, resulting in four records: 3 Dec 1930, Reelfoot L. (collected) (MIG 2:7); 31 Dec 1930, Johnson City (shot) (MIG 2:7); 21 Dec 1930, Paris (collected) (Thompson 1937); and one bird killed by a farmer in a pasture in Sullivan Co. during the winter of 1930-31 (Coffey 1964b). The next sighting was of one bird observed on 11 Nov 1954 at Eagle Creek bay, Henry Co., near Paris Landing S.P.; this bird was later shot around mid Dec in Benton Co. (Cypert 1955a). A bird observed briefly on the Cumberland/White Co. line on 1 Dec 1956 was identified as this species (Kellberg 1956). Then, on 18 Dec 1960, one imm. bird was found at Nash. and later captured on 5 Jan 1961; it died on 26 Feb 1961 (Munro 1961). The most recent sighting is of one imm. bird at the Barkley WMA, Stewart Co., on 5 Jan-6 Feb 1987 (MIG 58:56-57). Owl pellets cast by this bird were analyzed and found to contain remains of a Pied-billed Grebe, prairie vole, a duck the size of a Mallard and an American Coot (Robinson 1988). Dec and Jan appear to be the best two months of the year to look for this species.

Substantiation: Specimen: 1, Nash., Davidson Co., 5 Jan 1961 (CSM, AV-324).

Barred Owl, *Strix varia*

Status: Regular.

Abundance: East: uncommon permanent resident.

Middle and West: fairly common permanent resident.

Remarks: Found in wooded areas, especially bottomland woods and wooded swamps. Widely distributed across the state, it is least detectable east of the Cumberland Plateau, especially in the eastern mountains. Usually nests a little later than the Great Horned Owl; however, a nest with two eggs found on 2 Mar 1975, Lawrence Co. (MIG 46:71) was not unusually early. During the late winter and early spring adults become highly vocal. A dramatic increase in the number of owls found on CBCs occurred in the 1970s corresponding with the increased popularity of "owling." High counts: twenty-four on 19 Dec 1981, Lebanon CBC (MIG 54:13) and seventeen on 20 Dec 1986, Reelfoot L. CBC (MIG 58:3).

Substantiation: Specimen: 1 female, Madison, Davidson Co., 14 Nov 1925 (LSUMZ, 75835).

Long-eared Owl, *Asio otus*

Status: Extremely Rare.

Remarks: Found in coniferous woods and in mixed coniferous/deciduous woods; usually occurs in areas of dense vegetation. Also found roosting in a magnolia tree at Memp. (Landis 1955). Frequently allows close approach by observers. This is an extremely rare winter resident owl, usually found from mid Dec to mid Mar. There are about thirty state records (Bierly 1980). Earliest published record is of one bird on 12 Jan 1923, at Belle Meade, Davidson Co. (Ganier 1940).

Arrivals: 4 Nov 1972, Lawrence Co., MIG 44:23

10 Dec 1939, near Murfreesboro, (Ganier 1940)

13 Dec 1987, Henry Co., MIG 59:65

22 Dec 1974, Cheatham L. dam, MIG 46:71

Departures: 25 Mar 1975, Greeneville, MIG 46:46, 68

3 Apr 1954, Memp., (Landis 1955)

9 Apr 1958, Memp., (Irwin 1958)

10 Apr 1975, Bristol, MIG 46:70

Substantiation: Specimen: 1 female, Halls, Lauderdale Co., 21 Jan 1944 (LSUMZ, 75838).

Short-eared Owl, *Asio flammeus*

Status: Irregular.

Abundance: Rare migrant and winter resident.

Fall: Arrives by late Nov.

Arrivals: 12 Oct 1955, Memp., MIG 27:16

25 Oct 1930, Knox Co., (Howell and Monroe 1958)

29 Oct 1977, Bedford Co., MIG 49:19

Winter: More sightings have been made for the mid to late Dec period than for any other period of the winter. This period coincides with the CBC season and effectively illustrates that the species is readily detected with a proper amount of observer effort.

Spring: Departs by mid Mar. There are two May records: 5 May 1955, Buena Vista Marsh (BNA:30) and 5 May 1956, Nash. SBC (MIG 27:33).

Departures: 3 Mar 1974, Knox Co., MIG 45:24

17 Apr 1954, Nash., (Ganier 1954a)

17 Apr 1954, Penal Farm, (Coffey 1955a)

Remarks: Found in open areas, especially in open, brushy fields. Forms communal roosts on the ground. Over 80% of the published records are for the middle and west; rarely recorded in the east, where it has been found in the following counties: Carter, Greene, Jefferson, Knox, and Washington. Two sight records also exist for the Nickajack L. area. High count: twenty-five on 5 Apr 1954, Nash. (Ganier 1954a).

Substantiation: Specimen: 1 female, Nash., Davidson Co., 1 Nov 1953 (LSUMZ, 75837).

Northern Saw-whet Owl, *Aegolius acadicus*
Status: Irregular. (Map A-28)
Abundance: East: locally rare permanent resident.
Middle and West: rare migrant and winter resident.
Remarks: A locally rare permanent resident of the GSMNP, this species is
rarely observed outside of that area. Ironically, the first published state
record was at Memp. on 1 Mar 1936 (Coffey 1936). Only one nest record:
two ad. and two fledglings on 8-11 May 1988, Claiborne Co. (George W.
McKinney, J. B. Owen). No nests have been documented in the GSMNP. In
the GSMNP, Savage (1965) found these birds calling primarily during the
Apr-June period at eight sites including Clingman's Dome and Newfound
Gap. They are known to inhabit the dense spruce and fir forests of the
Canadian zone in the Park (Alsop 1980). There were no known records for
Roan Mt., where suitable habitat is present, until one bird was found there
on 12-27 Apr 1985 (MIG 56:82). Eleven other published records from outside the GSMNP are listed below:
  4 Jan 1986, Nickajack L. CBC, MIG 58:3
  13 Mar 1985, Nash., MIG 56:77
  16 Mar 1940, Nash., (Ganier 1940)
  18-22 Mar 1988, Memp. (*fide* MGW)
  23 Aug 1975, Two Jays, (Riggins 1977)
  25 Oct 1983, Bell's Bend, Davidson Co., MIG 55:21
  28 Oct 1968, Two Jays, MIG 39:90
  13 Nov 1983, Montgomery Co., MIG 55:21
  1-21 Dec 1986, Memp., MIG 58:53
  6 Dec-8 Mar 1952/53, Williamson Co., (Goodpasture 1954)
  28 Dec 1981, Hickman Co., MIG 53:45
Also known from middle Tennessee by fossil evidence in Maury Co. (Parmalee and Klippel 1982).
Substantiation: Specimen: 1, Memp., Shelby Co., 26 Dec 1986 (UTMB, 410).

ORDER CAPRIMULGIFORMES

FAMILY CAPRIMULGIDAE: Goatsuckers

Common Nighthawk, *Chordeiles minor*
Status: Regular.
Abundance: Common migrant, fairly common summer resident, rare winter
visitor.

Common Nighthawk, continued

Spring: Arrives by mid Apr.

Arrivals: 4 Mar 1985, Nash., MIG 56:77

31 Mar 1968, Greeneville, MIG 39:45

16 Apr 1978, Memp., MIG 49:66

Summer: A fairly common summer resident across the state. May be locally common in certain metropolitan areas. Published nest records range from near Washington Co. ca. 1930 (Lyle and Tyler 1934) to Shelby Co. in 1947 (Coffey 1948a).

Fall: Departs by early Oct; may linger well into Nov.

Departures: 1 Nov 1986, Reelfoot L., MIG 58:21

11 Nov 1979, Chat., MIG 51:42

30 Nov 1983, Davidson Co., MIG 55:21

Winter: There are over ten Dec records, primarily from the Nash. area:

2 Dec 1971, Davidson Co., MIG 43:25

5 Dec 1983, Davidson Co., MIG 55:46

8-10 Dec 1957, Radnor L., (Parmer 1957)

9 Dec 1986, Nash., MIG 58:57

11 Dec 1984, Williamson Co., MIG 56:52

12 Dec 1978, Clarksville, MIG 50:43

12 Dec 1984, Davidson Co., MIG 56:52

12 Dec 1987, Wilson Co., MIG 59:67

18 Dec 1976, Lebanon CBC, MIG 48:32

20 Dec 1986, Chat. CBC, MIG 58:3

22 Dec 1987, Madison Co., MIG 59:65

There are no records of overwintering birds.

Remarks: Found in urban areas, where it often nests on rooftops. Locally distributed in (and sometimes absent from) predominantly rural areas during June and July. Also nests on exposed limestone, cedar glades and other similar habitats. Active both day and night; often seen at dusk and may be heard calling throughout the night, especially in metropolitan areas. Large numbers of birds can be observed migrating in the fall, usually from late Aug to early Sept. High counts: 4,000 on 26 Aug 1978, Fentress Co. (MIG 50:21); 3,500 on 8 Sept 1971, Nash. (MIG 42:92) and 2,500 on 5 Oct 1956, Chickamauga L. dam (MIG 27:50).

Substantiation: Specimen: 1 male, near Germantown, Shelby Co., 9 May 1943 (LSUMZ, 8704).

Chuck-will's-widow, *Caprimulgus carolinensis*

Status: Regular.

Abundance: Fairly common summer resident.

Spring: Arrives by late Apr.

Arrivals: 29 Mar 1953, Decatur Co., (Nicholson 1980)

5 Apr 1965, Bristol, MIG 36:66

6 Apr 1939, Clarksville, MIG 10:32

Chuck-will's-widow, continued

Summer: Nests are difficult to find; published records exist for the following
counties:

Dyer, 1979, nest with young, MIG 50:86

McMinn, ca. 1900, nests and eggs, (Ijams and Hofferbert 1934)

Rutherford, 1936, nest with eggs, (DeVore 1975)

Sullivan, 1960, nest with young, (Nunley 1960)

near Washington, ca. 1930, nest and eggs, (Lyle and Tyler 1934)

Becomes difficult to find once singing ends in late July. Many surveys have
been made of this species in Tennessee (e.g., forty-four birds on 8 June 1979
from twenty-seven of seventy-three stops on a 69 km route in Lauderdale
Co. [Coffey and Coffey 1980]). Birds can be found in most areas throughout
the west and middle regions of the state, but in the east they are generally
restricted to elevations below 460 m MSL (MIG 27:64, 65, 82). One bird at
Watauga L. was found at 610 m MSL on 29 May 1962 (Herndon 1962); and
in Sullivan Co. a nest record at 485 m MSL was documented in 1960
(Nunley 1960). Also recorded at about 500 m MSL near Signal Mt. at Chat.
(West and West 1960).

Fall: Departs by late Aug; fall migration is hard to detect.

Departures: 31 Aug 1958, Kingsport, MIG 29:58

23 Sept 1934, Nash., MIG 5:45

5 Oct 1984, Knox Co., MIG 56:25

Remarks: Found in open deciduous and coniferous wooded areas. Primarily
nocturnal, but one bird in Cannon Co. was found singing for three-and-a-
half hours after sunrise on 19 June 1971 (Bierly 1972a). High counts: 157 on
30 May 1988, McNairy Co. (BBC, LCC); 149 on 30 May 1988, Chester Co.
(BBC, LCC); and 138 on 7 June 1979, Fayette Co. (Coffey and Coffey 1980).

Substantiation: Specimen: 1 female, Camden, Benton Co., 23 July 1963
(LSUMZ, 75843).

Whip-poor-will, *Caprimulgus vociferus*

Status: Regular.

Abundance: Fairly common summer resident.

Spring: Arrives by late Mar.

Arrivals: 7 Mar 1954, Signal Mt., Chat., MIG 25:34

9 Mar 1974, Hardin Co., MIG 45:20

23 Mar 1967, Williamson Co., BNA:30

Summer: Nests are difficult to locate; published records exist for the following
counties:

Campbell, 1978, nest with eggs, MIG 49:69-70

Sullivan, 1982, nest with eggs, MIG 53:70

near Washington, ca. 1930, nest and eggs, (Lyle and Tyler 1934)

Williamson, 1962, nest and eggs, (Goodpasture and Douglass 1964)

A nest with young was also found in Stewart Co. in 1987 (Robinson and
Blunk 1989). May be heard singing as late as Sept or Oct. Many surveys

have been made of this species, primarily in western Tennessee and upper east Tennessee. In contrast to the preceding species, the Whip-poor-will is frequently found at elevations of 610 m MSL or higher in east Tennessee.

Fall: Departs by early Oct.

Departures: 30 Sept 1949, Memp., MIG 21:12

7 Oct 1951, Knoxville, (Howell and Tanner 1951)

27 Oct 1979, Williamson Co., MIG 51:16

Remarks: Found in wooded areas; often seen along roadsides at night. Calling birds are heard most often at dusk and just before dawn. A freshly dead specimen was found in Memp. on 25 Nov 1968 (MIG 40:19). High counts: 171 on 30 May 1988, Chester Co. (BBC, LCC) and 112 on 30 May 1969, Holston Mt., Sullivan and Carter Co. (Bridgforth 1969).

Substantiation: Specimen: 1 female, Nash., Davidson Co., 15 June 1966 (LSUMZ, 75851).

ORDER APODIFORMES

FAMILY APODIDAE: **Swifts**

Chimney Swift, *Chaetura pelagica*

Status: Regular.

Abundance: Common migrant and summer resident, very rare winter visitor.

Spring: Arrives by late Mar.

Arrivals: 7 Mar 1944, Clarksville, MIG 15:17

18 Mar 1945, Memp., MIG 16:11

23 Mar 1988, Washington Co. (James W. Brooks)

Summer: A widely distributed species; nests throughout the state. Primarily found in residential areas, but is easily detected in rural or wooded areas (including the eastern mountains) where it undoubtedly occasionally still nests in hollow trees.

Fall: Departs by mid Oct.

Departures: 31 Oct 1972, Knoxville, MIG 43:102

13 Nov 1977, Radnor L., MIG 49:42

17 Nov 1984, Memp., MIG 56:17

Winter: One record: 5 Dec 1972, Daus, Sequatchie Co. (MIG 44:26).

Remarks: Found in a wide variety of urban and rural habitats. Concentrations of migrating birds in the fall can be spectacular when several hundred birds spiral into a roost in a chimney. Over 108,000 swifts were banded between

1928 and 1944 at banding stations in Chat., Knoxville, Nash., Clarksville and Memp. (Ganier 1944). Most of these birds were banded in the fall at evening roosts. This work was largely instrumental in the discovery of the wintering grounds of this species in northeastern Peru: eight of thirteen birds recovered there in Dec 1943 had been banded at Memp. and Nash. (Coffey 1944). High count: ten thousand on 11 Oct 1933, Nash. (MIG 4:49).
Substantiation: Specimen: 1 female, Nash., Davidson Co., 13 Apr 1940 (LSUMZ, 75856).

FAMILY TROCHILIDAE: **Hummingbirds**

Ruby-throated Hummingbird, *Archilochus colubris*
Status: Regular.
Abundance: Fairly common migrant and summer resident.
Spring: Arrives by early Apr.
Arrivals: 24 Mar 1979, Nash., MIG 50:69
               25 Mar 1954, Shelby Co., MIG 25:51
               7 Apr 1954, GSMNP, (Stupka 1963)
Summer: Encountered regularly from the eastern mountains to the Mississippi River valley. Nests are difficult to locate, but sixty-one nests were found by Richard Gettys in McMinn Co. between 1897 and 1909 (Ijams and Hofferbert 1934)! These nests were placed in a variety of trees including pine, white oak, hickory, sweetgum, chestnut, and sycamore trees.
Fall: Departs by early Oct. One Dec record: 28 Nov-3 Dec 1978, Murfreesboro (MIG 50:43).
Departures: 1 Nov 1986, Knox Co., MIG 58:28
               4 Nov 1968, Reelfoot L., MIG 40:19
               24 Nov 1973, Nash., MIG 45:21
Remarks: Found along woodland edge, brushy fields and residential areas, especially where feeders have been established. Often seen feeding on columbine flowers in the spring, mimosa flowers in the summer and jewelweed in the fall. Utilizes feeders more often in late summer and fall than in the spring. All late fall hummers should be closely scrutinized as western hummingbirds, especially the Rufous Hummingbird, are known to wander at this time of year. High count: sixty on 20 Sept 1955, Jocelyn Hollow, near Nash. (Abernathy 1955).
Substantiation: Specimen: 1 male, Nash., Davidson Co., 20 July 1950 (LSUMZ, 75862).

Rufous Hummingbird, *Selasphorus rufus*

Status: Accidental.

Remarks: Two records: an imm. male was present at Murfreesboro, Rutherford Co., on 6-8 Sept 1983 (Erwin 1986). This bird was photographed. A well-described male was in Elizabethton, Carter Co., on 27 Sept and 11-12 Oct 1985 (Clark 1986). Two other records of hummingbirds in the genus *Selasphorus* are known, both of which cannot safely be identified as either Allen's Hummingbird (*S. sasin*) or Rufous Hummingbird. One of these records is of a freshly dead female specimen found at Memp. on 9 Nov 1976; the other bird, an imm., was photographed in Memp. on 26-29 Sept 1983 (Erwin 1986).

Substantiation: Photographs: 1, Murfreesboro, Rutherford Co., 6-8 Sept 1983 (MLB—on file, The Wood Thrush Shop, Nashville, TN).

ORDER CORACIIFORMES

FAMILY ALCEDINIDAE: Kingfishers

Belted Kingfisher, *Ceryle alcyon*

Status: Regular.

Abundance: Fairly common permanent resident.

Remarks: Found along creeks and streams and along the edges of lakes, ponds and rivers. Nests in burrows in exposed stream or river banks, road cuts and other similar areas. Usually found singly or in pairs; however, larger numbers can often be recorded dispersed in suitable habitat, especially in the winter. High counts: 142 on 2 Jan 1982, Hickory-Priest CBC (MIG 53:7) and 60 on 18 Dec 1982, Knoxville CBC (MIG 54:13).

Substantiation: Specimen: 1 male, Ashland City, Cheatham Co., 7 June 1916 (LSUMZ, 75865).

ORDER PICIFORMES

FAMILY PICIDAE: Woodpeckers

Red-headed Woodpecker, *Melanerpes erythrocephalus*

Status: Regular.

Abundance: East and Middle: uncommon permanent resident.

Red-headed Woodpecker, continued
West: fairly common permanent resident.

Remarks: Found in open wooded areas, wooded swamps, and river bottoms; appears to prefer areas where dead trees are present, including beaver-impounded wetlands. Nests throughout the state. Considered by Rhoads (1895) and Ganier (1933) to be abundant in middle Tennessee throughout most of the year; but large numbers are currently only reported from the west, primarily at Memp. and Reelfoot L. Considered by Ganier (1933) to be a fairly common summer resident in the east, but it currently is only reported from scattered localities and in generally low numbers throughout the Cumberland Plateau, eastern Tennessee River valley and eastern mountain regions. Presence anywhere in the state is often influenced by migratory movements and the availability of mast on northern breeding areas. High counts:

    27 on 21 Dec 1985, Cross Creeks NWR, MIG 57:10

    75 on 7-8 May 1966, Crossville SBC, MIG 37:37

    132 on 29 Oct 1978, Shelby Co., MIG 50:19

    199 on 17 Dec 1983, Reelfoot L. CBC, MIG 55:9

    341 on 30 Oct 1983, Shelby Co., MIG 55:18

Substantiation: Specimen: 1 male, Dyersburg, Dyer Co., 28 Aug 1949 (LSUMZ, 75924).

Red-bellied Woodpecker, *Melanerpes carolinus*
Status: Regular.

Abundance: Fairly common to common permanent resident.

Remarks: Found in open woodlands. Widely distributed; nests throughout the state. Less detectable in the east, especially in the winter and at high mountain elevations (e.g., three birds on 27 Dec 1975, Bristol CBC, MIG 47:36). High counts: 129 on 23 Dec 1972, Reelfoot L. CBC (MIG 44:11); 129 on 30 Dec 1978, Nash. CBC (MIG 50:11); and 128 on 21 Dec 1980, Memp. CBC (MIG 52:14).

Substantiation: Specimen: 1 male, Clarksville, Montgomery Co., 19 Apr 1942 (LSUMZ, 75895).

Yellow-bellied Sapsucker, *Sphyrapicus varius*
Status: Regular.

Abundance: East: fairly common migrant and winter resident, locally rare summer resident.

Middle and West: fairly common migrant and winter resident.

Fall: Arrives by late Sept.

    Arrivals: 25 Aug 1975, Memp., MIG 47:17

                27 Aug 1977, Savannah Bay, MIG 49:21

                9 Sept 1980, Nash., BNA:30

Winter: Found widely distributed across the state during the winter. Abundance varies between winters; in some years large numbers are recorded at sites

Yellow-bellied Sapsucker, continued

along major rivers (e.g., thirty-nine on 22 Dec 1963, Knoxville CBC, MIG 34:83; and forty-one on 22 Dec 1973, Reelfoot L. CBC, MIG 45:12).

Spring: Departs by early May.

Departures: 11 May 1958, Reelfoot L. SBC, MIG 29:31
                  19 May 1980, Montgomery Co., MIG 51:56
                  29 May 1972, Knox Co., MIG 43:79

Summer: A rare and local resident at high elevations in the mountains of east Tennessee. Reported by Alsop (1980) as having nested at least once in Unicoi Co. Stupka (1963) described a 1935 nest record in Sevier Co. and a 1938 nest record in Blount Co., both in GSMNP. Several representative summer sightings include:

    24 June 1978, Iron Mt., Carter Co., MIG 49:95
    25 June 1955, Elizabethton, Carter Co., MIG 26:51
    6 July 1974, Cherokee National Forest, Monroe Co., MIG 45:104
    21 July 1972, GSMNP, MIG 43:80

Remarks: Found in wooded areas and in open woods of towns and parks. High counts: sixty-nine on 26 Dec 1977, Nash. CBC (MIG 49:7) and sixty-one on 21 Dec 1975, Memp. CBC (MIG 47:36).

Substantiation: Specimen: 1 female, Nash., Davidson Co., 31 Dec 1957 (LSUMZ, 75953).

Downy Woodpecker, *Picoides pubescens*
Status: Regular.
Abundance: Common permanent resident.
Remarks: Found in wooded areas, residential areas and open areas with scattered trees. A widely distributed nesting species. Often seen searching for food on dead corn stalks in the fall and winter. Stupka (1963) described it as being more common than the Hairy Woodpecker in the GSMNP, usually at elevations below 1,065 m MSL; above that elevation the Hairy tends to outnumber the Downy Woodpecker. High counts: 148 on 26 Dec 1977, Nash. CBC (MIG 49:7); 147 on 27 Dec 1980, Nash. CBC (MIG 52:14); and 61 on 20 Dec 1986, Chat. CBC (MIG 58:3).

Substantiation: Specimen: 1 male, Clarksville, Montgomery Co., 15 Sept 1940 (LSUMZ, 76013).

Hairy Woodpecker, *Picoides villosus*
Status: Regular.
Abundance: Fairly common permanent resident.
Remarks: Found in wooded areas. Not as numerous as the Downy Woodpecker, nor as tame. A widely distributed nesting species. Found regularly in small numbers at elevations ranging from 760 m to 1,765 m MSL in the GSMNP (Bellrose 1938); tends to outnumber the Downy Woodpecker at elevations above 1,065 m in the GSMNP (Stupka 1963). High counts:

Hairy Woodpecker, continued
> 53 on 16 Dec 1979, Knoxville CBC, MIG 51:32
> 28 on 26 Dec 1977, Nash. CBC, MIG 49:7
> 27 on 4 May 1952, Greeneville SBC, MIG 23:27
> 17 on 2 Jan 1966, GSMNP CBC, MIG 36:88

Substantiation: Specimen: 1 male, Nash., Davidson Co., 24 Jan 1943 (LSUMZ, 75965).

Red-cockaded Woodpecker, *Picoides borealis*
Status: Irregular (Federally Endangered). (Map A-29)
Abundance: East: rare permanent resident.
Remarks: Found in open stands of mature pines. Formerly occurred occasionally in the middle and west, but is currently restricted to east Tennessee on the Cumberland Plateau, in the GSMNP, and the Cherokee National Forest in Polk Co. Nicholson (1977) summarized the past distribution of the species in the state, noted that the species had been found in the state as early as the time of John James Audubon, and estimated the state population to be between six and twenty-five birds. Former sightings from the west include at least six birds that were seen in McNairy and Hardeman Counties on 31 July and 6 Aug 1939 (Ganier 1962). Additional sightings from this area (east of Pocahontas) include five observations of one to four birds between 6 July 1947 and 30 Mar 1958 (Ganier 1962); observations of one to two birds on 24 Nov and 4 Dec 1963 (MIG 34:71); and a sighting of one bird on 14 May 1967 (Nicholson 1984). In Hardin Co., one bird was observed near Counce on 31 Mar 1946 (Counce 1946). In middle Tennessee, an observation of a single bird was made in Stewart Co. on 30 Oct 1937 during a museum collecting expedition; Ganier (1962) considered this sighting to be of a wandering individual due to the lack of pines in the area. In Pickett Co., a colony consisting of birds at three different areas was discovered in Pickett S.P. in June 1935 (Ganier 1962); and although no birds were seen there from 1943 to 1968, active nest sites were found in 1946 and ca. 1965, and two ad. feeding two young were observed there on 1 June 1969 (Nicholson 1977). Along the Cumberland Plateau, a bird was collected in Grundy Co. near Beersheba Springs in Dec 1921 (Ganier 1962), and at least two were found there on 8 Aug 1931 (Mayfield 1932). At Rockwood, Roane Co., two males and a female were seen by W. H. Fox on 10 Apr 1884 (Ganier 1962). Rhoads (1895) noted the birds "breeding" in the Allardt-Rugby area, Morgan and Fentress Counties, including nests with young at Allardt (Fentress Co.) on 8 June 1895. One to two birds were observed several times over a ten year period on the Stinking Creek road in Campbell Co. The earliest observation at this site was 13 June 1971 (Howell and Campbell 1972); and the latest on 3 June 1980 (MIG 51:94). A small breeding colony was regularly observed at the Catoosa WMA, Cumberland and Morgan Counties, from 1962 through the mid-1970s; a nest with eggs was found there on 20 May 1972 (Nicholson 1977). The latest sighting from that area is of one bird on

Red-cockaded Woodpecker, continued

27 May 1985 (MIG 56:80). East of the Cumberland Plateau, this woodpecker is known primarily from two areas, including the GSMNP area, Blount and Sevier Counties. In the Park, they were found up to an elevation of 670 m MSL (Ganier 1962), and were observed at least five times between 1935 and 1953. On 16 May 1965, a pair feeding young in a nest on Beard Cane Mt. (Blount Co.) was observed (Tanner 1965). Adults and young were also observed on Skunk Ridge (Blount Co.), GSMNP, in 1980 (MIG 51:96) and 1981 (MIG 52:75); and as many as five birds were observed in the Park on 4 Feb 1984 (MIG 55:51). A nest containing young was found in McMinn Co. on 3 May 1901 (Ijams and Hofferbert 1934); however, the accuracy of this record is questionable because the nest tree was described as an oak. A small colony was discovered in Cherokee National Forest, Polk Co., in 1986.

Substantiation: Specimen: 1 male, Pocahontas, McNairy Co., 31 July 1939 (LSUMZ, 76015).

Northern Flicker, *Colaptes auratus*

Status: Regular.

Abundance: Fairly common permanent resident.

Remarks: Found in wooded areas, along woodland edge and in open areas. Often found foraging on the ground. A widely distributed nesting species. More numerous in the winter due to arrival of migrants from northern breeding grounds. An apparent hybrid of the "Yellow-shafted" and "Red-shafted" forms of this species was observed in Memp. from 25 Dec 1959 to 1 Jan 1960 (MIG 30:60). On 18 Dec 1983, two birds were identified as being "Red-shafted" Flickers at Memp. (MIG 55:43). High counts: 221 on 21 Dec 1975, Memp. CBC (MIG 47:36); and 61 on 19 Dec 1976, Chat. CBC (MIG 48:32).

Substantiation: Specimen: 1 male, Clarksville, Montgomery Co., 31 May 1943 (LSUMZ, 75872).

Pileated Woodpecker, *Dryocopus pileatus*

Status: Regular.

Abundance: Fairly common permanent resident.

Remarks: Found in mature wooded areas. A widely distributed nesting species. Drumming sound is distinctive and more easily recognized than the drumming of other woodpecker species. High counts: 112 on 15 Dec 1979, Ashland City CBC (MIG 51:32); 60 on 18 Dec 1982, Reelfoot L. CBC (MIG 54:13) and 38 on 30 Dec 1984, GSMNP CBC (MIG 56:7).

Substantiation: Specimen: 1 male, Nash., Davidson Co., 20 Oct 1948 (LSUMZ, 75889).

[Ivory-billed Woodpecker, *Campephilus principalis*]
Status: Hypothetical (Federally Endangered).
Remarks: Ganier (1933), relying on records of this woodpecker's former occurrence in neighboring states, included this species on his state list, listing it as an exterminated (extirpated) species. John James Audubon saw two Ivory-billed Woodpeckers on the Mississippi River on 24 Nov 1820 north of Fulton, Lauderdale Co. (Deaderick 1940); however, there is no indication of whether the birds were observed on the east or west bank.

ORDER PASSERIFORMES

FAMILY TYRANNIDAE: Tyrant Flycatchers

Olive-sided Flycatcher, *Contopus borealis*
Status: Regular.
Abundance: East: rare migrant, locally rare summer resident.
Middle and West: rare migrant.
Spring: Early May to late May.
  Arrivals: 11 Apr 1965, near Greeneville, MIG 36:64
            24 Apr 1965, Radnor L., BNA:31
            7 May 1985, Fort Pillow S.P., MIG 56:74
  Departures: 24 May 1942, Shelby Co., MIG 13:43
            24 May 1954, Knoxville, MIG 25:54
            31 May 1986, Hickman Co., MIG 57:79
Summer: Has occasionally been found in the summer in Carter Co., but is more regularly reported from the GSMNP, where it is usually found at elevations of 1,060 m or higher (Stupka 1963). Representative sightings include:
  5-6 June 1979, GSMNP, MIG 50:90
  8 June 1975, GSMNP, MIG 46:91
  17, 19 June 1977, Roan Mt., Carter Co., MIG 48:107
  4 July 1972, GSMNP, MIG 43:80
  7 July 1972, Iron Mt., Carter Co., MIG 43:80
A nest, the only one documented for the state, was found on 30 June 1974 in the GSMNP near the Alum Cave Bluff trail, at 1,350 m MSL. The nest was placed in a red spruce 30 m above the ground and held three young (Williams 1976). Williams (1976) noted that he could not locate the birds from the Newfound Gap area to Clingman's Dome, where they were found more regularly in previous years (Stupka 1963).

Olive-sided Flycatcher, continued
Fall: Mid Aug to late Sept.
    Arrivals: 26 July 1969, Heaton Creek, Carter Co., MIG 40:70
                    30 July 1974, Grundy Co., MIG 45:102
                    8 Aug 1943, Memp., MIG 14:52
    Departures: 25 Sept 1979, Dyersburg, MIG 51:16
                    3 Oct 1983, Rutherford Co., MIG 55:21
                    6 Oct 1954, Johnson City, MIG 25:67
Remarks: Found along woodland edge and in clearings, usually at the top of a dead snag or limb. Formerly more numerous in the GSMNP (Stupka 1963). High count: four on 24 May 1986, Overton Co. (MIG 57:79).
Substantiation: Specimen: 1, Clarksville, Montgomery Co., spring 1964 (APSU, 1216).

Eastern Wood-Pewee, *Contopus virens*
Status: Regular.
Abundance: Common migrant and summer resident.
Spring: Arrives by mid Apr.
    Arrivals: 31 Mar 1968, Reelfoot L., MIG 39:42
                    1 Apr 1975, Knoxville, MIG 46:68
                    8 Apr 1978, Percy Priest L., MIG 49:68
Summer: A widespread woodland nesting species across the state. Commonly found at low elevations in the eastern mountains, but generally absent from elevations above 1,500 m.
Fall: Departs by mid Oct.
    Departures: 14 Oct 1967, Hardin Co., MIG 38:94
                    28 Oct 1984, Nash., MIG 56:21
                    20 Nov 1967, Elizabethton, MIG 38:101
Remarks: Found in wooded areas. Its song is often imitated by European Starlings. High count: fifty-nine on 5 May 1946, Elizabethton SBC (MIG 17:24).
Substantiation: Specimen: 1 female, Unicoi Mts., Monroe Co., 17 June 1946 (LSUMZ, 76083).

Yellow-bellied Flycatcher, *Empidonax flaviventris*
Status: Regular.
Abundance: Rare migrant.
Spring: Mid May to late May.
    Arrivals: 3 May 1983, Memp., MIG 54:60
                    6 May 1975, Daus, Sequatchie Co., MIG 46:68
                    9 May 1984, Radnor L., BNA:31
    Departures: 23 May 1968, Savannah, Hardin Co., MIG 39:63
                    23 May 1972, Erwin, Unicoi Co., MIG 43:80
                    26 May 1961, Nash., BNA:31

Yellow-bellied Flycatcher, continued

Fall: Late Aug to late Sept.

Arrivals: 8 Aug 1936, Nash., BNA:31

19 Aug 1942, Memp., MIG 13:43

19 Aug 1972, Roans Creek, Johnson Co. (*fide* RLK)

Departures: 9 Oct 1973, Johnson City, MIG 44:102

10 Oct 1981, Norris, MIG 53:20

14 Oct 1961, Nash., (Laskey 1962)

Remarks: Found in wooded areas and along woodland edge. All sight records should be based on singing birds; otherwise, should usually not be identified unless measurements of a bird in the hand are taken. Species appears to be encountered more often in bird banders' nets than it is found singing in the wild. High count: four birds found dead on 6 Oct 1954, Chat. (MIG 25:67).

Substantiation: Specimen: 1 female, Nash., Davidson Co., 17 Sept 1944 (LSUMZ, 76060).

Acadian Flycatcher, *Empidonax virescens*

Status: Regular.

Abundance: Fairly common migrant and summer resident.

Spring: Arrives by late Apr.

Arrivals: 11 Apr 1972, Nash., MIG 43:51

16 Apr 1967, Elizabethton, MIG 38:55

19 Apr 1975, Shelby Co., MIG 46:65

Summer: As a summer resident it is found nesting across the state. However, in the eastern mountains, it is usually not found at the higher elevations. An unusual record involved one bird as high as 1,200 m MSL on 9 June 1987, Roan Mt. (RLK). It is generally not found above 1,060 m MSL in the GSMNP (Stupka 1963).

Fall: Departs by late Sept.

Departures: 7 Oct 1951, Knoxville, (Howell and Tanner 1951)

16 Oct 1967, Nash., MIG 38:95

18 Oct 1972, Nash., MIG 43:100

Remarks: Found in mature forests and woodlands, especially in ravines and river bottom areas. High count: thirty-nine on 21 June 1980, Hatchie NWR SBC, (MIG 51:56).

Substantiation: Specimen: 1 male, Nash., Davidson Co., 3 Sept 1965 (LSUMZ, 76070).

Alder Flycatcher, *Empidonax alnorum*

Status: Irregular.

Abundance: East: rare migrant, locally uncommon summer resident.

Middle and West: rare migrant.

Remarks: Reported from west Tennessee without a description of song or other means of identification between 1950 and 1956. This species and the Willow Flycatcher were once considered a single species—the Traill's Flycatcher. First

Alder Flycatcher, continued

reliable sight record of an Alder Flycatcher was of a singing bird on 10, 16 May 1959 in Knox Co. (Elson 1960). There are at least eight sight records for middle and west Tennessee:

26-27 Apr 1975, Nash. SBC, MIG 46:57
11 May 1988, Cross Creeks NWR, MIG 59:98
14 May 1988, LBL, MIG 59:98
15 May 1976, Ashland City Marsh, MIG 47:76
19 May 1988, Cross Creeks NWR, MIG 59:98
19 May 1988, Shelby Co., MIG 59:95
29 May 1988, Cross Creeks NWR, MIG 59:98
31 May 1987, Lawrence Co., MIG 58:98

Found nesting at 1,500 to 1,800 m MSL on Roan Mt., Carter Co., on 24 June 1978 (MIG 49:95-96) and has been observed there annually thereafter; a nest with eggs was found in June 1988 (Brenda Hull). As many as seven singing males have been found at this site (MIG 55:95). The birds were found nesting in alder thickets (Lura 1979). The earliest arrival date at this breeding site is 14 May 1988 (MIG 59:103). The birds usually stay very low in thick vegetation (usually alder or blackberry shrubs) and are difficult to locate when not singing; they usually sing through mid July. Other sightings in east Tennessee include:

25-26 Apr 1981, Chat. SBC, MIG 52:65
14 May 1984, Cumberland Co., MIG 55:73
25 May 1987, Chat., MIG 58:103

Two birds collected on 23 May 1895 (BNA:31) and 7 Sept 1943 in Davidson Co. are reported to be this species. In the fall, Alder and Willow Flycatchers are not readily separated by bird banders, and are often identified as "Traill's." The presence of these birds at banding stations is often noted through late Sept, and occasionally into Oct.

Substantiation: Specimen: 1, near Nash., Davidson Co., 7 Sept 1943 (LSUMZ, 8769).

Willow Flycatcher, *Empidonax traillii*

Status: Regular. (Map A-30)
Abundance: East and Middle: uncommon migrant and summer resident.
West: rare migrant and summer resident.
Spring: Arrives by early May.
Arrivals: 20 Apr 1986, Stewart Co., MIG 57:79
                   7 May 1944, Carter Co., (Herndon 1950)
                   19 May 1988, Shelby Co., MIG 59:95
Summer: Nesting birds were first noted in 1958 in Carter Co. (Herndon 1958) and a general westward expansion took place thereafter with nesting birds being found in Davidson Co. by 1972 (MIG 43:76). Nesting has been documented in Blount, Campbell, Hancock, Johnson, Knox, Sullivan, and Washington Counties. Nests were also found in the HRA in 1969 (MIG

Willow Flycatcher, continued

40:70), and at Cross Creeks NWR (Stewart Co.) and Britton Ford (Henry Co.) in 1988 (JCR). In addition, in recent years birds have been found regularly during the summer months in Montgomery Co. (MIG 54:88), Maury Co. (MIG 56:110) and Shelby Co.

Fall: In the fall, Willow and Alder Flycatchers are not readily separated by bird banders, and are often identified as "Traill's." The presence of these birds at banding stations is often noted through late Sept, and occasionally into Oct. Singing Willows are not often found after July.

Departures: 1 Aug 1975, Maury Co., MIG 47:19
               1 Aug 1945, Carter Co., (Herndon 1950)
               17 Aug 1972, Davidson Co., (Goodpasture and Alsop 1972)

Remarks: Found in shrubby areas, usually near water or willow thickets. A bird collected at Memp. and identified as *E. t. trailli* on 27 Aug 1944 (Ganier 1945) is most likely this species. This species and the Alder Flycatcher were once considered a single species—the Traill's Flycatcher. Singing Willow Flycatchers were identified in Carter Co. as early as 7 May 1944 (Herndon 1950). Rarely recorded in the west, but observations there are increasing. Noted in June in Obion Co. and at Reelfoot L. in 1976 (Pitts 1982b), in 1981 (MIG 52:96) and in 1982 (MIG 53:87). Ten birds were found singing on 23 May 1987 in Henry Co. at Britton Ford (MIG 58:93); and one bird was heard on 31 May 1987 in Weakley Co. (MIG 58:137). High count: eleven on 30 May 1987, Cross Creeks NWR (JCR).

Substantiation: Specimen: 1, Nash., Davidson Co., 11 Sept 1948 (LSUMZ, 76074).

Least Flycatcher, *Empidonax minimus*

Status: Regular.

Abundance: East: uncommon migrant, locally uncommon summer resident. Middle and West: uncommon migrant.

Spring: Late Apr to late May.

Arrivals: 19 Apr 1968, Hardin Co., MIG 39:42
               20 Apr 1946, Gatlinburg, (Stupka 1963)
               23 Apr 1968, Nash., MIG 39:43

Departures: 26 May 1986, Jackson Co., MIG 57:79
               27 May 1971, Memp., MIG 42:68
               1 June 1985, Scott Co., MIG 56:113

Summer: Stupka (1963) noted it as an uncommon summer resident in the GSMNP and described nest records from Gatlinburg during the 1950-1953 period. Bellrose (1938) saw an ad. feeding young on 2 Sept 1938 at an elevation of 760 m MSL in the GSMNP; another observation of an ad. feeding young in the Park occurred at Siler's Bald, Sevier Co., on 7 July 1987 (MIG 58:147). On Roan Mt., where nesting evidence was found in 1981 and 1988 (RLK), it becomes a locally common summer resident at middle elevations (i.e., 900-1,500 m MSL). It is locally uncommon at similar elevations on

Least Flycatcher, continued

other mountain areas in northeast Tennessee. One to two birds were observed carrying nest material at an elevation of 550 m MSL in Carter Co. (Herndon 1950a) but no nest was subsequently found. Summer records of note are:

7 May-16 July 1950, Carter Co., (Herndon 1950a)

12 June 1988, Monterey, Putnam Co. (BHS)

22 June-23 July 1968, GSMNP, MIG 39:67

20-21 June 1987, Bledsoe Co., MIG 58:145

7, 21 June 1970, Campbell Co., MIG 41:71

Fall: Late Aug to late Sept.

Arrivals: 4 Aug 1949, Knox Co., (Howell and Monroe 1958)

17 Aug 1969, Two Jays, MIG 40:90

27 Aug 1944, Mud L., MIG 15:55

Departures: 1 Oct 1980, Norris, MIG 52:25

4 Oct 1968, Hardin Co., MIG 39:89

5 Oct 1965, Nash., BNA:31

Remarks: Usually found in brushy habitats and along woodland edge, but may also occur in woodland interior. All sight records, especially in the fall, should be based on singing birds; otherwise, should not be identified unless measurements of a bird in the hand are taken. The presence of this species on the Cumberland Plateau during the breeding season needs to be quantified. High count: thirty-two on 2 May 1954, Roan Mt. SBC (MIG 25:30).

Substantiation: Specimen: 1 female, Nash., Davidson Co., 27 Sept 1949 (LSUMZ, 76081).

Eastern Phoebe, *Sayornis phoebe*

Status: Regular.

Abundance: Fairly common summer resident, uncommon winter resident.

Remarks: Found along creeks and woodland edge, usually near water; nests statewide under culverts and bridges or in abandoned buildings and barns. Becomes slightly less detectable in the west where Coffey (1943) regarded it as not present in the summer from about Memp. southward. A common summer resident in the GSMNP up to an elevation of 900 m MSL (Stupka 1963). Coffey (1963) found phoebes up to elevations of 790 m MSL in northeast Tennessee, where the birds nest from Apr through July. A few individuals occasionally occur at higher elevations. Found in small but consistent numbers statewide during the winter, with fewer birds being found at the higher altitudes. Most sightings in the winter are made in Dec, primarily on CBCs; found in lower numbers in Jan, but an influx of birds is usually detectable by Feb. Representative winter records include:

25 Jan 1953, Elizabethton, MIG 24:17

8 on 31 Dec 1950, Kingsport CBC, MIG 21:76

22 on 30 Dec 1973, GSMNP CBC, MIG 45:12

24 on 1 Jan 1983, Hiwassee CBC, MIG 54:13

Eastern Phoebe, continued
>2 on 2 Jan 1987, Henry Co., MIG 58:53
>
>1 on 1 Feb 1987, Dyer Co., MIG 58:53
>
>3 on 14 Feb 1987, Reelfoot L., MIG 58:53
>
>High count: fifty-six on 30 Apr 1967, Knoxville SBC (MIG 38:33).

Substantiation: Specimen: 1 male, Reelfoot L., 8 May 1961 (LSUMZ, 76043).

Say's Phoebe, *Sayornis saya*
Status: Accidental.
Remarks: Two records: one bird was reported at Radnor L., Davidson Co., on
27 and 30 Sept 1984, and another bird was found on 29 Sept 1985 at Metro
Center, Nash. (MIG 57:28). Only the 1985 sighting was confirmed by the
Tennessee Bird Records Committee. Additional sightings, if they occur,
should also be in the fall.
Substantiation: Photographs: 1, Nash., Davidson Co., 29 Sept 1985 (TBRC).

Vermilion Flycatcher, *Pyrocephalus rubinus*
Status: Extremely Rare.
Remarks: At least nine state records. All of the records are of birds found near
major rivers, and all but two of the sightings are from the Mississippi River
floodplain. First recorded on 15 Oct 1961 when two males were present at
Reelfoot L. in Obion Co. (Smith 1965). Secondhand reports of birds found
at Reelfoot L. in Dec 1961, Dec 1966 and on 14 May 1960 are described by
Leggett (1969). All other sight records follow:
>20 Sept 1987, 1 imm. male, Island 13, MIG 59:32
>
>26-28 Sept 1987, 1 imm. male, Austin Springs, MIG 59:41
>
>30 Sept 1973, 1 female, Lauderdale Co., MIG 44:99
>
>21-22 Oct 1964, 1 imm. male, Knoxville, (Owen 1965)
>
>23 Nov-8 Dec 1968, 1 male, Reelfoot L., MIG 40:19
>
>1 Dec 1984, 1 imm. male, Shelby Co., MIG 56:48
>
>27 Dec 1967, 1 ad. male, Reelfoot L., (Hogg 1968)
>
>12 May 1970, Dyersburg, MIG 41:68

Substantiation: Adequately documented sight records.

Ash-throated Flycatcher, *Myiarchus cinerascens*
Status: Accidental (Provisional).
Remarks: Known from one record: one bird was found on the 22 Dec 1985
Kingsport CBC. The details of the sighting were accepted by the Tennessee
Bird Records Committee (Nicholson and Stedman 1988).
Substantiation: Adequately documented sight record (TBRC).

Great Crested Flycatcher, *Myiarchus crinitus*
Status: Regular.
Abundance: Fairly common migrant and summer resident.

Great Crested Flycatcher, continued
Spring: Arrives by mid Apr.
    Arrivals: 27 Mar 1954, Shelby Co., MIG 25:51
                        2 Apr 1967, Rutherford Co., (DeVore 1975)
                        11 Apr 1965, Chat., MIG 36:63
Summer: An inhabitant of most wooded areas throughout summer. In northeast Tennessee, it is regularly found up to about 1,600 m MSL (Eller and Wallace 1984). Ganier and Clebsch (1946) did not find it nesting at the higher altitudes in the Unicoi mountains, but noted one bird as high as 1,200 m MSL. Nests are described from near Washington Co. ca. 1930 (Lyle and Tyler 1934) and Hamilton Co. (Wight 1934) westward to Gibson Co. (Knox 1945) and Shelby Co. (MIG 14:40).
Fall: Departs by mid Sept.
    Departures: 27 Sept 1970, Nash., MIG 41:85
                        29 Sept 1984, Unicoi Co., MIG 56:27
                        8 Nov 1974, Woodbury, Cannon Co., MIG 46:71
Remarks: Found in wooded areas and along woodland edge. Nests in cavities and may sometimes utilize Wood Duck nest boxes or other artificial nest structures. Birds found in the late fall or winter should be closely examined since vagrant Ash-throated Flycatchers occasionally appear in the eastern U.S. at that time (Murphy 1982). High count: sixty-two on 26 Apr 1964, Knoxville SBC (MIG 35:46).
Substantiation: Specimen: 1 female, Winchester, Franklin Co., 7 June 1949 (LSUMZ, 76041).

Variegated Flycatcher, *Empidonomus varius*
Status: Accidental.
Remarks: A bird identified from photographs was present from 13-15 May 1984 at a site east of Reelfoot L. in Obion Co.
Substantiation: Photographs: 1, Obion Co., May 1984 (*Birding* 16(5): back cover, 1984 issue).

Western Kingbird, *Tyrannus verticalis*
Status: Extremely Rare.
Remarks: Usually found in open country. About 18 state records. First recorded on 24 May 1947, Shady Valley, Johnson Co. (Tyler and Lyle 1947). Only two other spring sightings: 10-11 May 1958, Reelfoot L. SBC (MIG 29:31), and 6 June 1988, Shelby Co. (JRW). All other records occurred in the fall, primarily from mid Sept to mid Oct. These sightings follow:
    24 Aug 1972, Reelfoot L., MIG 43:98
    3 Sept 1981, Nash., MIG 53:16
    5 Sept 1986, HRA, MIG 58:28
    14 Sept 1985, Island 13, MIG 57:23
    15-18 Sept 1987, Memp., MIG 59:32
    20 Sept 1983, Elizabethton, MIG 55:27

Western Kingbird, continued
>22-26 Sept 1988, Bartlett, Shelby Co. (JRW)
>
>25-26 Sept 1971, Percy Priest L., (Bierly et al. 1973a)
>
>28-30 Sept 1960, Davidson Co., MIG 32:4
>
>30 Sept 1978, Oak Ridge, MIG 50:23
>
>1-2 Oct 1957, Gatlinburg, (Stupka 1963)
>
>1-5 Oct 1983, Rutherford Co., MIG 55:21
>
>7-10 Oct 1968, Woodbury, Cannon Co., MIG 39:90
>
>8 Oct 1953, near Nash., (Goodpasture 1954a)
>
>9-16 Oct 1969, Clay Co., MIG 40:90

Most sightings are of one to two birds; high count: three on 10 Oct 1969, Lilydale, Clay Co. (MIG 40:90).

Substantiation: Adequately documented sight records.

Eastern Kingbird, *Tyrannus tyrannus*

Status: Regular.

Abundance: Common migrant and summer resident, very rare winter visitor.

Spring: Arrives by early Apr.

>Arrivals: 12 Mar 1961, Nash., MIG 32:5
>
>17 Mar 1964, Bristol, MIG 35:41
>
>31 Mar 1952, Memp., MIG 23:32

Summer: Nests throughout the state but is generally absent from the higher elevations of the eastern mountains.

Fall: Departs by mid Sept. There is one Nov record: 13 Nov 1971, Tennessee NWR, Humphreys Co. (MIG 43:25).

>Departures: 10 Oct 1965, Two Jays, MIG 36:94
>
>13 Oct 1974, Lawrence Co., MIG 46:20
>
>22 Oct 1972, Austin Springs, MIG 43:102

Winter: One record: 21 Dec 1968 to 30 Mar 1969, Norris (MIG 40:49).

Remarks: Found in open country and along field edges and roadsides. Often seen chasing and harassing crows and hawks. Occasionally, large numbers can be found in the fall (e.g., 1,000 on 28 Aug 1980, Memp., MIG 52:23; and 120 on 30 Aug 1984, HRA, MIG 56:25). A notable spring count was 322 on 15 May 1955, Memp. (MIG 26:47). High count: 5,000 on 5 Sept 1937, Mud L. (MIG 8:57).

Substantiation: Specimen: 1 female, Clarksville, Montgomery Co., 5 May 1940 (LSUMZ, 76029).

Scissor-tailed Flycatcher, *Tyrannus forficatus*

Status: Irregular.

Abundance: Rare migrant, very rare summer resident.

Remarks: Found in open country. About 40 state records, the majority of which has been made since 1980. This rare over-migrant can be expected anytime from Apr through Nov. First recorded on 26 Apr 1964 at Mud L. (Carpenter 1964). Nested unsuccessfully at Murfreesboro, Rutherford Co.,

Scissor-tailed Flycatcher, continued

where three young were found in a nest in July 1978 (MIG 49:92). At least one bird was found annually at this site from 1979 through 1985, with two juveniles being observed from 11 Aug-7 Sept 1983; no nest was found in 1983 (MIG 55:21). The only records from the east are of one bird on 18 May 1980, Jefferson Co. (MIG 51:94) and one to two birds observed in the southern Meigs Co./HRA/Blythe Ferry area each fall from 1983 through 1986. These birds were observed as early as 13 Aug 1986 (MIG 58:28) and as late as 24 Nov 1984 (MIG 57:35). A number of records also exists for the Memp. area and the Reelfoot L. area. Some representative dates include:

8 Apr 1975, Shelby Co., MIG 46:65
25 Apr 1985, Cedars of Lebanon S.P., MIG 56:110
5 May 1972, Sumner Co., MIG 43:51
12 May 1984, Old Hickory L., MIG 55:70
16 May 1970, Tiptonville, Lake Co., MIG 41:68
20 May 1976, Memp., MIG 47:99
24 June 1983, Haywood Co., MIG 54:86
15 Nov 1982, Lake Co., MIG 54:20

Substantiation: Photograph: 1 ad., LBL, Stewart Co., 1 June 1987 (Larry Doyle—TBRC).

FAMILY ALAUDIDAE: **Larks**

Horned Lark, *Eremophila alpestris*
Status: Regular.
Abundance: East and Middle: rare summer resident, uncommon winter resident.
West: fairly common permanent resident.
Remarks: Found in open country and agricultural fields. A year-round inhabitant of west Tennessee, especially within the Mississippi River valley between Memp. and Reelfoot L. Ganier (1933) regarded it as a fairly common winter resident in the east and middle, but the current winter abundance (Oct-May) of larks indicates it is not as numerous today as it was fifty years ago. Frequently not recorded on many of the CBCs east of the Tennessee River; of 138 CBCs conducted in the middle and east from 1980 through 1986, Horned Larks were only found on forty-nine (35%) counts. Rare outside of west Tennessee in the summer. Nesting in the east has been recorded as high as 1,800 m MSL on Roan Mt. (Tyler 1936). A review of *The Migrant* resulted in satisfactory breeding documentation in the following additional counties of east and middle Tennessee: Cumberland, Davidson, Franklin, Hamilton, Houston, Humphreys, Knox, Maury, Pickett, Rutherford,

Horned Lark, continued

Washington, and Williamson. Stupka (1963) described a nest record in 1953 in the GSMNP, Blount Co. The species may still nest in the east and middle at some of the large airports or fallow fields. The "Northern" race, *E. a. alpestris*, occurs in the state; as many as seventy-five were at Clarksville on 14 Nov 1942 (Clebsch 1943), and eight birds were noted in northeast Tennessee on 1 Feb 1936 (Tyler and Lyle 1936). High count: two thousand on 30 Jan 1978, Coffee Co. (MIG 49:43).

Substantiation: Specimen: 1 female, Nash., Davidson Co., 26 Jan 1936 (LSUMZ, 76109).

FAMILY HIRUNDINIDAE: Swallows

Purple Martin, *Progne subis*
Status: Regular.
Abundance: Fairly common to common migrant and summer resident.
Spring: Arrives by late Feb.

Arrivals: 2 Feb 1964, Chat., MIG 35:16
              8 Feb 1987, Memp., MIG 58:53
              12 Feb 1984, Byrdstown, MIG 55:46

Summer: A widespread nesting species but generally absent from the higher mountain elevations in the east. Beginning in late summer, large numbers gather into huge roosts prior to migrating south (e.g., 1,000 on 21 July 1956, Memp., MIG 27:67; 1,100 on 21 July 1968, Cookeville, MIG 39:64; and 810 on 31 July 1986, Stewart Co. [JCR]).

Fall: Departs by mid Sept.

Departures: 23 Sept 1988, Elizabethton (*fide* Glen D. Eller)
              1 Oct 1983, Ashland City, BNA:32
              12 Oct 1968, Reelfoot L., MIG 39:89

Remarks: Found in open and semi-open areas, frequently near water or where nesting structures have been erected. High counts: ten thousand on 30 July 1979, HRA (MIG 50:89) and six thousand on 30 July 1973, HRA (MIG 44:87).

Substantiation: Specimen: 1 male, Kingston Springs, Cheatham Co., 1 July 1916 (LSUMZ, 76144).

Tree Swallow, *Tachycineta bicolor*
Status: Regular. (Map A-31)
Abundance: Fairly common migrant, uncommon summer resident, very rare winter visitor.

Tree Swallow, continued
Spring: Arrives by early Mar.
    Arrivals: 10 Feb 1975, Tennessee NWR, MIG 46:44
                  23 Feb 1971, Savannah Bay, (Dubke 1975)
                  4 Mar 1987, Paris Landing S.P. (JCR)
Summer: Standing dead trees (snags) in or near water provide suitable nesting
    habitat. First nest of this species in Tennessee was discovered at Reelfoot L.
    on 22 May 1918 (Ganier 1964). No additional nests were reported until 1968,
    when active nests were found at the Norris L. dam, Anderson Co. (Olson
    1968) and at Monsanto Ponds, Maury Co. (Gray 1968). Nicholson and Pitts
    (1982) noted that only one nesting season observation of Tree Swallows was
    made between 1918 and 1960. Tree Swallow nests have been reported almost
    annually since 1967 (Nicholson and Pitts 1982) and the species has expanded
    its range with nests being recorded in the following counties: Benton,
    Blount, Cocke, Cumberland, Davidson, Dyer, Greene, Humphreys, Jefferson,
    Johnson, Knox, Lake, Lawrence, Shelby, Smith, Stewart, Warren, and
    Washington. Breeding in additional counties is likely.
Fall: Becomes locally common in west Tennessee along the Mississippi River,
    where flocks of a thousand or more birds can occasionally be found from
    Aug through Oct. Departs by late Oct.
    Departures: 16 Nov 1968, Holston River, MIG 40:23
                  26 Nov 1986, Cross Creeks NWR, MIG 58:24
                  28 Nov 1971, Reelfoot L., MIG 43:23
Winter: At least six records:
    20 Dec 1986, Reelfoot L. CBC, MIG 58:3
    24 Dec 1971, Reelfoot L. CBC, MIG 43:12
    27 Dec 1968, Reelfoot L. CBC, MIG 39:77
    6 Jan 1975, Savannah Bay, MIG 46:46
    17 Jan 1985, Chickamauga L., MIG 56:56
    19 Jan 1976, HRA, MIG 47:48
Remarks: Found near or over water. Occasionally nests in bluebird boxes or
    other artificial structures. High counts: 500,000 on 18 Oct 1970, Reelfoot L.
    (MIG 41:83); 80,000 on 18 Oct 1936, Shelby Co. (MIG 7:98); and 11,000 on
    12 Oct 1968, Reelfoot L. (MIG 39:89).
Substantiation: Specimen: 1 male, Reelfoot L., 22 May 1918 (LSUMZ, 76119).

Northern Rough-winged Swallow, *Stelgidopteryx serripennis*
Status: Regular.
Abundance: Uncommon migrant and summer resident.
Spring: Arrives by mid Mar.
    Arrivals: 1 Mar 1984, Maury Co., MIG 55:70
                  11 Mar 1986, Blount Co., MIG 57:85
                  17 Mar 1935, Mud L., MIG 6:12
Summer: Statewide in distribution. Nests in excavated burrows (dirt banks) or
    in crevices (rock banks). Breeding sites are often under bridges or in the

Northern Rough-winged Swallow, continued

banks overlooking streams, creeks or rivers; Bierly (1980) noted that rock cliffs created during the construction of interstate roads are also used for nesting sites. An ad. with three young was found in the GSMNP at an elevation of 1,600 m MSL (Savage 1964).

Fall: Departs by late Sept.

Departures: 23 Oct 1949, Shelby Co., MIG 20:68

3 Nov 1963, Greeneville, MIG 34:75

25 Nov 1983, Cross Creeks NWR, MIG 55:21

Remarks: Found along creeks and streams and, in migration, near or over water. High counts: 2,000 on 28 Aug 1968, Reelfoot L. (MIG 39:89) and 1,050 on 25 Apr 1987, Elizabethton SBC (MIG 58:82).

Substantiation: Specimen: 1 male, Perryville, Decatur Co., 28 June 1947 (LSUMZ, 19511).

Bank Swallow, *Riparia riparia*

Status: Regular. (Map A-32)

Abundance: Uncommon migrant, rare to uncommon summer resident.

Spring: Arrives by late Apr.

Arrivals: 21 Mar 1965, Coleman L., near Nash., BNA:32

9 Apr 1972, Erwin, Unicoi Co., MIG 43:54

12 Apr 1961, Dyer Co., MIG 32:41

Summer: Nesting birds are not frequently encountered, but several colonies exist at scattered locations, especially in west Tennessee. Two hundred nests were found at Heloise, Dyer Co., on 6 June 1954 (MIG 25:52) and 193 nests were counted at Island 21, Dyer Co., in 1978 (MIG 49:91). Nesting records have also been documented for Lake Co. (Pitts 1972), Lauderdale Co. (Coffey 1976) and Shelby Co., where the species was not found nesting until 1981 (Waldron 1981). Inactive nest holes were found in Cannon Co. in 1984 (MIG 55:92), and nesting reportedly occurred in Lawrence Co. sometime prior to 1986 (MIG 57:108). Active nest sites in isolated locations in Knox Co., Roane Co., Washington Co., and Hawkins Co. have been documented since about 1970. Nesting occurred as recently as 1986 at the Kingston Steam Plant (Roane Co.) and Mascot (Knox Co.) (MIG 57:113); and in 1988, an active breeding site was discovered at the John Sevier Steam Plant in Hawkins Co. (RLK). Nest burrows at the Roane Co. and Hawkins Co. steam plants were excavated in ash banks.

Fall: Departs by mid Sept.

Departures: 29 Sept 1980, HRA, MIG 52:25

14 Oct 1959, Bush L., MIG 31:11

26 Oct 1976, Shelby Co., MIG 48:18

Remarks: Found along rivers and exposed dirt embankments; nests in colonies. High counts: 5,000 on 27 July 1968, Reelfoot L. (MIG 39:64); 3,000 on 31 July 1978, Reelfoot L. (MIG 49:91) and 2,250 on 9 Sept 1980, Douglas L. (MIG 52:25).

Bank Swallow, continued
Substantiation: Specimen: 1 female, near Ashport, Lauderdale Co., 22 June 1947 (LSUMZ, 76124).

Cliff Swallow, *Hirundo pyrrhonota*
Status: Regular. (Map A-33)
Abundance: Fairly common migrant and summer resident.
Spring: Arrives by late Mar.
    Arrivals: 6 Mar 1974, Tennessee NWR, MIG 45:20
                    10 Mar 1987, Chat., MIG 58:104
                    30 Mar 1986, Paris Landing S.P., MIG 57:74
Summer: First reported nesting occurred in Stewart Co. and Decatur Co. in May 1936 (Ganier and Weakley 1936). Since then the species has greatly expanded its range eastward and northeastward with nesting colonies in upper east Tennessee being discovered by the 1970s (Alsop 1981). This expansion in breeding range appears strongly tied to areas along the Tennessee and Cumberland Rivers (Alsop 1981). Fewer nests are reported in the west. A review of *The Migrant* resulted in satisfactory breeding documentation for more than thirty counties throughout the state.
Fall: Departs by early Sept.
    Departures: 29 Sept 1980, HRA, MIG 52:25
                      23 Oct 1949, Memp., MIG 20:68
                      24 Oct 1958, Bush L., (Parmer 1959a)
Remarks: Usually found near water. Frequently nests under bridges, but may occasionally utilize the insides of barns, as well as exposed cliffs or rock bluffs and the mouths of large caves (West 1961a). High count: two thousand on 26 Aug 1936, Campbell Co. (MIG 7:73).
Substantiation: Specimen: 1 male, Savannah, Hardin Co., 4 July 1947 (LSUMZ, 19515).

Barn Swallow, *Hirundo rustica*
Status: Regular.
Abundance: Common migrant and summer resident, very rare winter visitor.
Spring: Arrives by late Mar.
    Arrivals: 5 Mar 1986, Lawrence Co., MIG 57:79
                    11 Mar 1974, Lamar, Washington Co., MIG 45:24
                    16 Mar 1977, Memp., MIG 48:75
Summer: Currently a widespread nesting species, although it was a very rare summer resident in the west ca. 1930 (Ganier 1933). Frequently found foraging around high elevation balds in the eastern mountains.
Fall: Departs by mid Oct.
    Departures: 3 Nov 1979, Savannah Bay, MIG 51:42
                      18 Nov 1983, Woods Res., MIG 55:21
                      19 Nov 1961, near Mud L., MIG 33:12

Barn Swallow, continued

Winter: Two records: 18 Dec 1976, Lebanon CBC (MIG 48:32) and 22-23 Dec 1978, Samburg, Obion Co. (MIG 50:41).

Remarks: Found in open country and agricultural areas, often near water. Frequently nests in open barns, under bridges or on the sides of buildings. High count: 1,080 on 25 Apr 1987, Elizabethton SBC (MIG 58:82).

Substantiation: Specimen: 1, Nash., Davidson Co., 10 June 1950 (LSUMZ, 76129).

FAMILY CORVIDAE: Jays and Crows

Blue Jay, *Cyanocitta cristata*

Status: Regular.

Abundance: Common permanent resident.

Remarks: Found in wooded and urban areas. Nests throughout the state. In the east, it is rare along the summits of Roan Mt.; however, Stupka (1963) reported it as breeding at all elevations in the GSMNP; and Ganier and Clebsch (1946) considered it fairly common in the Unicoi Mountains.

Migrant flocks can be found in the spring but are especially numerous in the fall; flocks of 200-240 were observed migrating in the fall of 1974 near Chat. (MIG 46:23), and over 600 were observed migrating on 24 Sept 1978 in Knox Co. (MIG 50:23). High count: 880 on 10 Oct 1982, near Chat. (MIG 54:25).

Substantiation: Specimen: 1 female, Nash., Davidson Co., 2 Sept 1966 (LSUMZ, 76162).

American Crow, *Corvus brachyrhynchos*

Status: Regular.

Abundance: Common permanent resident.

Remarks: Found in a variety of open country, urban and woodland edge habitats. Nests throughout the state. Generally less numerous on top of Roan Mt. during the nesting season. Regularly encountered at high elevations in the GSMNP. Often seen chasing and harassing owls and hawks. Winter roosts occur frequently and occasionally consist of over 10,000 birds. Roosts of 25,000 birds on 27 Dec 1960, Reelfoot L. CBC (MIG 31:76) and 35,000 birds on 26 Dec 1965, Nash. CBC (MIG 36:89) are particularly notable.

Substantiation: Specimen: 1 male, Memp., Shelby Co., 21 Dec 1952 (LSUMZ, 19160).

Fish Crow, *Corvus ossifragus*
Status: Regular.
Abundance: West: locally uncommon permanent resident.
Remarks: Found along the Mississippi River and in open and wooded areas adjacent to the River. Apparently the first state record was of two birds at Shelby Forest, Shelby Co., on 2 Aug 1931 (Coffey 1942). Nests are difficult to locate. Four nests were discovered in Shelby Co. in Apr 1980 (MIG 51:60); probably nests in small numbers in Dyer, Lauderdale and Lake Counties. Generally absent from the northern part of its range in the winter from late Oct through Feb, although it is occasionally observed at Reelfoot L. (e.g., 28 Dec 1966, MIG 37:65 and 26 Dec 1969, MIG 41:8); returns by mid Mar. Most winter records are from Shelby Co. Flocks exceeding a hundred birds have been recently observed in Lauderdale Co. Only one record outside of west Tennessee: four birds on 10 Apr 1979, Savannah Bay, Hamilton Co. (MIG 50:71). High count: 960 on 21 Dec 1987, Lauderdale Co. (MIG 59:65). Other representative records follow:
    21 Jan 1974, Hatchie NWR, MIG 45:20
    172 on 23 Dec 1967, Memp. CBC, MIG 38:88
    165 on 13 Jan 1987, Lauderdale Co., MIG 58:54
    112 on 15 Feb 1987, Lauderdale Co., MIG 58:54
    11 Mar 1973, Lake Co., MIG 44:22
    15 Mar 1986, Tigrett WMA, Dyer Co. (JCR)
Substantiation: Specimen: 1 female, Memp., Shelby Co., 31 May 1942 (LSUMZ, 76205).

Common Raven, *Corvus corax*
Status: Regular (State Endangered).
Abundance: East: locally uncommon permanent resident.
Remarks: Found in the eastern mountain regions of east Tennessee from Sullivan and Carter Counties southwestward to Blount Co. Usually occurs at elevations of 909 m MSL and higher (Alsop 1980). Consistently found throughout its range, but never in large numbers. Rhoads (1895) cited reports by W. H. Fox, who observed the species in Rockwood, Roane Co., in 1886 and considered ravens as common at Lookout Mt., Hamilton Co., in 1882. The first nest of this species, located on 4 May 1960 on a mountain ledge in the GSMNP, Sevier Co., was described by Ganier (1962a). Almost all other nest records are from this area as well, including a nest with seven eggs on 9 Mar 1974 and active nests in 1975 and 1976 (Williams 1980); a nest with one young on 16 May 1980 (MIG 51:96); and a nest with four young on 20-26 May 1986 (MIG 57:87). A nest was discovered on 27 Apr 1985 at Ripshin L., Carter Co. (MIG 56:82). Occasionally observed at low elevations, especially in the Johnson City-Austin Springs area, where there are a number of recent records (*fide* RLK); sightings of note include single birds at Johnson City (492 m MSL) on 3 May 1978 (Phillips 1979) and 10

Common Raven, continued

Jan 1983 (MIG 54:46), and two birds at Austin Springs on 18 Jan 1982 (MIG 53:48). High count: 17 on 28 Dec 1985, Bristol CBC (MIG 57:11).
Substantiation: Specimen: 1, Roan Mt., Carter Co., July 1936 (LSUMZ, 76202).

FAMILY PARIDAE: Titmice and Chickadees

Black-capped Chickadee, *Parus atricapillus*
Status: Regular.
Abundance: East: locally fairly common permanent resident.
Remarks: Found in wooded habitat at high mountain elevations. Range in Tennessee is primarily restricted to the GSMNP, but occasionally it is found on other sites in the eastern mountain chain:
4 Dec 1966, Big Bald Mt., Unicoi Co., MIG 38:23
4 May 1971, Hump Mt., Carter Co., MIG 42:72
21 Nov-29 Feb 1975/76, Bristol, MIG 47:50
14 June-13 July 1978, Roan Mt., MIG 49:96
29 Dec 1980, Roan Mt. CBC, MIG 52:14
In the GSMNP, Black-caps generally occur above 1,200 m MSL during the nesting season; and as low as 600 m MSL during the winter. A few remain at these low altitudes until about the first week of May, at which time they apparently return to the higher elevations (Tanner 1952).
Substantiation: Specimen: 1, near Cosby, Cocke Co., 21 June 1937 (USNM, 351088).

Carolina Chickadee, *Parus carolinensis*
Status: Regular.
Abundance: Common permanent resident.
Remarks: Found in wooded areas and semi-open and urban habitats. An abundant and widespread breeding species that nests in a variety of natural and artificial cavities. In the eastern mountains, it is generally absent from elevations above 1,200 m MSL, usually occurring up to about 852 m MSL; however, on mountains where Black-capped Chickadees are absent, Carolinas may be found as high as 1,200 m MSL in the summer and up to 1,125 m MSL in the winter (Tanner 1952). Where both species are present (GSMNP) an altitudinal gap of about 180 m usually exists where no birds occur, thus suggesting interspecific competition (Tanner 1952). Often found in mixed species feeding flocks during the fall, winter and spring; during the fall and spring, the presence of migrating warblers is often revealed by the

Carolina Chickadee, continued

sound of calling chickadees. High counts: 495 on 21 Dec 1985, Chat. CBC (MIG 57:11); 435 on 27 Dec 1980, Nash. CBC (MIG 52:14); and 300 on 17 Dec 1977, Kingsport CBC (MIG 49:7).

Substantiation: Specimen: 1 male, Nash., Davidson Co., 17 Sept 1966 (LSUMZ, 76221).

Tufted Titmouse, *Parus bicolor*

Status: Regular.

Abundance: Common permanent resident.

Remarks: A widespread woodland nesting species statewide; also found in semi-open and urban habitats. Nests in cavities (occasionally in bluebird boxes). A common summer resident in the GSMNP up to an elevation of about 1,500 m MSL (Stupka 1963). Also occurs regularly at similar elevations on Roan Mt. (Eller and Wallace 1984). Often found in mixed species feeding flocks during the fall, winter and spring. High count: 417 on 28 Dec 1985, Clarksville CBC (MIG 57:11).

Substantiation: Specimen: 1 female, Nash., Davidson Co., 10 Oct 1965 (LSUMZ, 76254).

FAMILY SITTIDAE: **Nuthatches**

Red-breasted Nuthatch, *Sitta canadensis*

Status: Regular.

Abundance: East: uncommon migrant and winter resident, locally fairly common summer resident.

Middle and West: uncommon migrant and winter resident.

Fall: Migrants arrive by mid Sept.

Arrivals: 25 Aug 1968, Chat., MIG 39:93-94
               28 Aug 1968, Nash., BNA:33
               9 Sept 1975, Memp., MIG 47:17

Winter: An irruptive winter resident, appearing in large numbers during "invasion" years and present only in small to moderate numbers in other winters. Often found in mixed species feeding flocks with chickadees, titmice and creepers.

Spring: Departs by early May.

Departures: 10 May 1958, Reelfoot L. SBC, MIG 29:32
               14 May 1986, Knoxville, MIG 57:85
               20 May 1978, Nash., MIG 49:92

Summer: A permanent resident of the spruce-fir forests at the higher elevations in the eastern mountains. It is readily detected in the summer on Roan Mt.,

Red-breasted Nuthatch, continued

where Lyle and Tyler (1934) considered it an abundant species. Also occurs regularly during the summer in the GSMNP where Tanner (1955) found it above 1,060 m MSL in the Le Conte Creek Valley. Nests have been described from Roan Mt. (Carter Co.) at an elevation of 1,800 m MSL (Ganier 1936), and in the GSMNP (Sevier Co.) at an elevation of 1,860 m MSL (Ganier 1962a). The only nest record outside of the mountain elevations occurred at Knoxville in 1977 (Owen 1979).

Remarks: Found in wooded areas, primarily in coniferous woodlands. May also occur in deciduous woodlands, especially during migration. High counts: 175 on 1 Jan 1950, GSMNP CBC (MIG 20:62); 128 on 30 Dec 1981, Roan Mt. CBC (MIG 53:8); 122 on 21 Oct 1977, Roan Mt. (MIG 49:23); and 55 on 5 Jan 1958, Chickasaw S.P. (MIG 29:7).

Substantiation: Specimen: 1, Nash., Davidson Co., 5 Oct 1957 (LSUMZ, 76290).

White-breasted Nuthatch, *Sitta carolinensis*
Status: Regular.
Abundance: Fairly common permanent resident.
Remarks: Found in wooded areas. In the eastern mountains, where it is very infrequently encountered in the spruce-fir forests, Tanner (1955) found this species up to 1,370 m MSL in the Le Conte Creek Valley of the GSMNP during the breeding season; occurs elsewhere in the GSMNP up to 1,675 m MSL (Stupka 1963). It is generally found at similar elevations on Roan Mt. Often occurs with other woodland birds in mixed species feeding flocks. Breeding Bird Survey results from the 1966-1987 period indicate a general increase in the population across the state. High count: 112 on 22 Dec 1984, Nash. CBC (MIG 56:8).

Substantiation: Specimen: 1 male, Nash., Davidson Co., 24 Jan 1943 (LSUMZ, 76263).

Brown-headed Nuthatch, *Sitta pusilla*
Status: Regular.
Abundance: East: locally uncommon permanent resident.
Remarks: Found in open stands of mature pines; in Tennessee, appears to prefer shortleaf pine and loblolly pine (Haney 1981). First valid record of this species involved two birds on 14 Dec 1968 in Hamilton Co. northeast of Collegedale (Basham 1969). One bird was found again near this locality on 14 Mar 1971, and the species has been regularly reported in loose colonies in adjacent areas throughout the 1970s and 1980s. These sightings are considered to represent a recent extension of the species' breeding range (Haney 1981). Nesting evidence is supported by a nest with eggs found on 10 May 1977 at McDonald, Hamilton Co. (MIG 48:78), and an active nest at Cleveland, Bradley Co., in 1985 (MIG 56:80). Nesting has also been described for the Chickamauga L. dam area and Chester Frost Park, Hamilton Co.; eggs

Brown-headed Nuthatch, continued
are generally laid in late Apr or early May (Haney 1981). The only record
outside of the Hamilton Co. area is of five birds on 29 July 1974 at Fall
Creek Falls S.P., Van Buren Co. (MIG 45:102). Haney (1981) estimated the
1981 Tennessee population to be about 50-70 birds. High count: twenty on
21 Dec 1985, Chat. CBC (MIG 57:11).
Substantiation: Photograph: 1, Hamilton Co., 12 Apr 1981 (J. Christopher
Haney, MIG 52:81).

FAMILY CERTHIIDAE: **Creepers**

Brown Creeper, *Certhia americana*
Status: Regular.
Abundance: East: uncommon migrant and winter resident, locally uncommon
summer resident.
Middle and West: uncommon migrant and winter resident, very rare summer
resident.
Fall: Migrants arrive by early Oct.
Arrivals: 12 Aug 1982, Nash., MIG 54:22
                29 Aug 1986, Knoxville, MIG 58:29
                27 Sept 1941, Milan, Gibson Co., MIG 13:44
Winter: Generally found in small numbers statewide during the winter, even at
high mountain elevations. Occasionally, large numbers are reported on CBCs
(e.g., 31 on 30 Dec 1962, GSMNP CBC, MIG 33:69).
Spring: Departs by late Apr.
Departures: 10 May 1937, Reelfoot L., (Pickering 1937)
              10 May 1980, Murfreesboro SBC, MIG 51:56
              21 May 1969, Elizabethton, MIG 40:70
Summer: Breeds in the GSMNP where active nests were found as early as 1886
(Stupka 1963). Found by Tanner (1955) to occur generally above 1,200 m
MSL in Le Conte Creek Valley, GSMNP, during the breeding season. A nest
with six young was found at Bays Mt., Sullivan Co., on 19 May 1987 (MIG
58:104). It is only occasionally seen on Roan Mt. during the breeding
season. Sightings of birds during the summer outside the eastern mountains
are rare but becoming more regular. A nest with two ad. and five young was
found at Radnor L. on 13-17 May 1976 (Bierly 1978), and a nest with four
young and at least three ad. was documented at the Tigrett WMA, Dyer
Co., on 14-15 May 1979 (Criswell 1979a). Ford (1987) found one to two birds
at locations in Lake, Fayette, Madison, Henry, and Shelby Counties during

Brown Creeper, continued

the summers of 1985 and 1986; most of the birds found were identified as singing males and all of the sites were over permanent water.

Remarks: Found in coniferous and deciduous wooded areas. High count: thirty-six on 26 Dec 1936, Memp. CBC (MIG 8:8).

Substantiation: Specimen: 1 female, Nash., Davidson Co., 24 Feb 1946 (LSUMZ, 76301).

FAMILY TROGLODYTIDAE: **Wrens**

Rock Wren, *Salpinctes obsoletus*

Status: Accidental.

Remarks: Known from two records. One bird on the 23 Dec 1956 Memp. CBC was collected (MIG 27:69). One bird at Chattanooga's Point Park (Bierly 1980) was photographed on 5 Nov 1965.

Substantiation: Specimen: 1 female, Memp., Shelby Co., 22-23 Dec 1956 (LSUMZ, 76384).

Carolina Wren, *Thryothorus ludovicianus*

Status: Regular.

Abundance: Common permanent resident.

Remarks: Found in woodlands, shrubby thickets and residential areas. Nests throughout the state, usually in cavities; occasionally is found in Wood Duck nest boxes. Generally restricted to elevations below 1,200-1,500 m MSL in the eastern mountains. Cold weather frequently has a negative impact on this species, and overall abundance will temporarily decline after especially severe winters. High counts: 244 on 30 Apr 1972, Knoxville SBC (MIG 43:46) and 243 on 19 Dec 1976, Memp. CBC (MIG 48:32).

Substantiation: Specimen: 1 male, Nash., Davidson Co., 26 Dec 1943 (LSUMZ, 76364).

Bewick's Wren, *Thryomanes bewickii*

Status: Regular (State Threatened).

Abundance: Rare permanent resident.

Remarks: Found in dry brushy areas and in rural and suburban habitats. Formerly more numerous in east and west Tennessee where it is now rarely observed. Most recent records have been from the middle region. Becomes less detectable in late summer and throughout the fall and winter. Rhoads (1895) recorded the species in every county he censused, and he observed a singing bird on Roan Mt. at an elevation of 1,200 m MSL. In the GSMNP, these wrens were generally recorded below 610 m MSL (Coffey et al. 1942).

Bewick's Wren, continued

Beginning in about the early 1940s, a general population decline was noted by many amateur ornithologists throughout the state (Coffey et al. 1942). Breeding Bird Survey results for the 1966-1987 period have also documented an overall decline across the state. The cause of this decline is unknown although it was suspected that the severity of several winters in the 1940s and 1950s, along with competition from the concurrently expanding House Wren population, was responsible (Alsop 1980). However, Laskey (1966a) noted that the decline of the Bewick's Wren at Nash. occurred prior to the House Wren's becoming established as a nesting species. Nests are usually built in Mar and Apr, but have been recorded as early as late Feb (Coffey et al. 1942). Singing birds are most often heard from Mar through July. Nests are documented for a number of east Tennessee counties through the late 1960s; in the west, breeding has been documented as recently as 1980 when a nest with four young was found in Dyersburg (MIG 51:92). In 1986, Bewick's Wrens were reported at seventeen sites in nine counties in middle Tennessee (MIG 57:105); and twenty-one birds were found utilizing slash piles in forest clear cut areas in Stewart Co. during July 1987 (MIG 58:141). These most recent sightings indicate a resurgence in the population level of this species. High count: twenty-eight on 14 May 1955, Nash. SBC (MIG 26:30). Other representative counts follow:

12 on 23 Dec 1934, Nash. CBC, MIG 6:8
12 on 24 Apr 1949, Greeneville SBC, MIG 20:35
13 on 3 May 1953, Kingsport SBC, MIG 24:37
26 on 5 May 1968, Savannah SBC, MIG 39:35
1 on 8 Apr 1975, Johnson City, MIG 46:68
1 on 8 Apr 1978, Knoxville, MIG 49:70
5 on 2 Jan 1983, Duck River Res. CBC, MIG 54:13
1 on 15 June and 3 July 1984, Camden, MIG 55:88
1 on 21 Dec 1986, Memp. CBC, MIG 58:4

Substantiation: Specimen: 1 male, Nash., Davidson Co., 1 Jan 1936 (LSUMZ, 76337).

House Wren, *Troglodytes aedon*
Status: Regular.
Abundance: East: fairly common migrant and summer resident, rare winter resident.
Middle: fairly common migrant, uncommon summer resident, rare winter resident.
West: fairly common migrant, rare summer and winter resident.
Remarks: Found in hedgerows, dense shrubby areas, and urban habitat. Usually present from mid Apr through late Oct; however, there are records for each month of the year, including more than fifty winter records. Most winter records are from Dec and probably represent lingering migrants. Birds found in late Mar are probably early spring migrants. Over the last fifty years the

House Wren, continued

House Wren's status in Tennessee has changed from that of a rare transient (Ganier 1933) to a regular breeding bird in most of the east and middle regions. The House Wren's breeding population in the state began increasing in upper east Tennessee ca. 1940 and has moved southward and westward since. First known nest was near Johnson City in 1913 (Tyler and Lyle 1947). Breeding was not noted again until 1947 when a nest with two eggs was found in Shady Valley, Johnson Co. (Tyler and Lyle 1947). By 1950, House Wrens were nesting in Knox Co. (MIG 21:52) and Sullivan Co. (MIG 22:49). Breeding in Davidson Co. at Nash. in 1957 was preceded by two singing territorial males in 1956 (Laskey 1966a). In 1979, breeding records were established for Shelby and Dyer Counties in the west (MIG 50:86), and breeding wrens were documented for Stewart and Montgomery Counties in the 1980s. Nesting attempts in the Chat. area were reported as early as 1978 (MIG 49:94) and successful nests were described from Bradley and Blount Counties in 1986 (MIG 57:114). The current breeding range of the House Wren extends from a line running diagonally from Chat. through Nash. up to Stewart Co. and all points east. Breeding records west of this line should become more regular if the species' current range expansion continues. High count: fifty on 8 May 1988, Elizabethton SBC (*fide* RLK).

Substantiation: Specimen: 1, Nash., Davidson Co., 4 Oct 1964 (LSUMZ, 76311).

Winter Wren, *Troglodytes troglodytes*

Status: Regular.

Abundance: East: uncommon migrant and winter resident, locally common summer resident.

Middle and West: uncommon migrant and winter resident.

Fall: Migrants arrive by early Oct.

    Arrivals: 14 Sept 1972, Nash., MIG 43:100

                    21 Sept 1968, Hamilton Co., MIG 39:94

                    3 Oct 1984, Dyersburg, MIG 56:17

Winter: The breeding population in the eastern mountains makes an altitudinal migration to lower elevations in the winter, although some individuals remain at high elevations (Coffey et al. 1942). On warm winter days its song can occasionally be heard.

Spring: Migrants depart by mid Apr.

    Departures: 3 May 1952, Nash., MIG 23:52

                    7 May 1974, Nash., BNA:33

                    13 May 1961, Kingsport SBC, MIG 32:31

Summer: Locally common in the eastern mountains, where it is found breeding at elevations above 900 m MSL (Coffey et al. 1942; Tanner 1955). One sing-

Winter Wren, continued

ing male was found at an elevation of 730 m MSL on 16 June 1983 in Shady Valley, Johnson Co. (RLK). Prime breeding areas include Roan Mt. and the GSMNP, where birds are often found in considerable numbers. It is somewhat less numerous on other mountain sites in northeast Tennessee. Nesting has been documented for Carter Co. (Ganier 1936) and Sevier Co. (Coffey et al. 1942).

Remarks: Found in wooded areas with dense underbrush, in flooded timber and swamps, and along woodland creeks. High count: sixty on 24 Dec 1971, Reelfoot L. CBC (MIG 43:12).

Substantiation: Specimen: 1 male, Clarksville, Montgomery Co., 17 Oct 1941 (LSUMZ, 76316).

Sedge Wren, *Cistothorus platensis*

Status: Regular.

Abundance: Uncommon migrant, rare winter resident.

Spring: Late Apr to mid May.

Arrivals:	6 Apr 1977, Memp., MIG 48:75
	19 Apr 1976, Chat., MIG 47:78
	20 Apr 1963, Cookeville SBC, MIG 34:32
Departures:	26 May 1975, Cheatham L., BNA:33
	28 May 1949, Reelfoot L., Lake Co., (Mengel 1965)
	2 June 1972, Knox Co., MIG 43:79

Fall: Late July to late Oct. One late June record: 30 June 1964, near Greeneville (MIG 35:64).

Arrivals:	3 July 1966, Amnicola Marsh, MIG 37:55
	23 July 1988, Britton Ford (JCR, Todd Fink, Doug Robinson)
	24 July 1985, Cross Creeks NWR, MIG 57:28
Departures:	29 Oct 1984, Penal Farm, MIG 56:17
	9 Nov 1975, Buena Vista Marsh, MIG 47:46
	25 Nov 1942, GSMNP, (Stupka 1963)

Winter: Every few years this species is found during the winter, especially in the middle and western regions. It is usually found when mild weather conditions persist into early winter. Most of the sightings are made in Dec, primarily on CBCs when observer effort is at a peak. Late winter observations are extremely rare; representative sightings include:

23 Jan 1944, Clarksville, MIG 15:17

2 Feb 1980, Fayette Co., MIG 51:38

26 Feb 1950, Hiwassee Island, MIG 21:14

14 Mar 1986, Cross Creeks NWR, MIG 57:79

23 Mar 1947, Radnor L., BNA:33

Sedge Wren, continued

Remarks: Found in grassy or shrubby fields and wet meadows. More detectable in the fall when it is found singing in July and Aug. Actual breeding has not been satisfactorily documented for the state. However, some birds found singing in mid July may actually be establishing breeding territories, as evidenced by two "dummy" nests found by Alfred Clebsch, Jr., in Montgomery Co. on 25 July and 7 Aug 1936 (MIG 7:70). Mengel (1965) described several breeding records for Kentucky. High count: twenty-four on 7 Aug 1936, Clarksville (Coffey et al. 1942).

Substantiation: Specimen: 1 female, Nash., Davidson Co., 7 Oct 1951 (LSUMZ, 76382).

Marsh Wren, *Cistothorus palustris*

Status: Regular.

Abundance: Uncommon migrant, rare winter resident.

Spring: Late Apr to mid May.

    Arrivals: 12 Apr 1975, Cheatham L., MIG 46:66

                   17 Apr 1975, Kingsport, MIG 46:68

                   1 May 1954, Memp. SBC, MIG 25:30

    Departures: 26 May 1940, GSMNP, (Coffey et al. 1942)

                   26 May 1975, Cheatham L., MIG 46:88

                   28 May 1985, Britton Ford, MIG 56:74

Fall: Late Sept to late Oct. There are at least three Aug records, possibly of summering birds: 5 Aug 1936, Nash. (Coffey et al. 1942); one collected in Hardeman Co. on 9 Aug 1939 (Calhoun 1941); and 10 Aug 1985, HRA (MIG 57:34).

    Arrivals: 8 Sept 1976, Austin Springs, MIG 48:107

                   14 Sept 1961, Ashland City Marsh, MIG 33:12-13

                   25 Sept 1983, Shelby Co., MIG 55:18

    Departures: 1 Nov 1986, Shelby Co., MIG 58:21

                   11 Nov 1978, Maury Co., MIG 50:43

                   16 Nov 1986, Monroe Co., MIG 58:31

Winter: Every few years this species is found during the winter, especially when mild weather conditions persist into early winter. It can also be found where suitable habitat is created by warm water discharge (e.g., by steam plants). Most winter sightings are made in Dec, primarily on CBCs when observer effort peaks. Late winter observations are extremely rare; representative sightings include:

    22 Jan 1980, Reelfoot L., MIG 51:38

    28 Jan 1917, near Nash., BNA:33

    14 Mar 1987, Nash., MIG 58:98

    31 Mar 1974, HRA, MIG 45:78

Marsh Wren, continued

Remarks: Found in shrubby fields and marshes; also in dense cattails. High count: twenty-six on 1 Oct 1978, Nash. (MIG 50:21).

Substantiation: Specimen: 1 male, Nash., Davidson Co., 29 Apr 1944 (LSUMZ, 76369).

FAMILY MUSICAPIDAE: **Kinglets, Gnatcatchers and Thrushes**

Golden-crowned Kinglet, *Regulus satrapa*

Status: Regular.

Abundance: East: locally common summer resident, fairly common migrant and winter resident.

Middle and West: fairly common migrant and winter resident.

Fall: Migrants arrive by early Oct.

    Arrivals: 13 Sept 1952, Nash., BNA:33

                    22 Sept 1966, Chat., MIG 37:83

                    22 Sept 1967, Hardin Co., MIG 38:94

Winter: Often observed in winter feeding flocks with Ruby-crowned Kinglets, chickadees, titmice and nuthatches.

Spring: Migrants depart by mid Apr.

    Departures: 5 May 1951, Kingsport SBC, MIG 22:25

                    5 May 1984, Radnor L., BNA:33

                    6 May 1984, Montgomery Co. SBC, MIG 55:60

Summer: A locally common summer resident in the eastern mountains, where it is found breeding at high elevations on Roan Mt. and at the GSMNP. Although present at these sites for many years, nesting was not documented until two ad. and seven young were found on Roan Mt. at Carver's Gap on 17-20 June 1980 (MIG 51:96). In the GSMNP, a nest with young was found at Clingman's Dome on 2 July 1984 (MIG 55:95). A low elevation breeding season record involved a pair of birds at 850 m MSL on 20, 29 June 1988 at Shady Valley, Johnson Co. (RLK).

Remarks: Found in wooded areas; at times may be locally common in pine or cedar groves. High count: 189 on 4 Jan 1976, GSMNP CBC (MIG 47:37).

Substantiation: Specimen: 1 male, Nash., Davidson Co., 5 Oct 1957 (LSUMZ, 76480).

Ruby-crowned Kinglet, *Regulus calendula*

Status: Regular.

Abundance: Fairly common migrant, uncommon winter resident; very rare summer visitor in east.

Fall: Arrives by late Sept.

Arrivals: 1 Sept 1976, Iron Mt. Gap, Unicoi Co. (*fide* RLK)
9 Sept 1974, Nash., MIG 46:20
19 Sept 1976, Memp., MIG 48:18

Winter: Becomes less numerous in most areas of the state by midwinter. It is best found at this time in coniferous forests where it joins Golden-crowned Kinglets, titmice, chickadees, nuthatches and Brown Creepers in winter feeding flocks.

Spring: By early Mar, Ruby-crowned Kinglets begin to return north in increasing numbers. Departs by early May.

Departures: 11 May 1958, Reelfoot L. SBC, MIG 29:32
11 May 1984, Knox Co., MIG 55:74
17 May 1938, Nash., BNA:33

Summer: Two records, both of single birds: 21 July 1972, GSMNP (MIG 43:80) and 21 June 1988, Roan Mt. (RLK).

Remarks: Found in wooded areas and along woodland edge. Its distinctive song is frequently heard in the spring during migration. High count: 124 on 21 Dec 1975, Memp. CBC (MIG 47:37).

Substantiation: Specimen: 1 male, Nash., Davidson Co., 22 Apr 1944 (LSUMZ, 76484).

Blue-gray Gnatcatcher, *Polioptila caerulea*

Status: Regular.

Abundance: Common migrant and summer resident, very rare winter visitor.

Spring: Arrives by late Mar.

Arrivals: 6 Mar 1986, Pickett Co., MIG 57:79
17 Mar 1945, Memp., MIG 16:11
19 Mar 1945, GSMNP, (Stupka 1963)

Summer: A common nesting species throughout most woodland areas of the state. Breeding evidence has been documented for all three regions. Found up to 800–900 m MSL in the eastern mountains.

Fall: Departs by late Sept. There are several Nov records that range from 7-9 Nov 1975, Old Hickory L. (MIG 47:46) to 27 Nov 1963, Boone L. (MIG 34:79).

Departures: 23 Oct 1976, Old Hickory L., MIG 48:19
30 Oct 1977, Hiwassee Island, MIG 49:22
31 Oct 1986, Coffee Co., MIG 58:24-25

Winter: There are over ten winter records. Dec sightings range from 12 Dec 1970, Knoxville (MIG 42:21) to 30 Dec 1978, Knoxville (MIG 50:45). Jan and Feb records include the following:

Blue-gray Gnatcatcher, continued
     10 Jan 1985, Knoxville, MIG 56:56
     11-12 Jan 1986, Knoxville, MIG 57:61
     7 Feb 1987, Lawrence Co., MIG 58:57
Remarks: Found in wooded areas and along woodland edge. High count: 185
     on 26 Apr 1959, Knoxville SBC (MIG 30:23).
Substantiation: Specimen: 1 male, Memp., Shelby Co., 12 July 1944 (LSUMZ,
     9619).

Eastern Bluebird, *Sialia sialis*
Status: Regular.
Abundance: Fairly common permanent resident.
Remarks: Found in open and semi-open areas. Prefers roadsides and
     fields/pastures with short-cut grass. Common to abundant ca. 1930 (Ganier
     1933), this species declined in numbers across all of Tennessee during the
     1940s, 1950s and 1960s. Reasons for continental population decline (in-
     cluding adverse weather, interspecific competition, and loss of habitat) are
     summarized by Zeleny (1976). Severe weather during the late 1970s caused a
     significant reduction in numbers in parts of the state (Pitts 1981a); however,
     during the last decade, bluebird numbers appear to be increasing in Ten-
     nessee, especially on SBCs and CBCs. A recent occurrence of weather-
     induced mortality involved an Apr 1987 snowstorm that resulted in the
     deaths of many bluebirds in northeast Tennessee (MIG 58:101, 105-106). The
     species nests throughout the state but occurs in fewer numbers at high eleva-
     tions in the east and in the riparian areas adjacent to the Mississippi River
     in the west. It is regularly encountered on Little Roan Mt., where Ganier
     (1936) found a pair feeding young on 25 June 1936 at an elevation of 1,760
     m MSL. High counts: 278 on 1 Jan 1985, Hiwassee CBC (MIG 56:8); 233
     on 28 Dec 1985, Buffalo River CBC (MIG 57:11); and 221 on 18 Dec 1976,
     Ashland City CBC (MIG 48:33).
Substantiation: Specimen: 1 female, Nash., Davidson Co., 5 Nov 1954
     (LSUMZ, 76472).

Veery, *Catharus fuscescens*
Status: Regular.
Abundance: East: uncommon migrant, locally common summer resident.
Middle and West: uncommon migrant.
Spring: Late Apr to mid May.
     Arrivals: 11 Apr 1972, Nash., MIG 43:51
                      25 Apr 1952, Gatlinburg, (Stupka 1963)
                      26 Apr 1979, Memp., MIG 50:68
     Departures: 23 May 1981, McNairy Co., (Nicholson 1984)
                      28 May 1958, Nash., BNA:34
                      30 May 1986, Knoxville, MIG 57:85

Veery, continued

Summer: Locally common summer resident in the eastern mountains, where it is generally found above 1,060 m MSL. Breeds in deciduous and coniferous forests at high elevations. Probably most numerous on Roan Mt. and in the GSMNP. Fewer birds are found on other mountain areas in northeast Tennessee. Nesting evidence has been documented for Carter Co. on Roan Mt. (Ganier 1936), for the GSMNP (Ganier 1962a), and for Monroe Co. in the Unicoi Mountains (Ganier and Clebsch 1946). Singing birds were noted in Morgan Co. as late as 9 June 1986 on Frozen Head Mt. (Nicholson 1987); and one bird was found in Campbell Co. on Cross Mt. on 2-25 June 1977 (MIG 48:106).

Fall: Early Sept to late Sept.

Arrivals: 18 Aug 1971, Davidson Co., MIG 42:93

               24 Aug 1969, Two Jays, MIG 40:90

               27 Aug 1985, Norris, MIG 57:34

Departures: 10 Oct 1984, Chat., MIG 56:25

               11 Oct 1952, Radnor L., BNA:34

               11 Oct 1954, Nash., BNA:34

Remarks: Found in wooded areas. High count: forty on 28 June 1987, Roan Mt. (RLK).

Substantiation: Specimen: 1 male, Nash., Davidson Co., 7 Sept 1943 (LSUMZ, 8875).

Gray-cheeked Thrush, *Catharus minimus*

Status: Regular.

Abundance: Uncommon migrant, very rare summer visitor.

Spring: Late Apr to late May.

Arrivals: 6 Apr 1939, Clarksville, MIG 10:32

               12 Apr 1985, Memp., MIG 56:74

               25 Apr 1987, Greeneville SBC, MIG 58:83

Departures: 21 May 1973, GSMNP, MIG 44:88

               26 May 1963, Memp., MIG 34:49

               26 May 1963, Nash., MIG 34:50

Summer: One record, most likely of a late spring migrant: 16 June 1949, Nash. (BNA:34).

Fall: Early Sept to mid Oct.

Arrivals: 27 Aug 1985, Tennessee River Gorge, MIG 57:34

               4 Sept 1980, Nash., BNA:34

               8 Sept 1969, Savannah, Hardin Co., MIG 40:88

Departures: 24 Oct 1967, Holston Mt., MIG 38:103

               30 Oct 1972, Nash., (Goodpasture 1974)

               8 Nov 1984, Nash., MIG 56:21

Remarks: Found in wooded areas. High count: twenty-three on 29 Apr 1984, Memp. SBC (MIG 55:60). A total of fifty-eight birds was killed at the Smyrna airport on 24 Sept 1955 (Laskey 1956).

Gray-cheeked Thrush, continued
Substantiation: Specimen: 1 male, Nash., Davidson Co., 20 Sept 1969 (LSUMZ, 76454).

Swainson's Thrush, *Catharus ustulatus*
Status: Regular.
Abundance: Fairly common to uncommon migrant, very rare winter visitor.
Spring: Late Apr to late May.
  Arrivals: 2 Apr 1972, Roan Mt., MIG 43:55
                 6 Apr 1986, Nash., MIG 57:79-80
                 11 Apr 1977, Memp., MIG 48:75
  Departures: 27 May 1954, Knoxville, MIG 25:55
                 30 May 1971, Savannah, Hardin Co., MIG 42:68
                 3 June 1940, Nash., BNA:34
Fall: Early Sept to mid Oct.
  Arrivals: 27 Aug 1955, Ashland City Marsh, BNA:34
                 1 Sept 1963, Two Jays, MIG 34:51
                 4 Sept 1939, GSMNP, (Stupka 1963)
  Departures: 31 Oct 1978, Memp., MIG 50:19
                 23 Nov 1975, Old Hickory L., MIG 47:46
                 26 Nov 1966, Knox Co., (Alsop 1967)
Winter: One documented record: 29 Dec 1965, Reelfoot L. CBC (MIG 36:84).
Remarks: Found in wooded areas. May be locally abundant for brief periods
  during spring or fall migration. Usually most numerous in the spring, but
  concentrations can also occur in the fall. High counts: 199 on 27 Sept 1980,
  Elizabethton Fall Bird Count (*fide* RLK) and 150 on 7 May 1978, Knoxville
  SBC (MIG 49:57).
Substantiation: Specimen: 1 female, Nash., Davidson Co., 24 Sept 1965
  (LSUMZ, 76451).

Hermit Thrush, *Catharus guttatus*
Status: Regular.
Abundance: Uncommon to fairly common migrant and winter resident, very
  rare summer visitor.
Fall: Arrives by early Oct.
  Arrivals: 20 Sept 1970, Memp., MIG 41:83
                 27 Sept 1931, Radnor L., BNA:34
                 27 Sept 1980, Roans Creek, MIG 52:27
Winter: Often associates with kinglets, chickadees, Tufted Titmice and Brown
  Creepers in winter feeding flocks. Presence is often revealed by its blackbird-
  like "chuck" note.
Spring: Departs by late Apr.
  Departures: 11 May 1958, Reelfoot L. SBC, MIG 29:32
                 11 May 1985, Lawrence Co., MIG 56:69
                 14 May 1981, Knoxville, MIG 52:74

Hermit Thrush, continued

Summer: There are about three summer records from the spruce-fir forests (elevation 1,700 m MSL or higher) on Roan Mt.:

7 June 1979, Roan Mt., MIG 50:90

10 June-8 July 1983, Roan Mt., MIG 54:92

17 May, 6 June 1986, Roan Mt., MIG 57:115

The 1983 and 1986 sightings involved one to three singing birds.

Remarks: Found in coniferous and deciduous woodlands. The only brown-backed thrush to be expected in the winter in Tennessee. High count: sixty-six on 24 Dec 1939, Memp. CBC (MIG 11:22).

Substantiation: Specimen: 1 male, Nash., Davidson Co., 12 Dec 1943 (LSUMZ, 76440).

Wood Thrush, *Hylocichla mustelina*

Status: Regular.

Abundance: Common migrant and summer resident, very rare winter visitor.

Spring: Arrives by mid Apr.

Arrivals:　　1 Apr 1969, Savannah, Hardin Co., MIG 40:45

1 Apr 1955, Gatlinburg, (Stupka 1963)

3 Apr 1929, near Nash., BNA:34

Summer: A common nesting species statewide in suitable woodland habitat. Seldom found above 1,060 m MSL in northeast Tennessee. Occurs up to about 1,500 m MSL in the GSMNP during the summer (Stupka 1963). There is a narrow range of overlap in the eastern mountains where this species and the Veery may both be found.

Fall: Departs by mid Oct.

Departures:　5 Nov 1976, Knoxville, MIG 48:50

6 Nov 1962, Nash., MIG 34:9

10 Nov 1966, Memp., MIG 37:80

Winter: One record: 17 Dec 1978 to 1 Jan 1979, Memp. (MIG 50:41).

Remarks: Found in lowland forests and other wooded areas. High count: 177 on 30 Apr 1972, Knoxville SBC (MIG 43:46).

Substantiation: Specimen: 1 female, Memp., Shelby Co., 17 Aug 1944 (LSUMZ, 9688).

American Robin, *Turdus migratorius*

Status: Regular.

Abundance: Common permanent resident.

Remarks: Found in a variety of urban, rural and woodland habitats. A common statewide nesting species. Can be found breeding on the summits of Roan Mt. (ca. 1,900 m MSL). Ganier and Clebsch (1946) also found robins to be common on the summits of the Unicoi Mts. in Monroe Co. A withdrawal from some breeding areas occurs during the winter, but the species remains readily detectable throughout the winter period. A northward migratory movement is usually evident by mid Feb. Large winter roosts have

American Robin, continued

occasionally formed, including 50,000 on 22 Dec 1984, Columbia CBC (MIG 56:8), and 500,000 on 29 Dec 1962, Nash. CBC (MIG 33:69). Ten thousand were observed migrating on 18 Sept 1977, Bristol (MIG 49:21). High count: 800,000 on 31 Dec 1960, Nash. CBC (MIG 31:76).

Substantiation: Specimen: 1 male, Memp., Shelby Co., 12 Feb 1944 (LSUMZ, 9247).

FAMILY MIMIDAE: Thrashers and Mockingbirds

Gray Catbird, *Dumetella carolinensis*

Status: Regular.

Abundance: Fairly common migrant and summer resident, rare winter resident.

Spring: Arrives by mid Apr. There are a few Mar records ranging from 9 Mar 1972, Johnson City (MIG 43:27) to 25 Mar 1988, Davidson Co. (Margaret L. Mann).

Arrivals: 2 Apr 1951, Lebanon, MIG 22:28

3 Apr 1955, Knoxville, MIG 26:50

18 Apr 1941, Gibson Co., MIG 12:37

Summer: Nests throughout the state. In northeast Tennessee, it occurs up to the summits of Roan Mt. (ca. 1,900 m MSL). Ganier and Clebsch (1946) found catbirds up to 1,520 m MSL in the Unicoi Mts., Monroe Co.

Fall: Departs by mid Oct.

Departures: 23 Nov 1985, Stewart Co., MIG 57:28

26 Nov 1961, Chat., MIG 33:15

29 Nov 1931, Memp., MIG 3:9

Winter: Every three out of four winters, on average, at least one catbird can be expected somewhere in the state during the Dec-Feb period. Most winter records occur in Dec, especially on CBCs when observer effort is at a peak. Significantly fewer birds are observed in Jan. Notably late records include: 16 Jan 1943, near Clarksville (Clebsch 1943a), and 26 Jan 1961, Gatlinburg (Stupka 1963). There appears to be very few records of this species successfully overwintering anywhere in the state; most birds can not be relocated after early Jan.

Remarks: Found in shrubby, second growth areas and along woodland edge.

High count: 118 on 7 May 1950, Elizabethton SBC (MIG 21:27).

Substantiation: Specimen: 1 male, Nash., Davidson Co., 12 Aug 1916 (LSUMZ, 76393).

Northern Mockingbird, *Mimus polyglottos*

Status: Regular.

Abundance: Common permanent resident.

Remarks: The state bird of Tennessee. Found in semi-open areas, hedgerows and shrubby thickets in a variety of urban, suburban and rural habitats. A widely distributed nesting species and year-round permanent resident. Generally absent from the higher elevations of the eastern mountains. Frequently imitates the songs and calls of other bird species present in its immediate breeding area. High count: five hundred on 26 Apr 1959, Knoxville SBC (MIG 30:23).

Substantiation: Specimen: 1 female, near Germantown, Shelby Co., 25 Dec 1943 (LSUMZ, 9095).

Brown Thrasher, *Toxostoma rufum*

Status: Regular.

Abundance: Fairly common summer resident, uncommon winter resident.

Remarks: Found in shrubby thickets, hedgerows and along roadsides. Nests throughout the state, but is less numerous in (and sometimes absent from) the higher elevations of the eastern mountains. Occasionally found on the grassy balds of mountain summits. Becomes less detectable in the winter when many birds withdraw from summer breeding areas; withdrawal is especially evident in northeast Tennessee where it becomes difficult to locate thrashers in the winter. Spring migrants are observed moving back north by early Mar. High count: 157 on 26 Apr 1964, Knoxville SBC (MIG 35:47).

Substantiation: Specimen: 1 female, Nash., Davidson Co., 24 Oct 1966 (LSUMZ, 76401).

FAMILY MOTACILLIDAE: **Pipits**

Water Pipit, *Anthus spinoletta*

Status: Regular.

Abundance: Fairly common to uncommon migrant and winter resident.

Fall: Arrives by early Oct.

Arrivals: 23 Aug 1984, HRA, MIG 56:26
                 11 Sept 1937, Warner Parks, Nash., BNA:34
                 24 Sept 1984, Island 13, MIG 56:17

Winter: Becomes locally common in suitable habitat by midwinter, usually in the southern part of the state. Representative counts include: 254 on 23 Dec 1933, Memp. (MIG 5:9) and 492 on 21 Dec 1985, Knoxville CBC (MIG 57:11).

Water Pipit, continued
Spring: Departs by late Apr.
  Departures: 9 May 1926, Warner Parks, Nash., BNA:34
            10 May 1958, Reelfoot L. SBC, MIG 29:32
            20 May 1984, Roan Mt., MIG 55:75
Remarks: Found in open areas, pastures, and agricultural fields with little or no vegetation. Often occurs near water. Occasionally observed in migration in the eastern mountains where there are several records for Roan Mt. and Chilhowee Mt. in Carter and Blount Counties. High count: 746 on 1 Jan 1986, Hiwassee CBC (MIG 57:11).
Substantiation: Specimen: 1 female, Murfreesboro, Rutherford Co., 22 Feb 1935 (LSUMZ, 76488).

Sprague's Pipit, *Anthus spragueii*
Status: Accidental.
Remarks: Found in large, open fields with short grass. At least sixteen state records. First recorded in the state in 1953 when two to five birds were found by Coffey (1953) on 21 Feb, 22 Mar and 17 Apr 1953 at the Penal Farm in Shelby Co. Recorded annually thereafter through 1957, after which it was only found at the Penal Farm on 18 Oct and 7 Nov 1959 (MIG 31:11), and in Lauderdale Co. near Golddust on 31 Jan 1976 (MIG 47:45). Suitable habitat, though not as abundant as it was in the 1950s, is still available. All sightings have occurred in west Tennessee. High count: seven on 23 Dec 1956, Memp. CBC (MIG 27:73). Additional records follow:
  12 Oct 1955, Penal Farm, MIG 27:16
  20 Oct 1956, Penal Farm, MIG 28:6
  29 Oct 1955, Penal Farm, MIG 27:16
  22 Dec 1957, Memp. CBC, MIG 28:66
  26 Dec 1954, Memp. CBC, MIG 25:78
  27 Dec 1953, Memp. CBC, MIG 24:78
  2 Feb 1957, Dyersburg airfield, MIG 28:7
  6 Feb 1954, Memp., (Coffey 1954)
  21 Apr 1957, Penal Farm, MIG 28:26
Substantiation: Specimen: 1 female, Memp., Shelby Co., 6 Mar 1954 (LSUMZ, 76489).

FAMILY BOMBYCILLIDAE: Waxwings

Cedar Waxwing, *Bombycilla cedrorum*
Status: Regular.
Abundance: East: fairly common migrant, uncommon summer and winter resident.

Cedar Waxwing, continued

Middle and West: fairly common migrant, uncommon winter resident, rare summer resident.

Remarks: Found in a variety of semi-open and urban habitats. Middle and west Tennessee occur along the southern limits of the waxwing's continental breeding range. In these two regions, the waxwing is a fairly common migrant and uncommon winter resident from about mid Sept to late May. However, a number of sightings exists for June, July and Aug, with fewer reports from the western region of the state. Attempted and/or successful nests have been documented in middle Tennessee for Pickett Co. in 1937 (Ganier 1937a), Cheatham Co. in 1984 (MIG 57:111), Davidson Co. in 1928 (BNA:34), Clay Co. in 1971 (MIG 42:70) and Stewart Co. in 1986 (Robinson and Blunk 1989). In east Tennessee the Cedar Waxwing is an uncommon breeding bird on the Cumberland Plateau and in the Eastern Ridge and Valley, but is more abundant in the eastern mountains during the nesting season (Bierly 1980). Documented nest records exist for Anderson Co. in 1979 (MIG 50:89), Hamilton Co. in 1961 (West 1961), McMinn Co. between 1897 and 1909 (Ijams and Hofferbert 1934), Washington Co. in 1973 (MIG 44:87), Johnson Co. in 1962 (Coffey 1964c) and in 1965 (MIG 36:69), Carter Co. in 1981 (MIG 52:99), Scott, Grundy and Knox Counties in 1987 (MIG 58:146), and the GSMNP (Stupka 1963). In 1988, nesting evidence was found in an additional eight counties of east Tennessee. Waxwings often move in flocks and are at times erratic in terms of abundance and distribution, especially during the fall and spring migration periods. High counts: 2,500 on 28 Feb 1986, Memp. (MIG 57:51); 2,000 on 15 Mar 1980, Davidson Co. (MIG 51:39-40); and 1,007 on 26 Dec 1981, Elizabethton CBC (MIG 53:50).

Substantiation: Specimen: 1 female, Nash., Davidson Co., 7 May 1941 (LSUMZ, 76494).

FAMILY LANIIDAE: **Shrikes**

Northern Shrike, *Lanius excubitor*

Status: Accidental.

Remarks: Known from one record: an imm. female was observed at Bristol on 9 Nov 1964 and collected on the following day. It was observed attacking a Mourning Dove on 10 Nov (Coffey 1964a).

Substantiation: Specimen: 1 imm. female, near Bristol, Sullivan Co., 10 Nov 1964 (LSUMZ, 76523).

Loggerhead Shrike, *Lanius ludovicianus*

Status: Regular.

Abundance: East: uncommon permanent resident.

Middle and West: fairly common permanent resident.

Remarks: Found in open areas and along roadsides and fencerows. Usually encountered singly or in pairs; small flocks consisting of recently fledged young can be found from late May through Aug. Nests throughout the state. Ganier (1933) described the Loggerhead Shrike as a rare summer resident in the middle and east. Today it is apparently more detectable in most parts of middle Tennessee, but it is still found in low numbers in the east. The frequency of sightings generally increases as one moves west. At least 35 and 65 active territories were found between Apr and July 1986 in Lawrence and Williamson Counties, respectively (MIG 57:109). However, Breeding Bird Survey data from the 1966-1984 period show a 50% decline in the number of shrikes in Tennessee (Stedman 1986a). High count: fifty-three on 21 Dec 1941, Memp. CBC (MIG 13:20).

Substantiation: Specimen: 1 male, near Germantown, Shelby Co., 10 Dec 1943 (LSUMZ, 9001).

FAMILY STURNIDAE: **Starlings**

*European Starling, *Sturnus vulgaris*

Status: Regular.

Abundance: Common permanent resident.

Remarks: Found in a variety of urban and rural habitats, usually near human dwellings. Introduced into the United States in the late 1800s. The species was still spreading westward through the state in the early 1930s. During the six 1932 June SBCs conducted at Reelfoot L., Memp. (two counts), Nash., Knoxville and Johnson City, the European Starling was recorded on only the last three counts, with the birds at Nash. being seen only on the day before the count (MIG 3:15). As late as 1933 there were still no breeding records for west Tennessee; and Albert F. Ganier and Ben B. Coffey, Jr., reported seeing no starlings on drives to Reelfoot L. on 27 May 1933 from Nash. and Memp., respectively (MIG 4:22). The European Starling is now an abundant bird throughout the state, although it is uncommon at high elevations in the eastern mountains. High count: 2 million on 29 Dec 1962, Nash. CBC (MIG 33:69).

Substantiation: Specimen: 1 male, Memp., Shelby Co., 2 Mar 1942 (LSUMZ, 6833).

FAMILY VIREONIDAE: Vireos

White-eyed Vireo, *Vireo griseus*
Status: Regular.
Abundance: Common migrant and summer resident, very rare winter visitor.
Spring: Arrives by early Apr.
    Arrivals: 6 Mar 1988, Warner Parks (David F. Vogt)
                  21 Mar 1972, Memp., MIG 43:49-50
                  26 Mar 1973, Greeneville, MIG 44:53
Summer: A conspicuous breeding bird statewide, it is frequently heard long
    before it is seen. Usually not found at the higher mountain elevations in the
    east. In the GSMNP, it generally nests below 900 m MSL, but post-breeding
    sightings may occur up to 1,675 m MSL (Stupka 1963).
Fall: Departs by mid Oct.
    Departures: 22 Oct 1944, Memp., MIG 15:77
                  13 Nov 1979, Johnson City, MIG 51:43
                  21 Nov 1967, Nash., MIG 38:96
Winter: There are three winter records, all of which probably represent linger-
    ing fall migrants:
        26 Dec 1926, Nash. CBC, (Walker 1932)
        5-14 Dec 1948, Carter Co., (Herndon 1950)
        23 Dec 1977, Reelfoot L. CBC, MIG 49:8
Remarks: Found in shrubby and second growth areas. At times is abundant
    during the spring migration. High counts: 108 on 27 Apr 1975, Knoxville
    SBC (MIG 46:57); 100 on 22 Apr 1967, Nash. SBC (MIG 38:34) and 92 on
    27 Apr 1986, Memp. SBC (MIG 57:68).
Substantiation: Specimen: 1 male, Nash., Davidson Co., 26 Apr 1966 (LSUMZ,
    76533).

Bell's Vireo, *Vireo bellii*
Status: Extremely Rare.
Remarks: Found in shrubby areas, usually near water and/or willow trees. Six
    state records. First record involved a pair at Memp. on 24-30 June 1935 that
    nested unsuccessfully (Coffey 1935a). Has not been reported in the east.
    Only report from the middle region is 6 May 1978, Clarksville (MIG 49:93).

Bell's Vireo, continued

This species breeds in southern Illinois and western Kentucky; additional records from west Tennessee are likely. All remaining records follow:

12 May 1984, Reelfoot L., Obion Co., MIG 55:68
27 May 1976, southeast Obion Co., (Pitts 1983)
27 June 1971, Mud Island, Shelby Co., MIG 42:68
7 July 1946, Natchez Trace S.P., (Coffey 1946)

Substantiation: Adequately documented sight records.

Solitary Vireo, *Vireo solitarius*

Status: Regular.

Abundance: East: fairly common migrant and summer resident, very rare winter visitor.

Middle and West: uncommon migrant; very rare winter visitor in west.

Spring: Late Mar to mid May.

Arrivals:	11 Mar 1974, GSMNP, MIG 45:26
	28 Mar 1986, McNairy Co., MIG 57:74
	30 Mar 1946, Nash., BNA:35
Departures:	18 May 1963, Nash., MIG 34:50
	18 May 1935, Memp., MIG 6:33
	21 May 1937, Nash., BNA:35

Summer: Found as a summer resident on the Cumberland Plateau and in the eastern mountains; locally distributed in the Ridge and Valley. Nesting records: Roan Mt. in Carter Co. (Ganier 1936); GSMNP in Sevier and Blount Co. (Stupka 1963); near Washington Co. ca. 1930 (Lyle and Tyler 1934); and on Frozen Head Mt. in Morgan Co. (Nicholson 1987). In the GSMNP usually found breeding at elevations above 600 m MSL (Stupka 1963; Tanner 1955); in northeast Tennessee, it is regularly found above 900 m MSL, but becomes less numerous between 600 and 900 m MSL; the nests in Morgan Co. on the Plateau occurred at elevations ranging from 610–914 m MSL (Nicholson 1987).

Fall: Early Oct to early Nov.

Arrivals:	29 Aug 1942, Nash., MIG 13:46
	9 Oct 1985, Hatchie NWR, MIG 57:23
	12 Oct 1968, Reelfoot L., MIG 39:89
Departures:	14 Nov 1986, Memp., MIG 58:21
	23 Nov 1985, Woods Res., MIG 57:28
	30 Nov 1985, Sullivan Co., MIG 57:34

Winter: About 15 winter records, two-thirds of which are from Memp. There are no middle Tennessee winter records. Representative sightings include:

24 Feb 1962, Bays Mt., Sullivan Co., MIG 33:17
3 Jan 1987, Kingsport CBC, MIG 58:4
20 Dec 1986, Chat. CBC, MIG 58:4
30 Dec 1979, GSMNP CBC, MIG 51:33
26 Dec 1941, Memp., MIG 13:20

Solitary Vireo, continued

Remarks: Found in wooded areas. Spring arrival dates in the eastern mountain region average one to two weeks earlier than elsewhere in the state. High count: forty-three on 26 Apr 1975, Elizabethton SBC (MIG 46:57).

Substantiation: Specimen: 1 male, Shady Valley, Johnson Co., 7 June 1934 (LSUMZ, 76562).

Yellow-throated Vireo, *Vireo flavifrons*

Status: Regular.

Abundance: Fairly common to uncommon migrant and summer resident.

Spring: Arrives by early Apr.

Arrivals: 28 Mar 1933, Memp., MIG 4:8

30 Mar 1975, Old Hickory L., MIG 46:66

3 Apr 1977, Tennessee River Gorge, MIG 48:78

Summer: Rhoads (1895) found this species at every stop he made between Samburg (Obion Co.) and Johnson City (Washington Co.). As a breeding species, it appears to be less numerous today throughout Tennessee. In the eastern mountains it is usually found breeding below an elevation of about 900 m MSL.

Fall: Departs by mid Sept.

Departures: 26 Oct 1984, Murfreesboro, MIG 56:21

27 Oct 1984, Arrow L., Maury Co., MIG 56:21

29 Oct 1987, Claiborne Co., MIG 59:41

Remarks: Found in wooded areas. High count: thirty-six on 27 Apr 1958, Knoxville SBC (MIG 29:32).

Substantiation: Specimen: 1 male, Pocahontas, Hardeman Co., 17 June 1942 (LSUMZ, 76552).

Warbling Vireo, *Vireo gilvus*

Status: Regular.

Abundance: Uncommon migrant and summer resident.

Spring: Arrives by mid Apr.

Arrivals: 1 Apr 1975, Shelby Co., MIG 46:65

5 Apr 1921, Nash., BNA:35

15 Apr 1936, Knoxville, MIG 7:49

Summer: Not especially numerous anywhere in the state. However, Rhoads (1895) found this species at every stop he made between Samburg (Obion Co.) and Johnson City (Washington Co.). Considerably less detectable in the east. Stupka (1963) reported only two sight records for the GSMNP. It occurs regularly at a few local sites in northeast Tennessee. The highest concentrations of birds are found in west Tennessee. Breeding records are documented for all three regions of the state (Alsop 1980).

Fall: Departs by early Sept. There is one Nov record: 6-13 Nov 1949, Carter Co. (MIG 22:19).

Warbling Vireo, continued
Departures: 23 Sept 1967, Savannah, Hardin Co., MIG 38:94
                  10 Oct 1939, Knoxville, MIG 10:76
                  15 Oct 1964, Nash., (Laskey 1964)
Remarks: Found in open wooded areas with scattered trees, often near water.
High count: sixteen on 1 May 1954, Memp. SBC (MIG 25:31).
Substantiation: Specimen: 1 male, Clarksville, Montgomery Co., 31 May 1943
(LSUMZ, 76579).

Philadelphia Vireo, *Vireo philadelphicus*
Status: Regular.
Abundance: Uncommon migrant.
Spring: Late Apr to mid May.
Arrivals: 31 Mar 1945, Memp., MIG 16:11
                  7 Apr 1940, Knox Co., (Howell and Monroe 1957)
                  13 Apr 1936, Clarksville, MIG 7:46
Departures: 13 May 1986, Johnson City, MIG 57:85
                  20 May 1941, Memp., MIG 12:36
                  24 May 1954, Nash., BNA:35
Fall: Mid Sept to mid Oct.
Arrivals: 28 Aug 1972, HRA, MIG 43:102
                  3 Sept 1976, Old Hickory L., BNA:35
                  18 Sept 1977, Shelby Co., MIG 49:18
Departures: 12 Oct 1968, Reelfoot L., MIG 39:89
                  21 Oct 1980, Elizabethton, MIG 52:27
                  30 Oct 1964, Columbia, MIG 35:101
Remarks: Found in wooded areas and along woodland edge. High count: seven
on 20 Sept 1977, Shelby Co. (MIG 49:18). Thirty-seven were picked up at
Nash. after an airport tower kill on 7 Oct 1951 (Laskey 1951). Appears to be
less detectable in the east, where Stupka (1963) did not list it for the
GSMNP; it is very infrequently encountered each year in northeast Tennessee. However, twenty-seven were picked up at Chat. after an airport tower
kill on 6 Oct 1954 (MIG 25:68).
Substantiation: Specimen: 1 male, Nash., Davidson Co., 14 May 1967 (LSUMZ,
76570).

Red-eyed Vireo, *Vireo olivaceus*
Status: Regular.
Abundance: Common migrant and summer resident.
Spring: Arrives by mid Apr.
Arrivals: 30 Mar 1945, Nash., MIG 16:14
                  4 Apr 1986, Knoxville, MIG 57:85
                  7 Apr 1977, Shelby Co., MIG 48:75
Summer: Common throughout Tennessee as a nesting species. In the GSMNP,
it is commonly found up to an elevation of about 1,370 m MSL, but also

Red-eyed Vireo, continued
occurs in fewer numbers at higher altitudes (Stupka 1963). It is seldom found above 1,200 m MSL in the mountains of northeast Tennessee.
Fall: Departs by late Sept.
　　Departures:　　27 Oct 1984, Arrow L., Maury Co., MIG 56:21
　　　　　　　　　30 Oct 1964, Columbia, MIG 35:101
　　　　　　　　　9 Nov 1963, Kingsport, MIG 34:76
Remarks: Found in deciduous woodlands. High count: 212 on 27 Apr 1958, Knoxville SBC (MIG 29:32).
Substantiation: Specimen: 1 female, Nash., Davidson Co., 6 Oct 1953 (LSUMZ, 76568).

FAMILY EMBERIZIDAE

This large family is represented by many passerine species that were previously grouped under separate families. Included here are the warblers, tanagers, cardinals, grosbeaks, buntings, towhees, sparrows, longspurs, meadowlarks, blackbirds and orioles. Because of the large number of species that is treated here, each subfamily of birds will be recognized.

SUBFAMILY PARULINAE: Wood-Warblers

Blue-winged Warbler, *Vermivora pinus*
Status: Regular.
Abundance: East and West: uncommon migrant, rare summer resident.
Middle: fairly common to uncommon migrant and summer resident.
Spring: Early Apr to mid May.
　　Arrivals:　　27 Mar 1954, Shelby Co., MIG 25:51
　　　　　　　　1 Apr 1967, Williamson Co., MIG 38:49
　　　　　　　　7 Apr 1986, Claiborne Co., MIG 57:85
Summer: Found as a breeding bird primarily in middle Tennessee. In the west, it has primarily been recorded in the summer months in the counties bordering the Tennessee River (e.g., 13 June 1985, Benton Co., MIG 56:107; and 13 July 1985, Decatur Co., MIG 56:107). In the east, breeding was documented for Alcoa Marsh, Blount Co., in 1976 (MIG 47:102); and, in 1986, singing males were at Chat. (Hamilton Co.), South Holston L. (Sullivan Co.) (MIG 57:85, 87), and Polk Co. (MIG 57:115). A nest with four eggs was also

Blue-winged Warbler, continued

found on the Cumberland Plateau at Fall Creek Falls S.P., Van Buren Co., in 1940 (Ganier and Clebsch 1940).

Fall: Early Sept to late Sept.

Departures: 4 Oct 1986, Shelby Co., MIG 58:21
14 Oct 1968, Radnor L., MIG 39:90
31 Oct 1981, Elizabethton, MIG 53:23

Remarks: Found in shrubby and second growth areas. High count: thirty-three on 30 Apr 1983, Columbia SBC (MIG 54:53).

Substantiation: Specimen: 1 female, near Nash., Davidson Co., 17 Aug 1935 (LSUMZ, 76594).

Golden-winged Warbler, *Vermivora chrysoptera*

Status: Regular.

Abundance: East: uncommon migrant and summer resident.

Middle and West: uncommon migrant; very rare summer visitor in middle.

Spring: Late Apr to mid May.

Arrivals: 9 Apr 1986, Stewart Co., MIG 57:80
12 Apr 1947, Shelby Co., MIG 18:62
13 Apr 1948, Knox Co., (Howell and Monroe 1957)

Departures: 17 May 1953, Memp., MIG 24:55
22 May 1977, Radnor L., MIG 48:104
26 May 1935, Putnam Co., (Crook 1936)

Summer: A summer resident only in the east where it is found breeding on the Cumberland Plateau and in the eastern mountains. In northeast Tennessee, it is usually encountered between 760 m and 1,060 m MSL. Also breeds at low and mid altitudes in the GSMNP (Stupka 1963). Rhoads (1895) found it breeding in Roane Co. and Fentress Co. on the Cumberland Plateau. Successful breeding has also been documented for Carter Co. (MIG 48:107), Scott Co. (MIG 58:146) and Campbell Co. (MIG 44:87). An unsuccessful nest was found at Cumberland Mt. S.P., Cumberland Co., in 1962 (West 1962). There have been a few summer records of presumed non-breeding birds in middle Tennessee:

2-16 June 1979, Lewis Co., MIG 50:88
26 July 1936, Columbia, MIG 7:71
26 July 1954, Nash., MIG 25:53

Fall: Early Sept to late Sept.

Arrivals: 14 Aug 1969, Nash., MIG 40:91
17 Aug 1979, Nash., MIG 51:16
20 Aug 1942, Memp., MIG 13:43

Departures: 1 Oct 1986, Hatchie NWR, MIG 58:21
9 Oct 1965, Knoxville, MIG 36:96
15 Oct 1969, Nash., (Laskey 1969)

Remarks: Found in shrubby second growth areas and along woodland edge. High count: nineteen on 25 Apr 1971, Knoxville SBC (MIG 42:38).

Golden-winged Warbler, continued
Substantiation: Specimen: 1 male, Nash., Davidson Co., 10 Sept 1944 (LSUMZ, 76586).

Brewster's/Lawrence's Warblers, *Vermivora pinus* x *chrysoptera*
Status: Irregular (Hybrids).
Abundance: Rare migrant, very rare summer visitor.
Remarks: These are the hybrids resulting from cross breeding between the Blue-winged and Golden-winged Warblers. The recessive Lawrence's is less frequently observed and in Tennessee has been reported only about half as often as the Brewster's Warbler. There are about twenty records for the Brewster's and about ten records for the Lawrence's. First record of the Brewster's was on 30 Aug 1941, Memp. (Tucker 1941); and first record for the Lawrence's was on 29 July 1945, Watauga River (Herndon 1950). Most observations of these hybrids are made in the spring (late Apr to early May). Two singing, apparently territorial, Brewster's Warblers have been documented: 25 May-9 June 1974, Grundy Co. (Dubke and Dubke 1977); and 11 June 1973, Cumberland Co. (Alsop 1974). Fall records range from late Aug to late Oct. Representative sightings follow (L = Lawrence's; B = Brewster's):

    14 Apr 1951 (L), Memp., MIG 23:8
    17 Apr 1960 (B), Two Jays, (Ogden 1960)
    23 Apr 1971 (B), GSMNP, MIG 42:48
    29 Apr-2 May 1984 (L), Dyersburg, MIG 55:68
    2-3 May 1962 (L), Columbia, MIG 33:30
    30 May 1975 (B), Unicoi Co., MIG 46:91
    17 July 1979 (B), Cheatham Co., MIG 50:88
    13-18 Sept 1982 (L), Shelby Co., (McLean et al. 1983)
    21 Sept 1984 (L), Radnor L., MIG 56:21
    21 Oct 1968 (B), Knoxville, MIG 39:94

Tennessee Warbler, *Vermivora peregrina*
Status: Regular.
Abundance: Common migrant, very rare winter visitor.
Spring: Mid Apr to mid May.
    Arrivals: 4 Apr 1975, Memp., MIG 46:65
                 9 Apr 1986, Stewart Co., MIG 57:80
                 11 Apr 1965, Chat., MIG 36:64
    Departures: 24 May 1987, Henry Co., MIG 58:93
                 25 May 1975, Knoxville, MIG 46:90
                 26 May 1979, Nash., BNA:36
Fall: Late Aug to late Oct.
    Arrivals: 2 Aug 1980, Nash., BNA:36
                 9 Aug 1969, near Roan Mt., MIG 40:93
                 25 Aug 1941, Memp., MIG 12:59

Tennessee Warbler, continued

Departures: 11 Nov 1978, Memp., MIG 50:41

                    12 Nov 1984, Chat., MIG 56:26

                    28 Nov 1961, Nash., BNA:36

Winter: Three records:

      3 Jan 1936, Knoxville, MIG 7:24

      28 Jan 1950, Nash., (Laskey 1950)

      17 Nov-2 Jan 1934/35, Nash., (Mayfield 1935)

Remarks: Found in wooded areas and along woodland edge; also in second growth areas and shrubby thickets. At times, becomes locally abundant during the spring and fall migration periods. High counts: 140 on 1 Oct 1983, Elizabethton Fall Bird Count (*fide* RLK) and 135 on 6 May 1970, Memp. SBC (MIG 41:38). Transmitter tower kills include: 325 birds on 30 Sept 1972, Holston Mt. (Herndon 1973); and 254 birds on 14 Oct 1969, Nash. (Laskey 1969).

Substantiation: Specimen: 1 female, Nash., Davidson Co., 2 Oct 1950 (LSUMZ, 76599).

Orange-crowned Warbler, *Vermivora celata*

Status: Regular.

Abundance: Uncommon migrant, rare winter resident.

Spring: Mid Apr to early May. The peak of the migration occurs in late Apr. Two early Mar records include 2 Mar 1987, Penal Farm (MIG 58:93); and 5 Mar 1950, Elizabethton (MIG 21:15).

Arrivals: 23 Mar 1986, Tennessee NWR, MIG 57:80

                 5 Apr 1936, Memp., MIG 7:38

                 13 Apr 1969, Knoxville, MIG 40:50

Departures: 8 May 1983, Reelfoot L. SBC, MIG 54:53

                 15 May 1981, Johnson City, MIG 52:74

                 20 May 1949, Clarksville, (Clebsch 1950)

Fall: Late Sept to early Nov. Most sightings occur in Oct.

Arrivals: 7 Sept 1987, Radnor L., MIG 59:37

                 17 Sept 1956, Bristol, MIG 28:12

                 12 Oct 1968, Reelfoot L., MIG 39:89

Departures: 8 Nov 1986, Penal Farm, MIG 58:21

                 19 Nov 1967, Greeneville, MIG 38:100

                 25 Nov 1978, Nash., BNA:36

Winter: There are winter records for all three regions of the state. Most sightings probably represent lingering fall migrants. Birds that successfully spent the winter at feeders include:

      27 Jan-16 Apr 1983, Elizabethton, MIG 54:67

      13 Jan-4 Apr 1984, Elizabethton, MIG 55:75

      20 Jan-22 Mar 1987, Knoxville, MIG 58:104

Orange-crowned Warbler, continued

Remarks: Found along woodland edge and in coniferous woodlands and shrubby thickets. A very uncommon migrant, most sightings are of one or two birds. High count: five on 26 Oct 1975, Williamson Co. (Goodpasture 1977).

Substantiation: Specimen: 1 female, Nash., Davidson Co., 24 Oct 1966 (LSUMZ, 76601).

Nashville Warbler, *Vermivora ruficapilla*

Status: Regular.

Abundance: Fairly common migrant.

Spring: Mid Apr to mid May.

Arrivals:	1 Apr 1978, Ashland City, MIG 49:68
	7 Apr 1978, Memp., MIG 49:66
	11 Apr 1981, Tennessee River Gorge, MIG 52:74
Departures:	17 May 1979, Dyersburg, MIG 50:86
	17 May 1916, Nash., BNA:36
	18 May 1984, Roan Mt., MIG 55:75

Fall: Early Sept to mid Oct.

Arrivals:	18 Aug 1939, Hardeman Co., (Calhoun 1941)
	28 Aug 1968, Carter Co., MIG 39:96
	31 Aug 1971, Nash., MIG 42:93
Departures:	7 Nov 1977, Erwin, Unicoi Co., MIG 49:48
	17 Nov 1981, Radnor L., BNA:36
	24 Nov 1977, Dyersburg, MIG 49:41

Remarks: Found in wooded areas, along woodland edge, and in shrubby secondary growth. Usually encountered singly or in small groups; most sightings involve concentrations of five or fewer birds. High count: forty-four on 30 Apr 1972, Knoxville SBC (MIG 43:47).

Substantiation: Specimen: 1 female, Nash., Davidson Co., 5 Oct 1954 (LSUMZ, 76611).

Northern Parula, *Parula americana*

Status: Regular.

Abundance: Uncommon to fairly common migrant and summer resident.

Spring: Arrives by early Apr.

Arrivals:	23 Mar 1975, Shelby Co., MIG 46:65
	27 Mar 1986, Montgomery Co., MIG 57:80
	1 Apr 1985, Meigs Co., MIG 56:80

Summer: Fairly evenly distributed over most of west Tennessee, but becomes locally common at Memp., Reelfoot L. and along the Hatchie River. In the east, it is found fairly commonly in the mountains, but is less numerous in the Ridge and Valley. In the GSMNP, Stupka (1963) found it breeding up to approximately 1,580 m MSL. Fewer birds are found in the Central Basin

Northern Parula, continued

region of middle Tennessee (Bierly 1980). Breeding males usually sing two song types, one of which is nearly identical to the song of the Cerulean Warbler.

Fall: Departs by late Sept.

Departures: 17 Oct 1975, Memp., MIG 47:17
23 Oct 1956, Elizabethton, MIG 28:13
3 Nov 1984, Nash., MIG 56:21

Remarks: Found in wooded swamps and lowland forests near streams. Usually observed foraging and singing high in the forest canopy during the breeding season; often utilizes the forest understory and second growth areas in migration. High count: ninety-eight on 18 Apr 1971, Memp. SBC (MIG 42:39).

Substantiation: Specimen: 1 male, near Woodstock, Shelby Co., 9 Sept 1947 (LSUMZ, 19591).

Yellow Warbler, *Dendroica petechia*

Status: Regular.

Abundance: East and Middle: fairly common migrant and summer resident; very rare winter visitor in the east.

West: fairly common migrant, rare summer resident.

Spring: Arrives by early Apr.

Arrivals: 27 Mar 1938, Knox Co., (Howell and Monroe 1957)
30 Mar 1988, Cheatham Co. (Margaret L. Mann)
16 Apr 1941, Gibson Co., MIG 12:37

Summer: A readily detectable breeding bird throughout east and middle Tennessee. Found breeding up to about 940 m MSL in the GSMNP (Stupka 1963). In the west, where Rhoads (1895) did not record it during his statewide survey, it is a rare summer resident. Between 1971 and 1982, observations of more than one bird or of birds present for more than one year were made in Benton, Lauderdale and Shelby Counties and at the Reelfoot L. area; and a nest was found in Shelby Co. in 1981 (Nicholson 1982).

Fall: Becomes less detectable after singing ends in early Aug. Most birds depart by mid Sept. Sightings after Sept are very rare.

Departures: 11 Sept 1941, Shelby Co., MIG 12:71
3 Oct 1965, Elizabethton, MIG 36:100
9 Oct 1959, Nash., MIG 31:11

Winter: One record: 17 Nov-11 Dec 1985, Knoxville (MIG 57:61).

Remarks: Found along woodland edge and in open areas with scattered trees, usually near water; frequently observed in willow thickets. High count: 131 on 1 May 1949, Elizabethton SBC (MIG 20:36).

Substantiation: Specimen: 1 male, Nash., Davidson Co., 1 May 1937 (LSUMZ, 76619).

Chestnut-sided Warbler, *Dendroica pensylvanica*

Status: Regular.

Abundance: East: fairly common migrant, locally fairly common summer resident.

Middle and West: fairly common migrant, very rare summer visitor.

Spring: Late Apr to mid May.

Arrivals:　　2 Apr 1981, Radnor L., MIG 52:72

　　　　　　16 Apr 1964, Elizabethton, MIG 35:43

　　　　　　23 Apr 1932, Reelfoot L., MIG 3:15

Departures:　24 May 1987, Radnor L., MIG 58:98

　　　　　　26 May 1963, Memp., MIG 34:49

　　　　　　31 May 1949, Nash., (Parmer 1963)

Summer: As a summer resident it is a common breeding bird in the eastern mountains and also occurs in smaller numbers on the higher mountains of the Cumberland Plateau. Ganier and Clebsch (1946) found it to be the fourth most common species in the Unicoi Mts., Monroe Co. Stupka (1963) listed it as a common summer resident in the GSMNP, where it breeds above 900 m MSL. At Roan Mt., it is usually found breeding at elevations above 800 m MSL. On the Plateau, from one to seven birds have recently been seen in the summer in Scott Co. (MIG 57:114) and in Morgan Co. on Frozen Head Mt. (Nicholson 1987). A nest with young was found in Campbell Co. on Cross Mt. in 1970 at an elevation of 860 m MSL (Campbell and Howell 1970). Occasionally it is observed at lower altitudes, with sightings having been made in all three regions; representative observations include:

　　10 June 1979, Chat., MIG 50:89-90

　　11 June 1975, Nash., MIG 46:89

　　7 July 1978, Shelby Co., MIG 49:91

Fall: Late Aug to mid Oct.

Arrivals:　　18 Aug 1933, White Co., MIG 4:39

　　　　　　21 Aug 1964, Nash., MIG 35:62

　　　　　　26 Aug 1941, Memp., MIG 12:59

Departures:　15 Oct 1956, Kingsport, MIG 28:11

　　　　　　21 Oct 1941, Memp., MIG 12:71

　　　　　　2 Nov 1974, Old Hickory L., MIG 46:71

Remarks: Found in wooded areas and in second growth habitat. High count: 55 on 24 Apr 1976, Elizabethton SBC (MIG 47:92). A total of 115 birds was picked up after a transmitter tower kill at Nash. on 14 Oct 1969 (Laskey 1969).

Substantiation: Specimen: 1 male, Nash., Davidson Co., 19 Sept 1943 (LSUMZ, 76623).

Magnolia Warbler, *Dendroica magnolia*

Status: Regular.

Abundance: Fairly common migrant, very rare summer visitor.

Magnolia Warbler, continued

Spring: Late Apr to late May. There is one Mar record: 10 Mar 1951, Elizabethton (MIG 22:18).

Arrivals: 13 Apr 1944, Nash., MIG 15:32
     19 Apr 1969, Sequatchie Co., MIG 40:50
     25 Apr 1979, Dyersburg, MIG 50:86

Departures: 30 May 1963, Knoxville, MIG 34:52
     3 June 1963, Nash., MIG 34:50
     4 June 1979, Shelby Co., MIG 50:86

Summer: At least three records: 30 June-14 July 1975 (three singing males), Roan Mt. (MIG 46:91); 16 May-30 June 1971, Clay Co. (MIG 42:70); and 21 June 1988 (1 singing male), Roan Mt. (RLK).

Fall: Late Aug to mid Oct.

Arrivals: 13 Aug 1958, Kingsport, MIG 29:58
     14 Aug 1941, Memp., MIG 12:58
     21 Aug 1976, Two Jays, BNA:36

Departures: 22 Oct 1950, Shelby Co., MIG 22:13
     31 Oct 1956, Elizabethton, MIG 28:13
     6 Nov 1938, Nash., MIG 9:98

Remarks: Found in wooded areas and along woodland edge. Usually found in larger numbers in the fall. High count: 106 on 29 Sept 1968, Knoxville (MIG 39:94).

Substantiation: Specimen: 1 male, Memp., Shelby Co., 6 May 1942 (LSUMZ, 6798).

Cape May Warbler, *Dendroica tigrina*

Status: Regular.

Abundance: East: fairly common migrant, very rare winter visitor.

Middle and West: uncommon spring migrant, rare fall migrant, very rare winter visitor.

Spring: Late Apr to mid May.

Arrivals: 7 Apr 1974, Bristol, MIG 45:80
     15 Apr 1919, Nash., BNA:36
     27 Apr 1975, Shelby Co., MIG 46:65

Departures: 19 May 1983, Memp., MIG 54:60
     30 May 1963, Knoxville, MIG 34:52
     2 June 1946, Pickett Co., (Spofford 1948)

Fall: Mid Sept to mid Oct.

Arrivals: 20 Aug 1941, Memp., MIG 12:58
     27 Aug 1962, Kingsport, MIG 33:50
     6 Sept 1968, Nash., (Laskey 1969a)

Departures: 23 Oct 1966, Nash., (Laskey 1966)
     26 Oct 1982, Elizabethton, MIG 54:27
     22 Nov 1975, Knoxville, MIG 47:48

Cape May Warbler, continued
Winter: There are six winter records:
    17 Jan 1972, Bristol, MIG 43:28
    9 Jan 1975, Tennessee NWR, MIG 46:44
    24 Dec 1975, Johnson City, MIG 47:48
    2 Dec-3 Jan 1975/76, Memp., MIG 47:45
    23 Nov-28 Dec 1975, Bristol, MIG 47:50
    early Jan-9 Feb 1982, Knoxville, MIG 53:48
Remarks: Found in wooded areas and along woodland edge. More abundant in the eastern third of the state, where it is generally most numerous in the fall. High count: 250 on 8 Sept 1979, Roan Mt. (MIG 51:20).
Substantiation: Specimen: 1 male, Nash., Davidson Co., 15 May 1967 (LSUMZ, 76704).

Black-throated Blue Warbler, *Dendroica caerulescens*
Status: Regular.
Abundance: East: fairly common migrant, locally common summer resident. Middle and West: rare migrant.
Spring: Late Apr to mid May.
    Arrivals: 3 Apr 1982, GSMNP, MIG 53:71
                   7 Apr 1973, Reelfoot L., MIG 44:50
                   11 Apr 1972, Nash., MIG 43:51
    Departures: 12 May 1960, Nash., MIG 31:45
                   16 May 1978, Warren Co., MIG 49:92
                   30 May 1976, Center Hill L., MIG 47:100
Summer: Resident almost exclusively in the eastern mountain region at the higher elevations. In the GSMNP it is found commonly above 850 m MSL but may breed as low as 730 m MSL (Stupka 1963). Breeding on the Cumberland Plateau is rare. A nest with eggs was found in 1922 in Grundy Co. (Ganier 1956); and, after summering birds were present in 1983-1986 on Frozen Head Mt. in Morgan Co., a pair feeding young was observed there at 848 m MSL in 1986 (Nicholson 1987). Additional records from the Cumberland Plateau include one bird at Fall Creek Falls S.P. on 3 June 1975 (MIG 46:88-89); and a female found on 22 Aug 1978 in Warren Co. (MIG 50:21) (the latter date may represent an early fall migrant).
Fall: Late Sept to mid Oct.
    Arrivals: 9 Sept 1981, Nash., MIG 53:17
                   23 Sept 1961, Nash., MIG 33:13
                   2 Oct 1977, Natchez Trace S.P., MIG 49:18
    Departures: 24 Oct 1966, Nash., (Laskey 1966)
                   27 Oct 1985, Shelby Co., MIG 57:23
                   24 Nov 1981, Watauga L., MIG 53:23
Remarks: Found in deciduous and mixed deciduous-coniferous woodlands, usually in the understory. High count: 62 on 6 May 1951, Elizabethton SBC

Black-throated Blue Warbler, continiued
(MIG 22:26). On Holston Mt. 105 birds of this species were picked up after a transmitter tower kill on 30 Sept 1972 (Herndon 1973).
Substantiation: Specimen: 1 male, Nash., Davidson Co., 24 Sept 1965 (LSUMZ, 76638).

Yellow-rumped Warbler, *Dendroica coronata*
Status: Regular.
Abundance: Common migrant, fairly common winter resident, very rare summer visitor.
Fall: Arrives by late Sept.
  Arrivals: 11 Aug 1955, Chat., MIG 26:50
               28 Aug 1987, LBL, MIG 59:37
               27 Sept 1987, Penal Farm, MIG 59:32
Winter: Tennessee's only regular winter warbler. Wintering population fluctuates, and in some years the species is not as numerous. May sometimes be locally abundant (e.g., 364 birds on 1 Jan 1985, Hiwassee CBC, MIG 56:8).
Spring: Departs by mid May.
  Departures: 15 May 1960, Memp. SBC, MIG 31:32
               19 May 1966, Elizabethton, MIG 37:26
               24 May 1976, Nash., MIG 47:100
Summer: There are three summer records of non-breeding birds:
  1 June 1952, Johnson City, (Tyler and Lyle 1952)
  26 July 1984, Lawrence Co., MIG 56:21
  28 June 1977, Nash., MIG 48:104
The 1952 sighting was reported as an "Audubon's" Yellow-rumped Warbler, but the details are sketchy and not totally convincing (see Remarks below).
Remarks: Found in wooded areas and along woodland edge. In the winter, it is often observed feeding on poison ivy berries. A well-described individual of the "Audubon's" race was found on 15 Mar 1987 in LBL, Stewart Co. (Robinson 1988c). High count: 522 on 28 Apr 1968, Knoxville SBC (MIG 39:33).
Substantiation: Specimen: 1 male, Nash., Davidson Co., 21 Apr 1946 (LSUMZ, 76723).

Black-throated Gray Warbler, *Dendroica nigrescens*
Status: Accidental.
Remarks: An ad. male of this species was picked up on 2 Oct 1972 at the weather radar station on Holston Mt. (elevation 1,280 m MSL) after a radar tower kill that occurred on the night of 30 Sept 1972 (Herndon 1972).
Substantiation: Specimen: 1 ad. male, Holston Mt., Carter Co., 30 Sept 1972 (Milligan College, 184).

Black-throated Green Warbler, *Dendroica virens*
Status: Regular.
Abundance: East: fairly common migrant, locally fairly common summer resident.
Middle: fairly common migrant, rare summer visitor.
West: fairly common migrant.
Spring: Early Apr to mid May.
    Arrivals: 13 Mar 1967, Tennessee River Gorge, MIG 38:52
                     19 Mar 1933, Memp., MIG 4:8
                     20 Mar 1921, Nash., BNA:37
    Departures: 28 May 1950, Decatur Co., MIG 21:51
                     29 May 1919, Nash., BNA:37
                     4 June 1987, Benton Co., MIG 58:138
Summer: In middle Tennessee, wandering birds are occasionally found (e.g., 5 June 1983, Hickman Co., MIG 54:89; and 9 July 1967, Williamson Co., MIG 38:66). The following observations in Pickett, Putnam and White Counties may indicate resident birds along the western edge of the Cumberland Plateau:
    1, 22 June 1969, Pickett S.P., MIG 40:69
    12 July 1970, Pickett S.P., MIG 41:69
    13, 20 July 1933, White Co., MIG 4:39
    12 June 1988, near Monterey, Putnam Co. (BHS)
    16 June 1988, Scott Pinnacle, White Co. (BHS)
In the east it is found breeding on the Cumberland Plateau and in the eastern mountains. Stupka (1963) stated that this warbler is present in the hemlock and spruce-fir forests at all elevations in the GSMNP. On Roan Mt., it is generally absent as a breeding bird from the spruce-fir forests.
Fall: Late Aug to late Oct.
    Arrivals: 2 Aug 1960, Nash., MIG 31:46
                     2 Aug 1986, Memp., MIG 58:21
                     7 Aug 1937, Memp., MIG 8:58
    Departures: 25 Oct 1985, Claiborne Co., MIG 57:34
                     9 Nov 1975, Memp., MIG 47:45
                     12 Nov 1979, Nash., MIG 51:40
Remarks: Found in deciduous and coniferous woodlands and second growth areas. May occasionally be heard singing during the fall migration. High count: seventy-one on 29 Apr 1973, Knoxville SBC (MIG 44:47).
Substantiation: Specimen: 1 male, Nash., Davidson Co., 7 Oct 1951 (LSUMZ, 76689).

Blackburnian Warbler, *Dendroica fusca*
Status: Regular.
Abundance: East: uncommon migrant, locally common summer resident.
Middle and West: uncommon migrant.

Blackburnian Warbler, continued
Spring: Late Apr to late May.
  Arrivals: 4 Apr 1935, near Knoxville, MIG 6:38
                 8 Apr 1977, Shelby Co., MIG 48:75
                 12 Apr 1981, Nash., MIG 52:72
  Departures: 25 May 1950, Memp., MIG 21:51
                 30 May 1946, Nash., (Parmer 1963)
                 31 May 1984, Williamson Co., MIG 55:71
Summer: Found breeding in the higher elevations of the eastern mountains, primarily in the GSMNP and the Unicoi Mts. Lyle and Tyler (1934) and Ganier (1936) did not list this species among the breeding birds of northeast Tennessee and Roan Mt., respectively. However, a pair was present on McQueen Knob (1,100 m MSL), Johnson Co., during June 1988 (RLK). In the GSMNP it occurs at elevations above 900 m MSL (Stupka 1963), and in the Unicoi Mts. it was found above 1,200 m MSL. Recent evidence indicates it is to be found uncommonly on the Cumberland Plateau: on 16 June 1970 an active nest was found at Fall Creek Falls S.P. (MIG 41:69); and in 1987 a pair feeding young was observed at an elevation of 823 m on Frozen Head Mt. in Morgan Co. (Nicholson 1987). One bird was present at an elevation of 650 m on Cross Mt., Campbell Co., on 19 June 1971 (Howell and Campbell 1972).
Fall: Late Aug to mid Oct.
  Arrivals: 4 Aug 1955, Chat., MIG 26:50
                 4 Aug 1960, Nash., BNA:37
                 26 Aug 1941, Memp., MIG 12:59
  Departures: 28 Oct 1947, Knox Co., (Howell and Monroe 1957)
                 28 Oct 1941, Memp., MIG 12:71
                 30 Oct 1964, Nash., MIG 35:102
Remarks: Found in coniferous and mixed coniferous-deciduous woodlands.
  High count: forty-one on 27 Apr 1958, Knoxville SBC (MIG 29:32).
Substantiation: Specimen: 1 male, Clarksville, Montgomery Co., 18 Sept 1940 (LSUMZ, 76713).

Yellow-throated Warbler, *Dendroica dominica*
Status: Regular.
Abundance: Fairly common migrant and summer resident, very rare winter visitor.
Spring: Arrives by late Mar.
  Arrivals: 15 Mar 1977, Tennessee River Gorge, MIG 48:50
                 19 Mar 1933, Memp., MIG 4:8
                 21 Mar 1953, Williamson Co., BNA:37
Summer: Breeds throughout the state. Usually found below 760 m MSL in the east, where it is local in the mountains and generally uncommon in the

Yellow-throated Warbler, continued

Ridge and Valley. Lyle and Tyler (1934) found it breeding up to about 910 m MSL in northeast Tennessee. More widely distributed in middle and west Tennessee.

Fall: Departs by mid Sept.

Departures: 14 Oct 1967, Pickwick L. dam, MIG 38:94
              28 Oct 1984, Knoxville, MIG 56:26
              5 Nov 1970, Columbia, MIG 42:19

Winter: Two records: 26 Feb 1950, Reelfoot L. (Smith 1950), and 8 Dec 1984, Knoxville (MIG 56:56).

Remarks: Found in wooded areas, usually near streams; prefers pines, sycamore and cypress trees. High count: twenty-nine on 25 Apr 1964, Nash. SBC (MIG 35:48).

Substantiation: Specimen: 1 male, Memp., Shelby Co., 23 June 1944 (LSUMZ, 9413).

Pine Warbler, *Dendroica pinus*

Status: Regular.

Abundance: East and Middle: fairly common migrant, uncommon summer resident, rare winter resident.

West: uncommon migrant and summer resident, rare winter resident.

Remarks: Found in coniferous or mixed deciduous-coniferous woodlands. Breeding distribution is limited by availability of suitable habitat (mature pine forests). In the east it occurs up to the lower elevations (ca. 970 m MSL) of the eastern mountains. Nests throughout the middle and east, but becomes less numerous in the west. Recently nested in Benton Co. (MIG 42:43). Spring migration is usually evident by early Mar and the fall migration usually peaks in Sept. Obvious migratory movements include seventeen birds on 3 Mar 1974, Catoosa WMA (MIG 45:21) and twenty-five birds on 26 Sept 1968, near Johnson City (MIG 39:96). In recent years more winter observations of Pine Warblers have been recorded, probably due in part to the use of tape-recorded owl calls to attract birds within viewing range. Recent winter records from the northern tier of counties include:

3 Jan 1976, Kingsport CBC, MIG 47:37
16 Jan 1987, Henry Co., MIG 58:54
1 Jan 1987, Stewart Co. (JCR)

High counts: 63 on 13 Mar 1987, Hardin Co. (MIG 58:93) and 57 on 1 Jan 1987, Hiwassee CBC (MIG 58:4).

Substantiation: Specimen: 1 male, Pocahontas, Hardeman Co., 17 June 1942 (LSUMZ, 76656).

Kirtland's Warbler, *Dendroica kirtlandii*

Status: Accidental (Provisional) (Federally Endangered).

Remarks: Known from one record. A well described bird of this species was seen on 28 Sept 1956 at Greeneville, Greene Co. (Darnell 1956). Placed on

Kirtland's Warbler, continued
the provisional list of Tennessee bird species in 1983 (Nicholson 1983).
Substantiation: Adequately documented sight record.

Prairie Warbler, *Dendroica discolor*
Status: Regular.
Abundance: Fairly common to uncommon migrant and summer resident.
Spring: Arrives by early Apr.
Arrivals: 21 Mar 1972, Sequatchie Co., MIG 43:54
                4 Apr 1929, Nash., BNA:37
                7 Apr 1968, Savannah, Hardin Co., MIG 39:42
Summer: As a breeding species it is most abundant in middle Tennessee, where suitable habitat is plentiful. In the east, Stupka (1963) noted it breeding up to an elevation of 820 m MSL in the GSMNP, although it currently is not as abundant due to lack of early successional habitat. It is locally uncommon in northeast Tennessee, where a nest with eggs was found on South Holston L., Sullivan Co., on 12 June 1964 (MIG 35:64). Bierly (1980) listed it as a transient in the Roan Mt. area. It can be expected at lower elevations elsewhere in the east. In the west, the frequency of sightings decreases as one moves westwards from the Tennessee River. Nesting was documented in Benton Co. in 1973 (Alsop 1976).
Fall: Departs by mid Sept.
Departures: 17 Sept 1986, Pace Point, MIG 58:21
                19 Oct 1968, Knoxville, MIG 39:94
                19 Oct 1984, Percy Warner Park, Nash., MIG 56:21
Remarks: Found in shrubby second growth habitats. High count: eighty-eight on 26 Apr 1959, Knoxville SBC (MIG 30:23).
Substantiation: Specimen: 1 male, Cheatham Co., 22 May 1943 (LSUMZ, 76700).

Palm Warbler, *Dendroica palmarum*
Status: Regular.
Abundance: Fairly common migrant, rare winter resident.
Spring: Mid Apr to mid May. There are several Mar records ranging from 7 Mar 1987, Blount Co. (MIG 58:104) to 30 Mar 1963, near Nash. (MIG 34:50).
Arrivals: 1 Apr 1975, Penal Farm, MIG 46:65
                3 Apr 1976, Wilbur L., MIG 47:80
                10 Apr 1972, Davidson Co., MIG 43:51
Departures: 7 May 1937, Reelfoot L., (Wetmore 1939)
                31 May 1937, Cades Cove, GSMNP, MIG 8:41
                4 June 1988, Nash. (David F. Vogt)
Fall: Early Oct to mid Nov. There is one Aug record: 13 Aug 1975, Radnor L. (MIG 47:19).

Palm Warbler, continued

Arrivals: 5 Sept 1976, Cannon Co., MIG 48:19
                 7 Sept 1981, Knoxville, MIG 53:21
                 8 Sept 1955, Ashland City Marsh, BNA:37

Departures: 18 Nov 1939, Knoxville, MIG 10:76
                 25 Nov 1966, Nash., MIG 37:81
                 25 Nov 1984, Jefferson Co., MIG 56:26

Winter: More than fifty winter records, but seldom seen after mid Jan. The species could occur anywhere in the state. Peak winter counts are of fifteen birds on 29 Dec 1963, GSMNP CBC (MIG 34:84), and of twelve birds on 2 Jan 1982, Hickory-Priest CBC (MIG 53:8).

Remarks: Found in brushy woodland openings, brushy fields and thickets, and in agricultural fields. High count: 157 on 5 May 1968, Chat. SBC (MIG 39:33). In the fall it is most numerous in east Tennessee (e.g., one hundred on 2 Oct 1976, Austin Springs, MIG 48:22); Stupka (1963) reported a flock of several hundred birds on 16 Oct 1940 at the GSMNP, and he observed flocks of at least a hundred birds there on the following dates: 17 Oct 1941, 21 Sept 1942, 24 Sept 1943 and 9 Oct 1945.

Substantiation: Specimen: 1 male, Nash., Davidson Co., 17 Oct 1943 (LSUMZ, 76736).

Bay-breasted Warbler, *Dendroica castanea*
Status: Regular.
Abundance: Uncommon to fairly common spring migrant, fairly common fall migrant.
Spring: Late Apr to mid May.

Arrivals: 18 Apr 1988, Murfreesboro (Terry J. Witt)
                 20 Apr 1985, Knoxville, MIG 56:81
                 26 Apr 1981, Memp. SBC, MIG 52:66

Departures: 23 May 1987, Henry Co. (JCR)
                 24 May 1983, Johnson City (Martha Dillenbeck)
                 28 May 1982, Radnor L., BNA:37

Fall: Early Sept to late Oct.

Arrivals: 13 Aug 1953, Nash., BNA:37
                 20 Aug 1984, Van Buren Co., MIG 56:21
                 31 Aug 1955, Elizabethton, MIG 26:51

Departures: 2 Nov 1975, Johnson City (Sally Goodin)
                 7 Nov 1974, Memp., MIG 46:44
                 21 Nov 1925, Nash., BNA:37

Remarks: Found in wooded areas. High counts: 138 on 28 Sept 1985, Elizabethton Fall Bird Count (*fide* RLK) and 60 on 12 May 1973, Kingsport SBC (MIG 44:47). The following numbers of birds were picked up after ceilometer/transmitter tower kills: 63 birds on 7 Oct 1951, Knoxville (Howell and Tanner 1951); and 206 birds on 14 Oct 1969, Nash. (Laskey 1969).

Bay-breasted Warbler, continued

Substantiation: Specimen: 1 male, Nash., Davidson Co., 6 Oct 1946 (LSUMZ, 76760).

Blackpoll Warbler, *Dendroica striata*

Status: Regular.

Abundance: Fairly common spring migrant, rare fall migrant.

Spring: Late Apr to late May.

    Arrivals: 27 Mar 1954, Chat., MIG 25:54

                    10 Apr 1952, Nash., BNA:37

                    13 Apr 1968, Savannah, Hardin Co., MIG 39:42

    Departures: 24 May 1967, Hardin Co., MIG 38:47

                    2 June 1942, Nash., MIG 13:46

                    2 June 1968, Gatlinburg, MIG 39:67

Fall: Mid Sept to mid Oct.

    Arrivals: 5 Sept 1962, Nash., (Ganier 1962b)

                    8 Sept 1977, near Wilbur L., MIG 49:23

                    11 Sept 1959, Nash., (Laskey 1960)

    Departures: 14 Oct 1985, Paris Landing S.P., MIG 57:23

                    22 Oct 1986, Austin Springs, MIG 58:29

                    26 Oct 1975, Nash., (Goodpasture 1976)

Remarks: Found in wooded areas. In the fall, when migration takes place primarily along the Atlantic Coast, birds in Tennessee should be identified with care. High count: 178 on 8 or 9 May 1954, Reelfoot L. (MIG 25:27, 32).

Substantiation: Specimen: 1 female, Nash., Davidson Co., 19 May 1945 (LSUMZ, 76749).

Cerulean Warbler, *Dendroica cerulea*

Status: Regular.

Abundance: Uncommon migrant and summer resident.

Spring: Arrives by mid Apr.

    Arrivals: 29 Mar 1985, Williamson Co., MIG 56:77

                    5 Apr 1957, Memp., MIG 28:26

                    11 Apr 1965, Chat., MIG 36:64

Summer: Somewhat local in distribution. Becomes less detectable in the east, where Stupka (1963) listed it as a very uncommon summer resident in the GSMNP. It is rare in northeast Tennessee. Although it is found breeding throughout the state, it is not particularly numerous anywhere. However, Nicholson (1987) found thirty-eight singing birds along 13.3 km of trails in the Frozen Head State Natural Area, Morgan Co.

Fall: Departs by early Sept.

    Departures: 1 Sept 1939, near Hardeman Co., (Calhoun 1941)

                    4 Oct 1975, Washington Co., MIG 47:22

                    6 Oct 1979, Nash., BNA:37

Cerulean Warbler, continued

Remarks: Found in river or creek bottom forests in west Tennessee, and in mature upland deciduous forests in middle and east Tennessee; generally observed in the tops of trees. Fall migration is unremarkable and poorly documented. High count: fifty-five on 29 Apr 1973, Knoxville SBC (MIG 44:47).

Substantiation: Specimen: 1 male, Memp., Shelby Co., 23 Apr 1943 (LSUMZ, 7935).

Black-and-white Warbler, *Mniotilta varia*

Status: Regular.

Abundance: East: fairly common migrant and summer resident, very rare winter visitor.

Middle and West: fairly common migrant, uncommon summer resident, very rare winter visitor.

Spring: Arrives by late Mar.

Arrivals: 18 Mar 1922, Radnor L., BNA:37
              22 Mar 1982, Grundy Co., MIG 53:69
              25 Mar 1967, Hardin Co., MIG 38:47

Summer: During the breeding season it is very uncommon in the west where it has been primarily recorded in Shelby Co. and Chickasaw State Forest. Becomes more widespread in middle Tennessee and especially in the east. It is a common breeding species in northeast Tennessee; Ganier and Clebsch (1946) found at least two immatures in the Unicoi Mts., Monroe Co., above 1,200 m MSL; and Stupka (1963) reported it as a common summer resident which breeds primarily below 1,520 m MSL in the GSMNP.

Fall: Departs by early Oct.

Departures: 1 Nov 1986, Shelby Co., MIG 58:21
              6 Nov 1954, Radnor L., BNA:37
              9 Nov 1958, Kingsport, MIG 30:11

Winter: About seven records, all of which appear to represent lingering fall migrants:

      3 Dec-1 Jan 1923/24, Nash., BNA:37
      20-23 Dec 1941, Memp., MIG 13:20
      7 Dec 1963, Kingsport, MIG 34:76
      15 Dec 1973, Nash., MIG 45:21
      28 Nov-8 Dec 1975, Nash., MIG 47:46
      7-14 Dec 1975, Johnson City, MIG 47:48
      8 Dec 1983, Dekalb Co., MIG 56:53

Remarks: Found in mature or second growth wooded areas. High count: seventy-eight on 26 Apr 1980, Elizabethton SBC (MIG 51:57).

Substantiation: Specimen: 1 female, Memp., Shelby Co., 26 Aug 1942 (LSUMZ, 6920).

American Redstart, *Setophaga ruticilla*

Status: Regular.

Abundance: East: fairly common migrant, uncommon to fairly common summer resident.

Middle: fairly common migrant, rare summer resident.

West: fairly common migrant and summer resident.

Spring: Arrives by mid Apr.

Arrivals: 1 Apr 1967, Williamson Co., MIG 38:49

3 Apr 1967, Tennessee River Gorge, MIG 38:52

13 Apr 1979, Memp., MIG 50:68

Summer: As a breeding species the redstart is most easily found in the Mississippi and Hatchie River floodplains in the west. Population in middle Tennessee has declined since 1933, when Ganier (1933) considered it a fairly common summer resident in that region. However, in some areas of middle Tennessee, it is still a locally uncommon breeder. In east Tennessee, Lyle and Tyler (1934) found it to be a fairly common breeding species in northeast Tennessee; Stupka (1963) listed it as a fairly common breeding bird up to about 760 m MSL in the GSMNP; and Nicholson (1987) documented a notable concentration on the Cumberland Plateau in Morgan Co.

Fall: Departs by early Oct.

Departures: 1 Nov 1959, Two Jays, MIG 31:11

12 Nov 1953, Gatlinburg, (Stupka 1963)

18 Nov 1969, Nash., BNA:38

Remarks: Found in wooded areas, primarily river bottom forests; also in shrubby, second growth habitats. A very active warbler; often seen catching its prey on the wing, like a flycatcher. High count: fifty-three on 21 June 1980, Hatchie River SBC (MIG 51:57).

Substantiation: Specimen: 1 male, Memp., Shelby Co., 4 Aug 1944 (LSUMZ, 9665).

Prothonotary Warbler, *Protonotaria citrea*

Status: Regular.

Abundance: East: uncommon migrant and summer resident.

Middle and West: fairly common migrant and summer resident; very rare winter visitor in middle.

Spring: Arrives by early Apr.

Arrivals: 27 Mar 1977, Fayette Co., MIG 48:75

30 Mar 1977, Old Hickory L., MIG 48:76

6 Apr 1935, near Knoxville, MIG 6:38

Summer: Found breeding throughout the state, but in considerably fewer numbers in the east, where breeding has been documented in Washington Co., in Greene Co. in 1959 (MIG 30:38), and in Knox Co. in 1937 (Ijams 1937). It is especially uncommon in upper east Tennessee. More numerous and widespread in middle and west Tennessee.

Prothonotary Warbler, continued

Fall: Departs by early Sept.

Departures: 25 Sept 1985, Pace Point, MIG 57:23
19 Oct 1943, Elizabethton, (Herndon 1944)
24 Oct 1980, Nash., BNA:38

Winter: One record: 2 Dec 1985, Bear Creek WMA, Stewart Co. (MIG 57:57).

Remarks: Found in wooded swamps and other woodlands near water; occasionally found away from water along woodland edge, especially during migration. Observed on Roan Mt. at an elevation of 1,675 m MSL on 8 Sept 1979 (MIG 51:20). High count: eighty-seven on 29 Apr 1967, Reelfoot L. SBC (MIG 38:34).

Substantiation: Specimen: 1 male, Nash., Davidson Co., 6 Sept 1962 (LSUMZ, 76832).

Worm-eating Warbler, *Helmitheros vermivorus*

Status: Regular.

Abundance: East and Middle: uncommon to fairly common migrant and summer resident.

West: uncommon migrant, rare summer resident.

Spring: Arrives by mid Apr.

Arrivals: 27 Mar 1954, Shelby Co., MIG 25:51
5 Apr 1986, Knoxville, MIG 57:86
7 Apr 1956, Radnor L., BNA:38

Summer: Well distributed (but somewhat local) throughout the middle and east, occurring up to about 1,200 m MSL in the eastern mountains. In the west it is rarely seen or reported in the summer; when it is found, the sightings usually consist of one or two birds. There appears to be no documented breeding evidence in the west.

Fall: Departs by early Sept.

Departures: 17 Sept 1956, Memp., MIG 27:68
6 Oct 1954, Johnson City, MIG 25:68
18 Oct 1972, Nash., MIG 43:100

Remarks: Found on wooded hillsides and ravines. High count: thirty-one on 26 Apr 1987, Knoxville SBC (MIG 58:83).

Substantiation: Specimen: 1 female, Nash., Davidson Co., 19 Apr 1951 (LSUMZ, 76825).

Swainson's Warbler, *Limnothlypis swainsonii*

Status: Regular.

Abundance: East and West: uncommon migrant and summer resident.

Middle: rare migrant and summer resident.

Spring: Arrives by late Apr.

Arrivals: 1 Apr 1972, Sequatchie Co., MIG 43:54
11 Apr 1977, Memp., MIG 48:75
20 Apr 1941, Montgomery Co., (Collier 1941)

Swainson's Warbler, continued

Summer: Nesting has been documented in the following counties: Obion in 1941 (Pickering 1941); Shelby in 1941 (Tucker 1941a); Henry in 1986 (*fide* Brainard Palmer-Ball, Jr.); Montgomery in 1940-1942 (Clebsch 1942); Cheatham in 1942 (Clebsch 1942); McMinn in 1902 (Ijams and Hofferbert 1934); and Carter in 1979 (MIG 50:91). Breeding population is distributed locally throughout the west and in the eastern mountains, where it breeds up to an elevation of about 820 m MSL (Alsop 1980). Birds have also been regularly observed on the Cumberland Plateau (e.g., eight birds on 10 July 1971, Campbell Co., MIG 42:72 and two birds on 1-2 June 1979, Fentress Co. [Nicholson 1981]). In middle Tennessee, no nests have been found since the 1942 nests in Cheatham and Montgomery Counties; the birds are now observed in this region primarily as rare spring migrants; one of the few recent summer records include 10 May-7 Sept 1975, Nash. (MIG 47:19).

Fall: Departs by early Sept. Fall migration is unremarkable. Dates listed below are all ceilometer/transmitter tower kills.

Departures: 28 Sept 1970, Nash., BNA:38
                7 Oct 1951, Knoxville, (Howell and Tanner 1951)
                15 Oct 1969, Savannah, Hardin Co., MIG 40:88

Remarks: Found in wooded swamps with canebrakes (west and middle) and in *Rhododendron* thickets along mountain ravines (east). A persistent singer. However, due to the dense habitat in which it occurs, many birds are heard but never seen. High count: fourteen on 31 May 1986, Haywood Co. (MIG 57:74).

Substantiation: Specimen: 1 male, Germantown, Shelby Co., 18 Apr 1942 (LSUMZ, 76813).

Ovenbird, *Seiurus aurocapillus*

Status: Regular.

Abundance: East: common migrant and summer resident, very rare winter visitor.

Middle: fairly common migrant, uncommon summer resident, very rare winter visitor.

West: fairly common migrant, rare summer resident.

Spring: Arrives by mid Apr.

Arrivals: 31 Mar 1945, Memp., MIG 16:11
               1 Apr 1928, Nash., BNA:38
               5 Apr 1986, Knoxville, MIG 57:86

Summer: Rare in the west. Recent records include a single bird on 14 June 1984, Carroll Co. (MIG 55:88) and a pair with young in McNairy Co. on 26 May 1982 (MIG 53:66). Uncommon in middle Tennessee along the Highland Rim, but becomes more numerous on the western edge of the Cumberland Plateau; very uncommon in the Central Basin (Bierly 1980). A common summer resident in the east, where Stupka (1963) reported it nesting up to about 1,370 m MSL in the GSMNP.

Ovenbird, continued
Fall: Departs by mid Oct.
    Departures: 17 Oct 1975, Memp., MIG 47:17
                    26 Nov 1920, Davidson Co., BNA:38
                    30 Nov 1959, GSMNP, (Stupka 1963)
Winter: There are three records:
    15 Dec 1976, Watauga L., MIG 48:51
    14 Dec-8 Jan 1978/79, Nash., BNA:38
    21 Dec 1985, Chat., MIG 57:11
Remarks: Breeds in mature woodland forests; in migration occurs in a variety of woodland and second growth habitats. High count: 110 on 28 Apr 1984, Elizabethton SBC (MIG 55:61). The following numbers of birds were picked up after ceilometer/transmitter tower kills:
    187 on 24 Sept 1955, Smyrna, (Laskey 1956)
    220 on 14 Oct 1969, Nash., (Laskey 1969)
    387 on 7 Oct 1951, Knoxville, (Howell and Tanner 1951)
    625 on 28 Sept 1970, Nash., MIG 41:86
Substantiation: Specimen: 1 male, Nash., Davidson Co., 5 May 1949 (LSUMZ, 76775).

Northern Waterthrush, *Seiurus noveboracensis*
Status: Regular.
Abundance: Uncommon migrant, very rare winter visitor.
Spring: Mid Apr to mid May.
    Arrivals: 1 Apr 1967, Nash., MIG 38:49
                    10 Apr 1977, Tennessee River Gorge, MIG 48:78
                    24 Apr 1975, Shelby Co., MIG 46:65
    Departures: 17 May 1952, Reelfoot L., MIG 23:29
                    23 May 1966, Nash., MIG 37:21
                    24 May 1974, Carter Co., MIG 45:104
Fall: Late Aug to early Oct.
    Arrivals: 8 Aug 1962, Elizabethton, MIG 33:51
                    19 Aug 1971, Nash., MIG 42:93
                    21 Aug 1987, Reelfoot L. (JCR)
    Departures: 6 Oct 1940, Mud L., MIG 11:103
                    28 Oct 1984, Tennessee NWR, MIG 56:22
                    23 Nov 1982, Austin Springs, MIG 54:26
Winter: There are three winter records:
    24 Dec 1971, Reelfoot L. CBC, MIG 43:13
    23 Dec 1972, Reelfoot L. CBC, MIG 44:12
    20 Dec 1980, Reelfoot L. CBC, MIG 52:14
Remarks: Found near standing water in wooded areas and along woodland edge. Behaviorally, tends to be tamer and more approachable than the Louisiana Waterthrush. High count: thirteen on 29 Apr 1972, Nash. SBC (MIG 43:47).

Northern Waterthrush, continued
Substantiation: Specimen: 1 male, Nash., Davidson Co., 9 Sept 1945 (LSUMZ, 76793).

Louisiana Waterthrush, *Seiurus motacilla*
Status: Regular.
Abundance: Fairly common migrant and summer resident, very rare winter visitor.
Spring: Arrives by mid Mar.
Arrivals: 3 Mar 1986, Cherokee National Forest, MIG 57:87
             10 Mar 1974, Williamson Co., MIG 45:21
             16 Mar 1977, Memp., MIG 48:75
Summer: A widely distributed (but somewhat local) breeding warbler. In the GSMNP it is a summer resident up to an elevation of about 1,060 m MSL (Stupka 1963). It is encountered fairly commonly in northeast Tennessee. Rhoads (1895) listed it as a "cosmopolitan summer resident . . . as numerous in one locality as another."
Fall: Departs by mid Aug.
Departures: 23 Aug 1969, Savannah, Hardin Co., MIG 40:89
               26 Sept 1970, Williamson Co., BNA:38
               5 Oct 1974, Erwin, Unicoi Co., MIG 46:23
Winter: Stupka (1963) described a wintering individual at Gatlinburg, present from 8 Dec 1954 to 25 Jan 1955.
Remarks: Found along streams and creeks, usually in woods. In migration, found in a wider variety of woodland and semi-open habitats. High count: thirty-nine on 29 Apr 1961, Nash. SBC (MIG 32:33).
Substantiation: Specimen: 1 male, Clarksville, Montgomery Co., 27 Mar 1944 (LSUMZ, 76802).

Kentucky Warbler, *Oporornis formosus*
Status: Regular.
Abundance: Fairly common migrant and summer resident.
Spring: Arrives by mid Apr.
Arrivals: 25 Mar 1954, Shelby Co., MIG 25:51
             9 Apr 1963, Nash., MIG 34:50
             12 Apr 1967, Chat., MIG 38:52
Summer: A fairly common (and sometimes locally common) breeding species throughout the state. Occurs up to about 1,060 m MSL in the GSMNP (Stupka 1963).
Fall: Departs by mid Sept.
Departures: 7 Oct 1986, Austin Springs, MIG 58:29
               9 Oct 1982, Knoxville, MIG 54:26
               29 Oct 1983, Nash., MIG 55:22
Remarks: Found in mature upland and lowland woodlands. High count: sixty on 25 Apr 1982, Memp. SBC (MIG 53:56).

Kentucky Warbler, continued
Substantiation: Specimen: 1 female, Nash., Davidson Co., 5 May 1943
(LSUMZ, 76888).

Connecticut Warbler, *Oporornis agilis*
Status: Regular.
Abundance: Rare migrant, very rare summer visitor.
Spring: Late Apr to late May.
Arrivals: 18 Apr 1973, Chat. SBC, MIG 44:47
18 Apr 1981, Nash., MIG 52:72
23 Apr 1936, Memp., MIG 7:38
Departures: 16 May 1983, Penal Farm, MIG 54:60
27 May 1947, Knoxville, (Monroe 1948)
29 May 1981, Nash., MIG 52:97
Summer: Known from one record, most likely of a late spring migrant: 13 June
1976, Alcoa Marsh, Blount Co. (MIG 47:102).
Fall: Early Sept to mid Oct.
Arrivals: 3 Sept 1944, Nash., BNA:38
7 Sept 1986, Penal Farm, MIG 58:21
13 Sept 1976, Erwin, Unicoi Co., MIG 48:22
Departures: 6 Oct 1975, Memp., MIG 47:17
17 Oct 1946, Nash., BNA:38
19 Oct 1975, Washington Co., MIG 47:24
Remarks: Found in weedy and shrubby thickets and in wooded areas with
dense underbrush; usually stays low and close to the ground. Most frequently seen in the middle and east; extremely rare in the west. Very few fall
records; fall migration occurs primarily along the Atlantic coast. High
count: four on 16 May 1943, Nash. (Abernathy 1943).
Substantiation: Specimen: 1 male, Nash., Davidson Co., 15 May 1967 (LSUMZ,
76896).

Mourning Warbler, *Oporornis philadelphia*
Status: Regular.
Abundance: Rare migrant, very rare summer visitor.
Spring: Early May to late May.
Arrivals: 16 Apr 1954, Shelby Co., MIG 25:52
21 Apr 1972, Johnson City, MIG 43:54
26 Apr 1959, Two Jays, BNA:38
Departures: 31 May 1971, Memp., MIG 42:68
1 June 1967, near Knoxville, MIG 38:67
4 June 1936, Centennial Park, Nash., (Parmer 1963)
Summer: One non-breeding record exists: 25 June 1985, Putnam Co. (MIG
56:111).

Mourning Warbler, continued
Fall: Early Sept to early Oct.
    Arrivals: 18 Aug 1933, White Co., MIG 4:39
                     19 Aug 1944, Shelby Co., (Tucker 1950)
                     8 Sept 1946, Knox Co., (Howell and Monroe 1958)
    Departures: 5 Oct 1947, Carter Co., (Herndon 1950)
                     28 Oct 1959, Nash., (Laskey 1960)
                     2 Nov 1986, Penal Farm, MIG 58:21
Remarks: Found low and close to the ground in weedy and shrubby thickets, and in wooded areas with dense underbrush. There are more spring records than fall records. Most records are from middle Tennessee where it is found twice as often as it is observed in either the east or west. High count: five on 9 Sept 1973, Two Jays (MIG 44:100).
Substantiation: Specimen: 1 female, Nash., Davidson Co., 11 Sept 1948 (LSUMZ, 76903).

Common Yellowthroat, *Geothlypis trichas*
Status: Regular.
Abundance: Common migrant and summer resident, rare winter resident.
Spring: Arrives by early Apr.
    Arrivals: 3 Mar 1957, Chat., MIG 28:9
                     19 Mar 1975, Memp., MIG 46:65
                     28 Mar 1986, Stewart Co., MIG 57:80
Summer: A common and widespread nesting species. Encountered regularly in a great variety of habitats from the Mississippi River floodplain to the summits of Roan Mt. Stupka (1963) reported it as a common summer resident at all elevations within the GSMNP.
Fall: Departs by late Oct.
    Departures: 31 Oct 1987, Reelfoot L. (JCR)
                     29 Nov 1985, Nash., MIG 57:29
                     1 Dec 1981, Elizabethton, MIG 53:50
Winter: There are more than forty winter records. Most observations are made in Dec and probably represent late or lingering migrants. Late winter sightings are rare; representative observations include:
        25 Jan 1986, Stewart Co., MIG 57:57
        14 Feb 1987, Reelfoot L., MIG 58:54
        21 Feb 1977, Knox Co., MIG 48:50
Remarks: Found in marshes and shrubby or weedy second growth areas. High count: 137 on 30 Apr 1972, Knoxville SBC (MIG 43:47).
Substantiation: Specimen: 1 male, Nash., Davidson Co., 13 May 1949 (LSUMZ, 76857).

Hooded Warbler, *Wilsonia citrina*
Status: Regular.
Abundance: East: fairly common migrant and summer resident.
Middle and West: uncommon migrant and summer resident.
Spring: Arrives by early Apr.
  Arrivals: 29 Mar 1977, Memp., MIG 48:102
                31 Mar 1929, Radnor L., BNA:39
                4 Apr 1967, Tennessee River Gorge, MIG 38:52
Summer: Becomes more numerous on the Cumberland Plateau and throughout
  the east, where Stupka (1963) listed it as a common summer resident up to
  about 1,200 m MSL in the GSMNP. Although Ganier (1933) listed it as a
  common summer resident in middle and west Tennessee, it is currently less
  abundant in these two regions of the state, and its current distribution is less
  widespread (and often local).
Fall: Departs by late Sept.
  Departures: 21 Oct 1979, Nash., MIG 51:16
                29 Oct 1972, Lawrence Co., MIG 43:100
                29 Nov 1955, GSMNP, (Stupka 1963)
Remarks: Found on hillsides and ravines in mature woodland forests; also occurs in bottomland forests. High count: seventy-four on 26 Apr 1980,
  Elizabethton SBC (MIG 51:57).
Substantiation: Specimen: 1 male, Nash., Davidson Co., 11 Sept 1948 (LSUMZ,
  76911).

Wilson's Warbler, *Wilsonia pusilla*
Status: Regular.
Abundance: Uncommon migrant.
Spring: Early May to late May.
  Arrivals: 15 Apr 1976, Johnson City, MIG 47:78
                17 Apr 1954, Lebanon SBC, MIG 25:32
                1 May 1953, Memp., MIG 24:55
  Departures: 24 May 1941, Shelby Co., (Tucker 1941b)
                27 May 1957, Knoxville, MIG 28:43
                29 May 1981, Nash., BNA:39
Fall: Early Sept to early Oct.
  Arrivals: 4 Aug 1980, Nash., BNA:39
                12 Aug 1939, Knoxville, MIG 10:58
                19 Aug 1940, Memp., MIG 11:76
  Departures: 13 Oct 1956, Elizabethton, MIG 28:13
                24 Oct 1966, Nash., (Laskey 1966)
                2 Nov 1971, Memp., MIG 43:23
Remarks: Found in semi-open areas, along woodland edge, and in shrubby
  thickets, often near water. High count: fifteen on 22 May 1983, Radnor L.
  (MIG 54:62).

Wilson's Warbler, continued

Substantiation: Specimen: 1 male, Germantown, Shelby Co., 11 May 1941 (LSUMZ, 5775).

Canada Warbler, *Wilsonia canadensis*

Status: Regular.

Abundance: East: uncommon migrant, locally common summer resident. Middle and West: uncommon migrant.

Spring: Late Apr to late May.

Arrivals: 17 Apr 1969, Tennessee River Gorge, MIG 40:50

    22 Apr 1975, Shelby Co., MIG 46:65

    23 Apr 1960, Two Jays, BNA:39

Departures: 28 May 1971, Nash., MIG 42:70

    29 May 1971, Memp., MIG 42:68

    31 May 1954, Knoxville, MIG 25:55

Summer: Nests in the high mountain elevations, usually above 1,035 m MSL. Breeding has been documented for the GSMNP (Stupka 1963), and on Roan Mt., Carter Co., in 1936 (Ganier 1936). It is possible that this species occurs as a breeding bird in very limited numbers on the Cumberland Plateau, as evidenced by two to six birds observed in May, June and July (includes a pair carrying food) on Frozen Head Mt. in 1985 and 1986 (Nicholson 1987).

Fall: Late Aug to late Sept.

Arrivals: 31 July 1938, Nash., MIG 9:52

    5 Aug 1964, Knoxville, MIG 35:63

    11 Aug 1941, Memp., MIG 12:58

Departures: 12 Sept 1936, Memp., MIG 7:69

    12 Oct 1976, Giles Co., MIG 48:19

    21 Oct 1979, Knoxville, MIG 51:19

Remarks: Found in wooded areas and shrubby woodland thickets. One of the earliest of the fall migrant warblers. High count: thirty-six on 10 May 1953, Roan Mt. SBC (MIG 24:39).

Substantiation: Specimen: 1 male, Unicoi Mts., Monroe Co., 18 June 1945 (LSUMZ, 76923).

Yellow-breasted Chat, *Icteria virens*

Status: Regular.

Abundance: Common migrant and summer resident, very rare winter visitor.

Spring: Arrives by mid Apr.

Arrivals: 8 Apr 1953, Nash., BNA:39

    14 Apr 1967, Hardin Co., MIG 38:47

    15 Apr 1965, Chat., MIG 36:64

Summer: A widespread and common nesting species. In the eastern mountains it breeds at low to mid elevations.

Fall: Departs by late Sept.

Yellow-breasted Chat, continued
>Departures: 13 Oct 1982, Memp., MIG 54:20
>6 Nov 1983, Norris, Anderson Co., MIG 55:26
>15 Nov 1981, Nash., MIG 53:17

Winter: About nine winter records. Representative sightings are listed below:
>12 Dec 1971, Anderson Co., MIG 43:27
>15-29 Dec 1983, Memp., MIG 55:43
>22 Feb 1953, near Nash., (Goodpasture 1953)

Remarks: Found in shrubby fields and thickets, and in second growth areas. Can often be heard singing after dark; frequently imitates the call notes of other bird species. High count: ninety-two on 29 Apr 1972, Nash. SBC (MIG 43:47).

Substantiation: Specimen: 1 male, Memp., Shelby Co., 8 Aug 1944 (LSUMZ, 9668).

SUBFAMILY THRAUPINAE: **Tanagers**

Summer Tanager, *Piranga rubra*
Status: Regular.
Abundance: Fairly common to uncommon migrant and summer resident, very rare winter visitor.
Spring: Arrives by mid Apr.
>Arrivals: 11 Mar 1966, Hamilton Co., MIG 37:23
>4 Apr 1988, Montgomery Co. (Anne H. Heilman)
>5 Apr 1957, Memp., MIG 28:26

Summer: A widely distributed nesting species. In the eastern mountains, Stupka (1963) noted that it is found up to about 600 m MSL, with the Scarlet Tanager replacing it at higher elevations. It is less numerous in northeast Tennessee.
Fall: Departs by early Oct.
>Departures: 20 Oct 1950, Elizabethton, MIG 22:17
>7 Nov 1975, Putnam Co., MIG 47:19
>16 Nov 1974, Memp., MIG 46:44

Winter: There are four winter records:
>21 Dec 1969, Knoxville CBC, MIG 41:9
>18 Dec 1977, Murfreesboro CBC, MIG 49:8
>5 Dec 1977, Shelby Co., MIG 49:41
>2 Feb-15 Mar 1978, Memp., MIG 49:41

Summer Tanager, continued

Remarks: Found in upland deciduous or mixed deciduous/coniferous woodlands. High count: seventy on 28 Apr 1985, Memp. SBC (MIG 56:70).

Substantiation: Specimen: 1 male, Nash., Davidson Co., 15 May 1943 (LSUMZ, 77084).

Scarlet Tanager, *Piranga olivacea*

Status: Regular.

Abundance: East: fairly common migrant and summer resident.

Middle: fairly common migrant, uncommon summer resident.

West: fairly common migrant, locally uncommon summer resident.

Spring: Arrives by mid Apr.

Arrivals: 1 Apr 1969, Knoxville, MIG 40:50

3 Apr 1988, Maury Co. (Anne R. Lochridge)

8 Apr 1967, Hardin Co., MIG 38:47

Summer: More numerous in the east, where Stupka (1963) reported it as a common summer resident in the GSMNP between 450 and 1,520 m MSL. It is also found fairly commonly in northeast Tennessee. In middle Tennessee it is less numerous, but probably occurs in appreciable numbers on the Highland Rim (e.g., 11 birds in Stewart Co. on 29 June 1986 [JCR]). In the west, it occurs at scattered localities in small numbers. A notable count was 13 birds in Benton Co. on 3 July 1984 (MIG 55:88).

Fall: Departs by mid Oct.

Departures: 28 Oct 1985, Memp., MIG 57:23

7 Nov 1976, Johnson City (Martha Dillenbeck)

27 Nov 1974, Nash., MIG 46:71

Remarks: Found in mature woodlands. High count: one hundred on 7 May 1978, Knoxville SBC (MIG 49:58).

Substantiation: Specimen: 1 male, Memp., Shelby Co., 23 Apr 1943 (LSUMZ, 7970).

Western Tanager, *Piranga ludoviciana*

Status: Accidental (Provisional).

Remarks: About four state records. Placed on the provisional list of Tennessee birds in 1983 (Nicholson 1983). An ad. male was seen in Dyersburg on 23-24 Apr 1969 (Hudson 1969). Details are lacking or insufficient for three other records: 19, 21 June 1985, Reelfoot L., Obion Co. (MIG 56:107); 21 Oct 1970 at Woodbury, Cannon Co. (MIG 41:86); and two birds that were reportedly present at Reelfoot L. in 1963 (Hudson 1969). Future sight records should be thoroughly documented.

Substantiation: Adequately documented sight record (TBRC).

SUBFAMILY CARDINALINAE: Cardinals, Grosbeaks and Allies

Northern Cardinal, *Cardinalis cardinalis*
Status: Regular.
Abundance: Common permanent resident.
Remarks: Found in shrubby thickets and woodland edge in a variety of urban and rural habitats. An abundant breeding bird throughout the state. Occurs up to about 1,060 m MSL in the GSMNP (Stupka 1963); at Roan Mt., it is found regularly as high as 1,370 m MSL (Eller and Wallace 1984). In the winter, often forms loose flocks of fifty or more birds. Common at bird feeders. High counts:
  797 on 28 Dec 1985, Clarksville CBC, MIG 57:11
  790 on 26 Dec 1983, Nash. CBC, MIG 55:10
  704 on 26 Dec 1965, Memp. CBC, MIG 36:90
Substantiation: Specimen: 1 male, Nash., Davidson Co., 13 Oct 1946 (LSUMZ, 77096).

Rose-breasted Grosbeak, *Pheucticus ludovicianus*
Status: Regular.
Abundance: East: fairly common migrant, locally common summer resident, rare winter resident.
Middle and West: fairly common migrant, rare winter resident.
Spring: Mid Apr to mid May.
  Arrivals: 16 Mar 1984, Columbia, MIG 55:71
                  23 Mar 1971, Dyersburg, MIG 42:43
                  13 Apr 1980, Campbell Co., MIG 51:62
  Departures: 15 May 1960, Memp. SBC, MIG 31:33
                  31 May 1976, Cannon Co., MIG 47:100
                  10 June 1986, Williamson Co., MIG 57:110
Summer: Found breeding primarily in the eastern mountains, where Stupka (1963) listed it as a common summer resident between 975 and 1,520 m MSL in the GSMNP. Ganier and Clebsch (1946) found it breeding in the Unicoi Mts. (Monroe Co.), and a nest was found in Greene Co. on Camp Creek Bald in 1968 (MIG 39:68). In 1987, a nest was found on Roan Mt. (Fred J.

Rose-breasted Grosbeak, continued

Alsop, III). On the Cumberland Plateau, Bierly (1980) listed it as a rare breeder in Campbell Co., and a pair was found building a nest in 1986 on Frozen Head Mt., Morgan Co. (MIG 57:86). Occasionally, birds are seen at lower elevations in the east in late June and throughout July.

Fall: Mid Sept to mid Oct.

Arrivals: 8 Aug 1964, Knoxville, MIG 35:63
             19 Aug 1973, Lake Co., MIG 44:99
             29 Aug 1976, Two Jays, MIG 48:19

Departures: 28 Oct 1975, Sequatchie Co., MIG 47:22
             12 Nov 1983, Davidson Co., MIG 55:22
             14 Nov 1984, Shelby Co., MIG 56:17

Winter: More than twenty winter records, primarily from east and middle Tennessee. Birds which remained for a substantial period of time include:

18 Dec-22 Feb 1975/76, Anderson Co., MIG 47:48
29 Dec-7 Feb 1978/79, Nash., MIG 50:43
11 Dec-20 Jan 1982/83, Hamilton Co., MIG 54:46
19 Dec-10 Jan 1982/83, Columbia, MIG 54:44

Remarks: Found in wooded areas. Becomes abundant at times during migration. High counts: 621 on 27 Sept 1980, Elizabethton Fall Bird Count (*fide* RLK); 437 on 28 Sept 1980, Knoxville (MIG 52:26); and 1,322 on 27-28 Sept 1980, Nash. Fall Count (BNA:39).

Substantiation: Specimen: 1 male, Memp., Shelby Co., 29 Apr 1943 (LSUMZ, 7974).

Black-headed Grosbeak, *Pheucticus melanocephalus*

Status: Extremely Rare.

Remarks: About 11 state records. First recorded in the state when one bird, which was present in mid winter 1968/69 through 24 Apr 1969 at Sevierville, was photographed (Alsop 1969). There were six separate sightings during 1974 and 1975. This species should be identified with care and only in good light; all observations should be thoroughly documented. Note the yellow or greenish yellow wing linings. All other sight records follow:

6 Sept 1987, Lake Co., MIG 59:32
30 Dec-9 Jan 1973/74, Murfreesboro, (Hettish 1974)
2 Jan-21 Apr 1975, Sumner Co., MIG 46:67
11-15 Jan 1974, Knoxville, MIG 45:24
13-19 Jan 1975, Memp., MIG 46:44
19 Jan-1 Mar 1970, Shelby Co., MIG 41:21
15 Mar 1975, Nash., MIG 46:67
26 Mar 1975, Nash., MIG 46:67
25-26 Apr 1981, Chat. SBC, MIG 52:66
4 May 1986, Nash., MIG 57:80

Substantiation: Photographs: 1, South Tunnel, Sumner Co., 8 Mar 1975 (JPC–TBRC).

Blue Grosbeak, *Guiraca caerulea*

Status: Regular.

Abundance: East and West: uncommon migrant and summer resident; very rare winter visitor in east.

Middle: fairly common migrant and summer resident.

Spring: Arrives by late Apr.

Arrivals: 28 Mar 1972, Murfreesboro, MIG 43:51

14 Apr 1974, Elizabethton, MIG 45:80

15 Apr 1980, Memp., MIG 51:60

Summer: Breeding range in Tennessee has significantly increased over the last forty years. First reported nesting was in McNairy Co. in 1945 (Warriner 1945), and then in Knox Co. in 1951 (Howell 1951). By 1962, it was nesting in Sullivan Co. (MIG 33:50) and in Williamson Co. (Goodpasture 1968). It is now a summer resident throughout most of the state, being mostly absent from the higher elevations of the eastern mountains and Cumberland Plateau. It is most numerous in middle Tennessee.

Fall: Departs by late Sept.

Departures: 9 Oct 1977, Davidson Co., MIG 49:19

14 Oct 1967, Pickwick L. dam, MIG 38:94

17 Oct 1964, Bristol, MIG 35:105

Winter: One record: 27 Dec 1970, Knoxville CBC (MIG 42:10).

Remarks: Found in shrubby fields and semi-open areas; frequently observed along roadsides. High count: thirty-eight on 30 Apr 1967, Chat. SBC (MIG 38:35).

Substantiation: Specimen: 1 male, 3 km E La Grange, Fayette Co., 6 July 1947 (LSUMZ, 19668).

Indigo Bunting, *Passerina cyanea*

Status: Regular.

Abundance: Common migrant and summer resident, rare winter visitor.

Spring: Arrives by mid Apr.

Arrivals: 19 Mar 1966, Elizabethton, MIG 37:26

21 Mar 1986, Lawrence Co., MIG 57:80

13 Apr 1986, Tennessee NWR (JCR)

Summer: A widespread and abundant breeding species; conspicuous in a great variety of habitats. In northeast Tennessee, it is fairly common on the summits of Roan Mt. Stupka (1963) listed it as a common summer resident in the GSMNP, where it breeds at the lower and middle elevations.

Fall: Departs by mid Oct.

Departures: 28 Oct 1967, near Savannah, MIG 38:94

29 Oct 1967, HRA, MIG 38:99

13 Nov 1978, Columbia, MIG 50:43

Winter: Representative sightings of the close to twenty winter records for the state include:

Indigo Bunting, continued
> 16 Jan-15 Mar 1975, Sumner Co., MIG 46:71
> 20 Jan-15 Mar 1976, Anderson Co., MIG 47:48
> 27 Feb-5 Mar 1986, Memp., MIG 57:51

Remarks: Found in open areas, especially in shrubby thickets and fields, and along roadsides and woodland edge. Forms loose flocks in the fall (Sept-Oct), when it is often encountered in weedy grain fields (e.g., corn or milo crops overgrown with johnsongrass). High count: 317 on 28 Apr 1985, Memp. SBC (MIG 56:70).

Substantiation: Specimen: 1 male, Nash., Davidson Co., 8 June 1940 (LSUMZ, 77122).

Painted Bunting, *Passerina ciris*
Status: Regular.
Abundance: West: locally rare summer resident.
Remarks: Found in open areas in shrubby or brushy fields and thickets along the Mississippi River from late Apr to mid July. Range in Tennessee is primarily restricted to Shelby and Tipton Counties. First recorded on 26 May 1929 at Memp. by Coffey (1933), who also recorded the only sighting in Obion Co. on 15 July 1934 (Coffey 1934). It was also observed at Barr, Lauderdale Co., on 24-25 May 1975 (Coffey 1976). Breeding has been documented for Shelby Co. (Coffey 1933), and is suspected in Tipton Co., where birds have been occasionally seen since 1975. One middle Tennessee record: 7 May 1988 (1 male), Lawrence Co. (DJS). High count: ten on 31 May 1981, President's Island, Shelby Co. (MIG 52:96).
Substantiation: Adequately documented sight records.

Dickcissel, *Spiza americana*
Status: Regular.
Abundance: East: uncommon to rare migrant and summer resident, rare winter resident.
Middle: uncommon migrant and summer resident, rare winter resident.
West: fairly common to common migrant and summer resident, rare winter resident.
Spring: Arrives by early May (there are several Mar records).
> Arrivals: 9 Apr 1975, Madison Co., MIG 46:66
>   12 Apr 1962, Nash., BNA:40
>   27 Apr 1984, Knoxville, MIG 55:74

Summer: Absent from most of the forested areas of the eastern mountains and the Cumberland Plateau. Breeds in small numbers in the lower elevations of the eastern valley in Hamblen, Knox, Greene, Sullivan, and Hamilton Counties. Breeding birds are also scattered uncommonly in middle Tennessee, most notably at the Cross Creeks NWR, Tennessee NWR in Humphreys Co., Lawrence Co., Montgomery Co. and Robertson Co. In the west, it is a com-

Dickcissel, continued

mon summer resident and becomes locally abundant within the Mississippi River floodplain.

Fall: Singing ends by mid Aug, after which Dickcissels become less conspicuous. Most birds depart by late Aug; however, a few individuals linger well into late fall and (rarely) may attempt to overwinter.

Winter: There are close to forty winter records, primarily from middle and west Tennessee. Representative records include:

16-31 Jan 1968, Greeneville, MIG 39:22

1 Nov-6 Mar 1974/75, Murfreesboro, MIG 46:71

20 Jan-7 Feb 1984, Memp., MIG 55:43

Remarks: Found in weedy fields, agricultural (grain and hay) fields and along roadsides. High count: 612 on 6 May 1970, Memp. SBC (MIG 41:38).

Substantiation: Specimen: 1 male, Nash., Davidson Co., 6 June 1943 (LSUMZ, 77140).

SUBFAMILY EMBERIZINAE: Towhees, Sparrows and Longspurs

Green-tailed Towhee, *Pipilo chlorurus*

Status: Accidental.

Remarks: Known from three records. First recorded at Memp. on 21-25 Dec 1952 (Smith 1952a). Another bird was found at Memp. on 23 Dec 1956 (MIG 27:73), and one was trapped, banded and later released at Elizabethton where it was present from 24 Mar-26 Apr 1957 (Herndon 1957).

Substantiation: Adequately documented sight records.

Rufous-sided Towhee, *Pipilo erythrophthalmus*

Status: Regular.

Abundance: Common permanent resident.

Remarks: A widely distributed breeding species. Nests from the Mississippi River floodplain to the higher elevations in the eastern mountains. The "spotted" form of the western U.S. has been occasionally recorded in west Tennessee as follows:

20 Dec-28 Apr 1952/53, Shelby Co., (Seahorn 1953)

19 Nov 1955, Shelby Co., MIG 27:16

12-25 Dec 1975, Shelby Co., MIG 47:45

3 Dec-19 Mar 1976/77, Shelby Co., MIG 48:45

12 Jan-26 Feb 1978, Reelfoot L., MIG 49:41

Rufous-sided Towhee, continued
Formerly absent during the breeding season from the extreme southwest part of the state (Coffey 1941); it was first recorded breeding at Memp. in Apr 1945 (Hoyt 1945a). Waldron (1987) listed it as a common permanent resident in Shelby Co. High count: 394 on 29 Apr 1962, Knoxville SBC (MIG 33:31).
Substantiation: Specimen: 1 male, Nash., Davidson Co., 21 Apr 1949 (LSUMZ, 77192).

Bachman's Sparrow, *Aimophila aestivalis*
Status: Irregular (State Endangered).
Abundance: Rare summer resident.
Spring: Arrives by mid Apr.
Arrivals:　　　4 Mar 1921, Nash., BNA:40
　　　　　　　9 Mar 1960, Chat., MIG 31:15
　　　　　　　11 Mar 1961, Hardeman Co., MIG 32:4
Summer: Formerly a fairly common and widely distributed species, it is now rare and local. Rhoads (1895) described it as "numerous" in Fentress, Scott and Morgan Counties on the Cumberland Plateau. The number of birds found on SBCs declined in the 1960s, and no birds were found on SBCs conducted between 1969 and 1975 (Nicholson 1976). Breeding has been documented in the following areas: McMinn Co. ca. 1910, Shelby Co. ca. 1944, Fayette Co. in 1975, near Nash. in 1918 and near Johnson City in 1934 (Nicholson 1976). Recently fledged young have been observed in Rutherford Co. in 1953, in Greene Co. in 1950 (Nicholson 1976) and in Montgomery Co. in 1937 (MIG 8:61). This species will utilize clear-cut areas replanted to pines until the pine tree overstory and underbrush become too dense. Recently established colonies in this type of habitat have been found in Giles Co. in 1985 (MIG 56:111) and Hardin Co. in 1987 (MIG 58:138).
Fall: Departs by mid Aug.
Departures:　　22 Aug 1939, near Hardeman Co., (Calhoun 1941)
　　　　　　　25 Sept 1970, Elizabethton, MIG 41:89
　　　　　　　17 Oct 1920, Nash., BNA:40
Remarks: Found in open woods or old fields with an interspersion of bare ground and herbaceous cover (prefers *Panicum* and *Andropogon* grasses); also uses clear-cut areas replanted to pines. A very secretive sparrow; rarely found unless song or call notes are heard. High count: fifteen on 28 May 1988, Hardin Co. (DJS).
Substantiation: Specimen: 1 male, Nash., Davidson Co., 12 Apr 1941 (LSUMZ, 77321).

American Tree Sparrow, *Spizella arborea*
Status: Regular.
Abundance: Rare winter resident.

American Tree Sparrow, continued
Fall: Arrives by late Dec. Observations in Oct and Nov are rare.
  Arrivals: 19 Oct 1969, Reelfoot L., MIG 40:89
                 28 Oct 1969, near Roan Mt., MIG 40:93
                 11 Nov 1943, Montgomery Co., (Clebsch 1943)
Winter: An irruptive species; frequency of sightings increases during "invasion" years. Usually not seen in southern or eastern counties unless large numbers have invaded the state.
Spring: Departs by mid Mar. Observations after late Mar are extremely rare and should be fully documented.
  Departures: 18 Mar 1978, Penal Farm, MIG 49:40
                 24 Mar 1968, Knoxville, MIG 39:47
                 26 Mar 1978, Ashland City, MIG 49:68
Remarks: Found in weedy and brushy fields. Occurs more often in the west and middle regions of the state than in the east. High count: two hundred on 17 Jan 1977, Cheatham L. (MIG 48:48).
Substantiation: Specimen: 1 female, near Germantown, Shelby Co., 23 Dec 1942 (LSUMZ, 7273).

Chipping Sparrow, *Spizella passerina*
Status: Regular.
Abundance: Fairly common migrant and summer resident, rare winter resident.
Remarks: Found in open deciduous and coniferous woodlands, and in thickets and shrubby areas, especially in residential habitats. It is easily detected between early Mar and mid Oct, but is scarce in (south), or absent from (north), most areas from Nov through Feb. Recent notable winter records include:
      23 on 1 Jan 1985, Hiwassee CBC, MIG 56:8
      25 on 28 Dec 1985, Elizabethton CBC, MIG 57:11
      36 on 4 Jan 1986, Nickajack L. CBC, MIG 58:4
Spring migrants begin returning north in increasing numbers by mid Mar. The peak of the migration occurs in Apr. It is a fairly evenly distributed nesting species throughout the state. Breeds primarily at the lower elevations in the eastern mountains. Occurs in fewer numbers in the Shelby Co. area during the summer. A nest at Audubon Park, Shelby Co., was found in May 1980 (MIG 51:92). High count: 136 on 25 Apr 1965, Knoxville SBC (MIG 36:74).
Substantiation: Specimen: 1 male, Nash., Davidson Co., 1 Apr 1945 (LSUMZ, 77377).

Clay-colored Sparrow, *Spizella pallida*
Status: Accidental.
Remarks: Known from three records, two of which had acceptable details. A singing bird was at Johnson City on 30 Apr-2 May 1933 (Tyler 1933), and a

Clay-colored Sparrow, continued

first year male was caught in a mist net on 17 Oct 1969, near Savannah (Patterson and Patterson 1969).

Substantiation: Specimen: 1 male, Olive Hill, Hardin Co., 17 Oct 1969 (LSUMZ, 77386).

Field Sparrow, *Spizella pusilla*

Status: Regular.

Abundance: Common permanent resident.

Remarks: Found in grassy and brushy fields and along woodland edge. Breeds throughout the state. Found at the lower and middle elevations in the eastern mountains, but may occasionally range to the mountain summits (ca. 1,600-1,860 m MSL), especially during the spring or fall. Seems to be less numerous in the extreme southwest in the summer and in the northeast in the winter. High counts:

> 647 on 1 Jan 1983, Hiwassee CBC, MIG 54:14
> 617 on 19 Dec 1981, Ashland City CBC, MIG 53:9
> 512 on 21 Dec 1941, Memp. CBC, MIG 13:20

Substantiation: Specimen: 1 female, Nash., Davidson Co., 24 Oct 1966 (LSUMZ, 77394).

Vesper Sparrow, *Pooecetes gramineus*

Status: Regular.

Abundance: East: uncommon migrant, locally uncommon summer resident, rare winter resident.

Middle and West: uncommon migrant, rare winter resident.

Spring: Mid Mar to mid Apr.

> Arrivals: 1 Mar 1934, McNairy Co., MIG 5:11
>   2 Mar 1941, Knoxville, MIG 12:19
>   8 Mar 1936, Clarksville, MIG 7:46
> Departures: 13 Apr 1986, Tennessee NWR, MIG 57:74
>   2 May 1985, Montgomery Co., MIG 56:77
>   7 May 1950, Knoxville, MIG 21:28

Summer: During the breeding season, the Vesper Sparrow is primarily found at Shady Valley and on the balds of Roan Mt., usually above 1,520 m MSL. Rhoads (1895) stated he found this species breeding at Johnson City. Lyle and Tyler (1934) cited an observation of two pairs feeding young in Shady Valley, Johnson Co.; and a nest with eggs was found in Shady Valley again in June 1966 (MIG 37:55). Also observed at Cross Mt., Campbell Co., on 8 July 1972 (MIG 43:80).

Fall: May occur at low elevations in the east by late Aug (e.g., 22 Aug 1971, Savannah Bay, MIG 42:95). There is a handful of Sept records. Most migrants are observed between mid Oct and mid Nov.

Winter: There are many winter records, usually from the southern tier of counties, but also from northern areas such as Reelfoot L., Dover, Clarksville,

Vesper Sparrow, continued

Knoxville and Johnson City. There are more observations in Dec and Jan than in Feb. Recent notable counts include:

19 on 14 Dec 1986, Penal Farm, MIG 58:54
20 on 14 Jan 1986, Lawrence Co., MIG 57:57
21 on 4 Jan 1986, Nickajack L. CBC, MIG 58:4

Remarks: Found in grassy and weedy fields, stubbly or fallow agricultural fields and along roadsides. Usually encountered in loose groups of 5-15 birds during migration. High count: 75 on 15 Apr 1980, Austin Springs (MIG 51:63).

Substantiation: Specimen: 1 female, Nash., Davidson Co., 8 Apr 1945 (LSUMZ, 77312).

Lark Sparrow, *Chondestes grammacus*
Status: Regular.
Abundance: Rare migrant and summer resident, very rare winter visitor.
Spring: Arrives by mid Apr.

Arrivals:　　9 Mar 1957, Lebanon, MIG 28:9
　　　　　　22 Mar 1980, Knoxville, MIG 51:63
　　　　　　12 Apr 1962, Memp., MIG 33:47

Summer: Population has declined since Ganier (1933) listed it as a fairly common transient. Has bred in Sevier Co. in 1972 (MIG 43:79), in Obion Co. in 1974 (Pitts 1974), in Decatur Co. in 1978 (Nicholson 1980), in Marion Co. in 1987 (MIG 58:146) and in McNairy Co. in 1981 (Nicholson 1984).

However, most sightings and nesting records are from middle Tennessee.

Fall: Departs by mid Aug. There is a handful of Oct and Nov records.

Departures:　18 Aug 1952, Knoxville, MIG 23:54
　　　　　　 7 Nov 1970, Williamson Co., MIG 42:20
　　　　　　 9 Nov 1986, Penal Farm, MIG 58:21

Winter: There are about six winter records from middle and east Tennessee:

31 Dec 1955, Lebanon CBC, MIG 26:63
3 Jan 1964, Oak Ridge, MIG 34:74
14 Oct-10 Jan 1963/64, Knoxville, MIG 34:74
11 Jan 1971, Woods Res., MIG 42:20
8 Dec-18 Jan 1971/72, Lebanon, MIG 43:16
1 Feb 1984, Columbia, MIG 55:47

Remarks: Found in disturbed areas, cedar glades, and bare old fields or pastures with sparse vegetation (grasses and shrubs). High count: twelve on 9 July 1955, Wilson Co. (Ogden 1955).

Substantiation: Specimen: 1 male, McMinnville, Warren Co., 14 June 1945 (LSUMZ, 77319).

Lark Bunting, *Calamospiza melanocorys*
Status: Accidental.
Remarks: There are two records of this western species: a female was present at
Woodbury, Cannon Co., on 1-22 Apr 1966 (McCrary and Wood 1966a); a
male was near Elizabethton, Carter Co., on 26 Apr 1980 (MIG 51:64).
Substantiation: Specimen: 1 female, Woodbury, Cannon Co., 22 Apr 1966
(LSUMZ, 77224).

Savannah Sparrow, *Passerculus sandwichensis*
Status: Regular.
Abundance: Fairly common migrant, fairly common to uncommon winter resi-
dent; very rare summer resident in east.
Fall: Arrives by mid Sept.
    Arrivals: 15 Aug 1984, Austin Springs, MIG 56:26
                    1 Sept 1984, Tennessee NWR, MIG 56:22
                    12 Sept 1971, Tennessee NWR, MIG 42:91
Winter: Regularly encountered in all three regions of the state during the
winter, but distribution is somewhat local. Probably more numerous in the
southern half of the state, especially in midwinter.
Spring: Departs by mid May.
    Departures: 20 May 1981, Chat., MIG 52:98
                    23 May 1987, Britton Ford, Henry Co., MIG 58:93
                    28 May 1957, Two Jays, BNA:40
Summer: There are two breeding records. A nest with three young and as many
as three ad. was found on 29 June–10 July 1973 in Hawkins Co. near
Kingsport. The nest was placed in a field of orchard grass at an elevation of
about 333 m MSL (Alsop 1978). A pair with recently fledged young was
found in Washington Co. in 1987 (MIG 58:146). Non-breeding sight records
include 13 June 1972, Elizabethton (*fide* RLK) and one bird that was found
in Cocke Co. on 2 July 1988 (Jon A. Koella).
Remarks: Found in open areas, and fallow or grassy fields. High count: 344 on
21 Dec 1975, Memp. CBC (MIG 47:37).
Substantiation: Specimen: 1 female, Nash., Davidson Co., 23 Apr 1950
(LSUMZ, 77233).

Grasshopper Sparrow, *Ammodramus savannarum*
Status: Regular (State Threatened).
Abundance: Uncommon to fairly common migrant and summer resident, very
rare winter visitor.
Spring: Arrives by mid Apr.
    Arrivals: 4 Mar 1942, Knoxville, (Meyer 1942)
                    31 Mar 1923, Nash., BNA:40
                    2 Apr 1939, Memp., MIG 10:31

Grasshopper Sparrow, continued

Summer: Once a fairly common to common summer resident (Ganier 1933). As a breeding species, it is uncommon throughout much of middle and east Tennessee, but becomes locally fairly common in suitable habitat. Birds are present each year in the west, but nesting has been documented only in Shelby Co.

Fall: Present but inconspicuous throughout Sept. Departs by mid Oct.

    Departures: 4 Nov 1957, Nash., (Laskey 1957)
                     10 Nov 1968, Boone L., MIG 40:23
                     13 Nov 1966, Nash., (Laskey 1966)

Winter: There are two overwintering records: 27 Jan-25 Feb 1938, GSMNP (Stupka 1963); and 27 Feb-20 Mar 1960, Davidson Co. (BNA:40). Additional sightings total about ten records, most of which are in Dec. The only record from the west is of one bird at Reelfoot L. on 26 Dec 1955 (MIG 26:63).

Remarks: Found in grassy fields, meadows and pastures. Can occasionally be heard singing at night. High count: sixty on 2 May 1954, Knoxville SBC (MIG 25:33).

Substantiation: Specimen: 1 male, Clarksville, Montgomery Co., 31 May 1943 (LSUMZ, 77262).

Henslow's Sparrow, *Ammodramus henslowii*

Status: Extremely Rare.

Spring: Mid Apr to mid May.

    Arrivals: 1 Mar 1970, Memp., MIG 41:42
                     27 Mar 1949, Shelby Co., MIG 20:68
                     4 Apr 1957, Davidson Co., BNA:40
    Departures: 3 May 1971, Knox Co., (Alsop 1972a)
                     9 May 1971, Blount Co., (Alsop 1972a)
                     21 May 1961, Two Jays, MIG 32:42

Fall: Early Oct to early Nov.

    Arrivals: 28-29 Sept 1963, Knox Co., (Alsop and Wallace 1970)
                     2 Oct 1982, near Wilbur L., MIG 54:27
                     16 Oct 1955, Greene Co., (White 1956)
    Departures: 28 Oct 1933, GSMNP, (Ganier 1948)
                     2 Nov 1980, Greene Co., MIG 52:50
                     3 Nov 1981, Savannah Bay, MIG 53:21

Winter: There are two winter records: 22 Dec 1968, GSMNP (MIG 39:78) and 26 Dec 1941, Shelby Co. (MIG 13:23).

Remarks: Found in grassy fields. There are about twenty-two state records for this very rare migrant, including ten sightings each in the spring and fall. Two-thirds of the observations have been made in the east. No sightings have been made since 1982. First recorded in the state on 2 Aug 1936, Mud L. (Coffey 1936a). High count: six on 27 Mar 1949, Shelby Co. (MIG 20:68).

Substantiation: Adequately documented sight records.

Le Conte's Sparrow, *Ammodramus leconteii*

Status: Regular.

Abundance: Rare migrant and winter resident.

Fall: Arrives by early Nov.

    Arrivals: 25 Sept 1929, Nash., (Mayfield 1932a)

                    22 Oct 1983, Memp., MIG 55:18

                    11 Nov 1956, Elizabethton, (Langridge 1956)

Winter: Becomes less detectable in the east, where it is rarely reported. Most records are from middle and west Tennessee. Species is probably overlooked as it occurs in a habitat not frequently worked by observers. Overwintering records include:

    8 Nov-8 Mar 1952/53, Nash., MIG 24:14

    13 Dec-20 Mar 1954/55, near Knoxville, (Tanner 1955a)

    24 Jan-14 Feb 1982, Penal Farm, MIG 53:44

Spring: Departs by late Mar.

    Departures: 29 Mar 1986, Britton Ford, Henry Co., MIG 57:75

                      27 Apr 1963, Nash., BNA:40

                      28 Apr 1985, Knoxville SBC, MIG 56:81

Remarks: Found in grassy fields in open areas; seems to prefer foxtail and johnsongrass fields. High counts: fourteen on 7 Dec 1943, Memp. (MIG 14:77) and twelve on 26 Mar 1944, Montgomery Co. (MIG 15:17).

Substantiation: Specimen: 1 female, Clarksville, Montgomery Co., 1 Jan 1944 (LSUMZ, 77284).

Sharp-tailed Sparrow, *Ammodramus caudacutus*

Status: Irregular.

Abundance: Rare migrant.

Spring: Late Apr to mid May (all records listed).

    13 Apr 1979, Alcoa Marsh, Blount Co., MIG 50:71

    1 May 1988, Nash. (JCR)

    12-13 May 1956, Nash., (Weise 1958a)

    17 May 1975, Cheatham L., MIG 46:89

    18 May 1986, Stewart Co., MIG 57:80

    19 May 1971, Buena Vista Marsh, MIG 42:70

Fall: Late Sept to early Nov.

    Arrivals: 22 Sept 1983, Shelby Co., MIG 55:18

                    24 Sept 1955, Smyrna, (Laskey 1956a)

                    24 Sept 1977, Austin Springs, MIG 49:22

    Departures: 8 Nov 1986, Cross Creeks NWR, MIG 58:25

                      9 Nov 1986, Britton Ford, Henry Co., MIG 58:21

                    12 Nov 1970, Knoxville, MIG 42:21

Remarks: Found in dry or wet grassy or brushy fields in open areas, usually near water. Species is probably overlooked as it occurs in a habitat which is not worked frequently by observers. There are more than thirty state records.

Sharp-tailed Sparrow, continued
First recorded in the state on 23 Nov 1952, Elizabethton (Laskey 1956a).
High count: four on 4 Oct 1987 in Henry (3 birds) and Stewart (1 bird)
Counties (JCR, DWB).
Substantiation: Specimen: 1 female, Nash., Davidson Co., 24 Oct 1966
(LSUMZ, 77290).

Fox Sparrow, *Passerella iliaca*
Status: Regular.
Abundance: Uncommon migrant and winter resident.
Fall: Arrives by late Oct.
Arrivals:　　1 Oct 1965, Knoxville, MIG 36:96
　　　　　　　4 Oct 1965, Two Jays, MIG 36:94
　　　　　　　18 Oct 1937, Reelfoot L., (Wetmore 1939)
Winter: Encountered regularly in small numbers throughout most of middle
and west Tennessee. Becomes less detectable in the east. Found in large
numbers only at Memp. (e.g., 169 birds on 24 Dec 1939, Memp. CBC, MIG
11:22; and 173 on 26 Dec 1965, Memp. CBC, MIG 36:90). Sixty birds were
at Smyrna on 20 Jan 1977 (MIG 48:48).
Spring: Departs by early Apr.
Departures:　27 Apr 1980, Memp. SBC, MIG 51:57
　　　　　　　30 Apr 1967, Chat. SBC, MIG 38:35
　　　　　　　31 May 1976, Lawrence Co., (Williams 1978)
Remarks: Found in shrubby fields and along woodland edge; prefers multiflora
rose hedgerows. High count: 186 on 21 Dec 1980, Memp. CBC (MIG 52:14).
Substantiation: Specimen: 1 male, Memp., Shelby Co., 10 Feb 1942 (LSUMZ,
6827).

Song Sparrow, *Melospiza melodia*
Status: Regular.
Abundance: East: common permanent resident.
Middle: uncommon summer resident, common winter resident.
West: rare summer resident, common winter resident.
Remarks: Found in grassy and shrubby fields, along woodland edge, and in a
variety of residential habitats. Winter resident birds arrive by early Oct and
depart by Apr. In the late nineteenth century, Rhoads (1895) commented on
the absence of the Song Sparrow during the breeding season in middle and
west Tennessee; and he noted only a few in Johnson City. By the early
1930s, Ganier (1933) listed this species as a fairly common summer resident
in the east. Since that time the Song Sparrow has expanded its breeding
range westward in Tennessee to the Mississippi River. Nesting was noted in
Cumberland Co. in 1966 (Robinson 1966), Putnam Co. in 1968 (MIG 39:65),
Davidson Co. in 1970 (MIG 41:70), Maury Co. in 1984 (MIG 55:71), Rutherford Co. in 1986 (MIG 57:110) and Lake Co. in 1976 (MIG 47:99). During
the summer of 1986, active sites in middle Tennessee were documented for at

Song Sparrow, continued

least ten counties (MIG 57:110), and ten singing birds were found in Wayne
Co. in 1987 (MIG 58:143). There are also recent summer records for Shelby
Co. This species appears destined to breed throughout the state. During the
winter, it becomes one of the most abundant sparrows in the state. High
count: 956 on 18 Dec 1982, Knoxville CBC (MIG 54:14).

Substantiation: Specimen: 1 male, Nash., Davidson Co., 24 Mar 1947 (LSUMZ,
77482).

Lincoln's Sparrow, *Melospiza lincolnii*

Status: Regular.

Abundance: Uncommon migrant, rare winter resident.

Spring: Encountered very infrequently during Mar. Most migrants are observed
from mid Apr through mid May.

Departures:　15 May 1967, Amnicola Marsh, MIG 38:52

28 May 1988, Shelby Co. (JRW)

28 May 1940, Nash., BNA:41

Fall: Early migrants arrive by late Sept. The peak of the migration occurs in
Oct. The species is encountered infrequently in Nov (e.g., 30 Nov 1934,
Nash. [Calhoun 1934]). Some birds occasionally linger into the winter.

Arrivals:　8 Sept 1965, Knoxville, MIG 36:96

26 Sept 1976, Buena Vista Marsh, MIG 48:19

27 Sept 1985, Penal Farm, MIG 57:23

Winter: Occasionally winters in the state, with records fairly evenly distributed
among each of the three regions. Representative observations include:

28 Jan 1986, LBL, MIG 57:57

3-6 Feb 1965, Knoxville, MIG 36:10

12-28 Feb 1986, Memp., MIG 57:51-52

Remarks: Found in brushy and weedy fields, along woodland edge and
hedgerows. Usually encountered singly or in loose groups of two to four
birds. High count: eight on 26 Sept 1972, Johnson City (MIG 43:102).

Substantiation: Specimen: 1 female, Nash., Davidson Co., 12 May 1946
(LSUMZ, 77443).

Swamp Sparrow, *Melospiza georgiana*

Status: Regular.

Abundance: Common migrant and winter resident.

Fall: Arrives by late Sept.

Arrivals:　23 Sept 1988, Austin Springs (Glenn Swofford, et al.)

24 Sept 1968, Nash., MIG 39:91

4 Oct 1987, Britton Ford, Henry Co. (JCR)

Winter: A common, and sometimes abundant, wintering sparrow statewide, occurring in lower numbers in upper east Tennessee and along the Cumberland
Plateau.

Swamp Sparrow, continued
Spring: Departs by early May.
    Departures: 10 May 1959, Memp. SBC, MIG 30:24
                     19 May 1988, Stewart Co. (JCR)
                     30 May 1977, Austin Springs, MIG 48:106
Remarks: Found in marshes and in low grassy or brushy fields and meadows, often near water. High count: 502 on 26 Dec 1936, Memp. CBC (MIG 8:8).
Substantiation: Specimen: 1 male, Nash., Davidson Co., 1 Jan 1938 (LSUMZ, 77455).

White-throated Sparrow, *Zonotrichia albicollis*
Status: Regular.
Abundance: Common migrant and winter resident, rare summer visitor.
Fall: Arrives by early Oct.
    Arrivals: 16 Sept 1959, Nash., MIG 30:37
                    22 Sept 1971, Johnson City, MIG 42:95
                    23 Sept 1976, Memp., MIG 48:18
Winter: The most abundant of Tennessee's wintering sparrows, this species is widespread and easily detected across the state. Many birds will sing shortly after arriving in the fall, and throughout the winter and spring. Prime wintering areas may harbor over a thousand birds on a CBC (e.g., 1,177 on 17 Dec 1972, Knoxville CBC, MIG 44:12).
Spring: Departs by mid May.
    Departures: 22 May 1972, Knox Co., MIG 43:79
                     24 May 1974, Memp., MIG 45:101
                     28 May 1939, Clarksville, MIG 10:32
Summer: A rare summer visitor. There are more than twenty summer records, primarily from the middle and west. Representative dates include:
    6 July 1949, Memp., MIG 20:54
    20 June 1972, Elizabethton, MIG 43:80
    28 June 1977, Old Hickory L., MIG 48:104
    9 July 1977, Signal Pt., Hamilton Co., MIG 48:106
    31 May-23 June 1985, Sumner Co., MIG 56:112
    1 Aug-6 Sept 1981, Memp., (Coffey 1985a)
Remarks: Found in weedy and brushy fields, brushy woodland thickets and along woodland edge. High count: 2,284 on 26 Dec 1965, Memp. CBC (MIG 36:90).
Substantiation: Specimen: 1 female, Nash., Davidson Co., 31 Oct 1943 (LSUMZ, 77426).

White-crowned Sparrow, *Zonotrichia leucophrys*
Status: Regular.
Abundance: Uncommon migrant and winter resident.
Fall: Arrives by early Oct.

White-crowned Sparrow, continued
Arrivals: 19 Sept 1959, Nash., MIG 30:37
               22 Sept 1982, Austin Springs, MIG 54:26
               4 Oct 1987, Britton Ford, Henry Co. (JCR)
Winter: Found wintering statewide. Frequently heard singing throughout the
winter, especially on warm days. Generally less detectable in the east;
however, 250 were found in Washington Co. on 13 Feb 1976 (MIG 47:48).
Spring: Departs by early May.
Departures: 19 May 1978, Tipton Co., MIG 49:66
                21 May 1954, Knoxville, MIG 25:55
                1 June 1964, Nash., MIG 35:36
Remarks: Found in brushy or weedy fields, along woodland edge and
hedgerows; prefers multiflora rose thickets. High count: 262 on 28 Dec 1985,
Clarksville CBC (MIG 57:12).
Substantiation: Specimen: 1 male, Memp., Shelby Co., 26 Dec 1942 (LSUMZ,
7375).

Harris' Sparrow, *Zonotrichia querula*
Status: Irregular.
Abundance: Rare migrant and winter resident.
Fall: Arrives by mid Dec.
Arrivals: 30 Oct 1956, Memp., MIG 28:6
               6 Nov 1953, Memp., (Coffey 1956)
               10 Nov 1970, Montgomery Co., (Sexton and Harker 1972)
               17 Nov 1965, Nash., MIG 36:94
Winter: Most sightings are from middle and west Tennessee. Very rarely found
in the eastern half of the state. Winter records from the east include:
    10-26 Feb 1955, Blount Co., (Tanner 1955a)
    1 Feb-28 Apr 1969, Greeneville, MIG 40:50
    30 Dec 1972, Bristol CBC, MIG 44:12
    2 Feb-15 Mar 1976, Jefferson Co., MIG 47:48
Spring: Departs by mid Apr.
Departures: 21 Mar 1986, Britton Ford, Henry Co., MIG 57:75
                27 Apr 1969, Nash., MIG 40:47
                28 Apr 1953, Memp., (Coffey 1956)
                6 May 1966, Nash., MIG 37:21
Remarks: Found in brushy thickets and hedgerows; prefers multiflora rose
thickets. Often associates with White-crowned Sparrows. First recorded in
the state on 10 Dec 1933 at Nash. (MIG 5:15). This is Tennessee's largest
wintering sparrow. High count: eleven on 26 Dec 1954, Memp. CBC (MIG
25:79).
Substantiation: Specimen: 1 female, Nash., Davidson Co., 3 Jan 1957 (LSUMZ,
77399).

Dark-eyed Junco, *Junco hyemalis*
Status: Regular.
Abundance: East: common migrant and winter resident, locally common summer resident.
Middle and West: common migrant and winter resident.
Fall: Migrants arrive by early Oct.
Arrivals: 24 Sept 1972, Cross Creeks NWR, MIG 43:100
3 Oct 1967, Bristol, MIG 38:103
4 Oct 1968, Savannah, Hardin Co., MIG 39:89
Winter: A widely distributed and common winter resident statewide. Birds that nest in the eastern mountains make an altitudinal migration to lower elevations, but a few may be found on the summits throughout the winter months (Stupka 1963).
Spring: Migrants depart by mid Apr.
Departures: 10 May 1983, Memp. (CHB)
13 May 1923, Nash., BNA:41
17 May 1969, Knoxville, MIG 40:70
Summer: A conspicuous and very common bird at high elevations in the eastern mountains. This species was described as the most abundant breeding bird in the GSMNP (Stupka 1963), on Roan Mt. (Ganier 1936) and in the Unicoi Mts. (Ganier and Clebsch 1946). Generally breeds above 900 m MSL. Apparently does not breed in the Cumberland Mts. The first record for Holston Mt., Sullivan Co., was of three birds on 9 June 1969 (MIG 40:70).
Remarks: Found in grassy and brushy fields, along woodland edge and in residential areas. Several subspecies of the Dark-eyed Junco have been reported in the state. There are more than thirteen reports of the "Oregon" Junco, beginning with the sighting of four birds in Greene Co. on 10 Mar 1960 (Darnell 1960). DeVore (1974), however, noted that the variations in, and differences between, the plumages at the subspecific level often make it impossible to accurately separate the "Oregon" Junco from regularly occurring Dark-eyed Juncos unless the bird is in the hand. A "Gray-headed" Junco was reported in Maury Co. on 24 May 1982 (Anderson 1984), and two "White-winged" Juncos were reported at Nash. in Jan and Feb 1933 (Laskey 1933). High count: 1,700 on 4 Jan 1976, GSMNP CBC (MIG 47:37).
Substantiation: Specimen: 1 male, Nash., Davidson Co., 1 Jan 1941 (LSUMZ, 77346).

Lapland Longspur, *Calcarius lapponicus*
Status: Regular.
Abundance: Rare migrant and winter resident.
Fall: Arrives by mid Nov.
Arrivals: 23 Oct 1982, Austin Springs, MIG 54:26
25 Oct 1987, Cross Creeks NWR, MIG 59:37
4 Nov 1951, Penal Farm, MIG 22:71

Lapland Longspur, continued

Winter: Very rare in the east; most records are from areas west of Nash. Becomes more detectable in the west along the Mississippi River between Reelfoot L. and Memp. Usually not found in large numbers; however, notable counts include:

500 on 30 Dec 1983, Cross Creeks NWR, MIG 55:47
501 on 24 Dec 1961, Memp. CBC, MIG 32:71
600 on 1 Feb 1976, Lake Co., MIG 47:45

Spring: Departs by early Mar.

Departures: 29 Feb 1940, Montgomery Co., (Clebsch 1940)
8 Mar 1986, Cross Creeks NWR, MIG 57:81
11 Mar 1960, Oak Ridge, MIG 31:16

Remarks: Found in open areas, especially fallow or stubbly agricultural fields, and along roadsides. Most easily detected by call. Often occurs with Horned Larks. High count: 911 on 22 Dec 1940, Memp. CBC (MIG 12:8).

Substantiation: Specimen: 1 male, Memp., Shelby Co., 27 Dec 1940 (LSUMZ, 8988).

Smith's Longspur, *Calcarius pictus*

Status: Accidental.

Remarks: Found in grassy and weedy fields. All but one record of this species were reported from Shelby Co., where it was found in fields dominated by *Aristida* grass. First recorded on 22 Nov 1953, when one bird was found at the Penal Farm (Coffey 1954). It was recorded annually in Shelby Co. thereafter through 1958. The only report of this species since 1958 involved a single bird at Gallatin, Sumner Co., on 28 Mar 1975 (BNA:41). High count: thirty-seven on 27 Dec 1953, Memp. CBC (MIG 24:79). Additional Shelby Co. records follow (flock size ranged from one to thirty-five birds):

19 Nov 1955, Field 21, Woodstock, MIG 27:16
20 Nov 1955, Penal Farm, MIG 27:16
28 Nov 1953, Penal Farm, (Coffey 1954)
15 Dec 1956, Memp. area, MIG 28:6
21 Dec 1958, Memp. CBC, MIG 29:72
23 Dec 1956, Memp. CBC, MIG 27:73
26 Dec 1954, Memp. CBC, MIG 25:79
26 Dec 1955, Memp. CBC, MIG 26:63
6 Feb 1954, Penal Farm, (Coffey 1954)
14 Mar 1954, Penal Farm, (Coffey 1954)
16 Mar 1957, Penal Farm, MIG 28:7

Substantiation: Specimen: 1 female, Memp., Shelby Co., 6 Mar 1954 (LSUMZ, 77510).

Snow Bunting, *Plectrophenax nivalis*
Status: Irregular.
Abundance: Rare migrant and winter resident.
Fall: Arrives by mid Nov.
Arrivals: 24 Oct 1954, Big Bald Mt., Unicoi Co., (Behrend 1955)
2 Nov 1960, Memp., (Irwin 1961)
14 Nov 1984, Davidson Co., MIG 56:22
Winter: The majority of sightings of this rare species has been made on Big
Bald Mt. in Unicoi Co., and on Roan Mt. in Carter Co. It is seldom
reported in the middle or west; observations made in these two regions of
the state include:
19-20 Nov 1954, Bush L., (Goodpasture 1955)
16 Nov 1975, Buena Vista Marsh, MIG 47:46
6 Dec-16 Feb 1980/81, Percy Priest L., MIG 52:47
30 Dec 1983, Cross Creeks NWR, MIG 55:47
12 Nov 1984, Island 13, MIG 56:17
Spring: Departs by mid Feb.
Departures: 18 Feb 1970, Old Hickory L. dam, MIG 41:45
2 Mar 1979, Roan Mt., MIG 50:47
14 Mar 1965, Hump Mt., Carter Co., (Behrend 1965)
Remarks: Found in open areas; in the eastern mountains it occurs on the grassy
balds. First state record was on 21 Nov 1948, Big Bald Mt., Unicoi Co.
(Behrend 1948). Also found in the GSMNP on 22 Dec 1957 at an elevation
of 1,520 m MSL (Stupka 1963). Additional records are likely on the mountain summits in the east. High count: fifteen on 28 Dec 1969, Cherokee L.
(Etnier 1971).
Substantiation: Adequately documented sight records.

SUBFAMILY ICTERINAE: **Blackbirds and Allies**

Bobolink, *Dolichonyx oryzivorus*
Status: Regular.
Abundance: Fairly common spring migrant, uncommon to rare fall migrant,
rare summer visitor; very rare summer resident in east.
Spring: Late Apr to mid May.
Arrivals: 12 Apr 1964, Bush L., MIG 35:36
17 Apr 1953, Penal Farm, MIG 24:54-55
17 Apr 1982, Knoxville, MIG 53:69
Departures: 31 May 1988, Lake Co. (CPN)
8 June 1976, GSMNP, MIG 47:103
10 June 1988, Cross Creeks NWR (JCR)

Bobolink, continued

Summer: Only nesting record for the state occurred in Shady Valley, Johnson
Co., on 10 June 1962 (Dubke 1963). The nest was found at an elevation of
850 m MSL and had three young. Occasionally, Bobolinks are found at scattered locations across the state during June and July. Representative records
include:

21-22 June 1950, GSMNP, (Stupka 1963)
15 July 1977, Hawkins Co., MIG 48:106
14 June 1980, Jefferson Co., MIG 51:94-95
21 June 1980, Stewart Co. (DWB)
24 July 1983, Austin Springs, MIG 54:91

Fall: Late Aug to early Oct.

Arrivals: 6 Aug 1988, Tennessee NWR (SJS, James R. Peters)
8 Aug 1952, near Kingsport, MIG 23:56
9 Aug 1967, Amnicola Marsh, MIG 38:67

Departures: 4 Oct 1987, Britton Ford (JCR)
25 Oct 1987, Cross Creeks NWR, MIG 59:37
12 Nov 1956, Elizabethton, MIG 28:13

Remarks: Found in open grasslands and hay fields. Rarely reported from the
west in the fall. High count: two thousand on 15 May 1950, Memp. (MIG
21:50).

Substantiation: Specimen: 1 male, Nash., Davidson Co., 2 May 1942 (LSUMZ,
76949).

Red-winged Blackbird, *Agelaius phoeniceus*

Status: Regular.

Abundance: Common permanent resident.

Remarks: Found along roadsides and in grassy fields and marshes, often near
water. A common and widely distributed nesting species during the breeding
season. In the winter, large roosts often form, especially in west and middle
Tennessee. It is found in reduced numbers in upper east Tennessee during
the winter months. High count: 5 million on 30 Dec 1958, Reelfoot L. CBC
(MIG 30:16).

Substantiation: Specimen: 1 male, Nash., Davidson Co., 19 Jan 1946 (LSUMZ,
76977).

Eastern Meadowlark, *Sturnella magna*

Status: Regular.

Abundance: Common permanent resident.

Remarks: Found in grassy fields and pastures and along roadsides. Nests
throughout the state. In the winter meadowlarks often gather into loose
flocks of 25-50 or more birds at prime feeding/roosting areas. Usually
separable from the Western Meadowlark in the field only by voice, but some
males may sing songs of both species. High counts:

Eastern Meadowlark, continued
>754 on 22 Apr 1967, Nash. SBC, MIG 38:35
>680 on 30 Apr 1972, Knoxville SBC, MIG 43:47
>660 on 21 Dec 1975, Memp. CBC, MIG 47:37

Substantiation: Specimen: 1 female, 3 km S Germantown, Shelby Co., 23 Jan 1942 (LSUMZ, 6678).

Western Meadowlark, *Sturnella neglecta*
Status: Irregular.
Abundance: West: rare migrant and winter resident, very rare summer resident.
Fall: Arrives by late Oct.
>Arrivals: 15 Oct 1955, Penal Farm, MIG 27:16
>17 Oct 1971, Shelby Co., MIG 42:91
>20 Oct 1956, Penal Farm, MIG 28:6

Winter: Winter distribution in the west is primarily limited to Shelby and Lake Counties, where over 90% of the sightings have been made.
Spring: Reported from several areas in west Tennessee, including: Lauderdale Co. on 18 Mar 1956 (MIG 27:16); Fayette Co. on 10 Mar 1957 (MIG 28:7); and Dyer Co. on 14 Apr 1984 (MIG 55:68). There is only one record each for east and middle Tennessee: 19 Apr-23 May 1959, Knox Co. (Pardue 1959) and 5 Mar 1988, Cross Creeks NWR (MIG 59:99). Departs by mid Apr.
>Departures: 21 Apr 1957, Penal Farm, MIG 28:26
>8 May 1983, Reelfoot L. SBC, MIG 54:54
>26 May 1956, Penal Farm (*fide* MGW)

Summer: One breeding record: a nest with two ad. and six young was found at the Penal Farm on 20 May 1951 (Smith 1951).
Remarks: Found in open areas in grassy or fallow fields and along roadsides. First state record was on 11 Dec 1943, Shelby Co. (Burdick 1943). Recorded annually between 1950 and 1969; in recent years there have been fewer reports. Usually separable from the Eastern Meadowlark in the field only by voice, but some males may sing songs of both species. All sight records in middle and east Tennessee should be thoroughly documented. High count: eighteen on 26 Feb 1956, Penal Farm (MIG 27:16).
Substantiation: Specimen: 1 male, 3 km S Germantown, Shelby Co., 11 Dec 1943 (LSUMZ, 8993).

Yellow-headed Blackbird, *Xanthocephalus xanthocephalus*
Status: Extremely Rare.
Remarks: First verified state record was of one male on 10 Mar-3 May 1975 at Memp. (Coffey 1975). Currently there are about thirteen state records; however, Bierly (1980) noted there are a number of unconfirmed reports. Most of the sightings have been made in the Jan-Apr period. This blackbird of midwestern and western states should be looked for in large winter

Yellow-headed Blackbird, continued

blackbird roosts. Three east Tennessee records of doubtful validity were described by Alsop (1972). All other records follow:

3 Sept 1977, Pace Point, (Bierly 1980)
24 Oct 1987, Shelby Co., MIG 59:32
3-24 Jan 1979, Nash., MIG 50:43
14 Jan 1979, Williamson Co., MIG 50:43
14 Jan-5 Feb 1978, Clarksville, MIG 49:43
21 Jan 1985, Davidson Co., MIG 56:53
27 Jan 1985, Sumner Co., MIG 56:53
27 Jan-9 Feb 1985, Davidson Co., MIG 56:53
28 Jan 1982, Nash., MIG 53:46
4 Mar 1978, Nash., MIG 49:43
17 Apr 1984, Sumner Co., MIG 55:71
17 Apr 1982, Nash., BNA:42

Substantiation: Photographs: 1, Memp., Shelby Co., 1 Apr 1975 (JPC−TBRC).

Rusty Blackbird, *Euphagus carolinus*
Status: Regular.
Abundance: Uncommon migrant and winter resident.
Fall: Arrives by early Nov.
Arrivals: 26 Sept 1965, Knoxville, MIG 36:96
12 Oct 1968, Reelfoot L., MIG 39:89
16 Oct 1970, Nash., MIG 41:86
Winter: Found wintering throughout most of the state, but generally less numerous in east Tennessee. Flocks exceeding a hundred birds are rare. Usually encountered apart from other blackbird species; however, its occurrence with mixed species blackbird flocks or at blackbird roosts is not uncommon. A roost in Maury Co. has consistently been found to contain many thousands of these birds.
Spring: Departs by mid Apr.
Departures: 12 May 1974, Reelfoot L. SBC, MIG 45:44
23 May 1967, Chat., MIG 38:52
23 May 1983, Nash., MIG 54:63
Remarks: Found in wet woods, pastures, swamps and harvested grain fields. High counts: 240,000 on 30 Dec 1976, Columbia CBC (MIG 48:33); 3,000 on 18 Dec 1983, Knoxville CBC (MIG 55:10); and 1,819 on 28 Dec 1985, Clarksville CBC (MIG 57:12).
Substantiation: Specimen: 1 female, Nash., Davidson Co., 23 Dec 1945 (LSUMZ, 77010).

Brewer's Blackbird, *Euphagus cyanocephalus*
Status: Regular.
Abundance: East and Middle: rare migrant and winter resident.

Brewer's Blackbird, continued

West: uncommon migrant and winter resident.

Fall: Arrives by late Nov.

Arrivals: 27 Oct 1956, Memp., MIG 28:6

22 Nov 1969, Watauga L., MIG 41:24

30 Nov 1986, Lawrence Co., MIG 58:25

Winter: An uncommon to rare winter resident, it is found in most years in the western region of the state, primarily in Shelby and Obion Co. A recently discovered wintering area is located in the pasture fields of Wayne and Lawrence Co. The Lawrence Co. Buffalo River CBC recorded 157 Brewer's on 27 Dec 1986 (MIG 58:5). It is rare elsewhere in middle Tennessee and throughout the eastern region of the state.

Spring: Departs by late Mar.

Departures: 14 Apr 1957, Penal Farm, MIG 28:26

18 Apr 1959, near Nash., BNA:42

19 Apr 1974, Carter Co., MIG 45:80

Remarks: Found in barnyard feedlots and grassy pastures, usually in wet areas. First state record was on 20 Apr 1935, near Johnson City (MIG 6:73). Compare with Rusty Blackbird in all plumages. Male is separable in good light from the male Rusty Blackbird; female has dark eye and lacks pale throat patch and light breast streaks of female Brown-headed Cowbird. High count: 300 on 15 Jan 1972, Carroll Co. (MIG 43:23).

Common Grackle, *Quiscalus quiscula*

Status: Regular.

Abundance: Common permanent resident.

Remarks: Found in orchards and farmyards, along woodland edge and in a variety of urban and suburban habitats. Breeds throughout the state. Scarce at high elevations in the eastern mountains. May nest in loose colonies. Ganier and Clebsch (1942) found grackles nesting in the steel beams of the Kentucky L. bridge at Paris Landing S.P. between Henry and Stewart Co. Frequently forms large roosts with other blackbirds in the winter. High counts:

2,500,000 on 22 Dec 1957, Memp. CBC, MIG 28:66

2,000,000 on 29 Dec 1984, Murfreesboro CBC, MIG 56:9

1,600,000 on 29 Apr 1979, Knoxville SBC, MIG 50:59

Substantiation: Specimen: 1 male, Nash., Davidson Co., 15 Apr 1966 (LSUMZ, 77038).

Brown-headed Cowbird, *Molothrus ater*

Status: Regular.

Abundance: Common permanent resident.

Remarks: Found in open country, in woodlands and along woodland edge, and in urban and suburban habitats. A nest parasite; lays its eggs in other birds' nests. Rhoads (1895) found it to be rare in the summer throughout Ten-

Brown-headed Cowbird, continued

nessee, and Ganier (1933) also listed it as a rare to very rare summer resident. It was not recorded as a breeding bird in upper east Tennessee until
1932 when three parasitized nests were found in Knoxville and Johnson City
(Anon. 1932). Since that time, cowbirds have substantially increased in
numbers across the state and can even be found at high elevations in the
eastern mountains. In the winter, cowbirds frequently form large roosts and
may become locally abundant in some areas and scarce in other areas. High
counts:

    500,000 on 28 Dec 1962, Reelfoot L. CBC, MIG 33:70

    50,000 on 23 Dec 1923, Nash. CBC, (Walker 1932)

    1,200 on 28 Dec 1975, Knoxville CBC, MIG 47:37

Substantiation: Specimen: 1 female, Nash., Davidson Co., 8 July 1966
(LSUMZ, 77066).

Orchard Oriole, *Icterus spurius*

Status: Regular.

Abundance: Fairly common migrant and summer resident.

Spring: Arrives by mid Apr.

    Arrivals: 2 Apr 1945, Memp., MIG 16:11

                2 Apr 1951, Lebanon, MIG 22:28

                9 Apr 1965, Chat., MIG 36:64

Summer: A fairly common breeding species throughout the state, although it
generally avoids heavily forested areas. Absent from the higher elevations in
the east.

Fall: Departs by late Aug.

    Departures: 26 Sept 1974, Memp., MIG 46:19

                 30 Sept 1978, Elizabethton Fall Bird Count (*fide* RLK)

                 28 Nov 1971, Davidson Co., MIG 43:25

Remarks: Found in orchards, semi-open areas with scattered trees and along
woodland edge. Migrates south in the fall earlier than most summer
residents. High count: 117 on 22 Apr 1967, Nash. SBC (MIG 38:35).

Substantiation: Specimen: 1 female, Nash., Davidson Co., 7 Sept 1969
(LSUMZ, 76995).

Northern Oriole, *Icterus galbula*

Status: Regular.

Abundance: East and Middle: fairly common to uncommon migrant, rare summer resident and winter visitor.

West: fairly common migrant, locally common summer resident, rare winter
visitor.

Spring: Arrives by late Apr.

    Arrivals: 19 Mar 1966, Elizabethton, MIG 37:26

                8 Apr 1929, Nash., BNA:42

                11 Apr 1957, Memp., MIG 28:26

Summer: Formerly more common, this species is now a rare summer resident throughout most of the state. Rhoads (1895) described it as abundant and stated that "it was more numerous . . . than . . . elsewhere in the U.S." Population has since declined, and it is now encountered frequently only in the west, where it becomes locally common in the counties adjacent to the Mississippi River.

Fall: Departs by early Sept.

Departures: 18 Oct 1966, Bristol, MIG 37:84

4 Nov 1977, Dyersburg, MIG 49:41

8 Nov 1968, Nash., BNA:42

Winter: A rare winter visitor. There are more than twenty-five winter records, primarily from middle and east Tennessee. May be found at feeders, especially if fruit or suet is available. Representative sightings include:

20 Dec-26 Jan 1986/87, Clarksville, MIG 58:58

10 Jan-28 Feb 1983, Memp., MIG 54:42

13 Jan-4 Mar 1972, Johnson City, MIG 43:27

Remarks: Found in semi-open areas with scattered trees, and along wooded riparian areas; seems to prefer cottonwood and sycamore trees. High count: forty-seven on 1 May 1954, Memp. SBC (MIG 25:32).

Substantiation: Specimen: 1, Nash., Davidson Co., 20 Jan 1968 (LSUMZ, 77000).

FAMILY FRINGILLIDAE: **Cardueline Finches**

Purple Finch, *Carpodacus purpureus*

Status: Regular.

Abundance: Fairly common migrant and winter resident, very rare summer visitor.

Fall: Arrives by mid Oct.

Arrivals: 20 Sept 1970, Elizabethton, MIG 41:89

20 Sept 1975, White Co., MIG 47:19

26 Oct 1985, Henry Co. (JCR)

Winter: Winters in moderate numbers throughout the state. An irruptive species, it is more abundant during "invasion" years; in other years it may be noticeably uncommon.

Spring: Departs by late Apr.

Departures: 8 May 1983, Reelfoot L. SBC, MIG 54:54

19 May 1980, Montgomery Co. SBC, MIG 51:57

23 May 1986, Johnson City, MIG 57:86

Purple Finch, continued

Summer: Summer records exist only for Roan Mt., where birds have been found at an approximate elevation of 1,730 m MSL or higher. Representative records include:

1-15 July 1962, Roan Mt., (Behrend 1962)

12 May-7 July 1963, Roan Mt., (Behrend 1963)

16-19 June 1977, Roan Mt., MIG 48:107

Remarks: Found in woodland thickets, wooded bottomland and second growth areas; also frequently visits bird feeders. High count: 553 on 17 Dec 1977, Lebanon CBC (MIG 49:8).

Substantiation: Specimen: 1 male, Nash., Davidson Co., 27 Feb 1944 (LSUMZ, 77155).

*House Finch, *Carpodacus mexicanus*

Status: Regular.

Abundance: East: common winter resident, locally fairly common summer resident.

Middle and West: fairly common winter resident, locally uncommon summer resident.

Remarks: Found primarily in residential areas; also in shrubby fields and thickets and along woodland edge. Native to the western U.S., this finch was introduced to Long Island, New York, in 1940 and has since rapidly spread throughout the eastern U.S. First recorded in Tennessee on 24-26 Mar 1972 at Greeneville (Holt 1972). In middle Tennessee, it was found at Old Hickory L. on 17 Feb 1975 (MIG 46:71) and in the west it was first reported on 4 Dec 1979 in Shelby Co. (MIG 51:38). Nesting was first documented in Washington Co. on 31 Mar 1981 when a nest with three eggs was found (MIG 52:74). During the first ten years after its arrival in the state, the House Finch was principally observed during the winter months (Nov through Mar) and was scarce or absent during the Apr to Oct period. However, with the establishment of nesting populations, the number of nesting season observations has increased substantially. It is now a locally fairly common summer resident throughout the residential areas in east Tennessee and is an uncommon to rare summer resident in the Nash. area, at Clarksville and in Memp. The population is expected to continue expanding, and this species may soon become a locally common breeding bird throughout the state. High counts:

419 on 28 Dec 1985, Lebanon CBC, MIG 57:12

384 on 20 Dec 1986, Knoxville CBC, MIG 58:5

320 on 18 Dec 1982, Murfreesboro CBC, MIG 54:14

Substantiation: Specimen: 1 male, Nash., Davidson Co., 26 Jan 1988 (CSM, F88-3).

Red Crossbill, *Loxia curvirostra*

Status: Regular.

Abundance: East: rare winter resident, locally uncommon summer resident. Middle and West: rare migrant and winter visitor, very rare summer visitor.

Fall: Arrives by mid Nov.

Arrivals: 8 Aug 1981, Nash., MIG 53:17
18 Aug 1970, Sullivan Co., (Rowell 1972)
15 Nov 1981, Paris Landing S.P., MIG 53:15

Winter: An irruptive species, it is most likely to be seen during "invasion" years. In the GSMNP, it can be common in some winters and scarce or absent in other winters (Stupka 1963). West of the eastern mountains, the Red Crossbill becomes a rare winter visitor; there are no winter records for west Tennessee; representative sightings include:

26-28 Dec 1963, Knox Co., MIG 34:74
1 Jan 1964, Chat., MIG 35:16
1 Jan 1987, Stewart Co., MIG 58:58
15 Jan 1977, Cannon Co., MIG 48:48
11-17 Feb 1973, Cheatham Co., MIG 44:23

Spring: Departs by mid Apr.

Departures: 14 Apr 1974, Williamson Co., MIG 45:76
14 Apr 1974, Davidson Co., MIG 45:76
14 May 1985, Cumberland Co., MIG 56:81

Summer: Occurs fairly regularly at the GSMNP, where Stupka (1963) described it as a fairly common summer and early fall visitant. Many observations of adults feeding young have been made in the GSMNP, but no nests have yet been found there or elsewhere in the state. Breeding in the Park is suspected due to the fact that young birds with short tails and uncrossed mandibles (recently fledged young) have been observed (Stupka 1963). McNair (1988) described nesting activities of this species south of the GSMNP in western North Carolina. May also be found on Roan Mt. during the summer (e.g., 30 May-21 June 1970, Roan Mt., MIG 41:72). Summer records outside of the eastern mountains include:

27-28 July 1972, Lake Co., (Sumara 1972)
11 June 1973, east Cumberland Co., (Alsop 1974)
18 June 1973, Grundy Co., MIG 44:85
6 June 1976, Knox Co., MIG 47:102

Remarks: Found in spruce, hemlock and pine forests, where it feeds on the seeds of the cones. Highly nomadic, it may occur in unusual places at unusual times; generally follows the cone crop. Presence is often revealed by its distinctive call note. High count: 275 on 28 Dec 1969, GSMNP CBC (MIG 41:9).

Substantiation: Specimen: 1 male, S of Bristol, Sullivan Co., 5 Jan 1965 (LSUMZ, 82372).

White-winged Crossbill, *Loxia leucoptera*

Status: Irregular.

Abundance: East: rare migrant and winter resident.

Middle and West: very rare fall and winter visitor.

Fall: Arrives by late Dec.

Arrivals: 5 Nov 1975, Etowah, McMinn Co., MIG 47:48

28 Nov 1977, Martin, Weakley Co., MIG 49:41

20 Dec 1985, Oak Ridge, MIG 57:62

Winter: Most frequently found on Roan Mt. from late Dec through Apr. An irruptive species, it is most likely to be seen during "invasion" years (e.g., 88 birds on 20 Dec 1963, Roan Mt. CBC, MIG 34:89). Very rare elsewhere in the state; the only middle Tennessee record is of one bird at Clarksville, Montgomery Co., on 29 Nov 1977 (DWB); other records include:

1 Jan 1964, Cove L., Campbell Co., MIG 34:74

28 Dec 1969, GSMNP CBC, MIG 41:9

2 Dec 1977, Martin, Weakley Co., MIG 49:41

3 Feb-12 Apr 1985, Chat., MIG 56:81

Spring: Departs by mid Apr.

Departures: 21 Apr 1970, Roan Mt., MIG 41:47

25 May 1970, Roan Mt., MIG 41:72

5 June 1966, Roan Mt., MIG 37:56

Remarks: Found in spruce, hemlock and fir trees, where it feeds on the seeds of the cones. First recorded in the state at Memp. on 26 Dec 1954 (MIG 25:74). There are three west Tennessee records, one middle Tennessee record and more than twenty-five records from the east. High count: 210 on 29 Dec 1965, Roan Mt. CBC (MIG 36:92).

Substantiation: Specimen: 1 male, Roan Mt., Carter Co., 12 Dec 1965 (LSUMZ, 77183).

Common Redpoll, *Carduelis flammea*

Status: Extremely Rare.

Remarks: About ten state records. Most sightings have been made during the Dec to Jan period. First recorded during the winter of 1933-34 at Johnson City (Tyler and Lyle 1934). This species should be looked for in the winter when there are reports of redpolls "invading" northern states during the fall migration. May be found with flocks of other finches, especially siskins and goldfinches. High count: five birds on 2 Jan 1966, GSMNP CBC (MIG 36:90). There are no records for west Tennessee. All other observations follow:

10 Nov 1981, Clarksville, MIG 53:17

14 Dec 1965, GSMNP, (DeFoe 1966)

20 Dec-14 Mar 1985/86, Franklin Co., MIG 57:62

29 Dec 1968, Knoxville CBC, MIG 39:78

5 Jan 1986, Washington Co., MIG 58:30

9 Jan-11 Mar 1978, Nash., MIG 49:43

Common Redpoll, continued
>   10 Jan 1969, Knox Co., (Alsop and Wallace 1970)
>   21 Jan 1985, Stewart Co., MIG 56:53

Substantiation: Photograph: 1, Franklin Co., winter 1985-1986 (James R.
   Peters — TBRC).

Pine Siskin, *Carduelis pinus*

Status: Regular.

Abundance: East: uncommon to fairly common migrant and winter resident,
   locally rare summer visitor.

Middle and West: uncommon to fairly common migrant and winter resident.

Fall: Arrives by late Oct.

>   Arrivals: 18 Sept 1968, Hamilton Co., MIG 39:95
>   3 Oct 1987, Tennessee NWR, MIG 59:38
>   4 Oct 1987, Britton Ford, MIG 59:32

Winter: An irruptive species, its presence in the winter is erratic with greater
   numbers of birds being found during "invasion" years. It winters throughout
   the state and at times can be locally abundant in the eastern mountains
   (e.g., 1,820 on 20 Dec 1987, Roan Mt. CBC; and 1,387 on 19 Dec 1987,
   Elizabethton CBC, MIG 59:8). Seems to be more regularly reported than in
   former years, probably as a result of the increase in bird-feeding activity.

Spring: Departs by early May.

>   Departures: 31 May 1987, Wilson Co., MIG 58:99
>   6 June 1984, Memp., MIG 55:88
>   8 June 1984, Anderson Co., MIG 55:95

Summer: Summer records are usually restricted to the eastern mountains at the
   higher elevations. Most reports are from the GSMNP and Roan Mt., where
   birds have been found during the June to Sept period. Usually not found
   below an elevation of 1,460 m MSL (Stupka 1963). One bird was present on
   Signal Mt., Hamilton Co., on 1-18 Aug 1985 (MIG 57:34), and possibly summered there. There are no breeding records.

Remarks: Found in bottomland fields and woodland edge, where it feeds on the
   seeds of sweetgum and sycamore trees; also frequently observed in coniferous forests and in residential areas at feeders. Presence is often revealed
   by distinctive call notes, frequently given in flight. High counts: 4,813 on 2
   Jan 1966, GSMNP CBC (MIG 36:90) and 2,800 on 29 Dec 1963, GSMNP
   CBC (MIG 34:85).

Substantiation: Specimen: 1 female, Nash., Davidson Co., 21 Nov 1943
   (LSUMZ, 77169).

American Goldfinch, *Carduelis tristis*

Status: Regular.

Abundance: Common permanent resident.

Remarks: Found in weedy and brushy fields, along woodland edge, and in
   residential areas. A common and widespread nesting species; encountered at

American Goldfinch, continued

all elevations in the eastern mountains. Usually nests later than most other permanent residents. Stupka (1963) reported an incubating female as late as 18 Sept 1956 in Gatlinburg. Large flocks form during the winter, especially in areas where there is an abundance of natural food. By spring, it is not uncommon to find entire flocks of goldfinches in full song, often creating an indecipherable mixture of call notes and song. High counts:

> 2,000 on 22 Apr 1978, Highland Rim SBC, MIG 49:58
> 1,197 on 24 Apr 1971, Nash. SBC, MIG 42:39
> 1,120 on 3 Jan 1987, Nickajack L. CBC, MIG 58:5

Substantiation: Specimen: 1 male, Viola, Warren Co., 23 July 1937 (LSUMZ, 77173).

Evening Grosbeak, *Coccothraustes vespertinus*
Status: Regular.
Abundance: Uncommon migrant and winter resident; very rare summer visitor in east.
Fall: Arrives by mid Nov.

> Arrivals: 16 Sept 1986, Chat., MIG 58:29-30
> 27 Sept 1971, Nash., MIG 42:93
> 17 Oct 1979, Memp., MIG 51:16

Winter: Highly variable in numbers, the Evening Grosbeak is the classic example of an irruptive migrant. In some years, few or no birds are found and in other winters it "invades" the state. Notable counts include:

> 250 on 23 Feb 1955, Gatlinburg, (Stupka and Tanner 1955)
> 114 on 22 Dec 1985, Memp. CBC, MIG 57:12
> 64 on 21 Dec 1985, Cross Creeks NWR, MIG 57:12

There are fewer records for west Tennessee during the winter.
Spring: Departs by early May.

> Departures: 9 May 1973, Shelby Co., MIG 44:50
> 24 May 1986, Coffee Co., MIG 57:81
> 5 June 1962, near GSMNP, (Stupka 1962)

Summer: Two records: 15 June 1973, Elizabethton (MIG 44:88) and 29 July 1976, Knoxville (MIG 47:102).
Remarks: Found along woodland edge and in residential areas, where it is usually seen at bird feeders; feeds on the buds and seeds of maple, ash, box elder and elm trees. First verified record of this species in Tennessee was on 22 Nov 1945 at Elizabethton (Behrend and Behrend 1945). High count: 726 on 2 Jan 1972, GSMNP CBC (MIG 43:13).
Substantiation: Specimen: 1 male, Johnson City, Washington Co., 9 Mar 1969 (LSUMZ, 77150).

FAMILY PASSERIDAE: Old World Sparrows

*House Sparrow, *Passer domesticus*
Status: Regular.
Abundance: Common permanent resident.
Remarks: Found in residential areas and around farmlands; usually occurs in close proximity to human dwellings. An introduced species which was brought into the United States around the mid 1800s. In Tennessee it is a common and widespread nesting species. Rhoads (1895) found it "abounding in all larger towns and villages" as early as 1895. High counts:

2,190 on 23 Dec 1962, Memp. CBC, MIG 33:69

1,370 on 21 Dec 1985, Reelfoot L. CBC, MIG 57:12

Substantiation: Specimen: 1 female, Nash., Davidson Co., 19 Mar 1965 (LSUMZ, 76939).

Species Supported by Fossil Evidence

An archaeological site survey conducted at Cheek Bend Cave in Maury Co. during 1978–1979 was responsible for the discovery of fossil remains representing sixty bird species (Parmalee and Klippel 1982). The presence of several species in these fossil deposits suggested that a boreal habitat and climate occurred in Tennessee during the Pleistocene epoch. Noted below are four species that were found at the Cheek Bend Cave for which there are no other records for Tennessee. Additional archaeological investigations would undoubtedly result in the discovery of more species that have never been described for Tennessee. However, it is best not to include such species in the main species list.

Northern Hawk-Owl, *Surnia ulula*

Boreal Owl, *Aegolius funereus*

Gray Jay, *Perisoreus canadensis*

Pine Grosbeak, *Pinicola enucleator*

Literature Cited
in the Text

Abernathy, B. H. 1943. The Connecticut Warbler, a spring visitant. *The Migrant* 14(2):27-28.

———. 1955. Jewels in the jewelweeds. *The Migrant* 26(3):44.

Alsop, F. J., III. 1967. Observations at a unique farm in Knox County. *The Migrant* 38(1):1-3.

———. 1969. Black-headed Grosbeak in Tennessee. *The Migrant* 40(3):59-60.

———. 1970. Northern Phalarope in the Great Smoky Mountains National Park. *The Migrant* 41(2):39-40.

———. 1972. A preliminary list of Tennessee birds. *The Migrant* 43(3):57-64.

———. 1972a. Henslow's Sparrows in Blount and Knox counties. *The Migrant* 43(1):19-20.

———. 1974. June records of a Brewster's Warbler and Red Crossbills in Cumberland County, Tennessee. *The Migrant* 45(3):69-70.

———. 1976. The 1973 foray: Benton County. *The Migrant* 47(4):81-86.

———. 1978. Savannah Sparrow nesting in upper east Tennessee. *The Migrant* 49(1):1-4.

———. 1979. *Population status and management considerations for Tennessee's threatened and endangered bird species.* Kingsport: East Tennessee State University. Department of Biological Sciences.

———. 1980. Birds. p. A-1 - A-113 in D. C. Eagar and R. M. Hatcher, eds. *Tennessee's rare wildlife. Vol. 1, the vertebrates.* Nashville: Tennessee Wildlife Resources Agency.

———. 1981. The Cliff Swallow in Tennessee. *The Migrant* 52(1):1-11.

Alsop, F. J., III, and G. O. Wallace. 1970. Addendum: the birds of Knox County, Tennessee. *The Migrant* 41(1):1-4.

American Ornithologists' Union. 1983. *Check-list of North American birds.* 6th edition. Lawrence, Kansas: Allen Press.

———. 1985. Thirty-fifth supplement to the American Ornithologists' Union Check-list of North American Birds. *Auk* 102:680-86.

Anderson, K. G. 1984. First sight record of 'Gray-headed' Junco in Tennessee. *The Migrant* 55(3):64.

Anonymous. 1932. Cowbirds breeding in east Tennessee. *The Migrant* 3(3):38.

Barbig, H. T. 1953. Sandhill Cranes at Memphis. *The Migrant* 24(1):11.

Basham, B. 1969. Brown-headed Nuthatch. *The Migrant* 40(1):11.

Behrend, F. W. 1948. A record of the Snow Bunting in east Tennessee. *The Migrant* 19(4):64-66.

———. 1952. Fall migrations of hawks in 1952. *The Migrant* 23(4):62-65.

———. 1954. Horned Grebe and Double-crested Cormorant on Lake Phillip Nelson. *The Migrant* 25(3):49.

———. 1955. Evening Grosbeaks and Snow Buntings on Roan and Big Bald Mountains, Tennessee-North Carolina. *The Migrant* 26(1):14-16.

———. 1962. Northern finches summering on Roan Mountain. *The Migrant* 33(3):56.

———. 1963. Northern birds repeat their summer stay on Roan Mountain. *The Migrant* 34(2):38-39.

———. 1965. Snow Bunting on Hump Mountain. *The Migrant* 36(2):52-53.

Behrend, F. W., and M. F. Behrend. 1945. Evening Grosbeaks in northeast Tennessee. *The Migrant* 16(4):53-55.

Bellrose, F. 1938. Notes on birds of the Great Smoky Mountains National Park. *The Migrant* 9(1):1-4.

Bent, A. C. 1937. *Life histories of North American birds of prey.* Part 1. New York: Dover Publications.

Bierly, M. L. 1972. Whimbrel recorded at Nashville. *The Migrant* 43(4):92-93.

———. 1972a. Chuck-will's-widow singing in daylight. *The Migrant* 43(2):48.

———. 1976. King Eider recorded in Tennessee. *The Migrant* 47(1):14.

———. 1978. Brown Creeper nests in Nashville. *The Migrant* 49(4):86-87.

———. 1980. *Bird finding in Tennessee.* Nashville: Michael L. Bierly.

Bierly, M. L., K. A. Goodpasture, and M. L. Mann. 1973. Marbled Godwit and Willet observed in Nashville. *The Migrant* 44(2):40-41.

Bierly, M. L., R. O. Harshaw, and J. D. Parrish, Jr. 1973a. Western Kingbirds sighted in Nashville. *The Migrant* 44(1):18.

Blockstein, D. E., and H. B. Tordoff. 1985. Gone forever—a contemporary look at the extinction of the Passenger Pigeon. *American Birds* 39(5):845-51.

Blunk, D. W. 1984. Black-legged Kittiwake in Stewart County, Tennessee. *The Migrant* 55(1):15.

———. 1986. A Long-billed Curlew in Lake County, Tennessee. *The Migrant* 57(2):47.

Braun, M. J. 1988. Northern Gannet on I-65: second record for Kentucky, first record for Tennessee. *The Kentucky Warbler* 64:34-36.

Bridgforth, W. A., Jr. 1969. Whip-poor-will foray. *The Migrant* 40(3):66.

Brown, C. W. 1985. Hudsonian Godwits in Lake County, Tennessee. *The Migrant* 56(4):105.

Burdick, A. W., Jr. 1941. Mississippi Kite at Nashville. *The Migrant* 12(2):38.

———. 1943. A Western Meadowlark in Tennessee. *The Migrant* 14(4):77.

Butts, W. K. 1936. A Florida (Sandhill) Crane at Chattanooga. *The Migrant* 7(1):24.

Calhoun, J. 1934. Le Conte's and Lincoln's Sparrow. *The Migrant* 5(4):64.

Calhoun, J. B. 1941. Notes on the summer birds of Hardeman and McNairy Counties. *Journal of Tennessee Academy of Sciences* 16:293-309.

Campbell, J. M. 1967. Surf Scoters on Chickamauga Lake. *The Migrant* 38(1):16-17.

Campbell, J. M., and J. C. Howell. 1970. Observations of certain birds. *The Migrant* 41(4):73-75.

Carpenter, E. L. 1964. Scissor-tailed Flycatcher near Memphis. *The Migrant* 35(2):55.

Clark, R. 1986. Rufous Hummingbird in Carter County, Tennessee. *The Migrant* 57(4):99.

Clebsch, A. 1940. Mid-winter field ventures. *The Migrant* 11(1):5-8.

———. 1942. Swainson's Warbler nesting notes. *The Migrant* 13(2-3):45-46.

———. 1943. Some winter birds of the river bottoms. *The Migrant* 14(4):65-67.

———. 1943a. A Catbird in mid-winter. *The Migrant* 14(4):78.

———. 1950. Orange-crowned Warbler as spring migrant. *The Migrant* 21(2):29-30.

Clemens, W. 1963. Red Phalarope in Greene County. *The Migrant* 34(4):92-93.

Coffey, B. B., Jr. 1933. Notes on the Painted Bunting at Memphis. *The Migrant* 4(4):41-42.

———. 1934. Wayside notes from west Tennessee. *The Migrant* 5(4):59-60.

———. 1935. A Piping Plover at Memphis. *The Migrant* 6(2):35.

———. 1935a. Bell's Vireo at Memphis. *The Migrant* 6(3):67-68.

———. 1936. Saw-Whet Owl at Memphis. *The Migrant* 7(1):19-20.

———. 1936a. Henslow's Sparrow near Memphis. *The Migrant* 7(3):69.

———. 1939. Rare shorebirds at Mud Lake. *The Migrant* 10(1):15-16.

———. 1940. Mississippi Kite nesting in a city park. *The Migrant* 11(3):79.

———. 1941. Summer range of mid-south towhees. *The Migrant* 12(3):51-57.

———. 1942. Fish Crow at Memphis. *The Migrant* 13(2-3):42.

———. 1943. Phoebe tunnel. *The Migrant* 14(4):70-72.

———. 1944. Winter home of Chimney Swifts discovered in northeastern Peru. *The Migrant* 15(3):37-38.

———. 1946. Bell's Vireo and other Natchez Trace notes. *The Migrant* 17(3):46-47.

———. 1947. Franklin's Gull at Memphis. *The Migrant* 18(4):60-61.

———. 1948. Louisiana Heron recorded in Tennessee and north Mississippi. *The Migrant* 19(4):71-72.

———. 1952. Southwestern Tennessee heronries. *The Migrant* 23(3):45.

———. 1953. Sprague's Pipit in the mid-south. *The Migrant* 24(2):28-29.

———. 1954. Smith's Longspur in the mid-south. *The Migrant* 25(3):46-48.

———. 1955. The Knot recorded in Memphis. *The Migrant* 26(2):32-33.

———. 1955a. The Short-eared Owl in the mid-south. *The Migrant* 26(2):24-25.

———. 1956. Harris' Sparrow in the mid-south. *The Migrant* 27(2):37-39.

———. 1974. Brant in Shelby County. *The Migrant* 45(4):93-94.

———. 1975. Yellow-headed Blackbird in Memphis. *The Migrant* 46(1):15.

———. 1976. The 1975 foray: Lauderdale County. *The Migrant* 47(1):1-7.

———. 1979. Early records of the Mississippi Kite and a summary. *The Migrant* 50(4):83-84.

———. 1981. A past Green Heronry colony in Memphis. *The Migrant* 52(2):44.

———. 1981a. Prairie Falcon at Memphis. *The Migrant* 52(1):18.

———. 1985. First state records and nesting of Black-necked Stilts at Memphis, Tennessee. *The Migrant* 56(1):1-3.

———. 1985a. Summer records of the White-throated Sparrow in Memphis and near Samburg, Tennessee. *The Migrant* 56(1):15.

Coffey, B. B., Jr., and L. Coffey. 1980. A west Tennessee foray—June, 1979. *The Migrant* 51(1):12-14.

Coffey, B. B., Jr., et al. 1942. The wrens of Tennessee. *The Migrant* 13(1):1-13.

Coffey, B. B., Jr. (Mrs.). 1932. A trip to Mud Lake, Sept. 18, 1932. *The Migrant* 3(3):35-36.

———. 1939a. In the front yard of Memphis. *The Migrant* 10(2):28-29.

———. 1945. Further notes on Memphis nesting census. *The Migrant* 16(2):33.

———. 1948a. Nesting data from Memphis. *The Migrant* 19(1):11-12.

———. 1964. Cattle Egret nesting at the Dyersburg heronry. *The Migrant* 35(2):54.

Coffey, J. W. 1963. A nesting study of the Eastern Phoebe. *The Migrant* 34(3):41-49.

———. 1964a. Northern Shrike at Bristol—a new species for Tennessee. *The Migrant* 35(4):90-94.

———. 1964b. An additional Snowy Owl record for 1930. *The Migrant* 35(3):71.

———. 1964c. Cedar Waxwing nesting in Shady Valley. *The Migrant* 35(4):117.

———. 1966. Colonial nesting of the Green Heron. *The Migrant* 37(4):75.

———. 1970. Mute Swan in Sullivan County. *The Migrant* 41(3):59-60.

———. 1970a. Northern Phalarope in Washington County. *The Migrant* 41(3):66-67.

Collier, C. E., Jr. 1941. Snake in a Swainson's Warbler nest. *The Migrant* 12(2):28.

Counce, C. C. 1946. Red-cockaded Woodpecker in southwest Tennessee. *The Migrant* 17(1):13.

Crawford, D., and P. Crawford. 1977. Snowy Plover added to Tennessee state list. *The Migrant* 48(3):63-64.

Crawford, P. 1977. Black-hooded Parakeet in Sumner County. *The Migrant* 48(4):96-98.

Crawford, P., and D. Crawford. 1975. Purple Sandpiper sighting in Sumner County, Tennessee. *The Migrant* 46(4):80-81.

———. 1976. Second record of Northern Phalarope in Nashville area. *The Migrant* 47(4):94.

Criswell, W. G. 1979. A heron roost at Dyersburg. *The Migrant* 50(2):33.

———. 1979a. Brown Creeper nesting in west Tennessee. *The Migrant* 50(4):81-82.

————. 1986. Second Tennessee record of the Groove-billed Ani. *The Migrant* 57(3):70.

Crook, C. 1932. Early nesting of the Killdeer in Davidson County. *The Migrant* 3(1):11.

————. 1936. A late Golden-winged Warbler in the Cumberlands. *The Migrant* 7(2):48.

Crownover, M. 1965. Fulvous Tree Duck at Chattanooga. *The Migrant* 36(2):52.

Cypert, E., Jr. 1949. Three rookeries on Kentucky Lake. *The Migrant* 20(3):41-42.

————. 1955. Some interesting bird observations on Kentucky Lake. *The Migrant* 26(1):9-11.

————. 1955a. Snowy Owl on Kentucky Lake. *The Migrant* 26(1):12.

Darnell, C. B. 1960. Oregon Juncos near Greeneville. *The Migrant* 31(1):19.

————. 1966. A Ringed Turtle Dove in Greene County. *The Migrant* 37(4):73-74.

Darnell, M. 1956. Kirtland's Warbler. *The Migrant* 27(3):53.

Deaderick, W. H. 1940. Audubon in Tennessee. *The Migrant* 11(3):59-61.

DeFoe, D. H. 1966. Common Redpoll in GSMNP. *The Migrant* 37(1):11.

DeVore, J. E. 1966. Sandhill Crane near Chattanooga in August. *The Migrant* 37(1):15.

————. 1969. Brant and White-fronted Geese in east Tennessee. *The Migrant* 40(3):61.

————. 1972. The Sandhill Crane in Tennessee. *The Migrant* 43(2):29-34.

————. 1974. Dark-headed juncos in Rutherford and Wilson Counties. *The Migrant* 45(2):54.

————. 1975. Middle Tennessee ornithological records of the late H. O. Todd, Jr. *The Migrant* 46(2):25-37.

————. 1980. Status of the Sandhill Crane in Tennessee. *The Migrant* 51(3):45-53.

DeVore, J. E., and K. H. Dubke. 1966. Black Brant at Hiwassee Island. *The Migrant* 37(1):12.

Dinkelspiel, H. 1973. Monk Parakeet in Shelby County. *The Migrant* 44(3):82.

Dinsmore, M. O. 1975. Wood Stork seen in Stewart County. *The Migrant* 46(4):79.

Dubke, K. H. 1963. First nesting record of Bobolink in Tennessee. *The Migrant* 34(2):17-19.

————. 1963a. Unusually late spring waterfowl, shorebird, gull, and tern records — 1963. *The Migrant* 34(2):36-37.

————. 1968. Louisiana Heron and Glossy Ibis at Chattanooga. *The Migrant* 39(1):15-16.

————. 1968a. Red Phalaropes near Chattanooga. *The Migrant* 39(1):13.

————. 1974. Purple Gallinule nesting at Goose Pond, Grundy County. *The Migrant* 45(4):94-95.

————. 1975. Winter Tree Swallows at Savannah Bay. *The Migrant* 46(4):83.

Dubke, K. H., and L. H. Dubke. 1975. Red-necked Grebe sighted on Chickamauga Lake. *The Migrant* 46(4):75-76.

————. 1977. The 1974 foray: Grundy County. *The Migrant* 48(4):81-85.

Eller, G., and G. Wallace. 1984. *Birds of Roan Mountain and vicinity.* Elizabethton, Tenn.: Lee R. Herndon Chapter, Tennessee Ornithological Society.

Ellis, J. O. 1963. Two days at Reelfoot Lake. *The Migrant* 34(2):21-23.

Elson, J. 1960. Campus bird count — University of Tennessee, Knoxville. *The Migrant* 31(2):39.

Erwin, L. A. 1986. First sight record of Rufous Hummingbird in Tennessee. *The Migrant* 57(4):98-99.

Etnier, D. A. 1971. Snow Buntings, Oldsquaw, and White-winged Scoter in east Tennessee. *The Migrant* 42(1):5.

Fintel, W. A. 1974. First Masked Duck sighting in Tennessee. *The Migrant* 45(2):47-48.

————. 1974a. Band-tailed Pigeon sighting, Nashville, Tennessee. *The Migrant* 45(2):49-51.

Fleetwood, R. J. 1937. A Woodcock at high altitude in Great Smoky Mountains National Park. *The Migrant* 8(2):42.

Ford, R. P. 1987. Summary of recent Brown Creeper observations in west Tennessee. *The Migrant* 58(2):50-51.

Foster, G., Jr. 1936. Baird's Sandpiper at Caryville (Tennessee) Lake. *The Migrant* 7(4):102.

————. 1937. A Brown Pelican in East Tennessee. *The Migrant* 8(4):87.

————. 1937a. Notes on the water birds of Norris Lake. *The Migrant* 8(2):28-29.

Fowler, L. J. 1983. Shorebirds of Kingston Steam Plant. *The Migrant* 54(2):29-32.

————. 1985. Red-shouldered Hawk migration at Chilhowee Mountain: further clarification. *The Migrant* 56(4):100-102.

————. 1985a. Color phases of the Eastern Screech-Owl in Tennessee. *The Migrant* 56(3):61-63.

————. 1986. First east Tennessee record of Black-necked Stilt. *The Migrant* 57(1):19-20.

Ganier, A. F. 1917. *Preliminary list of the birds of Tennessee.* Nashville: State of Tennessee, Dept. of Fish and Game.

————. 1933. A distributional list of the birds of Tennessee. *Tennessee Avifauna* No. 1. Nashville: Tennessee Ornithological Society.

————. 1933a. Water birds of Reelfoot Lake, Tennessee. *Tennessee Avifauna* No. 2. Nashville: Tennessee Ornithological Society.

————. 1933b. A Swallow-tailed Kite. *The Migrant* 4(4):51.

————. 1935. Eared Grebe at Nashville. *The Migrant* 6(4):93.

————. 1935a. Goose Pond and its marsh birds. *The Migrant* 6(2):22-24.

————. 1935b. American Rough-legged Hawk near Nashville. *The Migrant* 6(1):13.

————. 1936. Summer birds of Roan Mountain. *The Migrant* 7(4):83-86.

————. 1937. A record of the Goshawk. *The Migrant* 8(4):85.

————. 1937a. Summer birds of Pickett Forest. *The Migrant* 8(2):24-27.

————. 1940. Notes on Tennessee birds of prey. *The Migrant* 11(1):1-4.

————. 1944. Swifts banded at southern stations. *The Migrant* 15(3):53.

————. 1945. Alder Flycatcher at Memphis. *The Migrant* 16(2):29.

————. 1948. Western Henslow's Sparrow in east Tennessee. *The Migrant* 19(2):28-29.

————. 1951. The breeding herons of Tennessee. *The Migrant* 22(1):1-8.

————. 1951a. Mississippi Kite and Golden Eagle in Overton Co., Tennessee. *The Migrant* 22(2):29.

————. 1951b. Some notes on Bald Eagles. *The Migrant* 22(3):37-39.

————. 1952. A Black Vulture roost. *The Migrant* 23(1):7.

————. 1952a. Purple Gallinules near McMinnville. *The Migrant* 23(3):46-47.

————. 1954. A Yellow Rail at Nashville. *The Migrant* 25(1):13.

————. 1954a. Spring water birds at Nashville—1954. *The Migrant* 25(2):21-23.

————. 1956. Nesting of the Black-throated Blue and Chestnut-sided Warblers. *The Migrant* 27(3):43-46.

————. 1960. A new heronry in northwest Tennessee. *The Migrant* 31(3):48-49.

————. 1962. The Red-cockaded Woodpecker in Tennessee. *The Migrant* 33(3):39-45.

————. 1962a. Some nesting records from the Smokies. *The Migrant* 33(1):1-6.

————. 1962b. Bird casualties at a Nashville T.V. tower. *The Migrant* 33(4):58-60.

————. 1964. A Tennessee nesting of the Tree Swallow. *The Migrant* 35(2):51.

————. 1968. Swallow-tailed Kite near Nashville. *The Migrant* 39(4):85.

Ganier, A. F., and A. Clebsch. 1940. Summer birds of Fall Creek State Park. *The Migrant* 11(3):53-59.

————. 1942. A week in west Tennessee. *The Migrant* 13(2-3):32-35.

————. 1946. Breeding birds of the Unicoi Mountains. *The Migrant* 17(4):53-59.

Ganier, A. F., and B. B. Coffey, Jr. 1934. A Hudsonian Curlew at Memphis. *The Migrant* 5(3):40-41.

Ganier, A. F., and S. A. Weakley. 1936. Nesting of the Cliff Swallow in Tennessee. *The Migrant* 7(2):29-30.

Gersbacher, E. O. 1939. The heronries at Reelfoot Lake. *Journal of Tennessee Academy of Sciences* 14:162-80.

Goodpasture, K. A. 1953. A chat near Nashville establishes first winter record for Tennessee. *The Migrant* 24(1):11.

——. 1954. Saw-Whet Owl wintering near Nashville, 1952-1953. *The Migrant* 25(1):13-14.

——. 1954a. Two Arkansas Kingbirds near Nashville. *The Migrant* 25(2):33-34.

——. 1955. Evening Grosbeaks and Snow Bunting found in Nashville area. *The Migrant* 26(1):12-13.

——. 1968. Summer occurrence of Blue Grosbeaks in middle Tennessee. *The Migrant* 39(1):1-3.

——. 1974. Fall 1972 television tower casualties in Nashville. *The Migrant* 45(2):29-31.

——. 1976. Nashville television tower casualties, 1975. *The Migrant* 47(1):8-10.

——. 1977. Fall banding at Basin Spring, 1975. *The Migrant* 48:65-69.

Goodpasture, K. A., and F. J. Alsop, III. 1972. Traill's Flycatcher nests at Nashville, Tennessee. *The Migrant* 43(4):81-84.

Goodpasture, K. A., and L. E. Douglass. 1964. Whip-poor-will nests at Basin Spring. *The Migrant* 35(4):100-101.

Gray, D. R., III. 1968. Tree Swallow nesting in Maury County. *The Migrant* 39(3):61.

Haney, J. C. 1981. The distribution and life history of the Brown-headed Nuthatch in Tennessee. *The Migrant* 52(4):77-86.

——. 1981a. First Tennessee fall record of Hudsonian Godwit. *The Migrant* 52(3):69.

Hassler, R. C. 1984. A Yellow Rail in Pickett County, Tennessee. *The Migrant* 55(1):15.

Hatcher, R. M. 1987. Bald facts about Bald Eagles in Tennessee. Nashville: Tennessee Wildlife Resources Agency.

Henry, E. O. 1937. Red-backed Sandpiper at Knoxville. *The Migrant* 8(2):40.

Herndon, L. R. 1944. Notes on Prothonotary Warblers. *The Migrant* 15(3):58.

——. 1950. Birds of Carter County, Tennessee. *The Migrant* 21(4):57-68.

——. 1950a. Least Flycatcher nesting near Elizabethton, Tennessee. *The Migrant* 21(3):49.

——. 1955. First record of Sanderling at Watauga Lake. *The Migrant* 26(3):43.

——. 1957. Green-tailed Towhee in Elizabethton, Tennessee. *The Migrant* 28(1):15.

——. 1958. Traill's Flycatchers breeding in Tennessee. *The Migrant* 29(3):37-42.

——. 1962. Chuck-will's-widow near Watauga Lake. *The Migrant* 33(2):35-36.

——. 1972. Black-throated Gray Warbler. *The Migrant* 43(3):67-68.

——. 1973. Bird kill on Holston Mountain. *The Migrant* 44(1):1-4.

Hettish, A. 1974. Report on Black-headed Grosbeak, Murfreesboro. *The Migrant* 45(3):72-73.

Hogg, G. E. 1968. Vermilion Flycatcher at Reelfoot. *The Migrant* 39(1):12.

Holt, J. G. 1972. House Finches at Greeneville. *The Migrant* 43(4):87.

——. 1979. Purple Sandpiper in west Tennessee. *The Migrant* 50(3):63.

Howell, J. C. 1951. Nest of the Blue Grosbeak in Knox County, Tennessee. *The Migrant* 22(3):44.

Howell, J. C., and A. J. Meyerriecks. 1948. Avocet seen in Knox County, Tennessee. *The Migrant* 19(4):73.

Howell, J. C., and J. M. Campbell. 1972. Observations of Campbell County birds. *The Migrant* 43(1):1-4.

Howell, J. C., and J. T. Tanner. 1951. An accident to migrating birds at the Knoxville airport. *The Migrant* 22(4):61-62.

Howell, J. C., and M. B. Monroe. 1957. The birds of Knox County, Tennessee. *Journal of Tennessee Academy of Sciences* 32(4):247-322.

——. 1958. The birds of Knox County, Tennessee. *The Migrant* 29(2):17-27.

Hoyt, J. S. 1945. White-fronted Geese at Memphis. *The Migrant* 16(1):10.

——. 1945a. Nesting records of the towhee at Memphis. *The Migrant* 16(3):40-41.

Hudson, C. 1969. Western Tanager in Dyer County. *The Migrant* 40(3):65-66.

Ijams, H. P. 1932. Black-bellied Plover at Knoxville. *The Migrant* 3(4):48.

————. 1934. A Sooty Tern at Knoxville. *The Migrant* 5(3):46.

————. 1937. Prothonotary Warblers. *The Migrant* 8(2):41.

Ijams, H. P., and L. A. Hofferbert. 1934. Nesting records of birds at Athens, Tennessee. *The Migrant* 5(1):1-4.

Imhof, T. A. 1986. Tennessee, Alabama, Mississippi Regional Summary. *American Birds* 40(4):1042-1044.

Irwin, O. F. 1958. Long-eared Owl at Memphis. *The Migrant* 29(3):59.

————. 1961. Snow Bunting at Memphis. *The Migrant* 32(3):49-50.

Johnson, W. N. 1935. A White Pelican at Knoxville. *The Migrant* 6(2):38.

Kalla, P. I., and F. J. Alsop, III. 1983. The distribution, habitat preference, and status of the Mississippi Kite in Tennessee. *American Birds* 37(2):146-49.

Kellberg, J. M. 1956. Snowy Owl. *The Migrant* 27(4):74.

Kiff, L. F. 1989. Historical breeding records of the Common Merganser in southeastern United States. *The Wilson Bulletin* 101(1):141-43.

Knox, M. 1945. Crested Flycatcher nestings. *The Migrant* 16(1):8-9.

Koella, J. A. 1985. Sight record of Gyrfalcon in Jefferson County, Tennessee. *The Migrant* 56(1):14-15.

Koella, T. 1975. Piping Plover seen in Cocke County. *The Migrant* 46(1):16-17.

Landis, H., Jr. 1955. Long-eared Owl in Memphis. *The Migrant* 26(2):33.

Langridge, H. P. 1956. Unusual sparrows for Carter County. *The Migrant* 27(4):74-75.

Laskey, A. R. 1933. Juncos with white wing-bars in Tennessee. *The Migrant* 4(1):9.

————. 1941. Spring record of a Goshawk at Nashville. *The Migrant* 12(3):61.

————. 1950. A Tennessee Warbler found in Nashville in January. *The Migrant* 21(2):29.

————. 1951. Another disaster to migrating birds at the Nashville airport. *The Migrant* 22(4): 57-60.

————. 1956. Bird casualties at Smyrna and Nashville Ceilometers, 1955. *The Migrant* 27(1):9-10.

————. 1956a. First specimen of Sharp-tailed Sparrow for Tennessee. *The Migrant* 27(1):13.

————. 1957. Television tower casualties. *The Migrant* 28(4):54-56.

————. 1960. Bird migration casualties and weather conditions—autumns 1958-1959-1960. *The Migrant* 31(4):61-65.

————. 1962. Migration data from television tower casualties at Nashville. *The Migrant* 33(1):7-8.

————. 1964. Data from the Nashville T.V. tower casualties autumn 1964. *The Migrant* 35(4): 95-96.

————. 1966. T.V. tower casualties at Nashville; spring and fall, 1966. *The Migrant* 37(4):61-62.

————. 1966a. Status of Bewick's Wren and House Wren in Nashville. *The Migrant* 37(1):4-6.

————. 1969. Autumn 1969 T.V. tower casualties at Nashville. *The Migrant* 40(4):79-80.

————. 1969a. T.V. tower casualties at Nashville in autumn 1968. *The Migrant* 40(2):25-27.

Layne, J. N. 1946. Field notes from the Smyrna area. *The Migrant* 17(2):19-21.

Leggett, K. 1969. Vermilion Flycatcher again recorded at Reelfoot. *The Migrant* 40(1):17.

————. 1969a. Groove-billed Ani. *The Migrant* 40(1):7-9.

————. 1970. Heronry at Dyersburg is no longer active. *The Migrant* 41(3):58.

Lewis, J. C. 1962. The status of Wild Turkeys in Tennessee. *The Migrant* 33(4):61-62.

Lochridge, O. B., and A. R. Lochridge. 1984. Immature Virginia Rail observed in Maury County. *The Migrant* 55(4):85.

Lura, R. 1979. Nesting Alder Flycatchers in Tennessee. *The Migrant* 50(2):34-36.

Lyle, R. B., and B. P. Tyler. 1934. The nesting birds of northeastern Tennessee. *The Migrant* 5(4):49-57.

M'Camey, F. 1935. August notes from North Lake. *The Migrant* 6(3):51-53.

————. 1936. A Brown Pelican at Memphis. *The Migrant* 7(2):38, 43.

Manlove, W. R. 1933. A roost of the wild pigeon. *The Migrant* 4(2):18-19.

Manning, D., and G. Manning. 1971. Hudsonian Godwit at Reelfoot Lake. *The Migrant* 42(3):58-59, 66.

Mayfield, G. R. 1932. The Red-cockaded Woodpecker in Grundy Co., Tennessee. *The Wilson Bulletin* 44:44.

———. 1932a. Le Conte's Sparrow in winter. *The Migrant* 3(1):10-11.

———. 1935. A Tennessee Warbler winters in Nashville. *The Migrant* 6(1):14.

Mayfield, G. R., Jr. 1981. Whimbrels on Big Bald Mountain, Tennessee. *The Migrant* 52(4):91.

McCrary, W. L., and M. Wood. 1966. Red Phalarope near Tullahoma. *The Migrant* 37(1):15.

———. 1966a. Lark Bunting in Tennessee. *The Migrant* 37(2):41-42.

McKinley, D. 1979. A review of the Carolina Parakeet in Tennessee. *The Migrant* 50(1):1-6.

McLean, H. K. 1982. First Tennessee record of Caribbean Coot. *The Migrant* 53(4):81-82.

McLean, R. G., M. E. Ritke, and E. Campos. 1983. A Lawrence's Warbler in Shelby County, Tennessee. *The Migrant* 54(2):38.

McNair, D. B. 1988. Red Crossbills breed at Highlands, North Carolina. *The Migrant* 59(2): 45-48.

Mengel, R. M. 1965. *The birds of Kentucky.* American Ornithologists' Union Monograph No. 3. Lawrence, Kans: Allen Press.

Meyer, H. 1942. Early arrival of the Grasshopper Sparrow. *The Migrant* 13(2-3):49.

Miller, R. A. 1979. *The geologic history of Tennessee.* Bulletin 74. Nashville: State of Tennessee, Department of Conservation, Division of Geology.

Monk, H. C. 1932. The water birds of Radnor Lake. *Journal of Tennessee Academy of Sciences* 7:217-32.

Monroe, B. L. 1944. Field notes from west Tennessee. *The Migrant* 15(4):76.

Monroe, M. B. 1959. Red Phalarope. *The Migrant* 30(4):56.

Monroe, R. A. 1948. The Connecticut Warbler in Knoxville. *The Migrant* 19(2):27-28.

Morlan, R. E. 1961. A Limpkin at Nashville. *The Migrant* 32(3):48-49.

Mount, J. 1945. Glossy Ibis near Memphis. *The Migrant* 16(3):44.

Munro, A. R. 1961. Snowy Owl. *The Migrant* 32(1):1-3.

Murphy, W. L. 1982. The Ash-throated Flycatcher in the east: an overview. *American Birds* 36(3):241-47.

Nevius, R. 1964. A Tennessee nesting of the Black Rail. *The Migrant* 35(3):59-60.

Nicholson, C. P. 1976. The Bachman's Sparrow in Tennessee. *The Migrant* 47(3):53-60.

———. 1977. The Red-cockaded Woodpecker in Tennessee. *The Migrant* 48(3):53-62.

———. 1980. Birds of Decatur County. *The Migrant* 51(1):1-10.

———. 1981. Birds of Fentress County, Tennessee. *The Migrant* 52(3):53-62.

———. 1982. The Yellow Warbler in west Tennessee. *The Migrant* 53(4):82-84.

———. 1982a. Further comments on the Caribbean Coot in Tennessee. *The Migrant* 53(4):82.

———. 1983. The official list of Tennessee birds. *The Migrant* 54(1):2-5.

———. 1983a. Barnacle Goose in Humphreys County, Tennessee. *The Migrant* 54(2):39.

———. 1984. Late spring and summer birds of McNairy County, Tennessee. *The Migrant* 55(2):29-39.

———. 1986. Alexander Wilson's travels in Tennessee. *The Migrant* 57(1):1-7.

———. 1987. Notes on high elevation breeding birds of Frozen Head State Natural Area, Tennessee. *The Migrant* 58(2):39-43.

Nicholson, C. P., and A. Morton. 1972. Glaucous Gull on Fort Loudon Lake. *The Migrant* 43(1):21.

Nicholson, C. P., and T. D. Pitts. 1982. Nesting of the Tree Swallow in Tennessee. *The Migrant* 53(4):73-80.

Nicholson, C. P., and S. J. Stedman. 1988. The official list of Tennessee birds: addendum I. *The Migrant* 59(1):1-4.

Nunley, H. W. 1960. Chuck-will's-widow. *The Migrant* 31(3):57-58.

Ogden, J. 1955. Lark Sparrows near Nashville. *The Migrant* 26(3):45-46.

———. 1959. Northern Phalaropes at Nashville. *The Migrant* 30(4):55.

———. 1960. Brewster's Warbler near Nashville. *The Migrant* 31(3):55.

Ogden, S. A. 1933. Raptore and water bird records from east Tennessee. *The Migrant* 4(4):46-48.

Olson, F. B. 1961. Cattle Egret—first Tennessee record. *The Migrant* 32(2):35.

———. 1961a. White-fronted Goose at Cove Lake. *The Migrant* 32(2):35-36.

———. 1965. Fulvous Tree Ducks below Norris Dam, Anderson County. *The Migrant* 36(4):104.

———. 1968. Tree Swallows nesting in east Tennessee. *The Migrant* 39(3):59-60.

Owen, J. B. 1960. Sandhill Crane wintering in Knox County. *The Migrant* 31(1):18-19.

———. 1965. Vermilion Flycatcher in Knox County. *The Migrant* 36(1):14-15.

———. 1979. First Tennessee breeding record of Red-breasted Nuthatch outside of mountains. *The Migrant* 50(2):36.

Palmer-Ball, B., Jr., and J. C. Robinson. 1987. First record of Ross' Goose in Kentucky. *The Kentucky Warbler* 63(4):66-67.

Pardue, P. S. 1959. A Western Meadowlark in Knox County, Tennessee. *The Migrant* 30(2):30-31.

Parks, J. T. 1985. Red-necked Grebe at Nickajack Lake, Tennessee. *The Migrant* 56(1):14.

Parmalee, P. W., and W. E. Klippel. 1982. Evidence of a boreal avifauna in middle Tennessee during the late Pleistocene. *Auk* 99:365-68.

Parmer, H. E. 1957. Nighthawks in December. *The Migrant* 28(4):67-68.

———. 1959. A rare visit of terns at Nashville. *The Migrant* 30(1):14.

———. 1959a. A late Cliff Swallow at Nashville. *The Migrant* 30(1):14.

———. 1960. Greater Scaup. *The Migrant* 31(3):50.

———. 1962. First middle Tennessee record for the Louisiana Heron. *The Migrant* 33(4):73-74.

———. 1962a. Further observations at Bush Lake. *The Migrant* 33(1):8-10.

———. 1963. Late warblers at Nashville. *The Migrant* 34(2):37-38.

Parmer, H. E., and H. C. Monk. 1969. Glaucous Gull. *The Migrant* 40(1):12-13.

Parmer, H. E., et al. 1985. *Birds of the Nashville area*. 4th edition. Nashville Chapter, Tennessee Ornithological Society.

Patterson, D. E. 1967. Spotted Sandpiper in February. *The Migrant* 38(1):16.

Patterson, D. E., and M. Patterson. 1969. Clay-colored Sparrow in Hardin County. *The Migrant* 40(4):84-85.

Peterjohn, B. G. 1987. Middlewestern Prairie Region. *American Birds* 41(1):93-99.

Petit, G. D. 1967. Fulvous Tree Duck at Kentucky Lake. *The Migrant* 38(3):60.

Phillips, R. A. 1979. Low altitude record of the Common Raven in Johnson City. *The Migrant* 50(3):65.

Pickering, C. F. 1937. A September visit to Reelfoot Lake. *The Migrant* 8(3):49-50.

———. 1941. Interesting days on Reelfoot Lake. *The Migrant* 12(2):24-26.

———. 1945. November notes from Reelfoot Lake. *The Migrant* 16(4):64.

Pitelka, F. A. 1939. "Cranetown" at Reelfoot Lake. *The Migrant* 10(2):26-28.

Pitts, T. D. 1972. Nesting of Bank Swallows in Lake County. *The Migrant* 43(2):48.

———. 1973. Tennessee heron and egret colonies: 1972. *The Migrant* 44(4): 89-93.

———. 1974. Lark Sparrows nesting in Obion County. *The Migrant* 45(4):86-87.

———. 1977. Tennessee heron and egret colonies: 1973-1975. *The Migrant* 48(2):25-29.

———. 1978. Comparison of American Woodcock courtship activities in Knox and Weakley counties, Tennessee. *The Migrant* 49(2):29-30.

————. 1981. European Wigeon at Reelfoot Lake, Tennessee in the early 1950s. *The Migrant* 52(3):68.

————. 1981a. Eastern Bluebird population fluctuations in Tennessee during 1970-1979. *The Migrant* 52(2):29-37.

————. 1982. Establishment of a new heron and egret colony at Reelfoot Lake, Tennessee. *The Migrant* 53(3):63-64.

————. 1982a. First record of occurrence and possible nesting of Black-bellied Whistling-Duck in Tennessee. *The Migrant* 53(1):1-3.

————. 1982b. Nesting season records of Willow Flycatchers in west Tennessee. *The Migrant* 53(4):84-85.

————. 1983. Bell's Vireo in Obion County, Tennessee. *The Migrant* 54(2):38.

————. 1985. The breeding birds of Reelfoot Lake, Tennessee. *The Migrant* 56(2):29-41.

————. 1987. Common Ground-Dove specimen from Weakley County, Tennessee. *The Migrant* 58(2):47-48.

Pullin, B. P. 1986. 1986 survey of wading bird colonies in the Tennessee Valley Region. Norris: Tennessee Valley Authority.

Pullin, B. P., J. Thomas, and S. Atkins. 1982. 1982 survey of wading bird colonies in Tennessee Valley. Norris: Tennessee Valley Authority.

Rauber, E. L. 1972. Roseate Spoonbill identified at Tennessee National Wildlife Refuge. *The Migrant* 43(3):67.

————. 1972a. Cinnamon Teal sighted at Tennessee National Wildlife Refuge. *The Migrant* 43(3):67.

Rhoads, S. N. 1895. Contributions to the zoology of Tennessee, No. 2. Birds. *Proceedings of the Academy of Natural Sciences of Philadelphia* 47:463-501.

Riggins, J. N. 1977. Fourth Nashville area record of Saw-Whet Owl. *The Migrant* 48(1):12-13.

Riggins, J. N., and H. Riggins. 1972. Second state record of Whimbrel. *The Migrant* 43(4):92.

Robbins, C. S., D. Bystrak, and P. H. Geissler. 1986. *The Breeding Bird Survey: its first fifteen years, 1965-1979.* Washington, D.C.: United States Fish and Wildlife Service, Resource Publication 157.

Robinson, J. C. 1982. Mid-continent observations of Ross' Geese. *Iowa Bird Life* 52(1):3-5.

————. 1988. First record of Snowy Owl in Stewart County, Tennessee. *The Migrant* 59(1):28-29.

————. 1988a. Heron and egret roost discovered near Memphis. *The Migrant* 59(4):118-19.

————. 1988b. First record of Ross' Goose in Tennessee. *The Migrant* 59(4):114-15.

————. 1988c. Audubon's Yellow-rumped Warbler in Tennessee. *The Migrant* 59(4):117.

Robinson, J. C., and D. W. Blunk. 1989. The birds of Stewart County, Tennessee. p. 70-103 in A. F. Scott, ed. *Proceedings of the contributed papers session of the second annual symposium on the natural history of lower Tennessee and Cumberland river valleys.* Clarksville: Center for Field Biology of Land Between The Lakes, Austin Peay State University.

Robinson, M. 1966. A westerly nest of the Song Sparrow. *The Migrant* 37(2):41.

Roever, K. 1951. Black-billed Cuckoo nesting near Jackson, Tennessee. *The Migrant* 22(2):30-31.

Rowell, A. B. 1972. Summer record of Red Crossbills for Sullivan County. *The Migrant* 43(3):73.

Ryan, C. 1968. Fulvous Tree Duck near Dover. *The Migrant* 39(1):16.

Savage, T. 1964. Rough-winged Swallow nesting in the Great Smoky Mountains. *The Migrant* 35(2):51.

————. 1965. Recent observations on the Saw-Whet Owl in Great Smoky Mountains National Park. *The Migrant* 36(1):15-16.

Schultz, V. 1953. Status of the Ruffed Grouse in Tennessee. *The Migrant* 24(3):45-52.

————. 1955. Status of the Wild Turkey in Tennessee. *The Migrant* 26(1):1-8.

Seahorn, C., Jr. 1953. Spotted Towhee at Germantown, Tennessee. *The Migrant* 24(2):42-43.

Sexton, J. W., and D. F. Harker, Jr. 1972. Harris' Sparrow in Montgomery County, Tennessee. *The Migrant* 43(1):20-21.

Shafer, W. L. 1972. First known record of a Ruff in Tennessee. *The Migrant* 43(4):86.

Sights, W. 1943. Hooded Merganser's nest on Reelfoot. *The Migrant* 14(1):16.

Simbeck, D. J. 1987. The 1986 Christmas Bird Count. *The Migrant* 58(1):1-10.

Smith, A. I. 1965. Vermilion Flycatchers at Reelfoot Lake. *The Migrant* 36(1):14.

Smith, P. W. 1987. The Eurasian Collared-Dove arrives in the Americas. *American Birds* 41(5):1370-79.

Smith, R. D., Jr. 1950. Winter record of Sycamore Warbler at Reelfoot Lake. *The Migrant* 21(3):49-50.

———. 1951. Western Meadowlark nesting at Memphis. *The Migrant* 22(2):21-22.

———. 1952. King Rail nest in Shelby County, Tennessee. *The Migrant* 23(3):46.

———. 1952a. Green-tailed Towhee in Memphis, Tennessee. *The Migrant* 23(4):76.

Snyder, D. H. 1974. Second record of Cinnamon Teal in Tennessee. *The Migrant* 45(4):94.

Solyom, V. 1940. The Chukar Partridge in Tennessee. *The Migrant* 11(1):11-12.

Spofford, W. R. 1941. A day at Reelfoot Lake. *The Migrant* 12(4):74.

———. 1942. A Black Vulture's nest at Reelfoot Lake. *The Migrant* 13(4):69.

———. 1945. Bald Eagle notes from Reelfoot Lake. *The Migrant* 16(4):65.

———. 1947. Another tree-nesting Peregrine Falcon record for Tennessee. *The Migrant* 18(4):60.

———. 1948. Some additional notes on the birds of Pickett Forest, Tennessee. *The Migrant* 19(1):12-13.

———. 1949. The accident to migrating birds at the Nashville airport. *The Migrant* 20(1):9-12.

Stedman, B. H., and S. J. Stedman. 1981. Notes on the raptor migration at Chilhowee Mountain. *The Migrant* 52(2):38-40.

Stedman, S. J. 1980. Recent records and status of the Whimbrel in Tennessee. *The Migrant* 51(4):88-89.

———. 1985. First record of Long-tailed Jaeger in Tennessee. *The Migrant* 56(3):64-66.

———. 1986. Songbird of prey: Loggerhead Shrike. *The Tennessee Conservationist* Sept/Oct: 9-11.

———. 1988. The Winter Roadside Raptor Survey in Tennessee: 1986-1987 results. *The Migrant* 59(1):14-21.

Stedman, S. J., and J. C. Robinson. 1986. First record of Parasitic Jaeger in Tennessee. *The Migrant* 57(2):44-46.

———. 1987. Documentation and submission of bird records in Tennessee. *The Migrant* 58(3):65-79.

———. 1987a. First record of Parasitic Jaeger in Tennessee: addenda. *The Migrant* 58(3):89-90.

Steenis, J. H. 1946. An Old Squaw duck on Reelfoot Lake. *The Migrant* 17(2):26.

Stringer, R. C. 1982. Southeast Tennessee occurrences of Mississippi Kite. *The Migrant* 53(3): 64-65.

Stupka, A. 1953. Some notes relating to the mortality of Screech Owls in Great Smoky Mountains National Park. *The Migrant* 24(1):3-5.

———. 1954. Golden Plover recorded from the Great Smoky Mountains National Park. *The Migrant* 25(2):33.

———. 1962. Late Evening Grosbeaks in Gatlinburg. *The Migrant* 33(2):35.

———. 1963. *Notes on the Birds of the Great Smoky Mountains National Park.* Knoxville: University of Tennessee Press.

Stupka, A., and J. T. Tanner. 1955. Evening Grosbeaks in the Gatlinburg-Knoxville area. *The Migrant* 26(1):13-14.

Sumara, B. 1972. Red Crossbills in Tiptonville. *The Migrant* 43(4):95.

Switzer, A. H. 1957. Observations at a fish hatchery. *The Migrant* 28(4):60-61.

Tanner, J. T. 1952. Black-capped and Carolina Chickadees in the southern Appalachian Mountains. *Auk* 69:407-24.

———. 1955. The altitudinal distribution of birds in a part of the Great Smoky Mountains. *The Migrant* 26(3):37-40.

———. 1955a. Le Conte's and Harris' Sparrows near Knoxville. *The Migrant* 26(1):20.

———. 1965. Red-cockaded Woodpecker nesting in the Great Smoky Mountains National Park. *The Migrant* 36(3):59.

———. 1985. An analysis of Christmas bird counts in Tennessee. *The Migrant* 56(4):85-97.

———. 1986. An analysis of spring bird counts in Tennessee. *The Migrant* 57(4):89-97.

Tennessee State Game and Fish Commission. 1959. Coturnix Quail. *The Migrant* 30(4):58.

Tennessee Wildlife Resources Agency. 1987. 1987 Wild Turkey report. *TWRA Technical Report* No. 87-4. Nashville: Tennessee Wildlife Resources Agency.

Terres, J. K. 1980. *The Audubon Society encyclopedia of North American birds*. New York: Alfred A. Knopf.

Thompson, B. 1937. Two Snowy Owl records. *The Migrant* 8(2):35.

Todd, H. O. 1937. Upland Plovers at Murfreesboro. *The Migrant* 8(3):64.

———. 1944. Some nesting records from Murfreesboro. *The Migrant* 15(2):21-23.

Trabue, L. O. 1965. A review of Tennessee Christmas counts. *The Migrant* 36(2):36-44.

Tucker, R. 1941. Brewster's Warbler at Memphis. *The Migrant* 12(4):77.

———. 1941a. Notes on the Swainson's Warbler at Memphis. *The Migrant* 12(2):28-29.

———. 1941b. Records of the Wilson's Warbler at Memphis. *The Migrant* 12(4):76-77.

Tucker, R. E. 1950. Notes of some specimens of birds from Shelby County, Tennessee. *The Migrant* 21(3):41-45.

Tyler, B. P. 1933. Clay-colored Sparrow at Johnson City. *The Migrant* 4(2):23.

———. 1936. Prairie Horned Lark nesting in northeast Tennessee. *The Migrant* 7(2):50.

Tyler, B. P., and R. B. Lyle. 1934. Additions to the list of winter birds of northeast Tennessee. *The Migrant* 5(1):14.

———. 1936. Additions to the list of winter birds of northeast Tennessee. *The Migrant* 7(1):25-26.

———. 1947. Two new birds for Shady Valley. *The Migrant* 18(2):28-29.

———. 1952. Audubon's Warbler, and other birds, at Johnson City. *The Migrant* 23(3):51.

Veit, R. R., and L. Jonsson. 1987. Field identification of smaller sandpipers within the genus *Calidris*. *American Birds* 41(2):212-36.

Waldron, M. G. 1980. Anhinga nesting at Big Hill Pond, McNairy Co. *The Migrant* 51(4):86.

———. 1981. First nesting of Bank Swallow in Shelby County, Tennessee. *The Migrant* 52(3):68.

———. 1982. Nest box utilization by Hooded Mergansers at Hatchie National Wildlife Refuge. *The Migrant* 53(1):13.

———. 1987. Seasonal occurrences of Shelby County, Tennessee birds. Memphis Chapter Tennessee Ornithological Society.

Walker, T., Jr. 1952. Summer birds of Camp Mack Morris, Benton County, Tennessee. *The Migrant* 23(1):5-6.

Walker, W. M., Jr. 1932. Nashville Christmas census for 17 years. *The Migrant* 3(4):42-43.

———. 1935. A collection of birds from Cocke County, Tennessee. *The Migrant* 6(3):48-50.

———. 1937. The Ospreys build a nest. *The Migrant* 8(3):53.

Wallace, G. O. 1971. A Ringed Turtle Dove in Knoxville. *The Migrant* 42(3):60-61.

Warriner, B. R. 1945. Some observations on the Blue Grosbeak. *The Migrant* 16(2):24-26.

Weakley, S. A. 1945. White Pelicans and Cliff Swallows on Tennessee River. *The Migrant* 16(2):33-34.

Weise, C. M. 1955. Spotted Sandpiper breeding in middle Tennessee. *The Migrant* 26(1):18-19.

————. 1958. Spring shorebird migrations at Nashville, 1954-56. *The Migrant* 29(3):42-50.

————. 1958a. Some noteworthy Nashville records. *The Migrant* 29(3):50-51.

West, E. M., and E. M. West (Mrs.). 1960. Whip-poor-will and Chuck-will's-widow census. *The Migrant* 31(3):56.

West, E. M. (Mrs.). 1957. Fall water birds at Chattanooga. *The Migrant* 28(4):57-58.

————. 1959. Brant in Chattanooga. *The Migrant* 30(4):54.

————. 1959a. Whistling Swan. *The Migrant* 30(4):56.

————. 1961. Breeding of Cedar Waxwings near Chattanooga. *The Migrant* 32(3):50.

————. 1961a. Cliff Swallow status in Chattanooga area. *The Migrant* 32(3):37-40.

————. 1962. Golden-winged Warbler building nest at Cumberland Mt. State Park. *The Migrant* 33(2):34.

————. 1963. First breeding record of Virginia Rail in Tennessee. *The Migrant* 34(2):20-21.

————. 1966. Harlan's Hawk is New Year present for Chattanooga. *The Migrant* 37(4):73.

Wetmore, A. 1939. Notes on the birds of Tennessee. *Proceedings of the United States National Museum* 86:175-243.

White, D., and R. W. Dimmick. 1979. The distribution of the Ruffed Grouse in Tennessee. *TWRA Technical Report* No. 79-6. Knoxville: University of Tennessee.

White, J. B. 1956. Birds of Greene County, Tennessee. *The Migrant* 27(1):3-8.

Whittemore, W. L. 1939. Reelfoot heronry notes. *The Migrant* 10(3):59-60.

Wight, E. M. 1934. Attracting birds at Chattanooga. *The Migrant* 5(3):46.

Wilds, C., and M. Newlon. 1983. The identification of dowitchers. *Birding* 15:151-66.

Williams, M. D. 1971. White Ibis in Giles County. *The Migrant* 42(3):58.

————. 1975. Common Gallinule nesting in east Tennessee. *The Migrant* 46(1):1-3.

————. 1976. Nest of Olive-sided Flycatcher in the southern Appalachian Mountains. *The Migrant* 47(3):69-71.

————. 1977. First breeding record of the Black Vulture in the Great Smoky Mountains National Park. *The Migrant* 48(1):11-12.

————. 1978. A late May sighting of the Fox Sparrow in Tennessee. *The Migrant* 49(4):87-88.

————. 1980. Notes on the breeding biology and behavior of the Ravens of Peregrine Ridge, Great Smoky Mountains National Park, Tennessee. *The Migrant* 51(4):77-80.

Witt, R. L. 1944. European Widgeons in west Tennessee. *The Migrant* 15(1):14.

Woodring, G. B. 1935. Radnor Lake notes. *The Migrant* 6(2):37.

Yeatman, H. C. 1955. Late spring record for Lesser Scaup duck. *The Migrant* 26(3):43.

————. 1965. Swallow-tailed Kite in Franklin County, Tennessee. *The Migrant* 36(3):58-59.

————. 1979. Harlan's Red-tailed Hawk and some other raptors at Sewanee. *The Migrant* 50(3):61-62.

————. 1980. Peregrine at Ashwood. *The Migrant* 51(4):88.

Zeleny, L. 1976. *The bluebird.* Bloomington: Indiana University Press.

Appendix:
Species Maps

Each of the following thirty-three species maps shows the counties in which the indicated species has bred *or* has been observed. An enclosed circle (•) indicates *breeding evidence* exists for the specified county. An open circle (○) indicates the species has been *observed* at least once in that particular county. Only one of these two codes is used on each of the maps.

Because it was not feasible to prepare maps for all of the species described in this book, only selected species of importance were chosen for inclusion in this Appendix. New information on bird distribution continually becomes available, and it is anticipated that many new locations not indicated on the following maps will be discovered in the near future. The soon-to-be completed Tennessee Breeding Bird Atlas Project will doubtless be an invaluable source for information on the distribution of all breeding species in Tennessee.

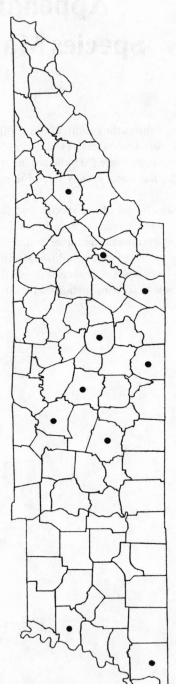

Map A-1. *Pied-billed Grebe* (breeding evidence)

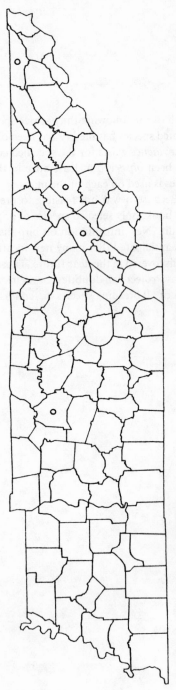

Map A-2. *Eared Grebe* (sight records)

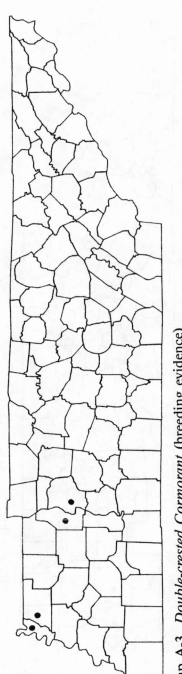

Map A-3. *Double-crested Cormorant* (breeding evidence)

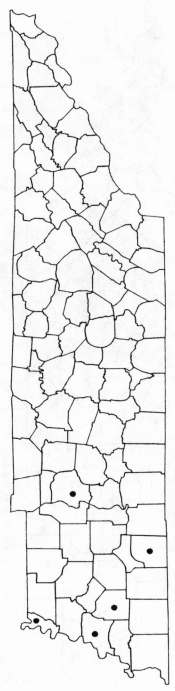

Map A-4. *Anhinga* (breeding evidence)

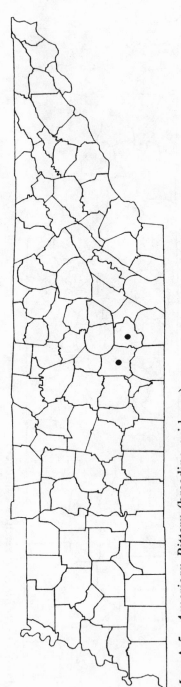

Map A-5. *American Bittern* (breeding evidence)

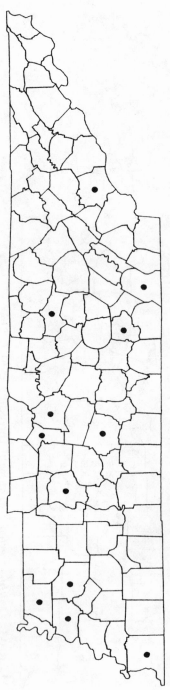

Map A-6. *Least Bittern* (breeding evidence)

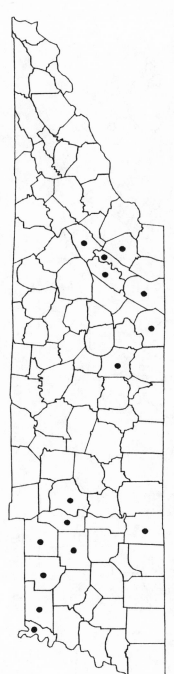

Map A-7. *Great Blue Heron* (breeding evidence)

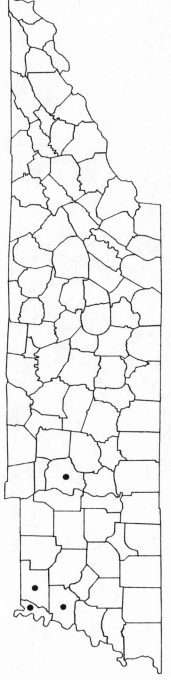

Map A-8. *Great Egret* (breeding evidence)

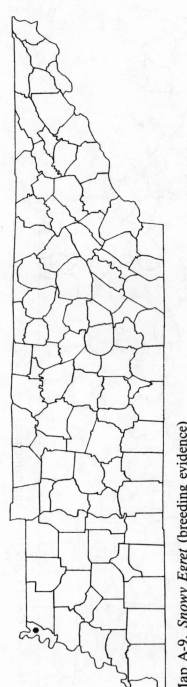

Map A-9. *Snowy Egret* (breeding evidence)

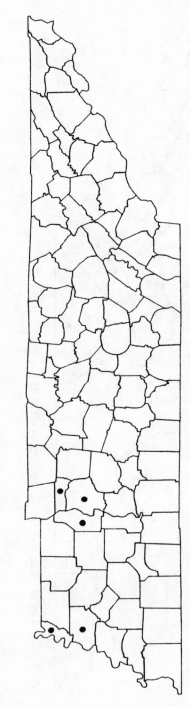

Map A-10. *Little Blue Heron* (breeding evidence)

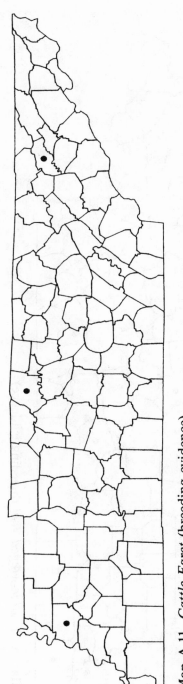

Map A-11. *Cattle Egret* (breeding evidence)

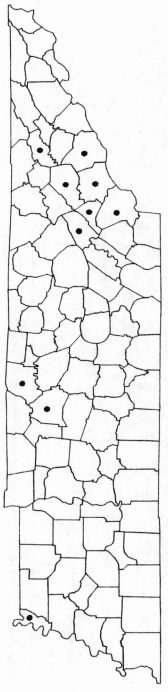

Map A-12. *Black-crowned Night-Heron* (breeding evidence)

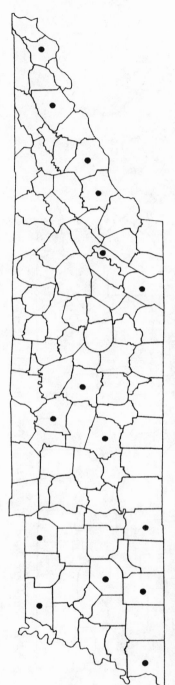

Map A-13. *Yellow-crowned Night-Heron* (breeding evidence)

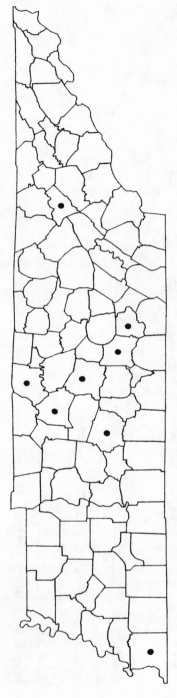

Map A-14. *Blue-winged Teal* (breeding evidence)

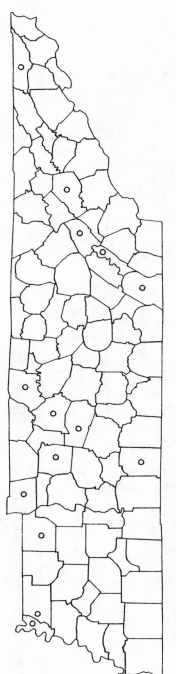

Map A-15. *Black Scoter* (sight records)

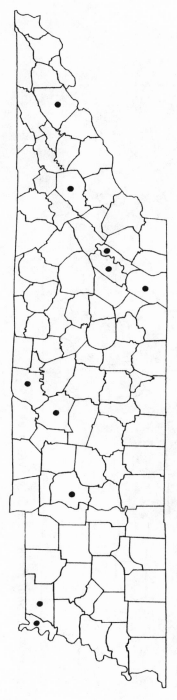

Map A-16. *Osprey* (breeding evidence)

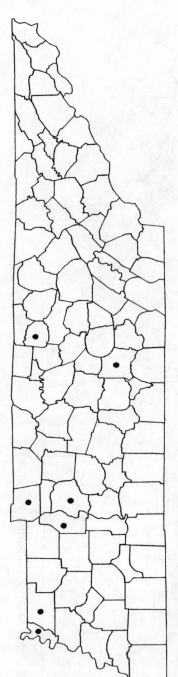

Map A-17. *Bald Eagle* (breeding evidence)

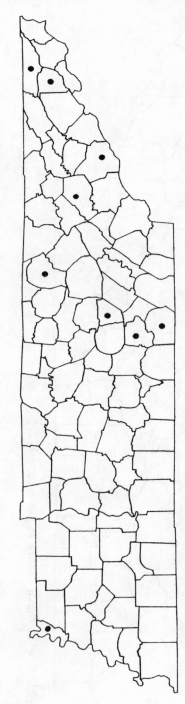

Map A-18. *Peregrine Falcon* (breeding evidence)

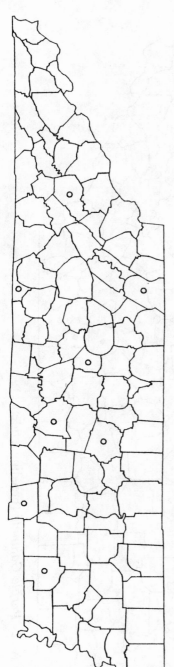

Map A-19. *Yellow Rail* (sight records)

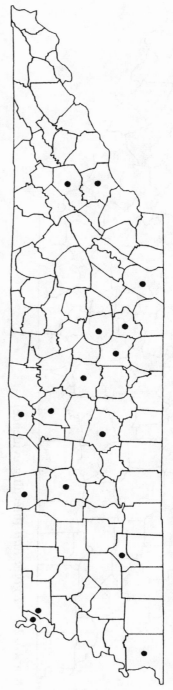

Map A-20. *King Rail* (breeding evidence)

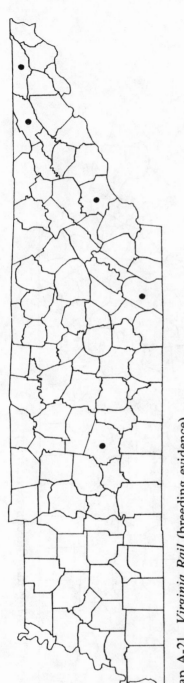

Map A-21. *Virginia Rail* (breeding evidence)

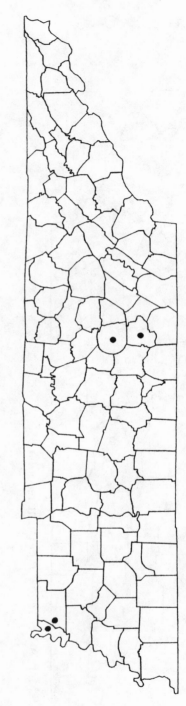

Map A-22. *Purple Gallinule* (breeding evidence)

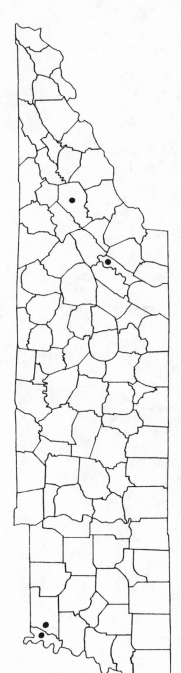

Map A-23. *Common Moorhen* (breeding evidence)

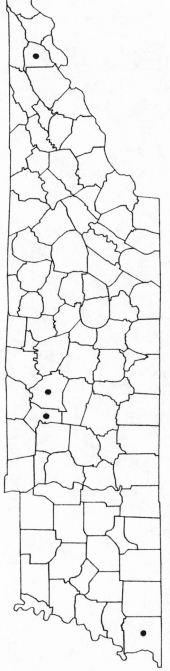

Map A-24. *Spotted Sandpiper* (breeding evidence)

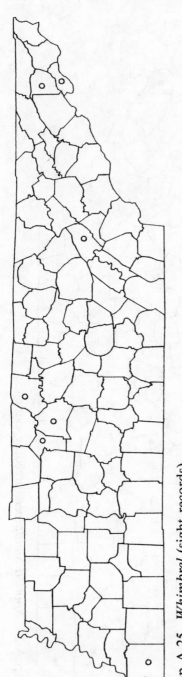

Map A-25. *Whimbrel* (sight records)

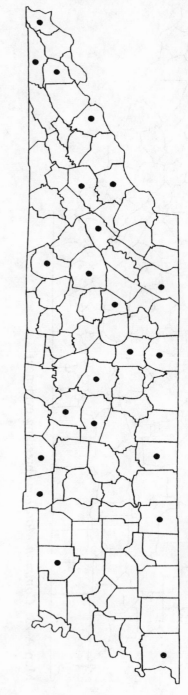

Map A-26. *American Woodcock* (breeding evidence)

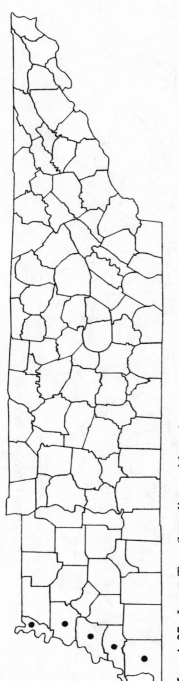

Map A-27. *Least Tern* (breeding evidence)

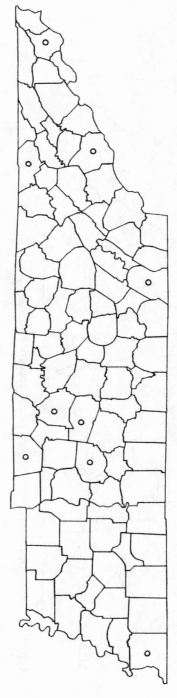

Map A-28. *Northern Saw-whet Owl* (sight records)

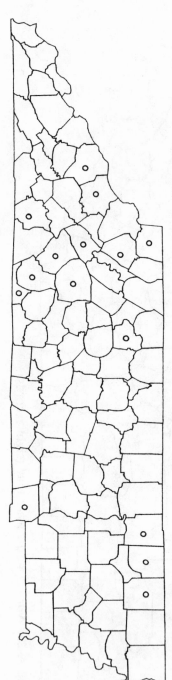

Map A-29. *Red-cockaded Woodpecker* (sight records)

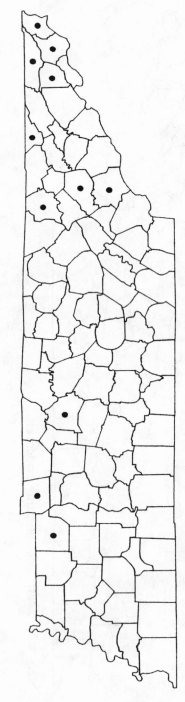

Map A-30. *Willow Flycatcher* (breeding evidence)

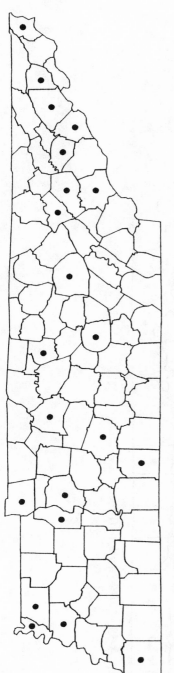

Map A-31. *Tree Swallow* (breeding evidence)

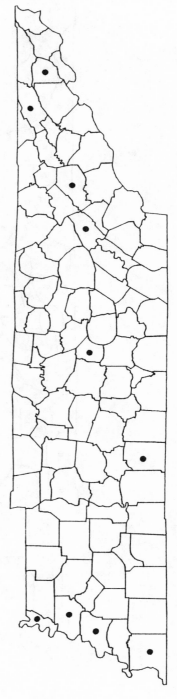

Map A-32. *Bank Swallow* (breeding evidence)

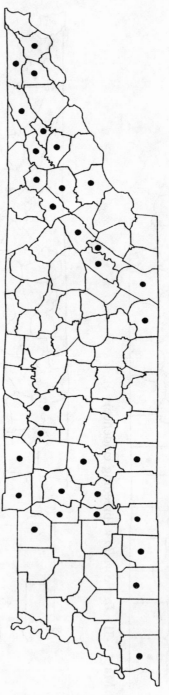

Map A-33. *Cliff Swallow* (breeding evidence)

Index
to Common Names

Following some species names are two page numbers; the first refers to the page where the species can be found in the *Species Accounts*, while the second refers to the page on which the species map appears.

An Annotated Checklist of the Birds of Tennessee was designed by Dariel Mayer, composed by Lithocraft, Inc., and printed and bound by BookCrafters, Inc. The book is set in Times Roman and printed on 50–lb Glatfelter Natural Antique.